Scottish Country Houses

1600–1914

Scottish Country Houses

1600–1914

edited by
IAN GOW
and
ALISTAIR ROWAN

RCAHMS

EDINBURGH UNIVERSITY PRESS

© Edinburgh University Press, 1995

Edinburgh University Press Ltd
22 George Square, Edinburgh

Typeset in Linotron Plantin Light
by Nene Phototypesetters Ltd, Northampton, and
printed and bound in Great Britain by
The University Press, Cambridge

A CIP record for this book is available from the
British Library

ISBN 0 7486 0499 5

The Publisher wishes to
acknowledge subsidy from
the Scottish Arts Council
towards the publication
of this volume.

Contents

Contents vii

Preface

In my introduction to the National Monuments Record of Scotland *Jubilee Guide to the Collections*, I paid tribute to the work of Kitty Cruft, who, in 1991, retired from her position as Curator of the NMRS. Following the award of an OBE for her outstanding contribution to Scottish historic architecture, this collection of essays by many of her friends and colleagues is further testament to the warm regard and high esteem in which Kitty has been held throughout her long career.

Starting in 1951 as a part-time research assistant with the small and struggling Scottish National Buildings Record (as it then was), Kitty rose to become Curator of an institution whose international standing was in large measure the result of her personal contribution to its work. Her knowledge and scholarship have not only been brought to bear on the study and practical application of architectural history, but have also been selflessly placed at the disposal of generations of other scholars and casual visitors alike. This generous spirit of enquiry and enthusiasm has underlain all her activities, contributing to an exceptional standard and style of public service, and creating the bond of numberless friendships.

On behalf of all the contributors, and those many other friends not included here, it is my great pleasure to offer this volume to Kitty as a tribute to her achievement, and as a modest repayment for all that she has invested in the subject. The extraordinary breadth of her own sympathies is reflected in the

wide range and nature of these contributions to the history of the Scottish
Country House, a theme that has long stood at the head of the catalogue of her
many architectural interests.

Crawford and Balcarres
Chairman, RCAHMS

List of Abbreviations

DNB	*Dictionary of National Biography*
FRIBA	Fellow of the Royal Institute of British Architects
NGS	National Galleries of Scotland
NLS	National Library of Scotland
NMRS	National Monuments Record of Scotland
NSA	*New Statistical Account*
OS	Ordnance Survey
PSAS	*Proceedings of the Society of Antiquaries of Scotland*
RCAHMS	Royal Commission on the Ancient and Historical Monuments of Scotland
RCHME	Royal Commission on Historical Monuments (England)
RHP	Register House Plans
RIBA	Royal Institute of British Architects
ROSC	*Review of Scottish Culture*
RSA	Royal Scottish Academy
SNBB	Scottish National Buildings Record (now NMRS)
SPAB	Society for the Protection of Ancient Buildings
SRO	Scottish Record Office

FIGURE 1.1 View of the Atholl Lodging at Balvenie after J. C. Nattes's engraved view, adapted by the author to restore the former harling.

A Plethora of Palaces

Some 'Castle-wise' Country Houses of Early Renaissance Scotland

CHARLES McKEAN

It began with Balvenie. To the modern eye, there seemed to be no military reason for the solitary, large-windowed round tower in the north-east corner of that dour quadrangular fortress of the Comyns by Dufftown, which the Earl of Atholl had incorporated when creating his Lodging around 1560. A conviction grew that Atholl had not incorporated an earlier round tower into his Lodging, but had built the block and round tower as a unity, *de novo*.

Drawings by R. W. Billings (c. 1847)[1] and J. C. Nattes (c. 1799)[2] sustain that view. They illustrate the Atholl Lodging as an elaborately decorated palace block, constructed of different masonry from the rest of the castle, and embellished with mottos and heraldry (see Figure 1.1). Lining the second storey is an array of beetling oriel windows (not a bow-shaped cill as the guide book has it,[3] but the remains of oriel windows of the Moray variant – compare Ballindalloch Castle and the Bishop's Palace, Elgin). The probability is that the Atholl Lodging was harled partly to conceal the indifferent rubble, and partly to highlight the heraldry and mottos. Above ground-floor vaulted cellarage, two floors of well-lit apartments occupy the entire width of the wing, reached by staircases projecting into the courtyard. There is indeed little military logic in the round tower: it is the last room in a ceremonial sequence of chambers.

Eftsoons (a good Renaissance word implying immediacy), the penny dropped. That round tower was a characteristic not of military endeavour, but of a more relaxed Renaissance way of life. Perhaps that was the case elsewhere. The guide book to Edzell Castle states that 'the circular tower in the corner is a reminder that there was still a need for defensibility'.[4] But that accords with neither the tower's big windows nor with its private turnpike stair down to the service rooms. The round tower in Edzell also contained an important room. So what could it have been? It has been suggested that the circular chambers might have been studies or closets; but their large windows facing different directions imply, rather, a principal bedroom or even gazebo. Whatever it was, it had a formal place in a procession of important chambers. The inspiration may well derive from France, as we may infer from the plans of Androuet de Cerceau and châteaux such as Chambord.

A similar, if much taller and more substantial, tower attached to a tall palace block can be seen in James Giles's painting of the Earl Marischal's double courtyard palace at Inverugie, by Peterhead, before it was blown up. Comparable forms are not uncommon elsewhere, and imply that a reconsideration even of houses such as Castle Fraser and Midmar could be useful.

The most ostentatious, however, was Huntly Castle (see Figure 1.2). Drawings by Nattes[5] reveal just how prodigious this free-standing château must have been when complete. The building of the palace block is dated to 1553, allegedly upon older foundations.[6] From that period dates the stacked horizontal plan of regularly fenestrated rooms in a procession of hall, 'grit chalmer' and 'ane round within the grit chalmer'. The large circular rooms within 'ane round' were linked vertically to their own internal staircase (as in Edzell); and the principal one is known to have been a bedchamber. It has been adduced that the block (like that at Inverugie) was on older foundations or incorporated older material.[7] That may be so, but it cannot be interpreted solely from the set-back at first-floor level, since that motif is also visible also in Boyne, Balvenie and Inverugie; and Boyne was new-built from scratch. It seems probable that thicker walls were required to contain the weight of the stone-vaulted ground floors, becoming thinner (and more economical) as they rose.

That this reinterpretation of well-known buildings is not entirely fanciful is supported by what happened to Huntly after 1594. After the Earl of Huntly's successful battle of Glenlivet in that year (the Catholics won the battle but lost the war), James VI required that efficient mason/architect William Schaw to slight both Slains and Huntly. Barely a gable survives of Slains. Nothing survives of the tower house at Huntly, which lay to the north. However, Schaw inflicted only token damage on the palace block. Clearly, he discounted its potential for military use; he could recognise a palace for what it was.

Huntly's rebuilding of the superstructure of his chateau in 1602 exalts the palace block into what seems to have been a Scottish response to the château

FIGURE I.2   Huntly Castle, conjectural restoration by the author.

of Amboise, not just in approximate shape and verticality, but also in the array of dormer windows recorded by Nattes. An effulgent superstructure rose from the palace block; and its use of expensive dressed stone implies that the remainder would have been harled, the better to set it off. Although the combination of harling and dressed stone had been used elsewhere (for example at Craigston by Turriff, but not to the degree originally planned), the achievement of Huntly was unmatched. Huntly Palace is impoverished by its current dereliction, which lends it a spuriously vertical and castellated appearance. There would be desirable logic in reflooring and reroofing it according to Nattes's drawing, so that we could once more experience the quality of living to which the Renaissance nobility of Scotland aspired.

Huntly is the most heroic exemplar of the early palace block, composed of a rectangle attached to a single asymmetrically-placed circular corner tower. It shares with the other versions of palace construction the characteristics of wings one room deep, ground floor of stone-vaulted cellarage or kitchens, and upper floors generally of two or three large apartments in a lateral arrangement. They seem usually to have been one or two storeys taller than the remainder of their encircling courtyards, as is implied by Tolquhon and by surviving illustrations of pre-classical Strichen and Glassaugh, and as was certainly the case at Balvenie, Pitsligo, Huntly and Inverugie. The round tower is usually at the end of the sequence of state apartments, and staircases almost invariably project in circular or square towers (squinched or corbelled upper stair turrets are not unknown). Tall windows were usually grilled. With the principal exception of the magnificence at Huntly, ornament is usually restricted to the customarily maverick stringcourses which wind up and down in defiance of any rigid canon, the processional entrance (not infrequently to the stair or stairtower, as was the case in Edzell), armorial panels, occasional aedicule window surrounds, and elaborate dormer windowheads.

Lustrous rooms within were probably sumptuously decorated: panelled, boarded, or in painted plasterwork according to period, status and location. Indeed, the rooms inside the palace at Huntly were painted by John Anderson, uncle of the artist George Jameson.[8] From M. R. Apted's 'Painted Ceilings of Scotland', supplemented by other elements of the period – the plasterwork in Winton, Auchterhouse or Craigievar, or the staircases at Glamis, Innes or Fyvie – we may infer the lost ambience of these abodes. The 1987 fire at Cullen House, which revealed the curiosity of *two* palace blocks projecting from the tower, also uncovered elaborately-painted plaster walls which, when first complete, must have been startlingly vivid. Our perception can also be enhanced by enjoying newly-recreated spaces within restored chateaux such as Peffermill, Terpersie or Carnousie, and by studying the records of visitors.

Sir William Brereton observed, as he passed through the Lothians in 1636, 'gentlemen's (here called lairds) houses built all castle-wise'.[9] Quite so. What a wonderfully English translation of the word 'chateau'. They were castle-wise stately dwellings, built between 1560 and 1660, whose purpose has been obscured by our preoccupation with the older towers to which so many were attached. Daniel Defoe's reaction to Gordon Castle (Bog o' Gight; see Figure

1.3) says it all: 'It is indeed a noble, large and ancient seat; as a castle much is not to be said of it, for old fortifications are of a small import as the world goes now: But as a dwelling or palace for a nobleman, it is very noble, spacious and royal building.'[10] Few of them have survived intact (unlike their contemporaries and clones on the Loire); many have been burnt out to become redesignated 'castle' ruins, and the remainder have been obscured by later baronialising.

Pitsligo, therefore, is instructive. Damned by the Minister of Aberdour along with Pittullie and Pittendrum as one of the three Pits of Hell in the early seventeenth century, Pitsligo was a 'castle' according to MacGibbon and Ross, and to the Ordnance Survey. Its grey ruins spotted with yellow lichen, hugging the northern slopes of Peathill overlooking the Moray Firth, seem, at first sight, to merit the description. But *Macfarlane's Geographical Collections* calls it neither castle nor tower: just Pitsligo or the place of Pitsligo;[11] and there are many similarities in the plan form to Edzell (the consistency within Macfarlane of the term 'place' or 'palace' being used for buildings around courtyards is striking). The curiously blank 1424 tower standing to the south (its windows blocked up) is all that really attracted MacGibbon and Ross, who dismissed the remainder of its buildings as being occupied as labourers' cottages.[12] It is customary to treat such a building as a 'tower with barmkin'.

FIGURE 1.3   The Castle of Gight (Gordon Castle): conjectural restoration of original appearance after John Slezer's engraved view.

Consider, if you will, the degree of the Forbes Lords Pitsligo. James Lascelles, the last Constable of Broadsea, watched Flemish troops drag countless cartloads of spoil from Pitsligo to Admiral Byng's ships at Fraserburgh in 1746.[13] The wealth which such booty suggests is vouched by the extravagently carved timber of the Pitsligo Loft, which the then laird installed in his new Episcopalian Parish Church on the top of Peathill in 1632; it is among the most gorgeous of its generation in Scotland. The Forbes of Pitsligo were evidentially warm men, as were many of their contemporaries in Buchan.

Their chateau of Pitsligo consisted of a stately courtyard built in stages between 1517 and 1663 to enfold the older tower. The courtyard plan, with parallels at Tolquhon, Balgonie, Drum, Cawdor and Dunrobin, is possibly the most habitual of this period in Scotland. The Pitsligo courtyard, entered beneath an arched pend in the west wing and revealed as cobbled during consolidation works by Douglas Forrest Architects for Malcolm Forbes, had apartments on the west and north wings on the first floor, above cellarage. They were reached by an outside stair against the north wing, and possibly by an internal turnpike reached from within the entrance pend. Nattes's 1800 view[14] attests that the north wing had only one principal floor with a garret above. It was roofed by stone flags or pantiles (impossible to distinguish which) edged by enormous stone skews. There is no evidence to suggest that the western entrance front was any taller, and no indication survives of how, if at all, the entrance archway was enhanced or identified. Indeed, the stonework implies that the entrance pend may be part of a later addition. By analogy with Tolquhon (1584–9), one of these wings may well have been a gallery. If so, by similar analogy, it would have been along the north wall.

Thus, to the west and to the north, the old tower was enfolded by a sweep of well-lit apartments and offices opening into each other. But what exalts Pitsligo to entirely another rank is the eastern range; for here are the remains of a diminutive palace block in full crumbling fig, with – like Balvenie – a round tower in the corner.

The foundations imply that the range extended the length of the east façade, but a new entrance was broken through in the eighteenth century, leaving a rump just the length, probably, of two apartments. Pending full excavation, it is not possible to ascertain what detail survives in the principal rooms. In the round tower there remain windows, fireplaces and the raggle of the conical roof rising around a typically sturdy chimney stack. As usual, the rooms in the palace block occupied its entire width, were tall and were well-lit; and those in the tower had large windows facing in different directions.

There is no evidence that the round tower was really defensive, as

FIGURE 1.4   A corner of the great garden at Edzell Castle after R. W. Billings, with the
harling reinstated over the rubble and the columns restored by the author.

MacGibbon and Ross suggest. Instead, it is likely to have contained the
private chamber or bedroom of Lord and/or Lady Pitsligo.

The clue to the quality of this chateau lies in the large-windowed stairtower,
possibly built around 1603. Square at the base, it is chamfered at the corner of
the second storey, where there appears to be a squinch for carrying a turret
above (as in Glenbuchat). Along with the rest of the palace block, it was

harled with dressed margins, stringcourses and armorial panels, as may be deduced not solely from the extensive remains of harl but also from the nature of the far too rough and rudimentary walling wholly to have been left visible, in the light of what the stairtower tells us about Lord Pitsligo's aspirations. Bearing stones for a now vanished but immense, presumably carved lintel stone or possibly even pediment still survive. A National Monuments Record photograph of the great stair (it is now in much worse condition than it was then) records a broad, sweeping staircase with transverse vaults, not far short in style of the exquisite 1603 structure in Fyvie Castle. There survives a large, sheltered walled garden to the north, and a pleasantly strange walled and gated pleasance to the west.

Pitsligo, whose current measured drawing programme by Douglas Forrest may uncover further details to assist in the interpretation, is instructive because it reveals a new style of living: the old tower unroofed and presumably derelict soon after 1700 (see Figure 1.6), yet the palace block in full occupation, as it remained until the 1745 Rebellion. Inverugie's palace block was only abandoned after the death of the last Earl Marischal's mother, her son being exiled abroad. It has been suggested that suites of rooms open-

FIGURE 1.5   The roofline of Glamis after R. W. Billings, with the harling restored by the author.

ing into each other were a medieval throwback, real adventurousness being displayed by the introduction of corridors. But there is no evidence to sustain the view that these buildings were abandoned because they were anachronistic at least until the late eighteenth century. Ian Gow's examination of the processional suite at Holyrood, and of how that pattern was translated by William Adam in the eighteenth century, confirms that we have stumbled across not so much an anachronistic survival as a formal and lofty way of life.

Seduced by the tower and persuaded by its turrets, historians have tended to ignore sixteenth- or seventeenth-century palace blocks. Their slight myopia has been encouraged by the fact that so many of the plans published in guidebooks are of the ground floors (i.e. the cellar floor) and not of the principal floor, from which the true purpose of these buildings could have been ascertained. It should come, therefore, as no surprise to read that 'the fortified private residence becomes obsolete after the Restoration'.[15] On the contrary, the fortified residence, as such, became obsolete many years before the Restoration. So how has this misconception arisen? People have been lured into the habit of concluding that what are really the ruins of 'chateaux' – castle-wise houses – are the ruins of 'chateaux forts', or castles. It fitted the view of Scottish culture as primitive, provincial and tardy. Yet Scottish culture was neither English nor British, at this stage, but mainstream European: and to judge by the quantity of architectural achievement, the Scottish economy was clearly flourishing.

Lindsay of Pitscottie has an amusing tale to tell about a similar misconception confounded during the progress made by King James V to hunt in Atholl in 1529. The Earl of Atholl caused to be constructed a 'fair palace of green timber, wind with green birks … which was fashioned in four quarters, and in every quarter and nook thereof a great round, as it had been a block-house, which was lofted and gested the space of three house height … there were two great rounds in each side of the gate and a great portcullis of tree'. Pitscottie recorded: 'The Ambassador of the Pope, seeing this great banquet and triumph which was made in a wilderness, when there was no town near by 20 miles, thought it a great marvel that such a thing could be in Scotland, considering that it was named The Arse of the World by other countries'.[16]

Pitscottie's description makes the timber palace at Atholl resemble a timber version of the ruined House of Boyne by Fordyce. Calling to one's aid the late Douglas Simpson, who prepared a naive reconstruction of it,[17] there is every reason to believe that Boyne was a rare sixteenth-century Scots palace built completely *de novo*. Yet John Dunbar states that Boyne 'shows the lengths to which native conservation could go', drawing attention to the 'high walls of enceinte and massive circular angle towers'.[18] The round towers are no more military than they were in other palace blocks, and the plan is a rather

grander and more sophisticated version of the customary courtyard plan of
the Scots Renaissance. Above the usual ground-floor cellarage and kitchens,
the principal apartments (above the set-back) are identified by large windows
and a stringcourse. Boyne did not strike the Rev. Alexander Hepburn as a
castle when he visited it in 1723, but rather as a stately house whose curious,
sunken, walled front garden was used for wild herbs. At that time, it was still
lived in occasionally by Lord Deskford and his family. It is arguable that what
remains at Dudhope, Dundee, is the mutilated survivor of a palace of
comparable aspiration for the Grahams of Claverhouse.

We need to review what constituted the architecture of the Scottish
Renaissance. Dominated by fortifications, towers and by MacGibbon and
Ross, we have failed to understand the palace block for what it was. Yet their
volumes imply a wealth of construction during this period of Scottish history.
The late eighteenth-century paintings of Francis Grose[19] and Robert
Riddell,[20] which record many such structures when still complete, confirm
that, and also hint at regional variations: the further south, the greater the
elaboration and carving around door or window, and the better the mason-
work (although the Medusa-head-like dormer windowheads of Cullen House
are as fanciful as any).

Residential blocks of greater or lesser grandeur, built for comfort or
magnificence between 1560 and 1670, were built in considerable quantities
and may be classified into groups. The villas which clustered in the
hinterland of major cities or Royal Palaces, frequently L-plan with the stair in
the re-entrant, were often miniature copies of their country cousins, and
shared common plan forms and characteristics until they developed their own
individuality. An unusual group of U-plan villas with elaborate decoration
existed in the vicinity of Edinburgh, of which the drawings by James Skene
imply the inclusion of the Wrychtes' Houses, Dean House, Moray House,
possibly Brunstane House and Pinkie House.[21] The free-standing block
usually adjacent to but detached from an older tower seems to have been
particularly vulnerable to change. That at Wester Powrie (by Dundee)
survives, whereas for example those of Elphinstone, Sauchie and Clackman-
nan have vanished. Some unusual palace blocks were sandwiched between
two towers, as possibly at Kellie (Fife), Cairnbulg, MacDuff's Castle and
Laurieston. The commonest is the palace courtyard, usually extending from
an existing tower, as in Cawdor, Glamis, Edzell, Balgonie, Tolquhon and
probably Drumlanrig.

The free-standing chateaux (in contradistinction to real towers like
Craigievar and Balmanno), such as Carnousie, Claypots, Peffermill, Elcho,
Edinample, Leslie and countless other homes misunderstood as towers, and
all the buildings like them, represented to their builders a refreshing advance

FIGURE 1.6   View of Pitsligo Castle from the entrance gateway, 1968.

in sophistication and culture over the old towers. Rather than piling room upon room in vertical mode for reasons of defence, their horizontal plans, as often as not enfolding a courtyard, represented a Scottish response to contemporary trends across the North Sea. A plethora of palaces? We don't yet know the half of it.

Most of these Renaissance palaces of Scotland (with the exception of the Royal ones which changed for different reasons) were altered or abandoned by the end of the eighteenth century. Why was this so? The probable answer, leaving aside social change and Jacobite forfeiture, lies in their verticality. It was curious of Scottish houses to have their balconies and their leads at the tops of buildings four, five or six storeys high, and even more curious to have the long gallery on the top floor as in Crathes; and quite extraordinary to have it on the top floor in a building as sophisticated as Duff House as late as 1735. By the late seventeenth century, plan forms were becoming more horizontal, particularly in England, as corridors appeared and servants became invisible. Horizontality can be extended easily: verticality cannot. Is it possible that the

Renaissance buildings of Scotland died – for the most part – because by going upward they were inflexible and thus atrophied?

ACKNOWLEDGEMENTS

Many people have assisted in my treasure hunt. They include Dr Iain G. Brown and Julian Russell of the National Library of Scotland Manuscripts Department; Miss Margaret Wilkes, Head of the Map Library; Miss Anne O'Connor, formerly at the Library of the National Museums of Scotland; Mungo Campbell of the Department of Drawings and Manuscripts at the National Gallery of Scotland; staff at Edinburgh Central Library; Colin MacLaren and his staff, Department of Manuscripts, the University of Aberdeen; Ian Gow, Simon Green and Kitty Cruft at the National Monuments Record of Scotland; and Donald Galbraith at the Scottish Record Office. Douglas Forrest initiated the interest in Pitsligo by querying what was so special about it. Aonghus Mackechnie and Dr Deborah Howard also tolerated the development of the notion and assisted with their advice, as did the late Colin McWilliam, whose encouragement is sorely missed.

NOTES

1. R. W. Billings, *The Baronial and Ecclesiastical Antiquities of Scotland*, 1852, plate 19.
2. J. C. Nattes, National Library of Scotland, MS 5205/3.
3. Iain MacIvor, *Balvenie Castle*, HMSO 1988, p. 17.
4. W. Douglas Simpson with Richard Fawcett, *Edzell Castle*, HMSO 1982.
5. J. C. Nattes, National Library of Scotland, MS 5205/30–34.
6. W. Douglas Simpson, *Huntly Castle*, HMSO 1960.
7. Ibid.
8. Ibid.
9. Sir William Brereton (1636), quoted in Hume Brown's *Early Travellers in Scotland*, James Thin, 1973, p. 148.
10. Daniel Defoe, *A tour through the whole island of Great Britain* (c. 1724–5), Folio Society, 1983, vol. 3, p. 288.
11. Sir Arthur Mitchell (ed.), *Geographical Collections relating to Scotland collected by Walter Macfarlane*, 3 vols, Edinburgh, 1906.
12. David MacGibbon and Dr Thomas Ross, *Castellated and Domestic Architecture of Scotland*, Mercat Press, 1971, vol. IV, p. 294.
13. Sir David Fraser (ed.), *Christian Watts Papers*, Caledonian Books reprint.
14. J. C. Nattes and James Fittler, *Scotia Depicta*, 1804, plate 3.
15. John Dunbar, *The Historic Architecture of Scotland*, Batsford, 1966, p. 76.
16. Lindsay of Pitscottie, *History of Scotland 1436–1565*, 3rd edn, 1778.
17. Aberdeen University Manuscripts: W. Douglas Simpson Collection.
18. Dunbar, op. cit., p. 52.
19. In the Department of Prints and Drawings at the National Gallery of Scotland.

20. In the Library of the Society of Antiquaries.
21. Drawings in the collection of Skene of Rubislaw at Edinburgh Central Library.

FIGURE 2.1   The principal front of Fyvie Castle, 1960.

2

Design Approaches in Early Post-Reformation Scots Houses

AONGHUS MACKECHNIE

In considering early Scottish country houses of the post-Reformation period, it should be stated at the outset that this topic begins more as a study of houses in the country than of any fully-developed 'country house' as the term is generally understood in the eighteenth- or nineteenth-century context. The full complement of country-house features did not come into being all at once, yet many of the most essential elements of the later houses, which set them apart as country houses rather than as any other class of building, either already existed or were being introduced into Renaissance Scotland, especially by the second half of the sixteenth century. Thus, as in other European nations, houses in the country were built to serve a purpose distinct from town houses as the principal residence within the rural estate. Often they were built close to the laird's tenantry – unlike later country houses, which were constructed a distance away or alternatively (as happened at Inveraray) were part of a greater plan which involved the relocation of the community to a new town or village further off. As the sixteenth and seventeenth centuries progressed, these houses demonstrate an increasing emphasis both on comfort and on pleasure with elaborate interior ornament, as at Kinneil and Newark, and rich furnishing such as is described in the inventories of Floors[1] and Hamilton Palace.[2]

There were also ornamental gardens, possibly the finest being royal gardens such as those which James IV created at Stirling, while the sketches on Pont's late sixteenth- and early seventeenth-century maps show clearly his recognition of the interrelationship between a house and its garden.[3] Late in our period, Balcaskie, a house of around 1629 in origin, is aligned on the Bass Rock, showing an interest in the use of an axial vista by that date, and the near-contemporary Staneyhill seems also to have been aligned similarly. At many houses, there were ornamental garden structures such as sundials (at Newbattle), well-heads (at Pinkie), garden pavilions (at Moray House) and gatepiers (at Merchiston and Staneypath), while sundials were especially popular in this country – possibly linked to the idea of a garden as a place for demonstration of the sciences. So, these Renaissance houses, the country houses of their time, are relevant in the genesis of the country house proper.

These early examples of country houses make it more than a little surprising that even as late as 1982 one author should confidently assert that 'the Scots [in contrast with England] did not build country houses before the Restoration'.[4] A moment's consideration of Culross Abbey House, for instance (1608) – a mainstream example of a European country house, having affinities with Courances in France (1606), or Villa d'Este in Italy – gives the lie to that assertion. Perhaps only English-looking houses were sought by that writer, for it is clear that even before the major and innovative series of works produced in the early seventeenth century, when Sir James Murray of Kilbaberton held the post of Master of the King's Works, there was a tremendous amount of building activity in Scotland producing structures which were undoubtedly the country houses of their period. Perhaps it is therefore time that they should be analysed using different criteria to the castellated conceptions of writers like MacGibbon and Ross and thus, perhaps, put into a context which will make the architecture of this period better understood.

From examination of the buildings of the period, two general points quickly emerge: first (and perhaps obviously), the different trends of fashion rendered the architecture of the previous generation old-fashioned; and, second, within a national context there were at least three distinct locations in which these developments were concentrated: the west, the north-east and east-central Scotland. It may be noted that all these areas are centred on university towns, and that they could even today, be said to determine distinctive cultural groupings.[5] The differences, when noted, should not be overstated, for strong links existed between all three regions, particularly between east-central Scotland and the other areas – a point which is well illustrated in the building trade by the number of mason apprentices coming from the west who were trained in Edinburgh.[6] East-central Scotland, however, was always set apart from the other regions as the place where political and administrative power lay. The royal palaces and favourite residences of the Scots kings (though little used after 1603) were all in this area. Here too (until the shift of emphasis arising from the expansion of the Clyde trade with the Americas from the second half of the seventeenth century) were the nation's principal burghs and trading ports, so that even Glasgow, in its eagerness to exploit the North Sea trade, used Bo'ness[7] as its port before Port Glasgow, acquired by the city in 1668,[8] became her principal outlet for trade. East-central Scotland continued as the centre of administration where Parliament met and foreign ambassadors stayed. Consequently, it is hardly surprising that, in general terms, the more sophisticated architecture of the period is seen there. The significance of this eastern or court architecture is discussed elsewhere.[9]

The Gaidhealtachd, or Gaelic-speaking Highlands, stood culturally apart – though not remote – from the rest of the country, though members of the Highland aristocracy could, of course, choose to adopt elements of lowland culture and fashions, either in the sometimes bicultural east or in the more solidly Gaelic west. Another point which emerges is that the buildings of one area type might be found in another area. An architect from east-central Scotland might be engaged in one of the other regions, but there is less evidence of this process being reversed. A case in point is Carnasserie (late 1560s) in Argyll which, with its particularly sophisticated detailing – of a character seen at, for instance, Mar's Lodging in Stirling, or Archbishop Hamilton's 1550s reconstruction of St Andrews Castle – looks out of place in the west; as indeed does Strathleven, of a century and a half later.

THE WESTERN SCHOOL OF THE LATER SIXTEENTH CENTURY: THE HAGGS–KENMURE GROUP

The first development to note is the type of ornament given to country houses in the west from about the 1570s, a style that remained popular for about twenty years. Now that Cowhill is gone and Blairquhan has been rebuilt, the style is yet represented by Haggs and Kenmure. Maybole, though well preserved, is not a mainstream example. This style is characterised by an emphatic use of distinctive ornamental detail. It uses revived early ornament, particularly a heavy cable-moulding, square-stepped or chequer-corbelling, dog-tooth and nail-head and figurative sculpture, including musicians. The panels for armorials are often rectangular and vertically-proportioned with T-shaped divides. The buildings could be enormous, like Kenmure, or small, like Gylen or the Crawford tomb chest at Kilbirnie. Excepting the last example, which is the only non-domestic structure thus far identified, all these buildings are asymmetrical, usually with an L-plan front, but with a fenestration in which is seen a tendency towards symmetry, being sometimes disposed in more or less regular bays. And yet, simultaneously, there is seen a movement away from the linear tower of symmetrical profile towards a wilful asymmetry of profile. The cable-moulding was sometimes, as at Blairquhan and Kenmure, run horizontally like a classical stringcourse, and sometimes carried up and round the windows. This amalgam of features is (or was) seen particularly at Kenmure and Haggs, Cowhill[10] and Blairquhan,[11] and in their 'symmetricalising' helps to underscore the classical basis to the buildings.

On most examples, a jamb (that is, a wing) is set at one end, usually the left, of the main front. Often the door is at its foot in the re-entrant angle, with the main stair within, usually a turnpike of generous proportions, leading to the principal apartments on the first and upper floors. The ground floor of the body of the house otherwise contains vaults and, if required, a corridor. This jamb may be square in plan, circular or semi-polygonal, but it is always square at the top floor and is usually corbelled outwards. Its top storey, which is set above or rises through the main eaves level, is sometimes of ashlar, or is otherwise given a more ornamental treatment than the lower floors of the house: a treatment which remained a characteristic of the national main-stream until at least the late seventeenth century. On the inside of the top floor was a wee room which must have had a special function, possibly a study or a library, as is suggested by the grandness of Maybole, which sports a large oriel at this level.[12] In this Western school of buildings, the stair to the top stage is not corbelled out from the re-entrant angle, as was commonly done elsewhere and in grand manner at, say, Ferniehurst: instead, it projects slightly from the outer wall, at the point of intersection between gable and jamb, and at Haggs these share the same wall-plane. Haggs, which was built about 1585 and reconstructed in the 1890s from a semi-ruinous condition, is one of the most elaborate examples, with a stair corbelled to square above the wall-head, perhaps to form a viewing platform. The impression is one of architectural elements climbing one on top of another: an arrangement further developed at Amisfield of 1600, which appears to be a late derivative of this Western school.

The decorated windows of Haggs and Blairquhan are paralleled at Maclellan's Castle, Kirkcudbright. These are framed by continuous mould-ings, encircling both the window opening and its pediment above (though sometimes not continued along the sill), and have a distinctive horned detail to emphasise the intersection of the vertical and raking members. The arrangements of a cable-moulding run continuously round the sides and top of an opening, and springing from corbels, seen at Blairquhan and Seagate Castle, Irvine,[13] is also seen on the armorial panel at Cornell, Ayrshire, thus linking this otherwise comparatively plain tower with the Western group. Another distinctive feature of the group is provided by the dormer heads at Blairquhan formed by three horseshoe-shaped arches, arranged in a triangu-lar pattern with one set centrally over the other two. Almost identical dormers appear at Maybole, and it is conceivable that the feature may derive from pediments of the long-demolished north wing at Falkland Palace, the detail of which is now known only from a rough survey drawing by Alexander Edward.[14]

Dunderave, of 1596, and Gylen, of 1582, though both lying within the Gaidhealtachd clearly belong to this Western lowland group. A contemporary inscription over the door at Dunderave is in Scots, pointing to the inroads made even in the sixteenth century by lowland culture and to the subordination of Gaelic more than a decade before the Statutes of Iona, yet only a generation after Carsewell – who, albeit a Gael, was a representative of the Establishment – chose Gaelic for the inscription at his house at Carnasserie.[15] Significantly, all three of these houses were built within Campbell-dominated territory. Not one recognised building by this western school is known in the east-central area, though further north it appears that the influence can be seen, as at Scalloway, where the overdoor panel has an inverted T-shaped divide (unless this shape is intended to conform with the glazing/shuttering pattern). On the other hand, there are parallels across the border in north-west England, first pointed to by Ian Fisher.[16]

Though it is not clear how this decorative fashion came about, it is important to recognise that its ornament marks a conscious revival of early forms – a fundamental of Renaissance architecture itself – using details which were almost completely abandoned by the close of the fifteenth century. Indeed, the revival of early forms was by this time a well-established phenomenon, as has recently been discussed elsewhere.[17] The essential point is that the use of this type of ornament in the Renaissance period in Scotland should not be viewed as old-fashioned: that, indeed, is one thing which it most certainly was not, for the conscious revival of ancient ornamental detail ties this group of buildings firmly to Renaissance values and not to any sort of 'Gothic survival'.

THE EASTERN COURT SCHOOL OF THE LATE SIXTEENTH CENTURY: FYVIE–BARNES GROUP

Given impetus by the royal works of James IV and James V, Renaissance influences spread, some ideas becoming quickly popular, including the use of details such as pediments which served a practical purpose as dormer heads, while baluster-shaped shafts were commonly used in architectural frames. Roundels were used in royal works at Stirling, Falkland, Linlithgow and Holyrood, and they were subsequently used elsewhere in the 1550s–70s, for example in stonework at Mary of Guise's House, Leith (1652),[18] Monimail Tower (1578), John Knox's House (1556) and Mar's Lodging, Stirling (1570–2). Again, these were used almost exclusively in east-central Scotland (Carsluith is an exception), pointing either to a school of craftsmen connected with the royal court or perhaps simply to a wish to share in the use of this fashion.[19] But it was not until about the early 1580s, following the unsettled mid-century years, civil war and the minority of Jamie Saxt, that there was a settled court to allow for the encouraging and flourishing of the Arts, i.e. once James was securely (he attained his majority in 1587) in the role of governing king. Coincidental (approximately) with this period up to the end of the century, two points can be noted which it is tempting to relate, viz. the period of William Schaw in the office of Master of the King's Works (i.e. 1583–1602), as well as the emergence of a new architecture which placed an emphasis, not seen in Scotland in the immediately preceding period, on symmetry both of plan and of elevation – though Drochil (1570s) and more particularly Mar's Lodging (1570–2) and Holyrood (particularly if John Mylne's information on James V's intention to duplicate the 'James V tower' is accurate) all pointed firmly in that direction. Within that group there is a diversity in design which most likely indicates the hand of more than one designer, pointing perhaps to a broad shift in educated architectural thought and not necessarily to the work of one individual alone. Definition of this group therefore contrasts with that for the Western school, the latter characterised in the main (as noted above) by a shared repertoire of ornament culled from native sources, for the Eastern group (perhaps most obviously seen at Fyvie) might use ornament culled from the local repertoire, while in its 'purer' Italianate detailing the Stirling Chapel Royal (1594) is of the highest quality for its time. Also in contrast to the Western school, examples of the group exist in the west (though not known in the Gaidhealtachd) and north-east, though the greatest concentration is in the east-central area. The linking element, evidently, is primarily the status of the patron, rather than simply a geographical or local convenience.

Since most identified buildings of this Eastern group are royal works or were for important political figures and courtiers, it is appropriate to label this group as a 'court style'. Examples such as Fyvie[20] (see Figure 2.1), Scone[21] and Barnes were conceived on a colossal scale and might be seen as the Scots equivalent of the great English prodigy houses or, more appropriately, the French Chateaux or the mansions of Northern Europe, while the building of the precocious Italianate Stirling Chapel Royal gave royal approval to this new style. Only one other church, at Burntisland (approx. 1589–96) – then a developing and prosperous burgh – adheres to these principles (its centralised plan indeed is advanced for its date even in comparison with Low Countries architecture), and most buildings of this group now known to us are (or were) country houses.

Although Fyvie (begun remodelling around 1596) was not the earliest example built, it is appropriate to consider it first. This is because it was built for Alexander Seton (from 1597 Lord Fyvie, from 4 March 1604 Earl of Dunfermline), who contributed a Latin epitaph to Schaw's memorial, where he described himself as Schaw's 'true-hearted friend';[22] but the obvious implication – viz. that Schaw helped with his friend's new house at Fyvie – lacks documentary substantiation.

Another point to note here is the significance of the Seton family as patrons of the court style, both during Schaw's period in office at Fyvie, Barnes and parts of Seton (the north-east quarter evidently executed by Schaw himself),[23] and in James Murray's period of office, early in the seventeenth century. The family aisle at Dalgety (c. 1610), Pinkie (begun 1613) and the Pinkie well-head (c. 1620–30), further work at Seton Palace (the south range at least), and Winton (1620–8) all date from Murray's period, and many – if not all – of these are perhaps attributable to him. At this point it is worth noting that the Dunfermline aisle at Dalgety and Culross Abbey house are possibly unique in Scotland for this period, having stone-panelled interior walls, and the similarity of the Culross mouldings to those seen at Murray's Edinburgh and Linlithgow palace blocks indicates a link between all these buildings. Indeed, Culross had a corbel table at its original wall-head, like those at the palace blocks, and spouts, suggesting that it too was originally flat-roofed and parapeted. Alexander Seton was himself described shortly after his death as having (among other virtues) 'great skill in architecture', an interest which (as evidently happened to James Smith over half a century later) might well have been aroused while he was a student at the College of Jesuits in Rome, although it might equally have been aroused during his service in France as a diplomat, or perhaps simply through his friendship with Schaw. Frustratingly, it is not known what his personal influence was on the development of the court style: that is, how far (if at all) it extended beyond providing the necessary patronage to perhaps providing an input to actual design.[24]

While (like so many other Scots houses) an earlier building was incorporated, Fyvie nonetheless was successfully given a big symmetrical palace front with regularly positioned openings, strings and classical details. The centre-piece is twin-towered, with parallels at Boyne, Dudhope (1580 onwards), Rowallan and Tolquhon (1584–9), but the Fyvie centrepiece is based much more on the triumphal arch theme, a feature repeated elsewhere (for instance at Craigston, 1607), the idea then being revived in the eighteenth century (for instance at Dun House). Another contemporary parallel is Saltcoats (1590), where an arch is thrown at a similarly high level between two turrets on one end wall.

William Adam's survey drawing of the 1720s shows that Fyvie had formerly a symmetrical courtyard plan, with recessed ranges linking corner towers; but the north and west ranges, described by Adam as 'ruinous vaults', may never even have been completed.[25] For its date, this plan was not quite unique in Scotland, for the great royal palace of Linlithgow had assumed a symmetrical and corner-towered quadrangular form by at least the time of James IV (1488–1513), and – as noted above – Holyrood appears from at least James V's time to have been intended to have a strictly symmetrical front with corner towers set forward and taller, its ground plan also symmetrical and quadrangular. The basic form of Fyvie was repeated in the next century for Heriot's and for Drumlanrig (both as reconstructed by James Smith, and as shown in 1608–18 plans of its proposed 'reformation'), though other forms of courtyard buildings – for example Tolquhon – certainly existed then. A feature seen on some of these examples (such as Drumlanrig) is a central entrance on the main front with an entrance door in the courtyard range opposite. Such an arrangement may have been intended for Fyvie, which would explain the positioning of the grand stair (see Figure 2.4) (cf. Drumlanrig); certainly it was used at Heriot's, and it is a feature characteristic of French house, or Hôtel, designs of the Renaissance period.

The south and east ranges of Scone were built for Sir David Murray of Gospetrie (created Lord Scone in 1605 and Viscount Stormont in 1621), who was given the confiscated Gowrie Lands in 1600, though it is not known when building work at Scone began. Both these ranges were given symmetrical fronts with the centre and ends advanced, and on plan, the ranges were set at right angles about a courtyard, reminiscent of Fyvie and of Barnes; but the retention at Scone of what appears to have been earlier ranges ruled out the possibility of precise symmetry in the courtyard plan, as was achieved at Fyvie, though the existence of the long fronts laid at right angles to one another on plan points to a similarly concern for symmetry. Culross Abbey House of 1608 comprised two ranges similarly arranged in an L-plan, and if it should be classed with this group (which it really post-dates) then the question arises of whether it too was intended to have been quadrangular, i.e. was only half-built.

Barnes Castle can also be linked to this courtyard group, though its 'courtyard' might more accurately be termed a walled forecourt. Its builder was Sir John Seton of Barnes (d. 1594), second surviving son of the 5th Lord Seton and so a brother of the future Earl of Dunfermline, builder of Fyvie. Barnes appears never to have been completed, but its plan is clear: strictly symmetrical, an enormous block with the ends advanced, a central entrance and square pavilions along the perimeter of the walled forecourt, rather like Montacute, Somerset (1580).

The next great house which requires mention here is that built in the 1590s for John Maitland of Thirlstane, Lord High Chancellor of Scotland, the foremost political figure in the country. Like Holyrood, Thirlstane was remodelled by Bruce and Mylne in the 1670s, but the basic form of the sixteenth-century house can still be seen: a tall rectangular-plan block with massive drum towers at the corners, giving the ends an appearance like the Fyvie centrepiece, while on the flanks is a series of buttress-like bays, semi-circular on plan, like the old wing at the royal chateau of Loches, near Tours, France, and linked at the eaves level by a shallow arcade which carries a parapet walk. It is not known whether the arcading originally carried along the west short end-wall in a way that might have made closer the comparison with Fyvie (there is a shallow triple-arched arcade on the east end), and neither is it known whether there were originally oriels above any of these 'rounds' (which would recall Schaw's work at Dunfermline). But, like the other houses mentioned here, Thirlstane was symmetrical both in plan and in elevation, and it had near-identical opposing elevations. The vertically-divided flat façade (seen here and at the gallery at Dunnottar) is a treatment particularly associated with French architecture, and best-known in this country from its use at Falkland (1537–9).

The precise symmetry of the buildings noted above features in the reconstruction of two buildings in the west which were first linked by MacGibbon and Ross on account of their having almost identical chimneypieces. These are Newark (dated 1597) and Spedlins (begun after 1600, associated 1605 datestone). The builder of neither was closely linked with the royal court.

At Newark, it is the centre range of what is (now) a U-plan block which is strictly symmetrical, both on its courtyard elevation and more particularly on its seaward front where the east and west ranges are treated as symmetrical recessed gables. With the exception of the exactly contemporary Crawford aisle at Kilbirnie (where identical moulding detail is seen), which could well be by the same architect, the 1597 work stands apart from other work of its date in the area on account of this strict symmetry as well as its pediment detailing on the upper floors, for the motif of a pediment-within-a-pediment is used, a sophisticated detail deriving from Michelangelo's Porta Pia of 1562.

As at Scone, there was a principal outer entry (although in an older block) leading into the courtyard directly opposite another entrance (in the case of Newark, the main door), and it is reminiscent in its planning of the Bishop's Palace, Kirkwall (1602), where, despite the sophistication of design, the same emphasis on symmetry was not made.

Spedlins was reconstructed following an Act of the Privy Council in 1600 for the better keeping of order in the west march, which directed that a series of houses, including Spedlins, be put in order.[26] The upper floors of the old tower were rebuilt on a double-pile plan (seen previously in symmetrical form only at Drochil); the centre walls and spinal corridor, ingeniously, carried on huge relieving arches which spring from the outer walls; the flanks were made twin-gabled and the roof M-shaped. Again, this work was strictly symmetrical, the opposing elevations near-identical. The use of a double-pile plan is unusual for this date, the next-built well-known example being Culross Abbey House, though Craigston of 1607, while a U-plan building, is, like Spedlins, double-pile at its upper level only. The next-dated double-pile buildings were James Murray's palace blocks of Edinburgh (1615–17) and Linlithgow (1618–21), while the double-tenement with M-shape roof remained a popular plan-type until the eighteenth century at least (at Marlefield of probably c. 1720, for example), late mainstream examples being the governor's houses at the castles of Edinburgh and Dumbarton. But consider the approach of the architect who designed Amisfield (or, perhaps more accurately, its remodelling, as an existing square tower appears to have been retained) in about 1600, where the elevations were made picturesquely asymmetrical, the detail a hangover from the Haggs–Kenmure repertoire of revivalist detail – indeed the distinctive bartizans with raised flats of ashlar continued on a raised wall-plane are paralleled at Kenmure (I have not noted the detail elsewhere). The overall effect at Amisfield is undoubtedly spectacular. But now to Spedlins: when it was remodelled – regardless of the difference in scale – the option must have been there to create a 'stacked' superstructure like that of Amisfield, but instead a totally different result was achieved, as a decision was evidently made to settle on a formal and much more classical response to a similar reconstruction exercise. This radically different outlook is seen on buildings whose datestones differ by only five years (building work could even have overlapped; Spedlins has an associated 1605 stone now at Denbie) and to houses only some ten miles from each other.

Other buildings of this group include Duntarvie (its symmetry now lost by the infilling of the western re-entrant angle) and Boyne – almost square in outline, a pair of parallel rectangular blocks – a formula which is paralleled at Saltcoats (above). Duntarvie is dateable to 1589, the date inscribed on four stones which were salvaged and taken to Hopetoun, where they were noted by the RCAHMS. The house is a long shallow rectangle in plan (as is Thirlstane), south-facing and well-lit with big windows in regular bays, *piano nobile* and the usual suite of three rooms as noted at (for example) the Earl's Palace and discussed below. The existing centre door architrave is not original, but probably marks the original entrance, as the stair – not a turnpike but, unusually, a straight flight – is directly within, and openings above are set between the floor levels. The top-floor windows (Duntarvie is three-storeyed) are lintelled at the eaves level, so the roof was probably unbroken at the eaves. Recessed to the rear, on each gable, is a single square pavilion, originally balustraded, the main walling between these almost unwindowed, but with a corbelled outset, asymmetrically placed, for the principal fireplace.

There are several houses whose dating to this period, or linking to this group, is less secure. These include Balcomie, Fife, which has a possible late sixteenth-century shallow rectangular-plan range (part of a courtyard with associated 1602 gatehouse) with square corner pavilions. A late sixteenth-century date is also possible for Glenbervie, again a shallow rectangular-plan block, the corners of the front wall this time with massive circular turrets, the staircase (as at Duntarvie) set central.[27] Inverugie, too, has big circular angle turrets at its front angles, as does Ardmillan. Is there a pattern emerging here? Note that Thirlstane can once again be cited by way of comparison, this time, though, with turrets at all four of its angles instead of at just two. Clearly these houses, composed of a rectangular main body plus two jambs/turrets, are different from the 'Z-plan' group identified by MacGibbon and Ross. And should we see in them links to the Baberton–Pitreavie formula of the 1620s–30s, which in outline plan is a full U-shape? Castle Kennedy (in progress, 1607) is a variant, the body of the house tower-like, with flanking jambs adjoining the front gable, but still set forward.

William Adam's published plan of Floors might also be mentioned here.[28] Rectangular-plan, spine-walled and with four square angle pavilions, Floors was rebuilt by Adam in about 1721–6. It was in 1724 referred to as 'an antient seat [which] ... begins to wear a new face', showing that the house was remodelled and not built anew, and examination of the plan suggests that what Adam did was to double up a long and narrow house of late sixteenth- or early seventeenth-century type. The northern (presumably added) pile (for Adam's plan is of a double-pile house) is deeper on plan and is more generously windowed throughout, even to the point where on the flanks symmetry is sacrificed by the requirement for light; and with the resultant squeeze for space of the flank windows, the spine wall also acts as ingoes.

If, then, the northern pile is discounted, that leaves a house comparable in outline plan with Duntarvie, especially with the paired turnpikes in the re-entrants expressed in elevation on the long front. Culross, too, would obviously be comparable: a long flat front with square angle pavilions, while one of these pavilions (the only one of the four at Floors) is shown to contain corner fireplaces, a feature first dateable in this country at Culross (1608), but deliberately avoided on the north pavilions. On the pavilions of the northern pile, the east/west-facing windows are placed directly opposite one another; on the southern pile they are not, and, indeed, the windows which face the opposing pavilions on the south wall are asymmetrically placed, as they are too at Culross.

Against this theory, there is a cross-wall placed dead-centre, where the main door would have been if the above theory is correct (Adam shows paired south-facing doors, separated by the cross wall), but that wall need not have been original.

It is difficult to know exactly how Birsay Palace fits in to this group. Its courtyard plan, at a glance, resembles Barnes, while it has a range of stacks over a single flue-bearing wall – a feature seen previously at Falkland and later at Pinkie (similarly, the spine walls at Culross and the Edinburgh and Linlithgow Palace blocks also carry the flues). The arrangement is often a consequence of having a long gallery, and presumably Fyvie too was given this treatment. But dating from 1574, this formal layout at Birsay is slightly earlier than the other dateable buildings in this series (the asymmetrical main block is retained from an earlier phase of building). This takes us back to the period of Mar's lodging (datestones 1570 and 1572). Maybe the conclusion to be drawn is that this developing emphasis on symmetry seen in these late sixteenth-century houses has a long background, more closely linked to James V's major Renaissance buildings than is usually claimed, but with an interruption of building (not a halt) in mid-century caused by the 'Rough Wooing', the lead up to and achievement of the Reformation, just as the period of civil war and interregnum halted the progress of architecture in the middle of the following century.

The above two groups of more sophisticated buildings (a north-east group is discussed by Charles McKean in Chapter 1), can be seen as evidence of diversity within the wider national mainstream of house-building, while at a national level we can note a basic pattern in internal planning which was widely used. Numerous variants notwithstanding, examples are basically similar in their layout and therefore, it would follow, in terms of the requirements which they fulfilled for their owners. Looking first at a series of houses classified by MacGibbon and Ross as 'Z-plan', there is a group which are particularly alike in their planning. Typified by Kilmartin, these houses have at basement level a tripartite division to the body of the house, made by two cross-walls, forming three rooms; only one room (usually the kitchen), at one end, is the full depth of the house, the depth of the other two rooms curtailed by a longitudinal corridor along the front wall (see Figure 2.2). The entrance door opens in to this corridor, usually beside the stair jamb, that is, at one angle, or else it is placed in the jamb itself.

At first-floor level is a suite of three rooms, the main stair opening in to the largest of these, the hall, which (on plan, a rectangle of roughly 3:2 proportions) occupies the greater part of that floor level; a room leading off is also rectangular, but this time narrower than it is deep, and often placed above the kitchen (see Figure 2.3). A third, much smaller, room is in the jamb beyond. Also, characteristically, a stair projects on the front wall of Kilmartin at the intersection of hall and room. On the floor(s) above are, mostly, bedrooms. Dargavel (1584) is another example, this time with the door placed near-centre; Hatton (Angus) follows the same formula, the door in the stair

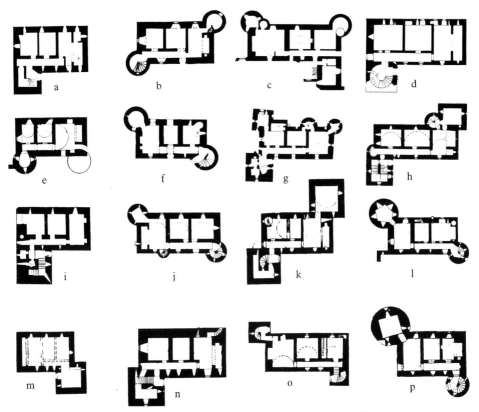

FIGURE 2.2   Ground-floor plans, showing commonalities of design in one group of houses
(not to scale): (a) Castle of Park (b) Dargavel (c) Cortachie (d) Haggs (e) Ardmillan
(f) Colliston (g) Elcho (h) Hatton (i) Dounreay (j) Kilmartin (k) Glenbucket (l) Kilcoy
(m) Forter (n) Finlarig (o) Fordell (p) Inchoch.

jamb; Kilcoy too is similar, and Fordell (1567) is a closely-related variant.
Glenbucket looks similar, but (presuming the interpretation by MacGibbon
and Ross to be correct) only in its secondary stage. Elcho, despite its very
different outline plan and elevational treatment, has basically this same plan,
but with more accommodation in the extra jamb at the north-west corner and
an unusual sophistication in its layout with individual access to virtually every
room. Castle Menzies and Notland have this same principal floor layout, and
so has Huntly (1602); but now we are dealing with something grander, a
major palace block, and again this class of building is discussed in Chapter 1
by McKean.

At any rate, what emerges is that these houses were fulfilling basically
similar requirements, whether on a grander or lesser scale: a way of living
which required a house with *piano nobile* and a suite of certainly two, perhaps

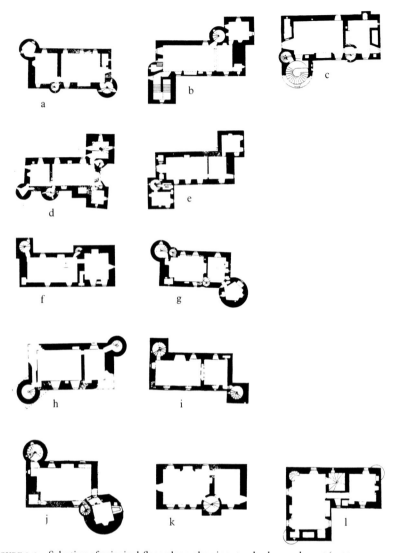

FIGURE 2.3   Selection of principal-floor plans, showing standard room-layout (not to
   scale): (a) Kilmartin (b) Hatton (c) Haggs (d) Elcho (e) Castle Menzies (f) Carnasserie
   (g) Kilcoy (h) Dairsie (i) Fordell (j) Inchoch (k) Blackhall (l) Gilbertfield.

three rooms (perhaps hall–chamber–closet; alternatively, hall–drawing-room–
chamber). Many 'L-plan', or splayed, buildings, for example Innerpeffrey
(c. 1610), also have this same three-room suite, while on other buildings –
usually those of smaller scale – there was no third room, but the principal two
were still of the same relative proportions. The owners of these houses too, in

other words, had basically similar requirements. Once again, there were many variant forms: both principal rooms might be in the body of the house as at Dairsie (where a stair occupied, it appears, both angle turrets) or Blackhall (classed as a 'T-plan' house by MacGibbon and Ross; basically a rectangle, its projecting main stair where the secondary stair is at Kilmartin); alternatively, the hall might occupy the entire body of the house at first-floor level, with the second room in a jamb, as at Gilbertfield (1607); or else, if there was insufficient room at the one level (as at Amisfield), the rooms were simply set one above the other, with room partitions at the bedrooms.

Returning to Blackhall, and to many other of the houses classed by MacGibbon and Ross as 'T-plan', this arrangement of having the stair at the axis of the two principal rooms takes on a new meaning when – unlike, say, Haggs – there is no grander staircase in a jamb or turret. That stair then becomes the main stair, and, when seen in that sense, 'L-plan' houses like Gilbertfield, where the rooms are separated essentially by the stair alone, appear suddenly to become much more closely related to 'T-plans' like Blackhall.

Duntarvie, too, can be noted here, as its centre stair (the principal stair, it will be recalled) also forms the axis between the two principal rooms, while at Haggs it is, as at Kilmartin, the lesser stair that is set at that axis. It is worth noting too that its basement plan is that of the Kilmartin type, and that the basement is not served by that secondary stair, although the lesser or private stair connecting the two lower floors is commonplace in buildings of this period. Johnby, in England, has this same basement plan. There are countless variations on this basic type of house plan; bigger houses might have more complex plans, like Tolquhon with its gallery, but even there a two/three-room suite still stands out distinctly on plan as it often does elsewhere, for example at Kilbryde or Melgund, although houses like Kenmure or Fyvie had more complex circulation patterns. But this discussion is only touching on what is a very large subject, pioneeringly but now quite inadequately covered by MacGibbon and Ross in five volumes. I hope to have shown that there are other ways of considering these buildings than through the classification which they identified.

One point suggested by the above is that this post-Reformation period witnessed a very substantial upswing in the level of building activity – small wonder that William Schaw saw the need to reorganise the governance of the mason craft if it had grown apace. But why this upswing? The answer must be that a period of relative social stability combined with an evidently greater availability of finance created an atmosphere conducive to house-building. However, this answer raises in turn another question, namely, how precisely this 'explosion' in building activity was financed. Manufactured goods in this period still contributed comparatively little to Scotland's

FIGURE 2.4   View of The Great Stair at Fyvie Castle, by James Giles, 1841.

economy: that is, it was not due to increased manufacturing industry alone. The explanation may lie in the fact of the Reformation itself, the severance with Rome and the subsequent redistribution of the Church's extensive wealth. This in turn would have the capacity to generate a greater level of credit advancement, enabling more to build, and the increased house-building activity must have brought with it a greater interest, and consequently skill, in estate management and development. The buildings themselves are the evidence of a wealthier and improving economy in the second half of the sixteenth century, a trend which, in broad terms, continued throughout the seventeenth century, culminating in extravaganzas like Drumlanrig and Hamilton Palace.

Returning, in conclusion, to the Fyvie–Barnes group: while this series of buildings pointed the way forward, it is interesting that the court style of the next generation did not always place the same emphasis on symmetry (though James Murray's Edinburgh and Linlithgow palace blocks, Baberton, Pitreavie and Heriot's all conform to these ideals), giving us buildings like Winton, Parliament House and Staneypath (these perhaps all by Murray). Indeed, splay-plan houses came to be about the commonest house-type built in that period; and (while favoured by Inigo Jones in seventeenth-century England, to little immediate direct effect) it was not until the late seventeenth century that these ideals were resurrected in Scotland, for example at Bruce's Hopetoun, Melville and the Smith designs in the RIBA. These go a stage further than the bulk of these late sixteenth-century houses in making the internal layout also symmetrical on paper (though cf. Spedlins and Barnes), which was the thinking that re-emerged in early eighteenth-century England through the one-time Scots lawyer Colen Campbell as Neo-Palladianism.[29]

NOTES

This chapter has been revised to take account of research carried out since it was written. A complete restructuring has not been possible. There are, therefore, some obvious omissions from this study, such as the court style of the mid-to-later sixteenth century, as characterised by Carnasserie, but whose relationship to the other house-groups had not been recognised by me then. This group of buildings has been discussed elsewhere (A. MacKechnie, *In-House*, Historic Scotland research paper, no. 1, July 1992).

As by far the greater number of the above buildings are described in the volumes listed below, it has not been thought necessary to footnote each building individually. Accordingly, buildings are footnoted only where descriptions are not contained in these volumes or where supplementary material is particularly helpful.

The basic sources are: D. MacGibbon and T. Ross, *Castellated and Domestic Architecture of Scotland*, 5 vols, 1887–92; RCAHMS, various county and City of Edinburgh *Inventories*; Historic Scotland *Official Guides* to monuments in care; Penguin Buildings of Scotland series, *Edinburgh* (1984); *Fife* (1988); *Lothian* (1978).

1. Accessible in Grant Simpson, *Scottish Handwriting*, 1986, document 30.
2. R. K. Marshall in *ROSC* 3, 1987.
3. The association of residence with garden/landscape was by no means new: for instance, King Robert I had a garden at Cardross early in the fourteenth century.
4. Richard Morrice, *Stuart and Baroque*, 1982, p. 34; Buildings of Britain series.
5. The Glaswegian's traditional view of Edinburgh – and the position vice versa – illustrates this point, and the different responses in architecture are obvious even into the twentieth century, as a glance at the work of Lorimer and Mackintosh, and of their contemporaries, shows. Compare for interest the linguistic divisions in Mairi Robinson (ed.), *The Concise Scots Dictionary*, 1985, p. xxxi.
6. R. S. Mylne, *The Master Masons to the Crown of Scotland*, 1883, p. 61.
7. T. C. Smout, *The Glasgow Merchant Community in the Seventeenth Century*, in *Scottish Historical Review*, vol. 47, 1968, p. 57.
8. *Extracts from the Records of the Burgh of Glasgow, 1663–90*, 1895, p. 101.
9. A. MacKechnie, *In-House* (Historic Scotland research paper no. 1, July 1992).
10. Francis Grose, *The Antiquities of Scotland*, vol. 1, 1789, p. 146.
11. NMRS – photographs collection.
12. Oriel windows at this time appear to be more a characteristic of the north-east.
13. *Muniments of the Royal Burgh of Irvine*, vol. 1, 1890, p. xxxixff.
14. Copy drawing in NMRS, FID/96/14.
15. R. L. Thomson, *Foirm na n-Urrnuidheadh*, 1970, p. lxxix; J. Bannerman, 'Two early post-Reformation inscriptions in Argyll' in *PSAS* 105, 1972–4, p. 307. Tradition tells that some of the sculptured stones at Dunderave came from the old MacNachton house at nearby Loch Shira (see D. MacKechnie, *Inveraray Tales and Traditions*, p. 6).
16. M. W. Taylor, *The Old Manorial Halls of Westmoreland and Cumberland*, 1892; RCHME, *Westmorland*, 1930.
17. An important new interpretation of the fifteenth-century Romanesque Revival has been made by Ian Campbell. He has compared the intellectual and political background to that phenomenon with the situation in early Renaissance Italy, and noticed strikingly close parallels between the two. His interpretation is to be published in *Architectural History*, forthcoming.
18. Demolished; two finely-executed salvaged stone panels are reset in the vestibule of South Leith parish church.
19. Timber panelling from Terregles (1583), now in the National Museum, is also decorated with roundels.
20. Published in Scottish National Portrait Gallery, *Treasures of Fyvie*, 1985 (exhibition catalogue).
21. David Walker, 'Scone Palace, Perthshire', in H. Colvin and J. Harris (eds), *The Country Seat*, 1970, p. 210.
22. *Treasures of Fyvie*, p. 11.

23. Cited by MacGibbon and Ross, vol. 2, p. 564, quoting *Memorie of the Somervilles*, vol. 1, p. 459.
24. For Seton's career, see M. Lee, 'King James's Popish Chancellor', in Cowan and Shaw (eds), *The Renaissance and Reformation in Scotland*, 1983; *Memoir of Chancellor Seton*.
25. Reproduced in *Treasures of Fyvie*, Figures 3 and 4.
26. *Register of the Privy Council of Scotland*, vol. 6, 1599–1604; 1894, p. 155.
27. W. D. Simpson, 'Glenbervie and its Castle', in PSAS 105, 1972–4, p. 255.
28. William Adam, *Vitruvius Scoticus*, plates 48 and 49.
29. For a background to these architectural developments in this period, see Howard Colvin, 'A Scottish Origin for English Palladianism?' in *Architectural History*, 1974; also his *Biographical Dictionary of British Architects*, 1978, p. 755; Alistair Rowan, *The Building of Hopetoun*, in *Architectural History*, 1984; also the relevant papers in *St Andrew's Studies in the History of Scottish Architecture and Design*, 1988.

FIGURE 3.1   East elevation of Kinneil House c. 1900, before its partial demolition in 1941. This was halted when the painted decoration was discovered.

3

'Scarce a Finer Seat in Scotland'

Kinneil Castle and the 4th Duke of Hamilton

ROSALIND K. MARSHALL

High on a slope above the burgh of Bo'ness stands Kinneil Castle (see Figure 3.1), once the property of the Dukes of Hamilton. Now in the care of Historic Scotland, it is most often visited because of the splendid wall-paintings (see Figure 3.2) in the sixteenth-century part, but no-one going to see it can ignore the large, ruined building which stands at right angles, to the south, handsome even now in its melancholy splendour.

This five-storey structure, with a plain parapet round the top and a four-storey pavilion at each side, was built in the 1670s by William, 3rd Duke of Hamilton, and his wife, the famous Duchess Anne. Because their principal seat was at Hamilton Palace in the west, Kinneil had been little more than a convenient stopping place for the family on their way to Edinburgh. Now, however, there seemed good reason to believe that it would be occupied permanently. Their eldest son James, Earl of Arran, was almost a man. He was away in Europe on the Grand Tour, but they hoped that when he returned he would take a Scottish wife and settle down at home. He would need his own establishment, and Kinneil seemed the obvious choice.[1]

As it stood, it was not nearly grand enough for the heir to Scotland's premier peer, and so the Duke resolved to extend it. All else apart, he would thereby gain useful experience of the problems of improvement. If he was successful at Kinneil, he and his wife intended to rebuild Hamilton Palace itself. Unfortunately, the contract and the accounts for the building work at Kinneil have not come to light among the Hamilton Archives, but there is

FIGURE 3.2   Painted decoration of the Arbour Room at Kinneil Castle after restoration.

good reason to suppose that the architect was James Smith, the man later
employed to redesign the Palace.

When the new castle was begun is not known, but by 10 November 1677
the Duke was able to tell his brother-in-law, the Duke of Queensberry:

> I have sent you a draught off the Tower of Kinneil, with the two new
> pavillions I have builded to itt, and ther is a scale will lett you know the
> measures. That with two stares was dearer than the other, being 1000
> merks Scots for the workmanship of the ston worke onely. The
> particulare agreement I could not send you, itt being att Kinneil . . .[2]

As the Duke's letter indicates, the south pavilion contained not only a
turnpike stair but also the main staircase of the house, leading from the Laigh
Hall up to the great first-floor Dining-Room.[3] The north pavilion room at that
level served as another, small, dining-room which led through to the
Drawing-Room and the Duchess's Bedchamber in the sixteenth-century
building. She and the Duke continued to occupy their previous quarters, his
apparently above hers. Their son and their younger children would sleep in
the other bedchambers which were situated in the upper storeys of the new
block, two to a floor, usually with their own closets or sitting-rooms.

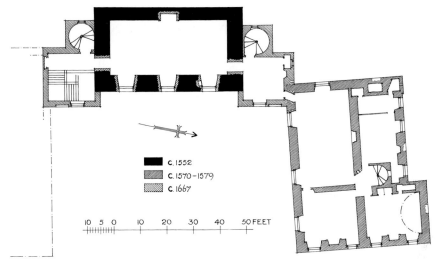

FIGURE 3.3   First-floor plan of Kinneil House.

The kitchens and the rest of the offices were separate buildings at the back, and extra accommodation was being erected there in the 1680s. On 13 September 1687, for instance, James Miller, mason in Kinneil, signed a contract with the Duke, agreeing to put up a new coach house at the end of the existing one. It would be the same length as the stable and the same height as the old coach house, and for this work Mr Miller would be paid £50 Scots and four bolls of meal.[4]

The proximity of the Hamiltons' burgh of Bo'ness to the castle proved a distinct advantage, for building materials could be brought in from Holland and Scandinavia and then carried the relatively short distance from the harbour. Richard Drury, skipper in Bo'ness, supplied a special consignment of Dutch 'leaded tyll' for the roof, Andrew Cowie's vessel carried loads of slates, and Richard Dauling, another Bo'ness skipper, provided several hundred deals for scaffolding, partitions, flooring, wheelbarrows, tables and beds.[5]

Most of the tradesmen employed at the castle were local men, like George Mitchell, smith in Bo'ness, Alexander Wilson, mason there, and Nicol Gardiner, one of the painters in Linlithgow. Sometimes an even more experienced craftsman was required, however, and in 1686 George Wallace, who had worked at both Holyroodhouse and Hamilton Palace, was busy using white lead, chalk, lamp black and '16 pynts of lintseed oyl for culloring thre great gates, stone and timber work within the tower head, old armes and blind window (painted like glass), all 3 times over', at a cost of £44 14s. He had been apprenticed to a herald painter originally, so he must have been particularly well-suited to the task of painting the coat of arms.[6]

By the spring of 1688, the Duke was satisfied with the new house. 'I wish you were here just now to see how sweet a place this is', he wrote to his eldest son. 'I am sure a little more charge bestowed on it wold mak it that there is scarce a finer seat in Scotland, and may compare with Hamilton itself, but I need not insist on this subject, for I fear you will hardly be prevailled on to thinke of a countrey life.'[7] If his tone was peevish, it was hardly surprising. Instead of returning meekly home, his heir had spent the last ten years living a riotous life in London. It was true that he had finally married; but his Countess, Lady Anne Spencer, was English and, as a lady-in-waiting to the Queen, was unlikely to wish to settle in Scotland.

Political events were about to supervene, however. Arran was a supporter of James VII, and with the Revolution he was imprisoned in the Tower of London. When his father eventually secured his release a year later, the Earl's creditors were quite literally waiting outside for him, and so he had to be smuggled secretly away from his prison. He had no alternative but to ride north, followed a few days later by his pregnant wife. Kinneil was hastily put in order for them, and at the end of December they moved in.

The Duke had prudently arranged for a complete inventory of the contents of the castle to be made, and it reveals the sequence of handsomely furnished chambers.[8] The Great Dining-Room, hung with tapestry and portraits of the Earl's forebears, had fourteen Russia leather chairs ranged round two square fir tables and an octagonal one. The Small Dining-Room had two tables and six chairs. In the Great Drawing-Room, twelve elegant cane chairs were set round a fir table and an old marble one. Duchess Anne's Bedchamber was dominated by a blue taffeta bed with eight chairs upholstered en suite, accompanied by two looking-glasses, a pair of stands and a walnut writing desk. This particular inventory does not identify the bedchambers used by the Duke, the Earl or the Countess, but each of the other rooms in the house was furnished in an equally suitable manner.

Pleasing though their new home might be, the Earl and his wife were not destined to stay there for long. They had already lost one baby daughter in infancy. Another was born at Kinneil on 13 March 1690, but, although she survived into childhood, her mother contracted puerperal fever and, to the great grief of everyone who knew her, died in the castle on 10 June. Heartbroken, the Earl of Arran shut up the house once more and went back to London.

For the next decade, his visits were brief. His chamberlain, Daniel Hamilton, was in charge of the day-to-day running of the estate, and the 3rd Duke doggedly continued his schemes for improvement. When he died in

FIGURE 3.4   Anne, 3rd Duchess of Hamilton, by Sir Godfrey Kneller.

1694, the Earl's brothers supervised the work. They considered carrying out their father's plan for a new south wing to balance the old sixteenth-century house, but they abandoned that scheme and instead concentrated their attention on the grounds. Spending a few days there in the early autumn of 1696, Lord John Hamilton was able to report to the Earl with satisfaction:

> Daniel Hamilton is building you a fine park wall and remooving your little town [of Kinneil] furder from you, without [outside] your park wall, and building it a regular town. There are five or six houses almost built. He is likewayes levelling your outer court and making a fine gravell walk thorow the midle of it . . .[9]

Lord John and the others constantly tried to involve the Earl in the improvements, plying him with designs for the gardens, deploring the condition of the roof and describing planting being undertaken. He paid little attention. It was probably he who somewhat inappropriately named the newly-enclosed land 'Hyde Park', but otherwise his interest was almost entirely financial. The property brought him in £6,000 sterling a year, for there were valuable coal and salt revenues, and he was anxious to have every penny to finance his extravagant life at Court.[10]

Because his mother was Duchess in her own right, the Hamilton estates had not come to him when his father died: they remained hers. She did, however, arrange for him to become 4th Duke of Hamilton when he married again in 1698. This was done so that he could represent the family in the vital pre-Union debates in Parliament. The new Duke therefore had a reason for coming north, and in 1700 he brought his petulant young English bride, Elizabeth Gerard, to stay at Kinneil.

When he saw the castle once more, he could not but be impressed, and he was soon telling people that he was sorry that he had stayed away for so long.[11] The roof was still giving trouble, it was true, but he was inspired to make a fresh round of improvements. A modern Lattermeat Hall for the servants was constructed, with a panelled dressing-room and closet for his Duchess, and he ordered that 'the two paviliones bee whitned, as the bodie of the hous is'.[12]

An inventory of 1712 reveals that the castle interior now bore the imprint of his ebullient personality.[13] The principal public rooms remained largely unaltered, but the Duke's own apartments were furnished with elegance and sophistication. His bed was hung with Indian calico lined with changeable

FIGURE 3.5   James, Earl of Arran, attributed to Ferdinand Elle.

silk. The walls of that room were draped with more of the Indian calico, and he had appropriated the big armchair with green cushions which used to stand in the Drawing-Room.

In his East Closet, he could recline in a striped silver armchair or lounge on a walnut couch, scrawl his deplorably spelled letters at the folding walnut writing table, take tea made in the japanned kettle on its stand or survey his policies through a conveniently placed telescope. He had a North Closet too, slightly smaller, but fitted out with another walnut desk, a large globe, a weather-glass and the usual selection of chairs and couches.

The walls of both his closets were hung with flowered silk, and on top of the flowered silk were pictures, dozens of them. He had a passion for art, and so this inventory records paintings and prints throughout the house, from the landscape and the night piece on the Great Stairs to the fifty-six paintings and fifteen miniatures in the North Closet. Even his wife had seventy-five small prints in her dressing-room, and there is little doubt that all these pictures had been chosen by the Duke himself.

His enthusiasm for his Scottish castle did not outlast the Union of the Parliaments, however. As soon as the treaty had been signed, he left Scotland, never to return, and on 15 November 1712 he was killed in a duel in Hyde Park, London.

ACKNOWLEDGEMENTS

The author is grateful to His Grace the Duke of Hamilton for allowing her to reproduce the portraits used as illustrations and to quote from his Archives, and thanks the Keeper of the Records of Scotland for permission to quote from the Hamilton Correspondence.

NOTES

1. The full story of the 3rd Duke and Duchess and their family is told in Rosalind K. Marshall, *The Days of Duchess Anne* (1973).
2. Scottish Record Office [SRO], Buccleuch Muniments, GD224/171, Queensberry Transcripts.
3. *10th Report and Inventory of Monuments and Constructions in the Counties of Midlothian and West Lothian* (Edinburgh 1929), 191–2.
4. Hamilton Archives, Lennoxlove, F1/442/2, F2/455/1, F1/548, F1/544, F2/458.
5. Ibid., F1/442/3, F1/443/4, F1/443/5, F1/51/515.
6. Ibid., F1/479, F1/557, F1/678, F1/548/17.
7. SRO, Hamilton Archives, GD406/1/6258.
8. Hamilton Archives, Lennoxlove, M12/8.
9. SRO, Hamilton Archives, GD406/1/6867.
10. Ibid., GD406/1/9047, 7402.
11. National Library of Scotland, MS 1031, f. 226.
12. Hamilton Archives, Lennoxlove, M10/53/9, 10.
13. SRO, Edinburgh Register of Testaments, 16 June 1722.

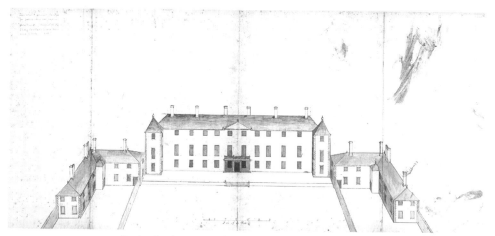

FIGURE 4.1   Design for the proposed west elevation of Kinnaird Castle by Sir William
    Bruce, c. 1695–8.

4

Two Late Seventeenth-Century Designs for Kinnaird Castle

JOHN G. DUNBAR

These designs form part of an album of some two dozen early architectural drawings preserved at Kinnaird Castle. The album was observed by Professor Alistair Rowan during a visit made to Kinnaird in 1976. Through the kindness of the late Lord Southesk, the volume was subsequently placed on temporary deposit with the Royal Commission on the Ancient and Historical Monuments of Scotland to allow photographic copies to be made for the National Monuments Record of Scotland. At the same time the album was examined by the present author and catalogued by Miss Cruft. This chapter seeks to review some of the provisional conclusions reached by these parties in 1976,[1] the present author alone, however, bearing responsibility for the views now expressed.

The album appears to have been compiled by James, 9th Earl of Southesk (1827–1905), whose bookplate it bears. It contains drawings relating to three main schemes for alterations to the castle and gardens of Kinnaird, together with a number of additional sheets. This chapter deals largely with the two earlier schemes, both of which can be ascribed to about the end of the seventeenth century, and is based mainly on the internal evidence of the drawings themselves. It is possible that further information about the circumstances in which the designs were produced is to be found in the Southesk family papers, but neither Sir William Fraser's *History of the Carnegies Earls of Southesk and of their Kindred* (1867) nor the Report of the National Register of Archives[2] gives any indication that this is the case, and the present author has not found it feasible to carry out a detailed search of the Kinnaird muniments.

The first scheme comprises some thirteen sheets of drawings, of which four (fols 2–5) relate to the castle and the remainder (fols 16–24) to the gardens and policies. A number of the drawings bear dates between 1695 and 1698, and all can be ascribed to about this period. Nor can there be much doubt about their authorship, at least so far as the design for the castle is concerned, for the ground-floor plan (fol. 3[r]) bears the inscription 'Aditions and amendments designd for the Earle of Southesks house of Kinnard by W.B. in Ap. 1698'. The reference is evidently to Sir William Bruce, the leading Scottish architect of the day, and another of the drawings, comprising floor-plans of the house as it stood in 1697 (fol. 4[r]), is inscribed in Bruce's own hand 'Ground draught of Kinnard house – as it is given me to amend & add as I think fit'. But the drawings themselves are delineated and annotated in another hand which, by comparison with known examples, can be recognised as that of Alexander Edward (1651–1708), who had acted as Bruce's draughtsman and assistant on a number of previous occasions.[3]

Bruce's scheme for Charles, 4th Earl of Southesk (1661–99), was designed to double the size of the house, regularise the plan and introduce a new entrance and forecourt on the west side. The germ of this idea was evidently in existence as early as January 1696, for the outline of the new house appears in one of Edward's garden plans of that date (fol. 22[r]). As at Kinross House, Kinross-shire, and Craigiehall, West Lothian, detailed plans for the house seem to have been drawn up only after the layout of the gardens and policies was already under way.[4]

Edward's plans of 1697[5] (fol. 4[r]) indicate that the existing house was a three-storeyed tower house of L-plan having later additions on the north side. The greater part of this building was to be retained in Bruce's scheme, which shows a three-storeyed double-pile block facing west on to a forecourt, with short return-wings at the rear, the overall plan thus being U-shaped. The principal elevation (see Figure 4.1) is of ten bays, the centre being emphasised by a four-columned entrance porch, with iron balustrade above, and a triangular pediment of unprepossessing size and appearance. Set forward from each corner of the façade are square pyramidal-roofed stairtowers which also communicate with two-storeyed offices flanking the inner angles of the forecourt.

Considering the difficulties involved in marrying the new building to the old, Bruce's plan must be adjudged a success. As at Bruce's own residence of Balcaskie, Fife, and at Brunstane, Midlothian, the house was to be enlarged by duplicating the earlier L-plan block, but the double-pile arrangement adopted at Kinnaird made for a much more convenient and flexible layout.

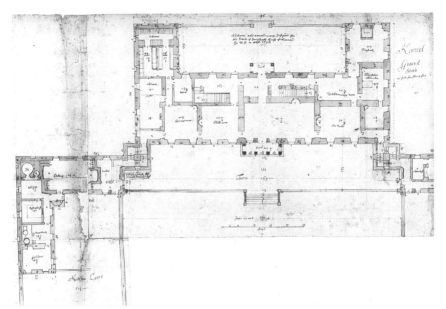

FIGURE 4.2   Proposed ground-floor plan for Kinnaird Castle by Sir William Bruce, 1698.

On the ground floor (see Figure 4.2), Bruce introduced an axial layout of front and garden entrances not unlike that at Kinross House, which may also have provided the model for the very spacious principal staircase. The usual ground-floor family apartment was reduced to two rooms (the bedchamber and closet presumably being on the first floor) to allow for a chapel and chaplain's lodgings. Probably this arrangement was chosen by Lord Southesk, whose wife was a keen Episcopalian and Jacobite,[6] in preference to the likely alternative of placing the chapel in a wing, as Bruce had done at her father's house, Thirlestane Castle, Berwickshire. The plan of the first floor is missing, but this no doubt included a state apartment, perhaps with the great dining-room set over the large ground-floor entrance-hall. The second floor contained another ten bedchambers, most of them provided with their own closets.

Externally, the design was less effective, for the house had an old-fashioned and piecemeal appearance, the tall square angle-towers recalling mansions of the previous generation, such as Panmure in Angus, and Balcaskie. Because so much of the original facework of the old house was retained, it is likely that the principal façade would have been harled, thus accentuating the general plainness of the composition.

In the event, Bruce's scheme for the house was not carried out, preparations evidently being brought to a halt by Lord Southesk's sudden death in

1699. Edward's landscape proposals fared little better, although there is evidence to suggest that planting was begun.[7]

The second scheme (fols 6–12), also unexecuted, comprises seven sheets, of which six relate to the house while the seventh is a plan for a garden layout. One is a first-floor plan of the house 'as it is at present', four are floor-plans of the proposed house (one being titled 'Dessein for Kennart'), while the sixth depicts the proposed front and rear elevations. None of the drawings is signed or dated, but on the evidence of the style of draughtsmanship and hand-writing they can be attributed to the Dutch or German military engineer, John Slezer, best known as the publisher of *Theatrum Scotiae*.[8] The plan for the garden layout is very similar to garden schemes produced by Slezer during the 1670s for the Duke and Duchess of Lauderdale in connection with their building operations at Ham House, Surrey, and at several of the Duke's Scottish houses, including Thirlestane Castle and Lethington, East Lothian.[9]

As in Bruce's scheme of the 1690s, the house was to be enlarged by duplicating the original L-plan castle and forming a double-pile block of U-shape. But Slezer's drawings show less regard for the integrity of the early house, with an entirely new range, three and a half storeys in height, being proposed as an addition to the west side of the building. The frontage (fol. 11; see Figure 4.3) was to be of thirteen bays, the middle five being contained within a shallow pedimented projection. The lowest floor, which is a semi-basement, is lit by distinctive oval windows similar to those on the south front of Ham House, of which Slezer had produced plans and drawings for the Lauderdales during the 1670s. The rear elevation, again of three and a half storeys, has a seven-bay centre and two-bay projecting ends.

These elevations are closely related to that depicted in an undated design drawing for a small country house, also attributable to Slezer, now in the National Monuments Record of Scotland. This last belongs to the group of Lauderdale building and garden drawings already mentioned, and probably represents a project for a member of the Lauderdale or Argyll family.[10] Alike in its general proportions, the treatment of the windows and the design of the high hipped roofs, the rear elevation of Kinnaird also bears a strong resemblance to the principal elevation of Melville House, Fife, erected to the design of James Smith, the distinguished Scottish architect, in 1697–1701. The resemblance is most marked with respect to the drawings of Melville that appear in *Vitruvius Britannicus*.[11] Bruce also prepared designs for Melville and may have contributed towards the final scheme.

Within, the remodelled Kinnaird House was to contain a spacious family apartment on the ground floor, together with a state apartment on the floor above. But the most remarkable feature of the plan (fol. 8; see Figure 4.4) is the very grand double-return staircase, placed axially to the principal

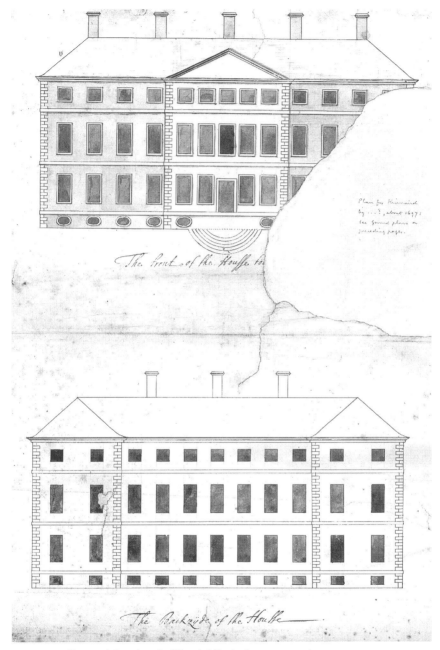

FIGURE 4.3   Proposed elevations for Kinnaird Castle, late seventeenth century.

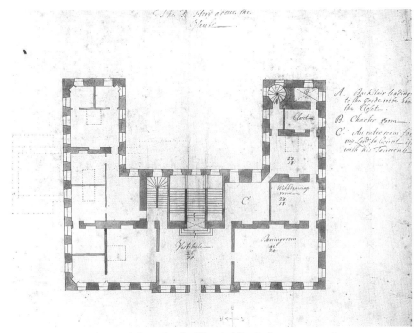

FIGURE 4.4   Proposed ground-floor plan for Kinnaird Castle, late seventeenth century.

entrance, but screened off from the vestibule. Such an arrangement would have been most unusual in late seventeenth-century Scottish or English architecture, but there are close precedents in Dutch classicist architecture,[12] with which Slezer presumably had first-hand acquaintance. Similar designs for staircases are likewise to be found in some of the theoretical house plans among the collection of James Smith's drawings now in the Royal Institute of British Architects.

The garden design (fol. 12; see Figure 4.5) is strongly Dutch in character. Modest in scale and made up of small self-contained areas hedged or walled off from one another, the garden has a distinctly piecemeal appearance. The design is not lacking in invention, however, for as well as a cherry garden (almost identical to those at Ham and Lethington),[13] a bowling-green and a parterre, there was to be a canal some 250 feet in length, with terminal pavilions. Slezer's notes also contain proposals for bringing cascades down to a second parterre above the canal, where there were to be 'statues supporting small beassens (basons) with *jets d'eau*'.

It seems likely that this garden layout was designed by Slezer himself, and his engineering skills would no doubt have equipped him to tackle the

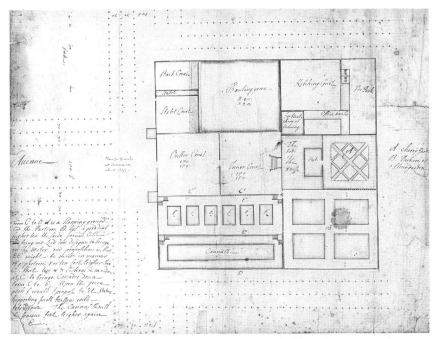

FIGURE 4.5   Proposed garden layout for Kinnaird Castle by John Slezer, late seventeenth century.

elaborate scheme of waterworks that was proposed. But was he also the author of the proposals to remodel the house, or was his role simply that of surveyor and draughtsman?

Slezer's somewhat chequered career[14] certainly reveals him as a man of many parts, but as yet we have no firm evidence of his employment as an architect designer. He is known to have acted as overseer of the Duke of Lauderdale's building operations in 1676–82, while at about the same time Lord Strathmore employed him to survey Glamis Castle, Angus, and possibly also to advise upon the building works there.[15]

Slezer's association with Lord Strathmore seems to have sprung from a visit made by Slezer to Glamis to prepare drawings for the *Theatrum Scotiae*. It is possible that his employment by the Southesk family originated in similar circumstances, but there is no record of any drawings of Kinnaird having been prepared or proposed for the *Theatrum*. More probably, Slezer's commission stemmed from the close links between the families of Southesk and Lauderdale. The Duke of Lauderdale was a cousin and confidant of Countess Anne, wife of Robert, 3rd Earl of Southesk (succeeded 1669, died 1688), while, as already noted, Charles, 4th Earl of Southesk, married a

daughter of the Duke's brother and successor, Charles, 3rd Earl of Lauderdale, who, as Lord Hatton, had himself employed Slezer during the 1670s.[16]

In the absence of clear evidence on these points, and in view of the fact that
the drawings themselves are undated, the circumstances of Slezer's association with the Southesk family and the precise nature of his role must remain
matters for speculation. It is possible that he was employed to draw out
proposals furnished by another designer, perhaps James Smith, as he had
been employed by Lauderdale to draw out William Samwell's designs for
Ham House and Sir William Bruce's and Robert Mylne's designs for
Thirlestane Castle. The links between the Kinnaird and Melville drawings
would point to a date in the 1690s, and the second Kinnaird scheme might
thus have been commissioned by the 4th Earl of Southesk at about the same
time as the first scheme.

There is, however, the alternative possibility that the second scheme
belongs to the time of the 3rd Earl and that Slezer himself had some
responsibility for the design. The similarity of the Kinnaird garden layout
(which is evidently contemporary with the plans and elevations of the house)
to Slezer's garden designs of the 1670s has already been noted. Moreover, all
Slezer's known drawings to which firm dates can be attributed belong to the
period before 1690. The Kinnaird elevations have links not only with Melville
but also with Ham and with the design for the unidentified Lauderdale/Argyll
house now in the National Monuments Record of Scotland. The annotations
on this latter drawing suggest that, in this case at least, Slezer was designer as
well as draughtsman.

At first sight, the drawings themselves are inconsistent with this view.
Slezer's plan of the old house of Kinnaird (fol. 6) shows a wing running
eastwards from the north end of the main block. This wing is absent from
Edward's plan of 1697 (fol. 4ʳ), but present in the mid-eighteenth-century
drawings that comprise the third scheme in the album (fols 13–15). Taken at
face value, this would indicate that Slezer's scheme post-dates Edward's, but
the wing in question does, in fact, appear in a block plan of the house
depicted in another of Edward's drawings (fol. 20ʳ). Slezer's scheme could
therefore be the earlier of the two.

Whatever the truth may be, the Kinnaird drawings associate Slezer more
closely than has hitherto been recognised with the small circle of designers,
surveyors and master craftsmen that dominated Scottish architecture during
the last quarter of the seventeenth century.

ACKNOWLEDGEMENTS

The figures are Crown Copyright, Royal Commission on the Ancient and Historical Monuments of Scotland. They are reproduced with the kind permission of Lord Southesk.

NOTES

1. NMRS, (Alistair Rowan), 'A Note on the bound volume of "Old Plans of Kinnaird" at Kinnaird Castle, Brechin, Angus'; (John G. Dunbar), 'A Note on the bound volume of early drawings of Kinnaird at Kinnaird Castle, Angus (supplementary to Dr Alistair Rowan's note of February 1976)'; (C. H. Cruft), 'Kinnaird Castle Drawings'.
2. National Register of Archives (Scottish Record Office), no. 792. Earl of Southesk.
3. H. M. Colvin, *A Biographical Dictionary of British Architects 1600–1840* (1978), 282–3.
4. J. Lowrey, 'Sir William Bruce and his Circle at Craigiehall 1694–1708', in (J. Frew and D. Jones), *Aspects of Scottish Classicism* (1988), 1–8.
5. Illustrated in D. Jones, 'A Seventeenth-Century Inventory of Furnishings at Kinnaird Castle, Angus', (J. Frew and D. Jones), op. cit., 50.
6. W. Fraser, *History of the Carnegies Earls of Southesk and of their Kindred* (1867), i, 170.
7. Edward's proposals are described in J. Lowrey, *'A Man of Excellent Parts'. Alexander Edward: Minister, Architect, Jacobite 1651–1708*, Catalogue of Exhibition at Crawford Centre for the Arts, University of St Andrews (1987), 11–14.
8. Cf. signed plans by Slezer of Dumbarton Castle (Public Record Office, MPF 244) and Stirling Castle (Public Record Office, MPF 246). This last is published in Royal Commission on the Ancient and Historical Monuments of Scotland, *Inventory of Stirlingshire* (1963), i, plate 56.
9. J. G. Dunbar, 'The Building-activities of the Duke and Duchess of Lauderdale, 1670–82', in *Archaeological Journal*, 132 (1975), 202–30.
10. NMRS B/18474; *Catalogue of 'Bute Sale' of Architectural Drawings*, Sotheby, 23 May 1951, Lots 22 and 23.
11. Colen Campbell, *Vitruvius Britannicus* (1715–25), ii, plate 50.
12. W. Kuyper, *Dutch Classicist Architecture* (1980), 110–11.
13. J. G. Dunbar, op. cit., plates XXVb and XXIVb.
14. On which see J. Jamieson, 'The Life of Slezer', in *Theatrum Scotiae* (1814), 1–13, and A. H. Millar, *The Book of Record, A Diary written by Patrick First Earl of Strathmore* (Scottish History Society 1890), 150–2.
15. J. G. Dunbar, op. cit., 211–12; A. H. Millar, op. cit., 42.
16. W. Fraser, op. cit., i, 152, 154, 162; J. G. Dunbar, op. cit., 211.

FIGURE 5.1   Garden (east) elevation of Hopetoun House by Sir William Bruce, engraved for William Adam's *Vitruvius Scoticus*.

5

Sir William Bruce's Design for Hopetoun House and Its Forerunners

DEBORAH HOWARD

The extraordinary story of the building of Hopetoun House has already been skilfully told by Alistair Rowan, who has unravelled the process by which Sir William Bruce's original design was steadily modified, first by Bruce himself, and subsequently by William Adam, who eventually obliterated all trace of Bruce's work from the entrance front.[1] On the exterior, Bruce's design survives only on the garden front, where the centre block emerges from its Adam wrapping (see Figure 5.1).

This article seeks to throw light on where Sir William Bruce may have found inspiration for his first scheme for Hopetoun, and to suggest why he chose such a radical and idealised plan. Bruce was already about seventy years old when he designed Hopetoun House for the young Charles Hope, then still a minor. The contract between Charles and his 'curators' and Tobias Bachope, the mason who was engaged to execute Bruce's design, was signed on 28 December 1698.[2] The document also mentions two small pavilions and a pair of office houses, although their exact position can only be guessed. The contract refers to the main house simply as an almost square block 'four score feet in length upon the east and west sydes and four score seven feet upon the south and north sydes'. Bruce's design was recorded, together with his own later additions and projected quadrant colonnades and service wings, in volume 2 of Colen Campbell's *Vitruvius Britannicus*, published in 1717 (see Figures 5.2 and 5.3).[3] Within fifty years of its inception, however, Bruce's entrance front had been transformed by William Adam from a square,

53

FIGURE 5.2   Principal (west) front of Hopetoun House designed by Sir William Bruce,
engraved for Colen Campbell's *Vitruvius Britannicus*, vol. 2.

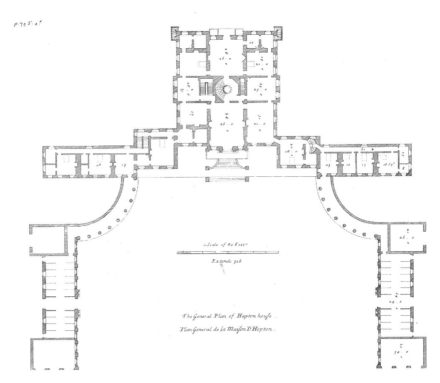

FIGURE 5.3   Sir William Bruce's principal floor plan of Hopetoun House, engraved for
Vitruvius Britannicus.

hipped-roofed block to a broad, sweeping façade topped by a balustrade.[4]

By the standards of contemporary fashion in Scotland, Bruce's scheme for Hopetoun was unusual, for few houses outside the towns were so deep and square. In his own house at Kinross, Bruce had adopted the modish French-style plan with apartments stretched out to right and left of a central axis.[5] Kinross seems to have rapidly earned a reputation within Scotland as a paradigm by which other buildings were compared. Both contracts and contemporary descriptions used Kinross as a point of reference, houses being described as 'like Kinross in miniature' and details such as chimneys or rustication being compared with those of Kinross.[6] Despite its evident success, Bruce himself must have pondered over the way in which the movement through the apartments ran at right angles to the grand central axis running through Kinross House and its park and terminating on Loch Leven Castle in the distance.

At Hopetoun, as at Kinross, the design is laid out on a grand, cross-country axis, in this case running ambitiously from North Berwick Law some thirty miles to the east to Abercorn Church to the west.[7] As at Kinross, the garden layout was conceived at the outset of the project, and it may even have been the very act of poring over garden plans that gave Bruce the original idea for the plan of the house at Hopetoun.[8] The layout for Kinross gives prominence to the form of the parterre, which is both larger and more clearly indicated than the house itself. It can hardly be coincidence that the ground-plan of Hopetoun House adopts the main characteristics of the Renaissance parterre, with its central Greek cross dividing the plan into four equal-sized corner sections, pivoted around a central focus.

If Bruce's first plan for Hopetoun bears an uncanny resemblance to a parterre – and it is suggested here that this may have been the original inspiration – he then drew on the full resources of his education, acquired through a lifetime of travel and reading, to develop and refine the idea.[9] As at Kinross, there were no earlier structures to be incorporated, allowing the architect's imagination to range freely. The design may have been difficult to appreciate in the Scottish context, but it grew out of the wealth of European tradition dating back more than two centuries. The Renaissance enthusiasm for the centralised plan has become a cliché, but its impact on domestic as well as religious architecture was fundamental. The idea of arranging four suites of rooms symmetrically around a central space appears to have originated in Giuliano da Sangallo's Villa Medici at Poggio a Caiano, outside Florence, designed for (and perhaps with the help of) Lorenzo il Magnifico.[10] This revolutionary villa, seminal not only for its unprecedented symmetry but also for the temple front on the façade, has a rectangular central hall and an H-shaped plan, raised on a square terrace (see Figure 5.4). At around the

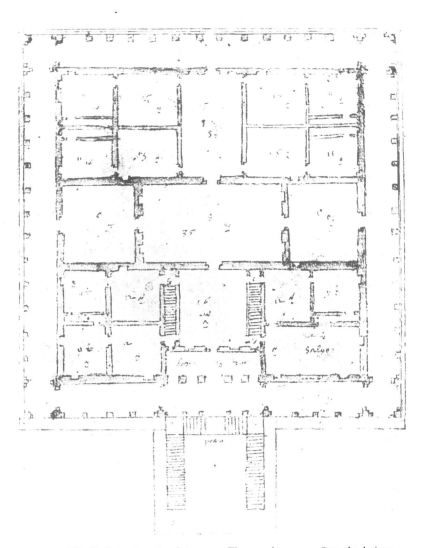

FIGURE 5.4   Villa Medici at Pioggio a Caiano near Florence, begun c. 1485 to the designs
of Giuliano di Sangallo. Plan of *piano nobile* from Giuliano's Siena sketchbook
reproduced from Falb, *Il Taccuino Senese* (1902).

same time, Francesco di Giorgio was experimenting with villa designs
focused around a circular central hall, and although his treatise remained
unpublished his ideas were taken up and developed by other architects.[11] The
theme reappears in the sixteenth century, for example in Falconetto's Odeo
Cornaro in Padua.[12]

However, it was not in Italy but in France, at Francis I's Château de Chambord (see Figure 5.6), begun in 1519,[13] that the idea of making the staircase the central focus of the plan seems to have taken root. The original design for Chambord, by a pupil of Giuliano da Sangallo, Domenico da Cortona, was drawn by Félibien before the model was broken up at the end of the seventeenth century. This shows that Domenico adopted his master's idea of the symmetrically-arranged corner apartments, but at the model stage the staircase was still in the entrance hall. The grand central staircase was certainly part of the original building, and it is suggested that Francis I himself may have suggested placing it centrally. This staircase is famous for its ingenious design with two independent flights, apparently an invention of Leonardo, who died at nearby Amboise in 1519.[14]

There is no evidence that Bruce himself visited France, but he certainly knew of Chambord. He had only to turn to Palladio's Book I (and we know he bought a copy of Palladio's *Quattro libri* in 1676) to read of the magnificent staircase at 'Sciambur luoco della Francia il Magnifico Rè Francesco in un Palagio da lui fabricato in un bosco'.[15] Palladio believed the stair to have four independent flights (in reality there are only two), each leading to one of the four corner apartments: 'è bellissima inventione, & nova'. A complete ground-plan of the Château de Chambord was illustrated in du Cerceau's *Les plus excellents bastiments de France*, where, again, the idea was warmly praised:

> La commodité du dedans a esté ordonnée avec raison & scavoir. Car au milieu & centre est vn escallier à deux montées, percé à jour, & entour iceluy quatre salles, desquelles l'on va de l'une a l'autre, en le circuissant. Aux quatre encoignneures d'entre chaque salle y a vn pavillon, garny de chambre, garderobbe, cabinet & montée.[16]

Chambord was one of the places visited by Bruce's son John on his Continental tour in 1681–3, recorded in letters and accounts still at Kinross House.[17] There can be little doubt that Bruce was consciously emulating this princely hunting lodge when he made his first design for Hopetoun, with its four corner lodgings arranged around a Greek cross with a grand, top-lit staircase in the centre. As John Lowrey has pointed out, he had already experimented with a top-lit, central staircase at the nearby house of Craigiehall, begun just one year earlier for Charles Hope's future father-in-law in 1698.[18]

The French qualities in Bruce's Hopetoun have already been mentioned. Colen Campbell noted that the façade was 'rusticated in the *French manner*'.[19] John Fleming described the house as 'seasoned with French motifs',[20] and Alistair Rowan has likened its channelled masonry to that of Le

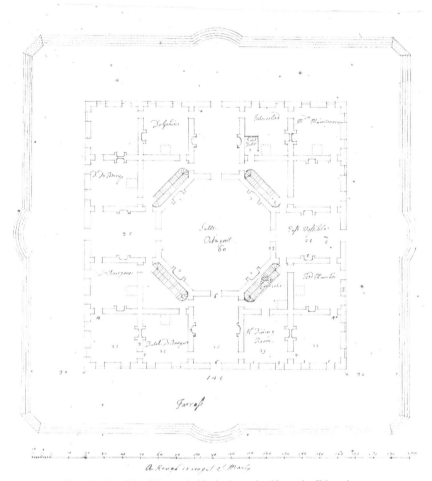

FIGURE 5.5   Ground plan of the Château de Marly drawn by Alexander Edward, 1701–3.
Ashmolean Museum, Oxford.

Vau's Hôtel Tambonneau.[21] Bruce's entrance façade bears a close resemblance to a French architectural drawing in the Hopetoun collection, measured in *Toises de France* and *Pieds du Roi*, showing the seven-bay façade of a two-storey house, with a three-bay pedimented centrepiece arcaded on the ground floor.[22] James Macaulay links the 'tight little semicircular pediment' on the garden front with the work of Le Muet.[23] Macaulay points to Marly as the source of the ground-plan, and we know that Bruce's associate Alexander Edward visited Marly on his own continental visit in 1701–3.[24] His drawing of the plan is preserved among the Gibbs drawings in the Ashmolean Museum, Oxford (see Figure 5.5). However, Edward's trip was made after

Bruce's first design for Hopetoun was begun, and it seems that the main block was substantially completed by the time that Edward returned. Although Bruce probably already knew of Marly, it seems more likely that both plans were drawing on similar sources of inspiration than that Marly was a direct prototype for Hopetoun. In particular, it is significant that the corner apartments at Marly consist of three rooms of similar size, whereas at Hopetoun they are made up of a chamber and two small closets (with the exception of the great dining-room in the north-east corner). A much closer parallel to Bruce's Hopetoun ground-plan can be found in a villa design in Serlio's Book VII. Serlio seems not to have thought of top-lighting for his central halls, and warns that this design would be 'freddissima' because of the lack of light in the hall.[25] It was Palladio in his Villa Rotonda who first demonstrated, inspired by the example of the Pantheon, that even a small roof-light could provide excellent illumination.[26]

It is a commonplace that the complete symmetry of the Villa Rotonda had enormous fascination for the eighteenth-century English Palladians. The Rotonda itself had serious disadvantages as a generalised villa design. In particular, the plan allows no direct access to the corner rooms from the central hall, a device used by Palladio to focus attention on the temple-like qualities of the building. Moreover, there are no closets in the corner suites, despite the fact that Palladio stated that a villa should have large, middle-sized and small rooms. And finally, vertical access is inconvenient and inconspicuous, making the Rotonda's design of limited usefulness for a house with more than one *piano nobile*. Nevertheless, Bruce showed himself fully aware of Palladio's repertoire, and it was no doubt the Palladian qualities of Bruce's Hopetoun that earned its inclusion in Colen Campbell's *Vitruvius Britannicus*. Campbell himself showed his admiration for the plan-form when he designed a smaller variant for his namesake Daniel Campbell's Shawfield House in Glasgow. This house, completed in 1712, but demolished before the end of the century, also had four corner chambers and a central staircase.[27] Significantly, plans of this type can also be found in drawings of Palladian-style houses by Bruce's contemporary James Smith, already signalled by Howard Colvin as a crucial formative influence on Campbell's Palladianism.[28] Indeed, there can be little doubt that Smith's keen interest in Palladio had a decisive impact on Bruce, as on Campbell.

Another feature of Hopetoun that can be traced back to Palladio is the expression of the central Greek cross by the placing of a pediment over the place where it emerges on the side of the building, anticipated by Palladio in his Villa Barbaro at Maser.[29] Although the *Quattro libri* illustration of the Villa Barbaro does not show this feature, it is possible that Bruce may have learned of its existence from James Smith, for the same feature appears on the side flank of Melville House, where the two architects were both involved.[30] The Villa Barbaro's deep central block projecting forward from straight flanking wings on either side, evident even in the *Quattro libri* illustration of Maser, bears a distinct resemblance to Bruce's Hopetoun design.[31]

That Bruce was attempting to emulate Palladian models in his design for Hopetoun is underlined by the way in which his disposition of the corner apartments recalls the layout of Inigo Jones's Queen's House at Greenwich, one of the flagships of the English Palladian movement.[32] By Bruce's time, the original H-plan of the Queen's House, not unlike that of Poggio a Caiano, had been transformed into a square by John Webb, although its peculiar bridge-like structure, spanning the main London–Dover road, survived. The Queen's House is shown in this state in a painting of Greenwich by Jan Wyck, painted together with its pendant depicting Jones's Banqueting House at Whitehall in about 1680; both pictures are now in the Red Drawing-Room at Hopetoun. If, as seems likely, the paintings were acquired soon after they were painted, this would indicate that the Hope family circle knew and probably admired Jones's work.[33] Bruce takes over one of the most practical of Jones's ideas from the Queen's House, that of placing a main chimney in the centre of each corner block, so that a chimneypiece can be placed on the inside wall of the principal chamber, with small fireplaces set diagonally across the corners of the closets.[34] Bruce, like Jones, evidently realised the unsuitability for a northern climate of placing chimneys on the outside walls, as Palladio preferred to do. In the beautiful tulip stair at the Queen's House, Bruce could also have found a precedent for his top-lit, cantilevered staircase.[35] Although circular, the spacious, open staircase at Hopetoun is far removed from the traditional Scottish turnpike stair, while most of the grander classical-style country houses in Scotland at this time had ample scale-and-platt staircases. How fortunate that William Adam never achieved his ostensible aim of displacing the main staircase at Hopetoun to one side, to the position of the present service stair!

The full subtlety of Bruce's plan for Hopetoun becomes clear when one begins to analyse the circulation patterns that he devised for the house. In spite of the impressive use of biaxial symmetry, he discouraged the use of the cross axis. To the right of the central axis running through the hall, staircase and garden parlour, and parallel to it, stretched a state apartment, consisting of the grand ceremonial dining-room at the front, the withdrawing-room and bedchamber, and finally at the rear two closets, probably one a study and one a service room. (The withdrawing-room and chamber have since been combined to form the library.) To the left, the private dining-room, preceded by two small service rooms at the front of the house, led into a withdrawing-room, followed by the Earl's private suite, consisting of bedchamber, closet and charter-room. The door from the charter-room to the garden parlour was slapped through in 1752,[36] but originally this room would have been inaccessible except through the Earl's private apartment. It is significant that it was not possible to leave the staircase hall to the left, and the exit to the right was clearly a service route only, to judge by the simple flagged floor and plastered walls of the passageway. In other words, although Campbell spoke approvingly of four corner apartments on each of the main stories of Hopetoun, the entrance floor in fact had *two* main apartments, each of which is arranged parallel to the main axis of approach. It seems that, in searching for a way of reconciling the conflict between two perpendicular axes of circulation that he experienced at Kinross, Bruce devised a layout in which sideways movement was discouraged, or even in places impossible.

It is not the intention here to deny Bruce's use of Dutch and French elements, at Hopetoun as elsewhere in his architecture. For example, Rowan's suggestion that Bruce may have found inspiration in William and Mary's Dutch country palace, Het Loo, seems entirely convincing. Both Bruce's façade elevation and the arrangement and form of the house and its wings are strikingly similar to this grand Netherlandish royal villa.[37] But it does seem clear that an Italianate taste was beginning to become extremely fashionable among the Hope family and their circle. John Lowrey has recently found a sheet in the Craigiehall archives, among papers of about 1699, inscribed with the name of a Venetian nobleman, Giacomo Leoni.[38] This Leoni appears to be too old to be identified with the architect of the same name, but the possibility of a connection is an intriguing one.[39] Bruce was building the nearby house at Craigiehall while he was working at Hopetoun, and the young Charles Hope married the daughter of the owner of Craigiehall, the Marquis of Annandale.[40] The Craigiehall inventory of 1733 shows that by this date all the main public rooms were hung with Italian paintings, apart from the family portraits in the dining-room. Most of the Dutch pictures, by contrast, were in store, 'locked up in the Library'.[41] At Hopetoun, too, Italian material, also apparently dating from about 1700, has turned up in the form of a series of miscellaneous architectural drawings.[42]

James Smith is the only figure in Bruce's circles known to have travelled in Italy, but Macky says in his *Journey through Scotland* (1729) that one could go nowhere in Italy without meeting Scots (he says the same of Germany, but the comment remains significant!).[43] The recently rediscovered painted ceiling in the dome of the staircase octagon at Hopetoun suggests that the fashion for Italian-style mural painting had already reached Scotland. Although we know the wall panels of the staircase to have been filled with paintings executed in the Netherlands, the author of the ceiling is still unidentified, although it is clear that the Edinburgh painter James Norie made substantial later embellishments in the 1730s and 1740s.[44] It is tempting to associate the ceiling with contemporary decorative schemes executed by Venetian painters in English

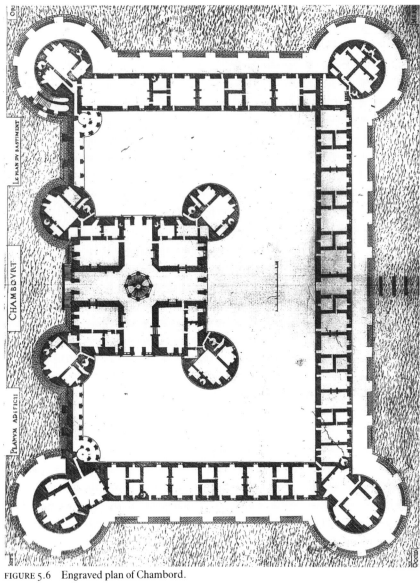

FIGURE 5.6   Engraved plan of Chambord.

country houses, such as those by Pellegrini at Castle Howard and Kimbolton Castle.[45] Certainly, the theme of the family's apotheosis, the playful illusionism with the figures looking out over a fictive balustrade and the bright palette, bring the Hopetoun staircase ceiling into the tradition of Veronese-style decoration that was so popular in villas and country houses, both in England and in the Veneto, in the early eighteenth century.

It has not been the intention here to suggest that Bruce selected prototypes for Hopetoun as one might choose the ingredients for a special recipe, but rather to demonstrate that his design forms part of the broader evolution of the centralised villa in Europe. The Italian qualities in Bruce's Hopetoun anticipated a fashion that was to accelerate after 1707, when the Union made travel to Italy more acceptable.[46] But however unambiguous its Italian characteristics, Bruce's design was a truly cosmopolitan one. His assimilation of Dutch, French and English architectural traditions during the travels of his youth had helped to form his distinctive personal style. At Hopetoun he sought not to suppress these northern European elements, but to reorganise them to create an idealised, Italianate, centralised villa. Centralised designs are not easily reconciled with the demands of domestic living, or with existing structures, and the type has therefore been largely confined to high-prestige commissions and open sites. It is no coincidence that most of the examples considered here – Poggio a Caiano, Chambord, Het Loo and the Queen's House among them – were built by powerful, if not royal, patrons. As a former surveyor-general to the Crown, Bruce would have been well aware of the cachet that such associations offered. Despite the complications of its subsequent remodelling by William Adam, Hopetoun has remained one of the grandest – and arguably the most sophisticated – country houses in Scotland.

ACKNOWLEDGEMENTS

I am grateful for advice and help to Professor Alistair Rowan and Basil Skinner; to John Dunbar, Kitty Cruft and Ian Gow of the Royal Commission on the Ancient and Historical Monuments of Scotland; to Aonghus Mac-Kechnie of Historic Scotland; to John Lowrey of Edinburgh University; to Captain Fox and the guides at Hopetoun; and to Peter Vasey and the staff of West Register House, Edinburgh.

NOTES

1. A. Rowan, 'The building of Hopetoun', in *Design and Practice in British Architecture: Studies in architectural history presented to Howard Colvin, Architectural History*, XXVII, 1984, pp. 183–209.
2. Contemporary copy of the original contract in SRO GD45/17/769; see also Rowan, op. cit., p. 185. Bundle 262 of the Hopetoun manuscripts,

which Rowan describes as containing all the documentation relating to Bruce's activity at Hopetoun, now contains only nineteenth-century material, possibly owing to a renumbering of the archive.

3. C. Campbell, *Vitruvius Britannicus*, vol. 2, London, 1717, p. 7 and plates 75–7.

4. Rowan, op. cit., pp. 189ff.; J. Gifford, *William Adam 1689–1748: A Life and Times of Scotland's Universal Architect*, Edinburgh, 1989, pp. 86–90.

5. J. G. Dunbar, 'Kinross House, Kinross-shire', in H. Colvin and J. Harris (eds), *The Country Seat: Studies in the History of the British Country House presented to Sir John Summerson*, London, 1970, pp. 64–9.

6. J. Macky, *A Journey through Scotland*, London, 1729, refers to both Melville House and Craigiehall as Kinross in miniature, and even describes Hopetoun itself as 'exactly after the model of the house of Kinross'. The 1698 contract for Hopetoun (see note 2, above) specifies that the chimney heads should be copied from those at Kinross in fine ashlar, and that the rustication should be either of the type used at Kinross or the channelled masonry of Craigiehall.

7. For contemporary descriptions of the landscape, see J. Macky, op. cit., pp. 202–3; and Sir R. Sibbald, *History Ancient and Modern of the Sheriffdome of Linlithgow*, Edinburgh, 1710, p. 21. William Adam's later contribution to the landscape is discussed in A. A. Tait, *The Landscape Garden in Scotland 1735–1835*, Edinburgh, 1980, pp. 27–9.

8. On Bruce's method of designing the landscape setting before the house, see J. Lowrey, 'Sir William Bruce and his circle at Craigiehall 1694– 1708', in *Aspects of Scottish Classicism: The House and its Formal Setting 1690–1750*, ed. J. Frew and D. Jones, St Andrews, 1989, pp. 1–8, esp. p. 2.

9. For details of Bruce's travel and library, see J. Dunbar, *Sir William Bruce 1630–1710*, Scottish Arts Council Catalogue, Edinburgh, 1970; H. Colvin, *A Biographical Dictionary of British Architects*, 2nd edn, London, 1978, pp. 151–5.

10. See P. Foster, *A study of Lorenzo de' Medici's Villa at Poggio a Caiano*, Yale University, 1974, Outstanding Dissertations in the Fine Arts, New York and London, 1978; F. W. Kent, 'Lorenzo de' Medici's acquisition of Poggio a Caiano in 1474 and an early reference to his architectural expertise', *Journal of the Warburg and Courtauld Institutes*, XLII, 1979, pp. 250–7; S. Bardazzi and E. Castellani, *La Villa Medicea di Poggio a Caiano*, 2 vols, Prato, 1981.

11. See, for example, Francesco di Giorgio Martini, *Trattati di architettura, ingegneria ed arte militare*, ed. C. Maltese, Milan, 1967, vol. 1, plate 166, fol. 89v; vol. 2, plates 199–201, fols 20–1.

12. See A. B. Alvarez, 'Le fabbriche di Andrea Palladio', in *Alvise Cornaro e il suo tempo*, exhibition catalogue, Padua, 1980.

13. W. Prinz, *Schloss Chambord und die Villa Rotonda in Vicenza: Studien zur Ikonologie*, Berlin, 1980.

14. J. Guillaume, 'Léonard de Vinci et l'architecture française', *Revue de l'art*, XXV, 1974, pp. 71–91; idem, 'L'escalier dans l'architecture française: la première moitié du seizième siècle', in J. Guillaume (ed.), *L'escalier dans l'architecture de la Renaissance*, Paris, 1985, pp. 27–47.

15. A. Palladio, *I quattro libri dell'architettura*, Venice, 1570, Book I, pp. 64–5. Bruce's purchase of Palladio's treatise in 1676 is recorded by a

bookseller's bill in the Kinross papers (Dunbar, op. cit., cat. nos 41, 57).

16. J. Androuet du Cerceau, *Le premier volume des plus excellents bastiments de France*, Paris, 1576. The quotation is from the 1607 edition, p. 7.

17. Dunbar, op. cit., cat. nos 44–6.

18. Lowrey, op. cit., p. 6.

19. Campbell, op. cit., vol. 2, p. 7.

20. J. Fleming, 'Hopetoun House, West Lothian – the seat of the Marquess of Linlithgow', *Country Life*, 5–12 January 1956, p. 17.

21. Rowan, op. cit., p. 186. Nevertheless, it should be remembered that channelled masonry of this type was also common in the Low Countries in the seventeenth century (see W. Kuyper, *Dutch Classicist Architecture*, Delft, 1980).

22. This drawing is among the collection of miscellaneous architectural drawings discussed in note 41 below.

23. J. Macaulay, *The Classical Country House in Scotland 1660–1800*, London, 1987, p. 21. See, for example, Le Muet's house for Mr de l'Aigle, illustrated in Jean Marot's collection of architectural engravings known as *Le Grand Marot*, facsimile edn, Paris, 1970 (unnumbered plates).

24. For Edward's career and his association with Bruce, see J. Lowrey, '*A Man of Excellent Parts': Alexander Edward: Minister, Architect, Jacobite 1651–1708*, Scottish Arts Council exhibition catalogue, Crawford Centre for the Arts, University of St Andrews, 1987, pp. 10–14.

25. S. Serlio, *Tutte l'opere d'architettura et prospetiva*, Venice, 1619, Book VII, pp. 16–17.

26. C. Semenzato, *La Rotonda di Vicenza, Corpus Palladianum*, vol. 1, Vicenza, 1968.

27. Campbell, op. cit., p. 51. See also G. Goodfellow, 'Colen Campbell's Shawfield Mansion in Glasgow', *Journal of the Society of Architectural Historians*, XXIII, 1964, pp. 123–8.

28. See H. Colvin, 'A Scottish origin for English Palladianism', *Architectural History*, XVII, 1974, pp. 5–13. The plan of Shawfield house is almost identical to several of the 'unidentified projects' by James Smith in the RIBA, recently discussed by Aonghus MacKechnie in 'James Smith's smaller country houses', in *Aspects of Scottish Classicism* (op. cit. above), pp. 9–16, plate 3.

29. Palladio, op. cit., Book II, p. 51.

30. See Macaulay, op. cit., pp. 29–31. The unusual placing of a pediment over *two* bays (rather than three or a larger odd number), used on the flanks of both Melville and Hopetoun, appears even more unexpectedly on the main façade of Bruce's Craigiehall (Dunbar, op. cit., pp. 17–18; Macaulay, op. cit., p. 19; and Lowrey, op. cit.). In each case, the placing of the pediment marks the internal room arrangement. As Aonghus MacKechnie has pointed out to me, flanking pediments had already been used in a similar way (although in this case across three rather than two window bays) at Fawley Court, Henley-on-Thames, a house that has been attributed to Wren.

31. Bruce's triple-arched loggia at the entrance to Hopetoun House has been linked by Macaulay (op. cit., p. 21) to Palladio's Villa Marcello (Gazzotti) at Bertesina. Several of Palladio's early villas, this one included, are entered through triple-arched loggias with the steps

leading only to the central bay, as in Bruce's Hopetoun façade, although in his *Quattro libri* Palladio preferred to correct this type of entrance to a single broad staircase, as in the Villa Godi. The staircase of the Villa Saraceno has even been altered to match that of the *Quattro libri*! John Lowrey has suggested to me that the unusual convex quadrant colonnades in Bruce's final project for Hopetoun (see Rowan, op. cit., p. 184, figure 1b, and plate Ib, opposite p. 202) may have been suggested to Bruce by his turning sideways Palladio's plan for the Villa Mocenigo (*Quattro libri*, Book II, p. 66).

32. See the plans, attributed to Wren, showing the Queen's House at this date, reproduced in J. Charlton, *The Queen's House, Greenwich*, London, 1976, p. 37.

33. These pictures, together with a third picture by Wyck in a slightly different format showing *Whitehall from the Horseguards*, may well be those mentioned in the Craigiehall inventory of 1733 in 'the little Dyning Room':
    No. 147 A Court of Guard Dutch picture
    No. 148 A Small Dutch Landskop [*sic*]
    No. 149 The Companion being a pice of architecture
    The Craigiehall collection has passed to Hopetoun House by inheritance.

34. This arrangement had already been used by Smith at Melville House.

35. Jones himself would have known Palladio's top-lit, cantilevered, spiral staircase, in this case oval in plan, at the Convento della Carità in Venice (see E. Bassi, *The Convento della Carità*, University Park and London, 1973, plates 48–55. As John Lowrey has pointed out (op. cit., p. 8, note 32), it was at Smith's Raith House, begun in 1694, that the top-lit staircase, though not here centrally placed, was probably introduced into Scotland.

36. Document exhibited in facsimile in the exhibition *William Adam at Hopetoun*, Hopetoun House, summer 1989.

37. Het Loo shared with Hopetoun the deep square plan, the tripartite main façade with pedimented centrepiece, the triple entrance with a staircase to the central bay only, the flanking pavilions linked by quadrant colonnades, and the formal gardens with ambitious axial vistas. Het Loo was begun about 1684, extended about 1690 and completed in 1692. (See W. Kuyper, *Dutch Classicist Architecture*, Delft, 1980, pp. 145–7, 181–3, figures 21–2 and plates 301–2.)

38. The sheet reads simply: 'Giacomo Leonni / Conte e Kavalier / à Santa Giustina / Venetia'.

39. The Leoni family came to Venice from Padua in 1652 and were admitted to the Venetian nobility in the following year (31 January 1652 *more veneto*). They had a *contea* (earldom) in Sanguineto. Giacomo Leoni, the son of Antonio, was born in 1650, perhaps married in 1677, and lived into the eighteenth century. (Information from the Barbaro genealogies in Venice: Biblioteca Marciana, MSS Ital., Cl. 7, no 926 (coll. 8595), vol. L, fol. 225; and Biblioteca Correr, vol. 4, fol. 169ff.) I am grateful to John Lowrey for showing me this document and to Catherine Puglisi of Rutgers University for providing information from Venice.

40. Dunbar, op. cit., pp. 17–18; Macaulay, op. cit., p. 19.

41. Copies of the Craigiehall inventories of 1733 and c. 1750 are in the

Scottish National Portrait Gallery, Edinburgh. I am grateful to Dr Rosalind Marshall for allowing me to see them.

42. Rowan, op. cit., p. 201, note 23. These drawings are now in the National Monuments Record of Scotland. They include the elevation and section of a villa measured in *piedi lucchesi* (Luccan feet) which Professor Rowan attributed to Andrea Pozzo. This intriguing find, however, turns out to be mistaken, for the inscription 'A. Pozzo' is the key to the drawing, indicating the *pozzo*, or well, marked by the letter A. Nevertheless, the collection is full of interest. In addition, it includes drawings of two three-bay centrepieces, a centralised, Palladian-style chapel, a town *palazzo*, and two small pavilions. There is also an explanatory double page showing how to insert a semicircular pediment into a cornice. French and Scottish drawings are also to be found in the same collection, and there are several engravings of English county seats. One of the French drawings has already been discussed earlier in this article.

43. Macky, op. cit., p. viii.

44. For example, in 1738 Norie was paid for gilding around the panels in the cupola. In 1741, he received a payment 'To painting the inside of the Cuppila with eight bunches of Festoons and painting an Astragal moulding around the whole, and a pannel below each window'. In 1763, his patron complained that Norie had charged £70 for the painting of the dome of the main stair below the cupola down to the cornice 'which seems very extravagant'. James Norie was primarily a painter of decorative landscapes rather than a history painter, and it is doubtful that he would have been responsible for the original painting of the dome. On Norie's career, see J. Holloway, *Patrons and Painters: Art in Scotland 1650–1760*, exhibition catalogue, Scottish National Portrait Gallery, 1989, pp. 61–5, 145–6.

45. See E. Croft Murray, 'Giovanni Antonio Pellegrini at Kimbolton', *Apollo*, November 1959. His fellow Venetian, Sebastiano Ricci, was working in England from 1712 to 1716. See G. Knox, 'Sebastiano Ricci at Burlington House: a Venetian decoration "alla Romana"', *The Burlington Magazine*, CXXVII, pp. 601–9.

46. Charles Hope's son John was one of the first young Scottish gentlemen to visit Italy on his Grand Tour. See Hopetoun Research Group Studies, Paper no. 1, *The Diaries and Travels of Lord John Hope 1722–1727*, Occasional Papers, Extra-Mural Department, University of Edinburgh, n.d.

FIGURE 6.1   View of Monymusk by James Giles from the Haddo Albums, c. 1848.

6

Organs, Orrerys and Others

A Commission for Monymusk[1]

MARY COSH

S ir Archibald Grant, 2nd baronet of Monymusk, who had lived at his family's ancient house on the Don (see Figure 6.1) since the age of sixteen, began to manage the estate for his father in 1716 when he was twenty years old, and succeeded to the baronetcy in 1722. The young man was to become a remarkable representative of the eighteenth-century amateur enthusiast: improver, cultivator, builder and 'man of parts'. He studied for the law and was admitted advocate in Edinburgh in 1717, and during the times of his absence the estate was managed by factors.[2] From 1722–32 he was MP for his county of Aberdeen. From 1734, however, back at Monymusk in the seat of management, he spent most of his long life in residence until his death in 1778 at the age of eighty-two – although with several unsuccessful efforts to regain a seat in Parliament.

It was not uncommon in Scotland to inherit a dilapidated, debt-laden estate. Sir Archibald's especial misfortune was that he was one of the trustees of the York Buildings Company, who, when its Secretary twice made fraudulent dealings in the company's name, became responsible for the primary debts. Loans from friends saved him from outright bankruptcy, but for the rest of his life he was struggling to repay these secondary debts. He introduced new farming methods of cultivation by fertilising, draining and enclosing, and planted trees. He improved his marches by judicious purchase and excambion agreements, made new farm buildings, and from the 1730s gradually transformed the whole estate with rurally-based products, achieving financial viability.

In the 1750s he gave valuable advice to the Aberdeen press on soil improvement and enclosures, and to his often surly and unresponsive son Archie he gave sound tips on how to make the most of the estate by timber sales from his maturing plantations, and – as a member of the local Turnpike Trust – on the improvement of the area's deplorable roads. He further tried to encourage manufactures, especially linen, attempted to revive a long-discontinued weekly market at Monymusk (useful for the county linen trade), and launched a society for the encouragement of agriculture in Aberdeen.

Yet he was perennially short of money, and there are signs that ideas sometimes outran efficiency of execution. Into the bargain, Sir Archibald had the true eighteenth-century enthusiast's interest in a wide variety of skills and sciences, music, astronomy, mining and mineralogy, all of which he encouraged or took part in to varying degrees. Like many such men of wide interests and enquiring minds, Sir Archibald had a strong dash of muddle-headedness, and was frequently in hot water financially as well as personally. A certain fecklessness about his transactions was the despair of his shrewd, peppery friend and kinsman Alexander Grant, a London merchant (later Sir Alexander Grant of Dalvey), whose prolific correspondence with Monymusk veers between affection and exasperation.

Sir Archibald was four times married, twice when young and – as he admitted later in a slightly rueful warning to his son – for love rather than policy. (He should perhaps have added, however, that his wives were all heiresses.) Most of his numerous family (see Figure 6.2), including his heir, were the children of his second wife Nancy Potts, who was the heiress of a Derbyshire mining magnate and, though dearly loved, a somewhat wayward and not always cooperative lady. She, however, died in 1742, and in 1751 Sir Archibald married his third wife, Elizabeth Clark, widow of Dr James Callender of Jamaica, who had not only inherited her husband's valuable estates but also had a pretty daughter Mary (Molly) in her early teens, with whom a few years later young Archie, back from travels and a brief military service with the East India Company, fell in love and whom he married, to the joy of their relatives. Grant's younger son Billy, although good-hearted and of a more agreeable disposition than Archie, was too heedless not to be a worry to his father, but eventually joined the Navy and, sadly, died in the Americas in 1755.[3]

Financially, matters had taken a more prosperous turn, although Sir Archibald had to embark on a troublesome and frustrating struggle with the agents of his new wife's estates to extract her due income from the plantations. But he was in a period of happy fulfilment, surrounded by a (mostly) loving family and, in spite of the occasional wrong-headed action,

FIGURE 6.2   The family of Sir Archibald Grant of Monymusk by William Robertson,
    early 1740s.

respected by Aberdeenshire contemporaries for his valued contribution to the
county's prosperity and improvement.

The Grant family enjoyed lively home activities and junketings, including
amateur theatricals, dancing and home concerts accompanied by harpsichord
and strings. Music was indeed one of their major interests, and by 1750 Sir
Archibald had joined the flourishing Musical Society of Aberdeen, of which a
leading figure was Andrew Tait,[4] who evidently joined in the family concerts
and advised on their instruments. Tait had since about 1735 been organist at
St Paul's Episcopal Chapel in Aberdeen and, from 1740, Master of the music
school there.

North-East Scotland had heard little enough church music, even unaccom-
panied, for the past generation. Even at Aberdeen, although it remained a
musical centre, St Nicholas's Church had lost its choir and was reduced to
'unharmonised singing' in unison, with a limit of some dozen tunes. Sir

Archibald made a collection of books of music, and started a choir at his own church at Monymusk, whom he helped to train in his own library. These sessions were apparently accompanied by a chamber organ, about whose origins nothing appears to be known, but it is mentioned in 1754 as needing repair, for which Tait was consulted.[5]

Early in 1755, Sir Archibald fell into a sharp dispute with the Rev. John Bisset at Aberdeen for attempting to introduce harmonised singing to the kirk, and was savagely denounced from the pulpit. When he observed mildly that he and his family, distressed by the 'usual discord' of sounds made by the congregation, merely wanted to promote 'the worship of God By praise In a more harmonious way', Bisset retorted that for this 'wicked Innovation' the Monymusk offenders would be 'Cursed of God, & would not Last to the 3d Generation'. Sir Archibald, understandably finding this rather un-Christian, asked if cleaning up the usually gloomy and dirty country churches to make them more light and cheerful would be equally blameworthy. He was persuaded, however, not to invite confrontation with the notorious Bisset, and the dispute ended with the Synod's agreeing to allow choirs and harmonised singing, while limiting the repertory to the statutory twelve tunes.[6]

As for organs, they seem in Scotland to have been confined to the Episcopal church, with St Paul's, Aberdeen, having installed theirs in 1722, and St Andrew's, Banff, by 1732.[7] But, for some 150 years after 1700 in England and Wales, the popular church instrument was the barrel organ (not to be confused with the type of street piano common in late nineteenth-century London, usually made and played by Italians). The instrument had ancient origins, and late in Queen Elizabeth's reign one had been exported from England to the Sultan of Turkey. From about 1700 they were used in English churches in place of the small band who performed in the gallery with the singers; or a smaller organ might be installed in the body of the church. By the middle of the eighteenth century, they had become quite sophisticated and their cases elaborately carved and gilded. Altogether more than 130 makers, many of them in London, are recorded in the period between about 1760 and 1840, although most surviving barrel organs date from the early nineteenth century. A number are still workable. The principle was of a handle-turned wooden barrel or cylinder, studded with brass pins that connected to keys corresponding with a mechanism communicating with 'pallets', that opened to admit wind to the pipes. The bellows might be worked either by the crank-handle or by a foot-pedal.

Their range was simple. Few were chromatic, and most – for reasons of space as well as cost – were limited to the keys of G and D, with fewest sharps. Larger instruments might hold three ten-tune barrels, mounted in a revolving frame, but on smaller organs the barrels were exchangeable. Although so largely used in churches, some had barrels that played secular tunes and country dances, and as a simple, more or less unskilled source of music, portable to gardens or fields where young people could dance al fresco, might seem an ideal home instrument.[8]

The acknowledged expert among organ-builders proper was the German, Johann Snetzler, who came to England in his thirties in about 1746, and from about 1760 acquired a near-monopoly of the manufacture. While Snetzler attempted few innovations except, reputedly, the 'dulciana' and 'German flute', his instruments were (says Sir John Sutton) 'remarkable for the purity of tone, and the extreme brilliancy of the Chorus-Stops'.[9]

Snetzler's organ-cases were usually bare and box-like, with a dignified architectural quality. Among his many chamber organs was one for the Duke of Devonshire (1756); his church organs included St Margaret's, King's Lynn (1754) and Peterhouse at Cambridge (1765).[10]

John Langshaw (1718–98), a maker employed by Snetzler, was in the 1760s to work on Lord Bute's organ installed at Luton Park, for which Handel composed. A minor London expert whom Sir Archibald was to consult was Joseph Mahoon of Golden Square, appointed harpsichord-maker to King George II in 1729, though his surviving instruments are mostly spinets.[11] Another maker consulted for Sir Archibald was E. Rostrand, of Orange Court, Leicester Fields, who advertised 'all sorts of Chamber-organs to play with fingers or barrels'; he later made a small one at Stanton Harcourt (1764).[12]

The late 1750s were a typically busy and fruitful time for Sir Archibald: 1757 opened with the birth of his first grandchild, Archie's daughter (another was born the following April), and young Archie spent some time in London, to establish himself with influential Whig courtiers and army officers. His father sent him kind, though hortatory, letters and memoranda, of deep sincerity and great length, their long-winded pages containing much practical and moral advice – not, alas, always patiently or productively received.[13]

The house and estate were always on Sir Archibald's mind. At Monymusk in May, he was ordering seeds from Murdoch Midleton, a Walton-on-Thames gardener, and, later, he was investigating details of the use of papier-mâché as a substitute for stucco ornament. The following spring (1758), when he was seeking a clerk, numerous poor gentlemen offered their skills, including the Collector of Elgin, who in what Sir Archibald endorsed as 'a Comicall Letter' addressed him as 'vir amplissime ... Vir dignissime', while naively apologising for his bad handwriting.[14]

Sir Archibald proposed to a sceptical Town Council in Aberdeen an elaborate scheme for employing the poor and vagrants, in useful industry such as linen and stocking manufacture. He himself was ever pursuing a halting timber industry, for whose products he maintained a fluctuating market in Newcastle; and at the end of the summer he was studying sketches of lime kilns, with proposals to burn lime at Aberdeen, and discussing as a possible tenant for his own mills a protégé of Cockburn of Ormiston – who might usefully introduce new 'implements of Husbandry'.[15]

He had many rival interests: he was busy collecting, and canvassing his friends for, scientific 'curiosities' to place in a 'musaeum' at the house, meanwhile encouraging senior members of his family, such as the judges, his brother William, Lord Prestongrange, and brother-in-law Lord Bankton, to have their portraits painted, while he tried to gather family portraits from various sources to hang at Monymusk.

Archie the younger was elected Preses of the Aberdeen Musical Society, at a critical juncture when it needed a good singing master: an appropriate choice, in view of the family's encouragement of 'vocall musick' in town and kirk. And that May comes the first hint of wanting a barrel organ for Monymusk, when on the back of a letter, the usual place for noting summaries and memoranda, Sir Archibald jotted down the words 'a Hand Organ'.[16]

A letter in December reminding Archie about the family portraits and other paintings contained an obscure reference to 'A good 2^d hand Barrell organ, with or wtout Keys – Your German At whose Concert I attended, hath undertaken the Enquiry at London'. He further adds, on the letter-fold, 'Marbles &c from Mr Adams for Musaeum'.[17] Although the 'German' is not further identified, Snetzler seems a fair guess. Archie may have encountered him in London the previous year, and Sir Archibald's concert visit may also have been in London.

At this time, an army officer of unusual articulacy and intelligence, whom Sir Archibald was later to enlist in the search for an organ, was stationed at Aberdeen. By 1758, Colonel Richmond Webb, of 'a genteel family in Kent', had spent three winters in the area, commanding sometimes one, sometimes two battalions, and became a close and valued friend of the Monymusk family. Helped by his father's friendship with the Duke of Chandos as well as his own natural ability, Webb had made a good career in the army, and purchased his lieutenant-colonelcy. He had served twenty-three years with General Leighton's regiment, the 32nd, thirteen of them as Field Officer, had been at Cartagena and in Cuba, and had been sent on 'hazardous Enterprizes' by General Wentworth. During the Forty-five, and later in Flanders, he was aide to General Huske, subsequently commanded the regiment in Gibraltar, and at the beginning of the Seven Years' War was ordered to Glasgow to review Highland battalions.

Webb, who had an agreeable wife and an ever-increasing family of children, had in the course of his service collected a leg-wound, three broken ribs and, through 'Colds' taken in his Scottish and West Indian service, 'a Disorder in his Side and a Deafness'. To his own misfortune, he now reluctantly followed the physicians' advice and sold out, retiring in the first instances to Greenwich – a place which he soon disliked exceedingly.[18]

Before long, his sudden poverty, addition to his family, longing to resume war service and – most galling of all – the unexpected cure of his deafness by the removal of a polyp, made Webb bitterly regret leaving the army. His father-in-law in Radnorshire dying suddenly, he left Greenwich for a few months to attend to the small estate at Downton near Presteigne, but returned home in November 1759 in time for his wife's confinement of a son, which brought his family to four girls and two boys, and presented them with a nice problem of maintenance. Desperately he considered turning author, but preferred almost literally any form of soldiering, even to raising a 'free Company' or joining the less fashionable East India Company service.

With his family, Colonel Webb now abandoned the superficial, materialistic society of Greenwich and moved to a house in Great Queen Street, Westminster, whence he made continuous but fruitless attempts to get companies raised in Aberdeenshire in which he might obtain a commission (the Secretary of State, Lord Barrington, assured him there was no Government money for such schemes), and other military enquiries, all abortive. Yet there was then a war in progress, which was to continue for four more years.[19]

At Monymusk, the Grant family had sustained a double misfortune. The kindly, warm-hearted Lady Grant, whose health had for some time been delicate, fell ill and died, apparently of rheumatic fever, which was rife in the sickly spring weather of 1759. Then, only two days after her mother's death, young Molly, pregnant a third time, miscarried. On top of this, a physician and all the servants fell ill, and the butler died.[20]

In the face of the sad loss of his wife, Sir Archibald appears to have thrown himself into yet greater activity. He had started the year with customary enthusiasm, and had been sending information on his ore-mining furnace to Garbet and Roebuck, who were building a furnace at Cockenzie and taking on the Bo'ness salt and coal works.[21] He was negotiating an apprenticeship for Sandy Sympson, the Monymusk minister's youngest son, with the Duke of Argyll's Inveraray clockmaker, Alexander Cumming – himself a skilled practitioner risen from obscure poverty through the Duke's patronage.[22] He was also helping to educate some young wards, children of clansmen and friends.[23] And, with an ironic timeliness, he had earlier started doing up the family burial place.[24]

In November, Sir Archibald was ordering a score of prints from the catalogue of Robert Fowles, the Glasgow printer, and suggested a long list of additions, including 'many British who meritt Busts & Prints': Newton, Gibbs, Bishop Burnet and (an obvious gibe here) the Duke of Argyll, 'who However Misled in some particulars, must be Esteemed by all for Generall and Extensive knowledge and abilities'.[25]

That same month saw the death of the Dowager Lady Stair, daughter of the 2nd Earl of Loudoun and widow of the 2nd Earl of Stair, and long a leading member of Edinburgh society; unfortunately, as some of his family thought, Sir Archibald received an advertisement of the sale of her effects to be held there early in February, 1760, including 'shells, and shell-work of all kinds'.[26] He also received notice of an organ. Being away from home at the time, he wrote to his eldest daughter Ketty (Katherine), one of his two children by his first wife, to make enquiries, thinking he might spend up to £25 on such an instrument.[27]

Miss Ketty was alarmed. Organs, let alone shells, she reminded him, were 'superfluous' to one short of money 'even for ye needful' – 'an organ & costly museum, are wt may easily be spared'. But Ketty was unfailingly loyal and obedient, and at her request Mrs McGill, a musical lady in Edinburgh skilled in the instrument, went to see it. Mrs McGill laughed at Ketty's naive assumption that it would be a barrel organ, 'foolish play things she said fit only for Children'. It was a keyboard chamber organ, and on her advice Ketty sent for 'a most ingenious' instrument-maker, Mr Johnston, who proved to be very familiar with the organ, which had once belonged to a clockmaker apparently named Dick (the name is conjectural). He explained some of the rudiments: 'plays by keys only, workes wth ye feet – ye pipes all wood'. It was old, 'in shape like a press', and the case, 3 feet by 2½ and 7 feet high, needed to be renewed, which in mahogany would cost at least £6 more. He further recommended installing lead pipes for yet another £6. It was a fairly standard model with five stops, diapason, 'open principall, a flut with a dubl in the middal, another flut an octave hayer, a fieften', and the range was from lower C to high D.[28]

Mr Johnston, who has in fact been no more identified than Mr Dick, valued the instrument at only £15 in view of the likely extra expense. Finally, the organ would have to be dismantled for transport to Aberdeen; but who was there to reassemble it on arrival? And where, begged Miss Ketty, could it *go*, unless where 'is now y[r] Buffate in Dining room'? Another, anonymous adviser who pencilled comments on Johnston's notes in a very cultivated hand, urged that Mrs McGill, as 'a Good Judge', should establish whether the instrument had a swell, an echo or a piano bellows, whether the last worked by the performer's foot, and whether indeed it was 'a Genteel Piece of Furniture'. 'Who', added this sceptic, 'is Mr Johnston, is he a Judge?'[29]

Sir Archibald had really started something, and the experts began to be called in. He had already consulted Andrew Tait in Aberdeen, who that spring (1760) at his request made exhaustive enquiries into available barrel instruments. Tait learned that the best cost about ten guineas, normally with three stops and capable of playing eight tunes, with additional tunes at two guineas each. An organ would be sold ready-equipped with one tune, the customer having choice of the rest. Second-hand organs, he added cautiously, were 'Always going Wrong', and new organs were a safer buy. Sir Archibald apparently asked him to undertake a few alterations, which Tait declined as 'too great an Undertaking for [his] Brain'.[30]

Further enquiries made in London, probably through John Langshaw, revealed that there the normal style was four stops and two barrels, each of eight tunes, the case of mahogany, and the average price fourteen guineas. In May, Sir Archibald thought he would order one.[31]

Langshaw, consulted about making such a 'box organ', supplied Johnston with his list of tunes and scale-range (middle or 'lower' C to top D, including C and F sharp). A two-barrel, four-stop organ (stopped diapason, principal, twelfth and fifteenth) might cost sixteen guineas, the extra two being for his 'trouble'; for twenty guineas, one could also have an open diapason and 'spiral' five- or six-inch-diameter barrels, which would hold '32 bars of a Country dance'. Sir Archibald's own suggested list, forwarded to Langshaw by Johnston, would run to six barrels; but, Langshaw explained, some of these would require a large barrel of nine-inch diameter,

> and even then, some of The Tunes must have only one part Repeated & others Neither, and there are that will take two Rounds, as the March in Saul, and the Minuet in Ariadne &c. which must have a Spiral Barrell, because the Common Barrels must finish the Tunes in one Revolution; And a 9 Inch Barrel will Contain 40, or to 46, but 50 are full too many Barrs of Alegro Time of 2 or 3 Crotchets in a Barr, and the Slower the time the fewer Number of Barrs in Proportion.

A few tunes on the list were too long for 'Common-Sized Barrels' and normal scale, needing more sharps and at least one more bass note; even then, 'all the Ends below B on the Midle Line Can have no Bass in the Close'. The minimum scale which Langshaw illustrated extended to B below middle C and included A and G sharps; with five stops, it would require six barrels, be nearly four feet high, and cost at least forty guineas.[32]

This gave Tait pause, and he prudently recommended the twenty-guinea version, to include only those tunes which it could easily accommodate, because most of the higher cost was for the extra bass notes, while each new barrel added two guineas, with two more for Johnston's fee. Tait called a halt in order to consult with 'the Captain' – Archie Grant the younger.[33]

Sir Archibald, who habitually pressed all possible allies into his heterogeneous army, had also been seeking help from Colonel Webb, by this time back at Old Radnor but shortly to return to London. Webb, with appropriate congratulations to the younger Archie for the birth of his first son in May, promised to seek the best advice on organs, and if he should buy a cheap instrument it 'shall be of ye very best sort and fit for Sir Archibalds Family which is all harmony and goodness'.[34]

There was plenty on order for Sir Archibald at this time: flowering shrubs, a fast-growing pine tree from a Camberwell nursery, a good new bellows for the smith, supplied by 'a famous man for Ventilators & Belows in Y[ork] Buildings In Strand', and, notably, maps of each quarter of the globe to cover a four-leaved canvas screen in Monymusk's library, together with 'proper prints, of Cronology, Astronomy, All parts & Terms of Ships, All D° fortifications & belonging to War, and other Curious or usefull Explanations, for Ocasional Recourse'.[35]

Moreover, Sir Archibald was corresponding with two painters, Cosmo Alexander in London about the maps, and Colin Morison, then in Rome, for 'curiosities' and for a collection of portrait medals. This somewhat inconvenienced Morison, who on 9 February had warned Sir Archibald: 'You ought either continue to increase the collection or accept of none I have already sent. They have cost me much study & pains which would be entirely to no purpose was it not continue further.'[36]

The problem was to find a quantity of maps large enough to fit the required space. At last, on 24 May, Cosmo Alexander found 'the latest & correctest Mapps' at Sayer's the printseller's, opposite St Dunstan's in Fleet Street, who had actually been 'Furnishing' such a screen. 'The 4 Quarters of the World each in 4 sheets best and correctest' were a mere four shillings each, with small sheets of the chief kingdoms at a guinea or so extra. For covering the leaves, as small uniform-sized maps could not be found, a suggested alternative was 'eight Two sheet mapps of the principall Kingdoms' at 1s 6d each. Sayer would send the maps to Aberdeenshire direct.[37]

As for his 'musaeum', Sir Archibald was choosy. It was not a matter of pieces suitable for a grotto, but 'Uncommonly Corded or Variegated, or petrifactions, or uncommon Shells Small or Great, or anything uncommon of Sea Weed, or fish or fowl, or Ingaets, Vegitables &c.' This request, made to

FIGURE 6.3   Chamber organ in the collection of the National Trust for Scotland's
Georgian House, 7 Charlotte Square, Edinburgh.

the Excise Officer at Dundee, Archibald Dunbar, was also passed on to any young officers leaving with their regiments for abroad.[38]

Friends and relatives continued the supply. Sir Archibald's newly-widowed sister, Mrs Jean Gordon, sent 'two polished pieces of Marbel ... got at Cadiz last Winter', which she had found among her late husband's possessions: it was the marble 'from the Granada Montons, for the ornamenting the New Church Building at Cadiz', together with a small piece of a transparent stone from the Leghorn marble quarries. Mr Gordon himself had been ashamed to send such trifles, but his widow had no such qualms.[39]

Colonel Webb, who on his return to London wasted no time, soon found that 'it is very hazardous meddling with second hand organs which may be near worn out or Damaged', while ready-made instruments were suspect as 'slight'. He was recommended to a 'very famous' organ-builder in the Strand named Ballie or Brillie[40] who had constructed a number of church and chapel organs, including that for Banff, and another privately for Lord Lothian. He quoted a starting price of £30: he had lately (he said) made a four-barrelled organ for £60, in an elaborately ornamented and gilded case, and 'he could have added another Barrel for the Money, if the Case had been plainer'. Extra barrels would cost about five guineas each, and he asked whether his customer wanted 'Jiggs Minuets Airs or Country Dances'. Like most schemes undertaken without a clear idea of what was involved, Sir Archibald's was running into ever-increasing expense.[41]

That was on 26 June. A couple of weeks later, Webb had some luck, apparently through yet another character in this highly peopled scene, Joseph Mahoon, who could supply a 'very Melodious' two-barrelled organ, in a plain mahogany case, for only ten guineas including packing cases. It would play eighteen tunes,

> and one Man may carry it any where, it's ye Size of a small Cabinet about 4 feet high & stands on a Mahogany frame of 4 Legs it has Gilt pipes in front ... it plays extreamly well true and strong but has no Bass.

A much finer one was offered for thirty-two guineas, of which the seller 'would not abate a farthing': it had only two barrels but included treble and bass,

> the first Barrell plays 2 peices of Musick and the other 12 Minuetts and Country Dances with their Bass, it is somewhat louder than the little one ... but not a great deal and has several Stops. its a fine Instrument and very prettily ornamented with Carved work and Gilding.

Alternatively, for the same price the builder could make such another, with Sir Archibald's own choice of tunes.

Webb recommended the cheaper job as perfectly adequate, 'to play in the Garden as it is Loud enough', and while for lack of a bass the tunes might be less 'agreeable to a Judicious ear', many seemed more distinct without it.

The first barrel included 'Handels Water peice', some minuets, a Handel jig, and a gavotte, and the second, another gavotte, a hornpipe, and popular airs such as 'Let's lose no time' and 'Lucy's Delight'.[42]

Sir Archibald agreed to order the cheaper organ, Webb drawing on Sir Alexander Grant for the money, but he asked that Mahoon inspect the instrument to see if they might add a bass and an extra barrel for new tunes from a list he sent. 'But he must give Directions for the use of it, and also any slight Repaires If needfull.'[43]

Colonel Webb applauded his prudence, it being 'extreamly necessary that a Man of skill should see and examine the Organ'. He feared the instrument might already be sold, as Mahoon had been out of town, and was now about to view it (in company with yet another expert) on his return. Luckily the maker could add a bass for an extra three guineas, and for fifteen guineas make a completely new three-barrelled organ of nine tunes each, with a bass 'as true as sweet & as Loud as any Organ in England of the price', which, provided it were kept dry and his instructions followed, would last for years.[44]

Letters flew back and forth. Mahoon himself had warned Tait of Aberdeen that to add the stops that Sir Archibald required would bring the cost to seventeen guineas, for an organ 'made in the Manner Mr Mahoon & his friend require': the friend being 'a very eminent Organ builder in a large way', between them they would (Webb reported) certainly look after Sir Archibald's interests.[45] The friend, who by a perverse unanimity among the correspondents is not named, must have been Snetzler, for towards the end of September Sir Archibald noted: 'Mahoon writes, the organ is forward, & he & Snetzler were to give directions, and would take Care to have it Good and Consult about one with Barrells & Keys'.[46]

That August, the estate at Monymusk suffered from appalling weather at the time of the new moon – 'a Perfect *Hurricane* these three days accompanied with heavy Squalls of Rain', wrote Archie on 15 August to his father, who was in Aberdeen. An ornamental obelisk in the grounds was blown over, the river Spey flooded the roads, and Archie, his uncle Francis and another guest were storm-bound at Monymusk. It was a few days before they could set off on an intended 'jaunt' to Glasgow and Edinburgh, taking in Argyll and Inveraray by the way – not without complaints from Archie of 'the Natural Weather of that

filthy climate, (Stinking Fogs, and Meazling rain)', which effectively silenced
any comments he might have made on the sights they visited.[47]

Colonel Webb now had to return once more to Radnorshire, but arriving
back in London in December he found Sir Archibald's organ ready, heard it
played, and reported it 'very musical'. Mahoon and 'freind' pronounced
it 'very well made'. Purpose-built packing cases pushed up the total cost to
nineteen guineas. So much for the hope of a cheap job for ten.[48]

The work took some time to complete. Eventually, the organ was packed
into its case, transported to the quayside and loaded on to the ship for Aberdeen, and there unloaded again and carried by cart to Monymusk. It was,
confusingly, Rostrand who wrote the detailed instructions for its use and
maintenance. It must not be kept in a damp place; to change the barrel, push
up the left-hand bolt below the keys, but beware of touching the pins; the
brass screws turning the barrel must occasionally be oiled. 'If you find the
Tunes play too quick', he added, 'its only turning the handle a little slower.'[49]

Colonel Webb, who paid over the nineteen guineas, was satisfied it could
come to no harm on the voyage, 'particularly as it has brass keys instead of
wooden ones'; equally, he was sure, it would 'Give great pleasure to the
Young Ladies and Gentlemen'. He admitted disappointment with the
instructions. 'They are very bald I own Sir but the fellow is a German and has
very little English', but their kernel seemed to be the urgent warning to keep
it dry.[50]

Sir Archibald, still impatiently awaiting news of maps and prints for the
library screen, was further anxious to acquire certain instruments. For this he
applied to James Ferguson, one of that number of natural geniuses from
obscure Scottish backgrounds, who were almost self-educated in science with
the occasional helping hand from amazed members of the gentry and nobility.
Ferguson, born near Rothiemay, had been established in London since about
1742, and besides making astronomical instruments was especially successful
with his astronomy lectures and educational textbooks for young people.[51]

Sir Archibald requested from Ferguson a 'horizontal dial' incorporating an
equation table ('the best'), provided with a pedestal because Monymusk had
no suitable stone; and a replacement for his worn-out air-pump. A tiresome
misunderstanding now arose, first over Ferguson's apparent failure to reply,
and then over his misinterpretation of the baronet's further request about an
orrery. Sir Archibald, irritated at this silence, set his sleuths on the track;
remarking not very resignedly how 'philosophers forget trivial things', he
asked Colonel Webb to bring in yet another clansman, Duncan Grant, an
Antigua merchant living in Red Lion Square, 'a Man of Genius – active
dissposition & a Large Fortune'.[52]

Ferguson had in fact already replied late in January 1761, but his letter quoting three guineas for a good dial of one foot diameter, and £10 for an air-pump, did not arrive until March. However, misunderstanding Sir Archibald's not very clearly-worded letter, he mistook his request for a print of an orrery (for the screen) as an order for an actual instrument, and was at pains to describe a thirty-six-guinea custom-built job, showing Venus and Mercury besides sun, moon and earth; and warned that it would take four months as 'These Machines are never made unless bespoke'. He also suggested suitable books, and described his own 'new astronomical Rotula for 5s 6d, 'shewing all ... except the rising and setting of the Sun, moon, and Stars', which 'takes in the whole affair of Solar and Lunar Eclipses ... for all Latitudes', and a three-shilling quarto pamphlet, with four plates, on the forthcoming transit of Venus. As for

> My new astronomical Instrument, shewing the change and age of the Moon, the places of the Sun and moon in the Ecliptic, the days of the month, and times of rising, southing, and setting, of the Sun, moon, and stars, it would be useless in your part of the country.[53]

Sir Archibald, not much mollified, repeated his request for maps, and queried why the rotula would not serve for Scotland. Books he could get from a book-seller; but, he conceded, 'if takeing them from you be any benefite to you, please send them' – an apparent condescension which in turn nettled the astronomer.[54]

Colonel Webb soon discovered both that Ferguson had already written and his confusion about the orrery ('a very expensive peice of Mechanism'). Duncan Grant next took a hand, and among other useful contributions sent Sir Archibald a remarkable collection of West Indian 'Triffels' for the museum: arrows from Dominica, petrified wood, a humming-bird's nest, a coconut from a tree which he himself had planted, a locust, an ear of maize with instructions for planting, a calabash, cashew nuts, and 'a walking Lance & Staff of an Indian prince'.[55]

But the misunderstanding was not fully clarified until June. It was not (as Sir Archibald supposed) that Ferguson was 'so much a philosopher, as not to be punctuall in Correspondence',[56] but that he had been almost totally incapacitated by two serious accidents. Ferguson described how, while hanging a hygrometer for a gentleman client, his ladder had slipped and he had fallen fifteen feet, nearly killed by the ladder falling across him. He was immobilised by his injuries for a long time.

> After that, I went out hastily to get some help for my daughter who was suddenly taken ill, and was accidentally met at turning a corner by a

man carrying a thick plank of wood on his shoulder, which struck against my breast and beat me down backward, and so I was taken up speechless, and since that time I have scarce been able to walk a quarter of a mile.

These Hoffnungesque disasters required a spell of recovery in Bristol – presumably to take the Hotwell waters – painful though the long journey must have been.

As for the rotula, Ferguson explained with a trace of impatience why it would be 'considerably out in your Latitude' for rising and setting times; and concluded with a brusque denial of any concern with stone pedestals, or even with the sale of his own publications, ending stiffly: 'Mr Miller sells all my books'.[57]

From this point, the story becomes fragmentary. It was June before Sir Archibald reported with annoyance that, although the organ had arrived, several pipes had been bent and keys broken through bad packing. With some difficulty they were mended, but he wanted two dozen new springs from the maker, and spare wire to mend barrels in case of need. Further, he hoped that the maker had kept a record, so that any new barrels required could be made without sending one back as a model. Finally, he was irritated to find that after all the instrument would not serve for outdoor entertainment, being too delicate for his servants to carry into the woods and fields. In fact, he was now enquiring about a further instrument, 'Chiefly to Resemble french Horn or Horns, and be tolerably Loud'. 'I Dont mean by this', he added ingenuously to the patient Colonel Webb, 'to Give you more Trouble, But if it fall In your Way I know you will Doe it.'[58]

Colonel Webb was too grateful for Sir Archibald's continuing support of his unavailing quest for a fresh army commission not to make immediate enquiries; but the organ-builder was mystified. He insisted that the organ, like all his instruments, had been carefully packed. Spare springs he could certainly supply, though none had been asked for; nor could they get lost, for if any fell off they were easily retrievable. Nor would the barrels' wire break. And finally, he maintained, the organ could be safety carried anywhere, provided it were never left in a damp place.[59]

Webb, though off to Wales again, promised to look out for yet another instrument, good and loud, but warned of the dangers of second-hand purchase. It seems as though there was talk of buying back the instrument they had had earlier, for still another technician, Andrew Lunan, writes from Aberdeen in December 1762 offering first refusal of his organ then at Crathes, which had been 'long in your Possession' and was now 'better in Tune and much fitter for use than at that time'. Mr Tait, sent to inspect it, was not impressed, but conceded that Lunan had made minor adjustments. The price was only eight guineas, 'but as he is Pinched Poor Fellow I believe 5/ or 6 would Doe' – not a very charitable suggestion. The instrument ought to be serviced locally, for sending it to London would cost more than it was worth, and the Banff organist had offered to undertake the job. Meanwhile, Tait had again been corresponding with Mahoon, but expressed little enthusiasm for revaluing an organ that he had already seen but forgotten.[60]

On this trickle, the story, after plunging so far in full flood, peters out. No further correspondence or references have yet come to light from Mahoon, Tait or Lunan, and curiously enough not even from Colonel Webb, last seen with a flat denial from the War Office and desperately contemplating the outside chance of the Governorship of Fort William. What became of the likeable, ill-starred officer has not so far been established.

There is no organ or barrel organ now at Monymusk, nor has there been within living memory; the odds are that Sir Archibald, in his disappointment, soon disposed of it. In the old Episcopal Church there, however, a later organ of the 1830s, by Henry Cephas Lincoln, was discovered in recent years. It seems to have been moved there from the house, and may originally have been installed in the library to replace Sir Archibald's. Part of the action for a barrel organ was lately discovered, during renovations, in the loft of the joiner's shop at the Home Farm.[61]

John Wesley, on one of his numerous extended gospel tours, visited Monymusk in July 1761, and recorded how impressed he was, not only by the estate improvements and the number of parishioners at church, but also by the quality of the singing.[62] The family, on their side, left surprisingly little comment on the visit.

Later that summer, Sir Archibald's daughter-in-law Molly gave birth to a second son, and in the winter he packed off the young couple to Bath for their health, with the revealing comment that 'their way of Life, Long in Bed, Uncomonly Hott In Rooms, thin in Cloaths and No Exercise, May, at least in part, account for these [ills]'.[63] He in fact found it advisable to separate his two eldest daughters from their younger half-brother. They had seen their father through his years of worst financial struggle, foregone matrimony for themselves and looked after their siblings; but Archie's difficult temperament made it uneasy for the large family to continue together.[64] Indeed, three generations, a young heir raising his own progeny, and elder sisters of so disparate an age, would make a delicate situation at the best of times.

For a few years, light plays brightly if fitfully on all these ventures and misadventures, and extended research may yet reveal an epilogue, when there has been opportunity to examine yet more of the vast, only partly sorted

Monymusk manuscript collection. Meanwhile, an interesting light can be thrown on a decade of the domestic life of the 2nd Baronet of Monymusk, and some illumination on the making of barrel organs in the mid-eighteenth century.

NOTES

1. This chapter is based on the Grant of Monymusk papers now at the Scottish Record Office, reference GD345. I am grateful to Sir Archibald Grant of Monymusk for permission to make use of the collection. In these notes, the prefix has been omitted; the chief sections consulted were 1163, 1179 and 1180. Background information was found in *Selections from the Monymusk Papers (1713–1755)*, ed. Henry Hamilton, Scottish History Society, 3rd series, vol. XXXIX, 1945, and David Johnson, *Music and Society in Lowland Scotland in the 18th Century*, Oxford University Press, 1972.

   The main works consulted on the technical side were: Cecil Clutton and Austin Niland, *The British Organ*, 2nd edn, EP Publications Ltd, 1976; *Dictionary of Scientific Biography*, New York, Charles Scribner's Sons, 1971, vol. 4 (on James Ferguson); *The New Grove Dictionary of Music and Musicians*, ed. Stanley Sadie, Macmillan, 1980, vols 2, 11, 17, 18; Lyndesay G. Langwill and Canon Noel Boston, *Church and Chamber Barrel-Organs*, 2nd edn, Edinburgh, 1970; Arthur W. G. J. Ord-Hume, *Barrel Organ: The Story of the Mechanical Organ and its Repair*; George Allen and Unwin, 1978; *The Organ* [monthly periodical], vols VI, XXXVIII, XLVII; Michael Wilson, *The English Chamber Organ, 1650–1850*, 1968. I must also express my thanks to the following, who kindly supplied me with useful information: Douglas Carrington, editor of *The Organ*; Christopher Hartley, of the National Trust for Scotland; and James Yorke, of the Furniture and Woodwork Department, Victoria and Albert Museum.

2. *Selections*, pp. lxxix, 171 (1746, 1748).
3. For Archie's marriage, 1179/270, 277; for Billy's career and death, 1179/284, 1174/3/60, etc.
4. Andrew Tait (c. 1710–78), b. Aberdeen, c.1735–75 organist at St Paul's Episcopal Chapel, 1740–c.1755 Master of Aberdeen Music School, 1748 a founder of Aberdeen Music Society. He collaborated with the printer James Chalmers on *A New and Correct Set of Church Tunes* (1749), at least one of which survives. *Grove*, vol. 18, pp. 528–9, and see e.g. 1179/257, 299.
5. 1179/156, 237 (April 1754); Johnson, pp. 176ff.
6. 1163/3/21–3, 28–31, 125–7. The Rev. John Bisset (1692–1756), b. New Deer, educated Marischal College, transferred to Aberdeen East Parish from New Machar in 1728. Zealous, controversial, and of a dreaded 'choleric disposition', he attacked George Whitfield from the pulpit during the latter's 1741 visit – for which the magistrates next day had to apologise – and once had to be excluded from his own church by the Provost. He was the founder of the Secession in Aberdeen, whose first (posthumous) congregation was formed in his church (*Fasti Eccles. Scot.*; and see Johnson, p. 178).
7. St Andrew's Episcopal Chapel, Banff, first built in the 1720s, had been

equipped with a loft organ at least by 1732, but it was burned with the
chapel in 1746 by order of the Duke of Cumberland, and part of the
church woodwork used for fuel by the soldiery. In 1752, the chapel was
rebuilt. During the incumbency of the Rev. Nathaniel Morgan (1755–
68), another organ was bought for £100, and a young man was sent to
London to learn how to play it. This organ continued to serve the
church, again rebuilt in 1880, until 1871, when it was sold for £25. (*The
Annals of Banff*, ed. William Cramond; Aberdeen, New Spalding Club,
1891, vol. ii, pp. 157, 159, 160. I am grateful to John Gifford for
providing me with this reference.) See also Johnson, p. 176. For its
unidentified builder, see n. 40.

8. The most comprehensive account of barrel organs is in Arthur Ord-
Hume's book (op. cit., pp. 53ff.), which, however, says little on the
work of eighteenth-century London organ-builders earlier than Benjamin Flight (1770s), and on church barrel organs is confined mostly to
the nineteenth century. See also Langwill and Boston, pp. 21ff.; *Grove*,
vol. 2, pp. 181ff.; Laurence Elvin, 'Barrel Organs', in *The Organ*, vol.
XXXVIII, no. 149, July 1958; J. P. Hall, 'A Bates Barrel Pipe Organ',
ibid., vol. XLVII, no. 185, July 1967; David Strong, 'Church Barrel-
Organs in General and Particular', ibid., vol. LV, no. 217, July 1976.

9. Sir John Sutton, *A Short Account of Organs Built in England from the
Reign of King Charles II to the Present Time*, London, 1847, p. 73.

10. Clutton and Niland, pp. 86–8; Groves, vol. 17, p. 427; Wilson, pp.
11–14, 101–12. Snetzler (sometimes wrongly described as Swiss) was
credited with a heavy Germanic accent which, though very Anglophile,
he never lost. A mythical story makes him retire in 1781 to his native
land but, homesick for England, attempt to return, only to die on the
journey.

11. For Langshaw, see *Grove*, vol. 2, pp. 181ff.; Ord-Hume, pp. 88f. It was
Langshaw who pinned the barrels of Lord Bute's organ, whose effect
was praised as 'masterly'. In 1772 he was appointed organist in
Lancaster, retaining the post until his death. For Mahoon, see Grove,
vol. 11, p. 533. Hogarth illustrates a Mahoon harpsichord in Plate II of
'The Rake's Progress' (1735).

12. Grove, vol. 2, pp. 181ff. A trade card is in the Monymusk papers,
1167/1/2.

13. 1164/3/32 and 6/20; 1179/361, etc.

14. 1179/377 and 364; 1165/1/11, 12 (John Cook to Sir Archibald, 8 May
1758).

15. 1165/83–5 (March/April 1758); ibid. 81 (July/August); ibid. 9, 70, 73
(August).

16. 1179/390, 410, 411 etc. (February 1758); 1165/74 (May).

17. 1180/21 (28 December 1758).

18. Richmond Webb's first appearance in the Monymusk papers is in 1755
(1179/193, 279). For his career, see Memorandum by Sir Archibald,
[?March 1759], 1165/3/86; Sir Archibald to Captain Rainy, 9 January
1761, 1166/1/89; Webb to Charles Townshend, Secretary at War, [1761],
1167/4/118; for his views on Greenwich, Webb to Sir Archibald, 28
October 1758, 1165/1/108.

19. Webb to Sir Archibald, 1165/2/89 and 44 (8 July, 15 December 1759);
1166/1/47, 64 (15 January, 5 February 1760).

20. Scroll, Sir Archibald to Webb, 28 May 1759, 1165/2/53; funeral account, 1 May 1759, 1165/1.
21. Francis Grant to his brother Sir Archibald, 6 March 1759, 1176/60 and 61.
22. Francis Grant to Sir Archibald, 4 January and to Alexander Cumming, 3 March 1759, 1176/3/59, 61; *Fasti Eccles. Scot.*, ad loc. Interestingly enough, it was Cumming who was called in when technical difficulties appeared in the Luton Park organ, though the work had gone too far for his proposals to be incorporated. A few years later, Cumming was to build an organ for Lord Bute's new house at High Cliffe, Hants (1782–7). Lord Bute was the nephew of the 3rd Duke of Argyll.
23. For example, Sir Archibald to Alexander Grant of Achoynanie, 8 March and 22 October 1759, 1165/3/47 and 49.
24. Archie Grant to Sir Archibald, 8 February 1759, 1173/3/44.
25. Scroll, Sir Archibald to Robert Fowles, 26 November 1759, 1165/2/63.
26. Balfour Paul, *Scots Peerage*, ad loc.; *Caledonian Mercury*, 23 January 1760; *Edinburgh Evening Courant*, 24 January 1760, and subsequent advertisements.
27. Katherine Grant to Sir Archibald, and endorsement, 7 January 1760, 1174/4/1. On his endorsement, Sir Archibald made a note to take the advice of 'Lady Kemnay & Miss Duce', and the writer of the comments on the organ (see below) may have been one of these. Lady Kemnay was Janet Burnett, second wife of George Burnett of Kemnay, and Miss Dyce was her elder sister. A Clementi barrel organ dated c. 1812 or perhaps later is in existence at Kemnay, although unfortunately no information has come to light about its purchase. I am grateful to Mrs Milton of Kemnay for this information.
28. Katherine Grant to Sir Archibald, 5 February 1760, 1174/6/28; ibid. 29; 'Mr Johnstons observations upon ye organ'. Johnston cannot be traced in *Grove*; nor can Dick (if that is the correct reading) in dictionaries of clockmakers; nor either in the Edinburgh apprentice and burgess records. Mrs McGill, mentioned in 1757 as recommending a spinet teacher (1164/6/48, 26 March), is not identified, but may well have been a relative of the architect Alexander McGill.
29. Anonymous note, 1174/6/29. The writer also recommends that 'Mess[rs] M[c]Pherson & Olivieri' examine the instrument.
30. Andrew Tait to Sir Archibald, 26 February and 27 March 1760, 1166/1/90, 127.
31. Andrew Tait to Sir Archibald, 12 May 1760, 1166/2/48.
32. John Langshaw to [?Andrew Tait], 29 May 1760, 1166/1/59.
33. Andrew Tait to Sir Archibald, 4 June 1760, 1166/2/76.
34. Col. Richmond Webb to Sir Archibald, Old Radnor, 31 May 1760, 1166/3/22.
35. Scroll, Sir Archibald to William Grant (of Aberdeen), [March 1760], 1166/1/101.
36. Colin Morison to Sir Archibald, Rome, 9 February 1760, 1166/1/117.
37. Cosmo Alexander to — Grant, London, 24 May 1760, 1166/2/61.
38. Sir Archibald to Archibald Dunbar, 15 September 1759, 1166/2/78.
39. Mrs Jean Gordon to Sir Archibald, Arndilly, [November 1760], 1166/4/ 71.

40. It has not been possible to establish either the name or the identity of this expert: Col. Webb's handwriting is unusually obscure at this point.
41. Webb to Sir Archibald, 26 June 1760, 1166/3/21.
42. Webb to Sir Archibald, 12 July 1760, 1166/3/23.
43. Sir Archibald to [Webb], 28 July 1760, 1166/3/18, and endorsement on Webb's letter of 26 June.
44. Webb to Sir Archibald, 12 August 1760, 1166/4/3(a).
45. Webb to Sir Archibald, 25 September 1760, 1166/4/3(b).
46. Sir Archibald, endorsement on note from Tait [Sept. 1760], 1166/4/3(c).
47. Archie Grant to Sir Archibald, 15 August and 5 September 1760, 1173/4/4 and 10.
48. Webb to Sir Archibald, 9 December 1760, 1166/4/88.
49. E. Rostrand to [?Andrew Tait], 29 November 1760, 1167/1/1.
50. Webb to Sir Archibald, 9 January and [late January] 1761, 1167/1/2 and 1167/4/126. There is great ambiguity here. Webb refers on 3 January to 'a paper of instructions sent down by Mr Mahoon to Mr Tate', but the instructions dated 29 November are by Rostrand, enclosing his trade card. Rostrand is not named in the correspondence; nor indeed is Snetzler, except by Sir Archibald (see n. 46).
51. *Dictionary of Scientific Biography*, vol. 4, pp. 565–6; F. Henderson, *Life of James Ferguson*, Edinburgh, 1867. There is no reference in these to the series of ludicrous accidents described by Ferguson in 1761. The chronology outlined by Henderson allows a bare space for these events: Ferguson is recorded as lecturing in Chelmsford in March, and as observing the transit of Venus on 6 June.
52. Sir Archibald to James Ferguson, 7 March 1761, 1167/1/63; Sir Archibald to [?Webb], 17 February, 1167/1/40, and 4 June, 1167/2/35.
53. James Ferguson to Sir Archibald, 27 January [1761 – wrongly dated 1760], 1167/1/53.
54. Sir Archibald to Ferguson, 7 March 1761, 1167/1/63.
55. Webb to Sir Archibald, 12 March 1761, 1167/2/47; Duncan Grant to Sir Archibald, 10 April 1761, 1167/2/35.
56. Sir Archibald to Webb, 12 June 1761, 1167/2/48.
57. Ferguson to Sir Archibald, 22 June 1761, 1167/3/13.
58. Sir Archibald to Webb, 12 June 1761, 1167/2/48.
59. Webb to Sir Archibald, 22 June 1761, 1167/3/8.
60. Andrew Lunan to [Captain] Archie Grant, 7 December 1762; Andrew Tait to [Captain] Archie Grant, 18 and 29 December 1762: all in 1180.
61. Repairs to the building in 1989 were followed in 1990 by restoration of the organ, which had not been in use since the Second World War. A charitable Trust, chaired by Lady Grant, was set up for the restoration and for raising a fund for the work. A sum of £10,000 was quoted for repairs to the organ alone. I am indebted to the present Sir Archibald Grant for supplying information on this later organ.
62. *The Journals of the Rev. John Wesley*, A.M., ed. Nehemiah Curnock, London 1938, vol. 4, pp. 451–2. See also 1167/3.
63. Sir Archibald to Sir Alexander Grant of Dalvey, 1 December 1761, 1167/4/89.
64. Memorandum by Sir Archibald on his children, n.d. but after July 1761, 1167/4/120.

FIGURE 7.1   1. First-floor plan and principal elevation of Alderman Fenwick's House, Newcastle-upon-Tyne. 2. Hypothetical ground- and first-floor plans and principal elevation of Gladney House, reconstructed from available evidence. 3. Hypothetical principal-floor plan and elevation of Marlefield House, Roxburghshire. 4. Principal-floor plan and elevation of Gallery House, Kincardineshire. RCAHMS.

7

An Account of the Reconstruction of William Adam's Design for Gladney House, with some Observations on Other Early Projects

JAMES SIMPSON

Gladney House, Kirkcaldy, was apparently designed and built in 1711 by William Adam for his future partner and father-in-law, William Robertson.[1] The Adam family subsequently occupied the house until their removal to Edinburgh sometime after Robert Adam's birth there in 1727. By 1927 it had descended to being a 'common lodging house', and its demolition was proposed to make way for a housing scheme. In response to an enquiry from the Society for the Protection of Ancient Buildings, Dr Thomas Ross wrote: 'it is in a most dilapidated and most lamentable condition; there is nothing inside but dirt and squalor, a slum of the slums. The sooner it is wiped off the face of the earth the better. I am very loath to report this, but so it is.'[2] By 1930 the site was cleared.

The loss of Gladney at about the same time as that of several other William Adam buildings, including Edinburgh Royal Infirmary and Dundee Town House, was most regrettable, the more so because it was not then thought necessary to record such structures in any detail. Gladney was a somewhat unusual house which, until a few years ago, was best known from the engraving reproduced by John Fleming in 'Robert Adam and his Circle'.[3] Two drawings and a description had, however, been included by Alexander MacGibbon and Dr Thomas Ross in *The Castellated and Domestic Architecture of Scotland*.[4] It was shown on the first and second editions of the Ordnance Survey map,[5] and two photographs by the Kirkcaldy photographer Violet Banks (see Figure 7.2) were published in the *Fife Free Press* on 30 April 1927.[6]

FIGURE 7.2   Photograph taken by Violet Banks of Gladney House before demolition.

FIGURE 7.3   Oblique view of Simon Montgomery's model of Gladney House, Kirkcaldy,
1986. Conjectural restoration of William Adam's original 1711 design.

In 1984, an attempt was made to reconstruct the design of Gladney in terms of plans and elevations, in the way that a crime, or a historical event, might be reconstructed from an examination of the evidence. Drawings were produced, which formed the basis of a 1:50 scale model (see Figures 7.1 and 7.3). To the extent that the evidence was incomplete, the reconstructed design and the plans in particular are speculative.[7]

Unfortunately, MacGibbon and Ross's account included no plan, so the starting point had to be the Ordnance Survey, which suggested a plan fifty feet square. Within the overall envelope, simple round-number dimensions fell easily into place: a recessed frontispiece twenty feet across left end bays of fifteen feet apiece, advanced ten feet from the plane of the main front. Allowing for an outside wall thickness, including finishes of about two feet six inches, these dimensions provided neatly for small rooms within the advanced end bays, presumably closets, ten feet square.

The next piece of evidence to be brought into play was the photographs, for what they showed of the roof form. They clearly indicated an 'M' roof, the front ridge slightly lower than the rear, but level with those of the side roofs, which ran from the advanced end gables of the frontage into the rear roof. The roof suggested a structural double-pile plan, that is with a spine wall beneath the centre valley gutter, supporting the wallplates and the inner rafter feet of the front and rear roofs. If all the pitches were equal, then the geometry of the roof forms suggested a front span of fifteen feet and a rear span of seventeen feet.

The disposition of rooms within the structural shell thus established was the next thing to be considered. In this, the positions of the stair, flues and windows were the significant factors, while it seemed reasonable to speculate on the possibility that the interior was controlled by a dimensional logic similar to that of the exterior. After testing various alternatives, there seemed to be only one reasonably probable position for the stair: placed centrally at the rear, it could be approached axially through an entrance vestibule, and could provide access at the centre of the upper floors to the various rooms. A solid-newel, scale-and-platt stair seemed a likely form in such a house. Following the principle, which may reasonably be assumed for rooms of this period, that windows, doors and fireplaces should be regularly disposed within rooms, the plan then fell naturally into place: the stair was flanked at each level by rooms seventeen feet square, with fireplaces on the gable walls between pairs of windows. The equal spacing of the gable windows dictated that there was only a central window at each end of the space contained in the front range, which must have been some forty-five feet long by fifteen feet overall. At the entrance and second-floor levels, this space seemed likely to have been divided into three rooms fifteen feet square, while on the principal floor the intriguing possibility of a single 'great room' emerged.

At this stage, or, to be honest, at a slightly earlier stage, comparison with the plans of two other houses began to suggest itself. Gallery[8] or Galleraw in Angus is dated 1680 on the weather vane, while Fenwick's House in Pilgrim Street, Newcastle-upon-Tyne,[9] seems to be the result of the remodelling of an earlier house in the early 1690s. In all significant respects, the plans of these houses are the same as that which has been postulated for Gladney. Gallery, though a country house, was built for a merchant; Fenwick's and Gladney were the town houses of prominent merchants; and all these were close to the east coast. In aspect and particularly in roof form, however, the three houses were quite distinct.

The plan-type, characterised by symmetrical double-pile arrangement, advanced closet towers and a first-floor 'great room' extending the full length of the frontage, seems to be rare, though the loss of substantial town houses of the period has been such that it may once have been less so. Marlefield in Roxburghshire[10] may have had a similar plan, though a full-length 'great room' there can only be considered to have been a possibility, and the closet towers linked to half-gables on the end elevations are strongly reminiscent of those at Panmure.[11] Comparison may also be made with the more common form of late seventeenth-century double pile, the 'U' or developed 'L' plan, in which, as at Cammo[12] and Bargany,[13] a balustraded flat roof is clasped between two front-facing gables. These variations on a double-pile, twin-gabled or closet-towered, recessed-centre theme may be seen as versions of a seventeenth-century form which gradually gave way to the more characteristi-cally Palladian pavilion-roofed, advanced-centred, tripartite plan, popula-rised in Scotland by James Smith in the 1680s and 1690s, of which his own house of Whitehill of c. 1686 – now Newhailes – is a representative example.

If Gladney was William Adam's first design, it was a worthy effort. However, it may not have been: the Grange at Earlsferry, also in Fife, is strikingly similar to Gladney and appears to have been built at about the same time, or perhaps a year or two earlier. The Grange was bought by James Malcolm, fourth son of Sir John Malcolm of Balbedie, in 1708, and it seems likely that the present house, which survives in ruins, was built shortly thereafter.[14] Like Gladney, the Grange is a regular classical house and has advanced closet towers with round-windowed gables; unlike Gladney, it is a single pile and has a walled forecourt with flanking pavilions. William Kay has established other links between Adam and Malcolm at this time, but it is not yet possible to prove that the Grange was the very first of what was to be a long line of Adam houses.

William Adam was, however, the builder and, in 1719, the author of revised plans for the neighbouring house of Kincraig.[15] In its recessed pedimented centre, in its general aspect and in certain details, Kincraig is again distinctly reminiscent of Gladney.[16] By comparison, however, it is no mere artisan work, but a polished and fully integrated piece of architecture, and this may begin to explain the reputation which William Adam was clearly acquiring at this time and which led to the great commissions for Floors and Hopetoun, by which his pre-eminent position in Scottish architecture from about 1720 until his death in 1748 was to be established.

Firm information on William Adam's early career continues to be elusive, but it may be that the earliest of his surviving drawings are those for Makerstoun in Roxburghshire, which are undated but which apparently superseded Alexander McGill's gabled Donibristle-style proposal of 1714.[17] The double-pile, advanced-centre plan is largely a consequence of the fact that the project was for the refronting of an existing extended tower house. The curvilinear pediment recalls the closet gables at Gladney and might be thought to pre-date serious study of the first volume of *Vitruvius Britannicus*, of 1715. Otherwise, the design was calmly up-to-date in its bell-cast, pavilion-roofed simplicity, much more so than McGill's.

If the Makerstoun drawings are of 1715 or thereabouts, it is surprising to find William Adam working so far from Fife at such an early stage in his career. It is perhaps even more so to find him in Roxburghshire again, being commissioned to build or rebuild Floors Castle for such an important patron as the 1st Duke of Roxburghe in 1721. There are two possible links, namely Sir William Bennet of Grubet and Marlefield and the Duke's factor Gilbert Ramsay, who may have been related to Andrew Ramsay of Abbotshall,[18] to whom the Adams were well known.

Bennet was a man of wide cultural interests, a patron of Allan Ramsay and acknowledged by James Thomson in his preface to *The Seasons* as his 'special friend'. Having rebuilt his own house of Marlefield, he seems to have been regarded locally as somebody to be consulted on such matters. In a letter to the Duchess of Roxburghe of 16 April 1721, Gilbert Ramsay wrote that Sir William Bennet 'spoke highly in praise of Mr. Adam',[19] and only a few weeks later William Adam was present at the founding of the new Floors Castle.

The plan of the centre block of Floors, to which the wings are somewhat awkwardly attached, is distincly like that of Marlefield, though on a much larger scale; it is fundamentally a double pile, with several flue-bearing cross-walls as well, and with closet towers at all four corners. It is tempting to suggest, on this basis, that Marlefield could also be attributed to William Adam. However, it is at least as likely that the plan of Floors and the building of Marlefield pre-dated Adam's appearance in Roxburghshire and that both houses may have been first conceived as buildings of the Panmure type, with steep-pitched roofs and ogee-topped closet towers. If so, links might be postulated with John Mylne, who designed Panmure, or with Alexander

Nisbet, who supervised its building. On some such basis as this, the relative awkwardness of the Wilton formula, derived from *Vitruvius Britannicus* and applied by Adam at Floors, becomes much more understandable.

The starting point for all these observations was the attempt to reconstruct the plan and the overall design of Gladney House and to relate this early project, attributed to William Adam by his grandson, to his other known works, which seemed, somewhat improbably, to begin with Hopetoun ten years later. While most of what has been suggested must remain speculative, the first stages of the career of Scotland's great early Georgian architect may be beginning to take some sort of shape.

ACKNOWLEDGEMENTS

I am grateful to Ian Gow and William Kay, with whom I have discussed aspects of this paper, and to Vicky Lennie for help with the illustrations.

NOTES

1. Blair Adam MSS; MS of William Adam of Blair Adam, 'Account of a Scotch Family from 1688 to 1838'.
2. SPAB; letter to the Secretary, A. R. Powys, 19 July 1927.
3. Op. cit., John Murray, 1962, facing p. 34.
4. Vol. 5, pp. 286–9.
5. OS 1:500, Kirkcaldy; Sh. XXXV.12.25, 1894.
6. SPAB; letter from Violet Banks to Mr McAndrew, 6 July (1927). Copies of four photographs referred to are in the Kirkcaldy Museum and Art Gallery.
7. Mahdad Saniee's drawings and Simon Montgomery's model are in the possession of Simpson and Brown, Architects. Their assistance is gratefully acknowledged.
8. NMRS; built by Thomas Wilkie, Mason in Edinburgh, for Sir John Falconer of Balmakelly, contract dated 1677; RCAHMS survey and record sheet, 1970.
9. Surveyed in 1981 by Simpson and Brown for the Tyne and Wear Building Preservation Trust Ltd.
10. Possibly built for Sir William Bennet of Grubet and Marlefield, patron of Allan Ramsay and James Thomson. Alterations and additions by George Paterson, 1754. The assistance of Mrs Mark Goodson, Kilham, is gratefully acknowledged.
11. William Adam, *Vitruvius Scoticus*, reduced facsimile edition, ed. James Simpson, (publ.) Paul Harris, 1980; plates 129–31 and note on p. 32. Panmure was designed by John Mylne, contract dated 28 February 1666. The work was supervised after Mylne's death by Alexander Nisbet.
12. William Adam, op. cit., plate 141 and note on p. 19. Built for John Menzies, dated 1693.
13. Built for the 2nd Lord Bargany between 1680 and 1693.
14. Ex inf. William Kay.
15. Contract of 1719; RCAHMS survey, photographs and record sheet, 1968;

ex inf. William Kay, to whom grateful acknowledgement is made. Kincraig was demolished in 1969.

16. Compare also Dryden House, the unattributed design for which, drawn by William Adam for *Vitruvius Scoticus*, plates 79 and 80, probably dates from before 1715 and closely parallels the Kincraig design, though on a grander scale.

17. Original drawings by Alexander McGill and William Adam in the possession of Christopher Scott, Esq. Parts of William Adam's frontage survived, embedded in later work, until 1973, when they were completely removed and a new frontage built after the same design but in a different position.

18. Ex inf. William Kay.

19. Floors Castle MSS; letter from Gilbert Ramsay of 16 April 1721.

The South Front towards the Garden.

These Fronts of the 2 Wings being more ornamented than the former are executing accordingly

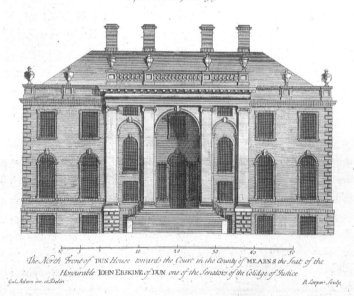

The North Front of DUN House towards the Court in the County of MEARNS the Seat of the Honourable JOHN ERSKINE of DUN one of the Senators of the Colidge of Justice

Gul. Adam inv. et Delin
R. Cooper Sculp.

FIGURE 8.1   William Adam's engraved elevations of the House of Dun from his *Vitruvius Scoticus.*

8

The Restoration of the House of Dun

DAVID LEARMONT

It was in 1730 that David Erskine, who became a judge of the Court of Session in Edinburgh, assuming the title of Lord Dun, commissioned William Adam to build the House of Dun (see Figure 8.1). Only four rooms, notably the saloon with its exuberant plasterwork by Joseph Enzer, survived the major alterations that were carried out in the early nineteenth century by two successive descendants – Alice Erskine, the eccentric 16th laird, and her nephew, John Erskine Kennedy-Erskine, who married Augusta, the natural daughter of the Duke of Clarence and the actress, Mrs Jordan. There are therefore two distinct architectural periods at Dun which overlap to some extent.

After the Second World War, the house was let as a hotel, and when Mrs Thomas Lovett, the 21st laird, died in 1980, she bequeathed the property to the National Trust for Scotland, together with two farms as the basis of an endowment.

Before any restoration work could start, an appeal was launched for £350,000 which was so successful that it became oversubscribed. With additional funds from the Historic Buildings Council for Scotland, the Scottish Tourist Board, the Countryside Commission for Scotland, the Manpower Services Commission and the Local Museums Purchase Fund, work began in 1984.

The first phase of the restoration programme was devoted to the complete rehabilitation of the adjacent courtyard and its buildings, which had degenerated into a ruinous state. These were wagon sheds, potting sheds, and a

FIGURE 8.2   The Saloon at the House of Dun in 1971, before restoration by the National
Trust for Scotland.

bothy, hen-houses and a late nineteenth-century kitchen surrounding a green,
edged with pleached limes, in the centre of which stood a charming wooden
game-larder raised on a central stilt. In the past, this part of the estate with the
stables beyond had underpinned the life of the house, and today, although the
bothy and the potting shed have been retained and displayed as they might
have appeared originally, the uses of the other buildings have changed in
order to support the business of opening a historic house to visitors. Thus the
wagon sheds on the north side have become lavatories, and those on the south
side house the looms which are still worked by the last handloom linen
weaver in Angus. The old kitchen is now the shop. The essential vernacular
style has been retained and as far as possible old materials used. It was not
until early in 1987 that work started on the house itself.

The roof had to be entirely reslated and releaded, chimney stacks rebuilt
and the south elevation refaced with rustication which had been removed
early in the twentieth century. This was quite tricky because it meant finding
exactly the right stone to match. The other major alteration was the replacement of the plate-glass windows installed in 1857 with the correct
glazing bars, to conform with the taste of the 1730s. Fortunately, those on an

FIGURE 8.3   The Saloon at the House of Dun after restoration by the National Trust for
Scotland.

internal window had survived and could be copied. It is quite astonishing
how much difference the right glazing makes to a historic house. The forlorn
air has disappeared and the façades are nicely articulated. A bold decision was
made to erect the balustrade on the cornice of the north front and also on the
south front, together with the arms of David Erskine, 1st Lord Dun, carved
on a massive central panel. These refinements had been intended by William
Adam but were not actually carried out.

The most satisfying and rewarding part of the entire programme, however,
was the rehabilitation and restoration of the interior of the house.

The Saloon, with its superbly executed plasterwork by Joseph Enzer and
probably one of the grandest rooms in Scotland, had been painted blue in the
early nineteenth century with the plasterwork dead white, together with
glossy white doors (see Figure 8.2). Scraping back layers of paint, a soft sage
green was discovered, and it was decided to reinstate this colour for the walls
and cove and then use a soft white for the plaster and woodwork, with the
exception of the doors, which were oak-grained. In the accounts for 1827,
there were references to marbling carried out by Lamont of Aberdeen for the
firm of Jap of Montrose. The flat of the skirting board was therefore marbled
here in order to give a rich base for such an exuberantly decorated room (see
Figure 8.3).

Also in the early nineteenth century, brass register grates had been installed at each end of the room, but only one of these had survived, which was not satisfactory because it would have been virtually impossible to find a match for it. Behind the surviving grate, some of the magenta Delft tiles of the 1740s had miraculously survived, and we were able to have them copied for both fireplaces. Years previously, I had picked up a pair of firedogs with the Carron mark cast into the uprights; a second pair was cast and thus the fireplaces match perfectly.

It was becoming more and more clear that the only way to present the Saloon was as an architectural masterpiece with a minimum of furniture arranged on the perimeter of the room. As far as possible, original furniture was used in order to retain the integrity of the house, and only where absolutely necessary were 'foreign' pieces introduced. Here, these included a generous loan of early Georgian chairs from the Duke of Atholl. A giltwood chandelier and a pair of pier glasses were specially made.

The dining-room lies to the east of the Saloon. It was created from the withdrawing-room and part of the 'bedchamber for the principal stranger'. There was never any serious question of restoring these lost rooms, although the idea had been discussed. Moreover, all the furniture supplied in 1828 by the Edinburgh firm of Young and Trotter had survived in various states of dilapidation. The curtains, with their long panels of needlework attributed to Lady Augusta, were still hanging in the room and only needed a good wash and a remake. The marble chimneypiece of 1740 with its glass above was still in place but fitted with a rather dreadful 'tiled surround'. I asked the builder to remove just this part and to excavate the rubble with which the opening was filled. On my next visit, the entire chimneypiece had been taken down and was lying forlornly on the floor. During its reinstatement, it was discovered that what had appeared to be a marbled cornice had originally been water gilt: obviously this had to be restored to its former appearance. For a grate, the surviving one from the Saloon was slightly reduced in width and is in perfect accord with the early nineteenth-century furniture which was supplied by Young and Trotter of Edinburgh in 1842. The pale blue colour scheme was retained, but the doors were mahogany-grained, and a chair-rail was put in to give the room a better sense of balance.

The Library to the west of the Saloon had also been created out of a group of smaller eighteenth-century rooms, this time the family bedroom and closets. Once again, all the bookcases, relegated to the basement, had survived, painted black with the remains of green cloth in the doors. The remaining library furniture was still in the house and just needed to be restored. The walls had been hung with flock wallpaper in the 1820s, but the cost of having it copied was prohibitive, and so wallpaper giving a very

FIGURE 8.4   The Entrance Hall at the House of Dun after restoration by the National
     Trust for Scotland.

similar effect was chosen. Under the black paint on the bookcases, there was
evidence of graining, and this was chosen in preference to the plain black.
The doors were relined with material for the simple reason that there were not
nearly enough books. The dark red leather on the chairs both here and in the
dining-room was specially produced as nearly as possible to the original.

The Parlour, which is next to the Library, retains almost all its William
Adam features despite its changes of use over the years. In the nineteenth
century, it was the smoking room, and the walls were oak-grained and hung
with a large collection of whips and riding-crops, being the collection of
Augustus Kennedy-Erskine, the 20th laird, who was a keen sportsman. More
recently, it had become a hotel bar, fitted with a Westmorland slate fireplace
and built-in seats round the walls. Underneath the graining and nicotine-
stained decoration, it was found that the original colour had been a pale buff
throughout, with no attempt to distinguish the relief plasterwork from the
background. After various trials, it was decided to pick out the decorative
areas in a soft white. A delightful hob grate with its stone surround had
survived, plastered over in the hotel pantry, dating from its day as a bedroom,
and this has suited the Parlour admirably. In the Charter room, which leads
off the Parlour, a panel of eighteenth-century wallpaper survives, as does the
built-in kneehole writing-desk.

The Entrance Hall (see Figure 8.4), when built, had been quite separate from the staircase, thus giving a formal approach to the Saloon. In the early nineteenth century, the two were opened up, which certainly created more space, but the eighteenth-century proportions were lost. Originally, the relief plasterwork on the walls had been treated in the same way as that in the Parlour, and then in recent years it had been picked out in pretty colours. In the restoration, the original warm buff colour was used, with the plasterwork painted soft white.

On the staircase, the walls had been divided into panels with egg-and-dart borders in trompe-l'oeil, which formed part of the 1828 decoration. This was all completely restored and a stair carpet specially woven incorporating the egg-and-dart motif.

Throughout the house, with only two exceptions, I chose Oriental carpets deliberately, for their mellowness and for the fact that they always look right with antique furniture. All the pictures, which include a good run of family portraits, were restored. These latter form a splendid display on the walls of the staircase.

The bedrooms upstairs are all furnished in a suitably old-fashioned way with furniture indigenous to the house, and, where beds were missing, by appropriate ones given to the Trust. Many of the delightful hob grates had been boarded up and had thus survived modernisation. Unsuitable grates of late date were replaced.

The Red Bedroom in the south-west corner retains its eighteenth-century panelling. It had been painted various colours and also oak-grained in the past, but it was felt that the cedar-graining which was the most recent treatment was the best background for the furniture. This includes the four-poster bed given to Lady Augusta by William IV on the occasion of her marriage. It is hung with needlework by Lady Augusta. The story goes that the background was all worked by Philippe Bordeaux, her chef. The dressing-room next door is furnished with an amazing Victorian shower-bath, a closed stool with blue and white china pan and a washstand supplied by Young and Trotter.

Mrs Erskine's bedroom, overlooking the garden to the east, had never really been completed; there was no cornice, and this was duly introduced. It is fitted with one of the early eighteenth-century chimneypieces, probably from downstairs. A pretty, patterned wallpaper was chosen, with glazed chintz of similar design for the half-tester bed hangings and the window curtains.

When Mrs Lovett had lived at Dun as a child at the beginning of the twentieth century, she had occupied a small bedroom with a corner fireplace overlooking the courtyard. We were given a small-size half-tester iron bedstead painted green and gold, which is ideal for this bedroom. It is hung with green chintz, being a copy of that used on Lord Byron's bed at Newstead Abbey.

The tapestry room is the only room on the first floor not to have been altered in the nineteenth century. The tapestries that now adorn the walls were hung for many years on the principal staircase; we moved them to their present position because the room was so obviously designed for them. During the restoration work, a wall that had been hung with wallpaper, which simulated gathered material and which had been hidden from view under later lining, was stripped bare despite instructions being given to preserve it. The furniture here, all late Stuart walnut and oak, came from a most generous bequest which could not have come along at a more opportune moment. The blue and white porcelain here and throughout the house is part of the House of Dun collection.

The Boudoir in the south-east corner was formed out of three small rooms early in the nineteenth century, and photographs show that it was furnished with French furniture; we have honoured this, and many of the same pieces are arranged here once again. The blue curtains with elaborate needlework form part of the early nineteenth-century Saloon decoration. The old curtains were quite rotten, so the needlework was all painstakingly reapplied – we owe a very great debt of gratitude to the Hill of Tarvit Conservation Group and to the Misses Sutherland for all their dedicated hard work.

I suppose the two major structural changes that the Trust made were the opening-up of the Porch room outside the old upstairs Library, thus showing off the pretty horseshoe stair to better advantage, and the recreation of the Library itself. It had been divided to make up two bedrooms and two closets when more bedroom accommodation was needed. It is once again one large room, panelled to dado level, comfortably furnished and with superb views over the Montrose basin to the south. Like the Saloon below, it has two fireplaces, and I managed to run to earth a pair of late eighteenth-century fire baskets. Much of the furniture is original to the house, but some generous gifts and bequests have helped enormously. The curtains were recut but do not bear close examination!

In the basement, the original vaulted kitchen, filled in to make a servants' hall in the nineteenth century, was excavated and the traditional arrangement of central open fire, hot plate and oven restored. The circular oven is late eighteenth century and is typically Scottish. The spit is turned by an early eighteenth-century clockwork mechanism which actually works. In the window bay will be seen a Regency charcoal stewing stove used for delicate cookery. Above the dresser is displayed the considerable copper *batterie de cuisine*, most of it marked 'Dun'. This is a remarkable survival.

The former nurseries below the family bedroom became the Housekeeper's

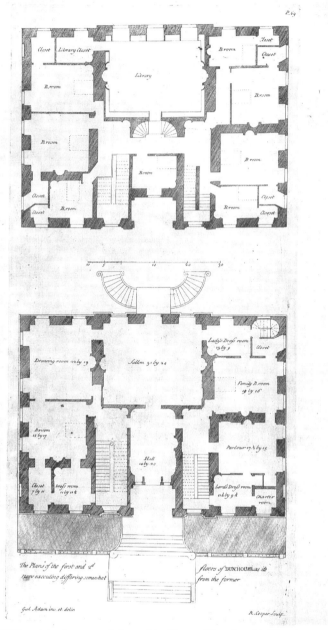

quarters in the nineteenth century, the built-in box-beds being used for the storage of linen. They are now shown in this latter form, with comfortable out-of-date furniture dominated by a splendid oak bureau cabinet. What had become a latter-day coal cellar is now restored as the Laigh Hall with a long central table and benches.

Two rooms have been set aside as gun and rod rooms to show the nineteenth-century sporting interests, which is a real innovation in a Trust property.

I think the House of Dun has been the most rewarding restoration project that I have had the pleasure of being involved with since I joined the Trust more than twenty years ago. Despite its use as a hotel since the Second World War, it was remarkably intact and untouched. The textiles, furniture, porcelain and even the copper had been faithfully looked after by Mrs Phillips, who had managed the House as a hotel. It was a constant thrill on the ever-increasing visits to the House to see what new secrets the 'old lady' had revealed: the walled-up bread oven complete with side flue in one of the basement rooms, original marbling behind a bookcase, a Regency chimneypiece under a later Victorian one. It is a delightful house with a happy atmosphere, and, because one can quite easily identify with it, most visitors from Queen Elizabeth down say that they would like to live there. I wonder whether there will be another house like it, waiting to be reawakened? I doubt it.

FIGURE 9.1   A view of part of the policies at Yester House, including the canal and cascades, by an unknown artist. Oil on canvas ($43\frac{3}{4}'' \times 35\frac{1}{4}''$).

9

Views in Scottish Houses, 1630–1770

JAMES HOLLOWAY

A surprisingly large number of seventeenth- and eighteenth-century houses in Scotland contain contemporary, or near-contemporary, painted decorative schemes. The wealth of early painted ceilings has already been very fully catalogued by M. R. Apted,[1] and many of the impressive illusionistic ceilings, typical of the Baroque, are well-known since they can be seen in such buildings as Hopetoun, Drumlanrig and Holyrood which are regularly open to the public.

The generally later landscape schemes, often painted for the walls of smaller houses, are however less well known, and their number is usually underestimated. Decorative schemes were produced for town as well as country houses, but, while many of those painted for Edinburgh, Glasgow and Aberdeen have been lost in the course of redevelopment, decorative schemes in the country have fared rather better.

One of the earliest and most interesting was commissioned by Charles I at the time of his Scottish coronation in 1633. Admittedly, the 'pictures of King's houses and townes in Scotland', which were drawn on the spot by Stalbemt and later transferred in oil on to panel by Alexander Keirincx, were destined not for a Scottish location but for the palace of the King of Scots in England. The Oatlands valuation of 1649–51, drawn up in the early days of the Commonwealth, is ambiguous about the precise number of landscapes painted, whether eight or ten, and some of these may have been English views. Until 1977, no Scottish subjects were known. The first to be discovered was a view of Falkland and the Howe of Fife. The palace, as shown by Keirincx, is a very accurate representation of the buildings largely completed by 1541: the south façade with twin towers flanking the entrance and the five distinctive buttresses, the east range shown shortly before it was badly burnt during the Cromwellian occupation. One feature of the façade which differs from the present-day building (and from the building in Slezer's engraving of 1693) is the form of the roofs on the two towers. It seems likely that Keirincx depicts what are termed 'prik ruiffis' mentioned in the building accounts for 1539–41, which would be steeper structures than the conical roofs which must have replaced them towards the end of the seventeenth century.[2]

Of almost equal interest to the buildings of the palace and town is the depiction of the countryside. Keirincx's views are the first Scottish landscapes known to have been painted, and the earliest by many decades. The second of the set, only discovered in 1986, is of even greater interest. It shows the rambling Medieval and Renaissance Palace of Seton where Robert Adam's Seton House now stands. The home of one of Scotland's greatest families was also one of the most important buildings in the country, but all that was hitherto known of its appearance had to be deciphered from a group of inadequate drawings made in the late eighteenth century by the amateur John Clerk of Eldin after the palace had fallen into ruin and decay. Both Seton and Falkland were visited by Charles on his royal progress round his native country. Leaving London on 13 May 1633 and following much of the route of the present A1, the king reached Scotland at Berwick a month later and travelled to Edinburgh via Dunglass, Seton and Dalkeith. He later visited Linlithgow, Stirling, Dunfermline, Falkland, Perth and Scone. He left Berwick for the journey south on 16 July. It is very much to be hoped that more of these exceptionally interesting landscapes can be identified and join the two recently acquired by the Scottish National Portrait Gallery.

The set of five late seventeenth-century landscapes painted for Yester are cruder and less sophisticated than the Keirincxes. They show views of the old house, its gardens and estate, like the earlier paintings, from a bird's-eye view (see Figure 9.1). The Yester paintings, four of which remain in the house, the fifth now owned by the Scottish National Portrait Gallery, are neither signed nor documented. They have been attributed, not implausibly, to Jacob de Wet, the Dutchman whom Sir William Bruce brought to Scotland around 1673 to paint decorative schemes at the Palace of Holyroodhouse. De Wet is not known to have painted landscapes – a point which would not necessarily rule out an attribution. The crudity and viewpoint of each of the Yester paintings suggest that the Tweeddales valued factual information more than aesthetic gratification.

FIGURE 9.2   Panorama of Taymouth and Loch Tay by James Norie and Jan Griffier II.
Oil on canvas (26″ × 52⅜″).

So too did Lord Glenorchy, though in commissioning James Norie to paint
his house and policies at Taymouth in 1733 he chose a more accomplished
painter (see Figure 9.2). Lord Glenorchy wanted his newly-planted gardens
recorded, and Norie obliged most beautifully. However, six years later with
his gardens redesigned, a second artist was instructed to record the alterations. Instead of using a fresh canvas, Jan Griffier II, on Lord Glenorchy's
instructions, merely painted over those parts of James Norie's landscape
which had been altered in the intervening years.[3]
    Lord Glenorchy was in fact rather old-fashioned, for by the 1730s there was
a new taste in decorative painting. Realistic views such as those painted at
Falkland, Yester and Taymouth were gradually supplanted by idealised
scenes with landscapes often more reminiscent of Italy than Scotland. Painted
sometimes on panel, sometimes on canvas, even directly on to the plaster, the
early eighteenth-century decorative landscapes were the production of firms
of house painters and interior decorators rather than specialist landscape
painters. In Edinburgh, the main firm at the beginning of the eighteenth
century was run by the Warrender family.[4] Bills for work, at Craigie Hall and
Hopetoun for instance, mention their landscape schemes as well as their work
marbelling and painting festoons of fruit and flowers, typical of any European
house painter of the late seventeenth or early eighteenth century. Landscapes
by either Thomas Warrender or his son John, however, are now unknown. In
fact, only one painting by a Warrender, a still life, can be identified today.
This is an accomplished if unoriginal composition, in the style of Edward
Collier. By 1720, the Warrenders had been eclipsed by a family whose
business came to dominate house painting and decorative work in Scotland.

So successful were James Norie senior and his sons that much that they never saw has been attributed to them by default. The Nories practised and perfected a type of decorative painting that had the great advantage of being both quick to produce and pretty to look at. Their colour schemes are normally a monochrome sage green or light purple. When newly cleaned to reveal their original state, they surprise by their freshness and elegance.

Typical of the Norie family's style of decoration is the newly-discovered series at Kemnay House. Ten grisaille panels are set into the panelling of a small ground-floor room. Three measure approximately $22'' \times 42''$, six approximately $7\frac{1}{2}'' \times 26''$ and one $4\frac{1}{4}'' \times 51''$. None of these paintings makes any reference to the local Aberdeenshire landscape; rather, the buildings and ruins in the paintings seem to be a recollection of those in the Italianate landscapes of the seventeeth-century Franco-Roman artist Gaspard Dughet.

Grander than the Kemnay cycle, and painted for a nobler and richer client, is the set of paintings, again a recent discovery,[5] which the Nories painted for Haddo. There, working in conjunction with the architect William Adam, the Nories introduced classical ruins and figure groups which even more obviously appear to have been copied from Continental models.

Occasionally, the source of the composition or component parts can be traced to particular prints. At Keir, where the Nories painted a set of six canvases, Gaspard's influence can be documented. Two of the set were copied from engravings by Vivares after Gaspard's oils, which were published in 1741.[6] But more often the Nories, in common with most British painters of the time, worked from whatever prints were most readily available, often reusing images a century old. At Moray House in the Canongate, for instance, where the Nories decorated a room with Roman scenes, they copied their designs from the engravings in François Perrier's *Icones* published in 1645.[7] A set of the Perrier prints had been in Edinburgh since at least 1730, when the young Allan Ramsay had copied from the volume as a student at the Academy of St Luke. They were presumably part of the large collection of Old Master prints that the first Treasurer and Master of the Academy, the Yorkshireman Richard Cooper, brought with him as a teaching aid, though it should be remembered that Allan Ramsay's father sold prints at his shop in the Luckenbooths and that sales of prints in Edinburgh were not uncommon.[8]

The use of Continental prints as a source for decorative painting was a British, not merely a Scottish, practice. Indeed, Francis Hayman, painting in the mid-1740s at Blickling, copied prints from the same source that the Nories used at Moray House. George Lambert and the young Thomas Gainsborough copied the engravings of Cornelis Visscher after Nicholas Berchem, and by the middle of the eighteenth century prints after seventeenth-century Dutch masters had come to share or even supplant those after the Italians like Panini and Ghisolfi on the canvases of British decorative painters.

Those Scottish artists who had the means travelled to Italy. In the seventeenth century, the two best-known artists to study there were John Michael Wright and William Gouw Ferguson, neither of them landscape painters. In the early eighteenth century, William Aikman, John Smibert, John Alexander and William Mosman all spent time in Rome. Not surprisingly, the decorative work of these Roman-trained artists reflects their studies and the opportunities they had to observe contemporary decorative painting in Europe's art capital. John Alexander spent the years between 1711 and 1720 in Rome, where he worked alongside Aikman's friend William Kent in the studio of G. B. Chiari. The ceiling that he painted on his return for the staircase at Gordon Castle is an adaptation of one of his master's ceilings in the Palazzo Barberini in Rome, though with Pluto and Prosperine rather than Apollo as its subject. Perhaps more typical of John Alexander's decorative work was the set of Roman landscapes, the Coliseum, Nero's Palace and an architectural subject, all approximately three feet by four feet, which were sold from Gordon Castle in 1938 and are now lost, like the great ceiling itself.

Until the recent discovery of a large figure composition and associated documents, it was not even known that Mosman had painted decorative schemes.[9] His landscape with Erminia, the heroine of Tasso's *Gerusalemme Liberata*, painted as part of his second decorative scheme for Patrick Duff at Culter House, is a very precious survival from the early eighteenth century – not, let it be said, for its quality as a work of art, which is negligible, but as the sole surviving example of large-scale Scottish decorative painting. Mosman's canvas, painted in the mid-1730s, is a straight copy of one of his master, Imperiali's paintings, though Mosman needed to make additions on each side to fit a predetermined space in Patrick Duff's saloon. To localise the painting, Mosman introduced a view of Culter House itself, as if Tasso's story had been relocated in rural Aberdeenshire.

James Norie may not have been able to afford to send his sons to Rome; instead, they were trained in London, Robert Norie certainly by George Lambert, his elder brother James very possibly by him as well.[10] The choice of Lambert was an interesting one. A leading landscape painter in both the traditional Italianate manner and a realistic, topographical style, Lambert was also one of the chief scenery painters in London. In the 1720s, he worked for the Lincoln's Inn Fields Theatre before moving in 1732 to the newly-built Covent Garden Theatre. Scenery painting may have been one aspect of the Norie sons' London training and a useful skill on their return to Edinburgh,

FIGURE 9.3   Landscape with a flock of sheep, by Robert Norie, at 79 High Street,
Dumfries. Oil on panel ($25\frac{3}{4}'' \times 57\frac{1}{4}''$).

where painters were needed to prepare the scenery for productions such as
The Tempest put on by the Edinburgh Company of Comedians in the Taylor's
Hall in January 1735 'with all the scenes, machines and other decorations'.[11]
Loss of all eighteenth-century theatrical sets as well as most large-scale
paintings has distorted our judgement of the work of the early landscape
painters.

James Norie junior died in 1736. If, as seems likely, the group of paintings
signed 'James Norie Edin' and dated in the early 1730s are by him, and not
his father, as is generally assumed, then Scotland lost its most promising
landscape painter at the age of only twenty-five. Robert, the younger brother,
did not return from his studies with Lambert until the early 1740s, when he
signed and dated several works, including the newly-discovered pair of
landscapes at 79 High Street, Dumfries (see Figure 9.3). The decline in
quality from the elegantly-composed canvases of the elder brother to the
clumsy and ill-coloured works of the younger is painful. Where Robert Norie
was best was when he was least original, and perhaps his finest paintings are
those at Johnstounburn House, Humbie, where in the two surviving
landscapes he took his compositions directly from prints. The Johnstounburn
paintings, in an oil medium on plaster, can be dated after 1762, when Boydell
published the two prints which Robert Norie used as his source. The first was
engraved by Vivares and Chatelain after Pietro da Cortona's *Call of St Peter*
now at Chatsworth, while the second, of *The Lake of Albano* (see Figure 9.4),
was also engraved by Vivares and Chatelain after an anonymous painting now
at Holyrood.

Perhaps Robert Norie's most original contribution to Scottish decorative
painting was to use features from the Scottish landscape in his own idealised

FIGURE 9.4   The Lake of Albano, by Robert Norie, at Johnstounburn House. Oil on plaster.

paintings. Ben Lawers appears in one of the canvases of 1741 now in the Hamilton apartments at Holyrood but probably commissioned for Taymouth. At Auchindinny, one of the six undated Norie panels shows a view of nearby Roslin.

At the end of his life, Robert Norie, and the firm which he ran after the death of his father in 1757, was overtaken by the superior skills of William Delacour. By the late 1750s, Delacour was established in Edinburgh, where he remained until his death in 1767. Where earlier James Norie had worked alongside William Adam, the Adam sons wisely preferred the more sophisticated Delacour, whose work can be seen at its best at Yester.

FIGURE 9.5   Sketch for a decorative overmantel at the Dower House, Corstorphine,
    Edinburgh, attributed to Jacob More. Gouache (9⅞″ × 15¼″).

A number of distinguished landscape painters passed through the Norie
workshop as apprentices. Alexander Runciman was bound to the firm in
1750. Jacob More became Robert Norie's apprentice in 1764. After the
latter's death two years later, he transferred his apprenticeship to Alexander
Runciman, who in 1767 left Scotland for Italy. More made his name that year
painting a set of scenery for the New Theatre in Edinburgh.

An exciting recent discovery, an overmantel at the Dower House, Corstorphine, is likely to be the sole surviving example of More's decorative work
still in situ. It is also unique among eighteenth-century Scottish decorative
paintings in that its preliminary sketch survives (see Figure 9.5). It shows
how much More's early style owes to Robert Norie. Shortly after painting
at Corstorphine, More left Edinburgh for good. By 1771, he had settled
permanently in Rome where, during the following decade, he was one of the
group of fashionable artists, including Mengs and Gavin Hamilton, commissioned by the Borghese family to redecorate their Roman villa. More's
twelve-foot-high *Landscape with the Metamorphosis of Daphne* was painted as
the backdrop for Bernini's *Apollo and Daphne*.[12]

But in Scotland the taste for such decorative landscape cycles had begun to
die as patrons reverted to the earlier practice of commissioning portraits of
their houses, a market supplied by painters such as Ibbetson or Alexander
Nasmyth. Increasingly popular were the picturesque landscapes by Nasmyth,

Knox and others which could be bought from artists' shops or from the walls of the new public exhibitions which became a regular feature of early nineteenth-century artistic life.

The change of taste as the Neo-Classical and Romantic movements succeeded the Rococo caused the destruction of many of the earlier decorative schemes and with them much of the early history of landscape painting in Scotland.

NOTES

1. M. R. Apted, *The Painted Ceilings of Scotland 1550–1650*, Edinburgh, 1966.
2. I am grateful for the help of Dr Duncan Thomson, who first researched this picture.
3. See J. Holloway and L. Errington, *The Discovery of Scotland*, Edinburgh, 1978, pp. 13–21.
4. For further information on the Warrender family and other eighteenth-century decorative painters, see J. Holloway, *Patrons and Painters: Art in Scotland 1650–1760*, Edinburgh, 1989.
5. The Haddo paintings were first identified by Christopher Hartley.
6. *Gaspard Dughet*, Greater London Council, Iveagh Bequest, Kenwood, 1980, p. 15.
7. *Icones et segmenta illustrium e marmore Tabularum quae Romae adhuc extant a Francisco Perrier delineata incisa et ad antiquam formam lapides exemplaribus passim collapsis Restitua.* The Moray House paintings, six Roman scenes each approximately three and a half feet square, are linked with friezes and antique heads. They may date from 1753 when the British Linen Bank took a lease on the Earl of Moray's Canongate house.
8. For instance, the collection of David Main, an art dealer, was sold in Edinburgh on 13 January 1752 and the following five days. It included 'some original paintings by Rembrandt, Hans Holbien, Snyders etc some miniature paintings and enamelings, set in Gold, India and other Curiosities, and a large Parcel of Drawings, Italian French and Flemish Prints. Books of maps, Prints and medals by the best engravers' (*Caledonian Mercury*).
9. See Holloway, *Patrons and Painters*, pp. 93–6.
10. J. Holloway, 'Robert Norie in London and Perthshire', in *Connoisseur*, January 1978.
11. Advertised in the *Caledonian Mercury*. The same month, January 1735, saw productions of *The Relapse* at the Edinburgh Theatre, *Henry IV* and *Oroonoko, or The Royal Slave* at Taylor's Hall.
12. More's canvas has disappeared, but his drawing for the picture survives. See J. Holloway, *Jacob More*, Edinburgh, 1987, p. 11.

FIGURE 10.1   View of the south front of Glamis by John Elphinstone, c. 1747.

10

John Elphinstone
and the Castle of Glamis

HARRY GORDON SLADE

The Hon. John Elphinstone, Master of Elphinstone 1706–53, was the son – eldest according to Burke, and second according to the *Scots Peerage* – of Charles, 9th Baron Elphinstone. Entering the army in 1740, he was commissioned as an ensign in Col. James Long's regiment of Foot. He joined the Corps of Engineers as a Practitioner Engineer in 1744 and was promoted to the rank of Sub-Engineer on 4 January 1748. He spent most of his military life in Scotland, and at the outbreak of the 1745 Rebellion was serving as one of only three engineers in the kingdom, the others being Dougal Campbell and Frederick Scott. Elphinstone had already published his *New and Correct Mercator's Map of North Britain* in March 1745, when in the Rebellion and in its aftermath he was caught up in the work that was eventually to lead to the *Military Survey of Scotland*. He seems to have been particularly concerned with fortifications. Like his more famous and younger compatriot, General William Roy,[1] he developed a taste for antiquities, and, apart from his purely military work, he produced drawings of the south front of Falkland Palace, Inverlochy Castle, Castle Lyon, Doune and Glamis Castle, all of which are in the Topographical Collection of George III, which is now preserved in the Map Library of the British Library. There may well be other unidentified drawings of Elphinstone's still in private collections.

The drawings of Glamis are important, for they give the most complete impression to survive of the castle after the building works of the 3rd Earl of Strathmore had been completed in 1695 and before the alterations, beginning with the demolition in 1775 of the west wing by the 9th Earl, had altered the appearance of the castle to its present form. There are two earlier views of the castle: one in the background of the De Wet portrait of the 3rd Earl and his sons (c. 1690), and the other Slezer's drawing of 1686, engraved by Robert White. Both show only the entrance front of the castle. Two similar views were made in 1746: one a roughish sketch by Thomas Winter as a decoration to his survey of the Mains of Glamis, and the other by Thomas Sandby (K. Top. XLIX 23b), which tidies everything up and refenestrates the castle with neat and elegant sashes.

Elphinstone's drawings (K. Top. XLIX 23a 1–6) are probably part of a larger set. They include the dedicatory plates, a plan of the second and third floors, and four external views. It is possible that at least one sheet of plans is missing, and it is likely that the drawings of Castle Lyon (K. Top. L 62), Lord Strathmore's other Scottish seat, would have been included.

The drawings, which are pen and ink, and wash, can be dated fairly closely. As they are signed *John Elphinstone Pract. Engin'*, they must fall between 1744, when he was promoted to that rank, and 4 January 1748, when he was promoted to the rank of Sub-Engineer. Since the dedicatory plate celebrates the victory of the Duke of Cumberland over the Pretender at Culloden in April 1746, they must have been drawn after that date. It is unlikely that Elphinstone would have been free before the early summer of the following year to have drawn so unmilitary a subject, and, since the drawings themselves suggest a summer scene, they were probably made in August or September 1747.

The dedicatory plate (K. Top. XLIX 23a 1) is a splendid assemblage of conceits and symbols. Dominating it is a framed portrait of the young hero. Supported by female angelic beings, and backed for no very good reason by a palm tree, the picture rests on a classical pedestal. On top of the pedestal and to the right of the picture is an insecurely-balanced cornucopia, and to the left is an animal which is, no doubt, intended as a loyal and admiring lion. It has all the appearance of a rather depressed mongrel. In the background on one side is a Triumphal Arch topped by an equestrian statue of the victor; on the other, a lively skirmish is taking place in a mountain landscape before a small castle which is defying all comers. The artillery is represented by two unattended cannon.

In front of the pedestal are a number of figures – 'the dear people stood at a distance and cheered, and were very loyal and respectful'. At the right are two loyal Highlanders, hands and eyes in attitudes expressive of admiration, knees much in evidence and tartan everywhere. They are joined by a female, clearly overwhelmed at finding herself in such company, who has dropped a large bouquet. To the right, a larger group, rather like the chorus line of an

Handelian opera, are also arranged in becoming attitudes. Some are immediately recognisable: Britannia, Mars, Mercury, Justice – who is hiding a pair of
weighted scales behind her back, and who seems to have lost her blindfold –
and Pallas Athene. It is not clear what is the role of the African who is holding
a club and a shield bearing the arms of England, Scotland, Ireland, France
and Hanover, and one prefers not to speculate on the reclining female nude
with a glowing orb in one hand, and her feet resting among John Elphinstone's surveying equipment.

The message of the centre and left foregrounds is unequivocal. A spotted
dragon, pierced with arrows like a grotesque St Sebastian, has expired on
three captured standards labelled *Lochiel, Athol and Tullibardine*, and *Rebellion*, and a captured cannon, marked with a fleur-de-lys to show that it was
supplied to the rebels by the French, bears the legend *Ultima Ratio Regum*.
The inscription on the pedestal reads:

> To His Royal Highness
> PRINCE WILLIAM
> Duke of Cumberland etc.
> The Drawings of the
> Castle of Glammis etc.
> are humbly dedicated
> By
> His Royal Highneſs's
> Most obedient and most dutiful
> Humble Servant
> John Elphinstone Pra^c Engin^y

and one can hardly say fairer than that.

The second drawing (K. Top. XLIX 23a 2; see Figure 10.2) is entitled:
'The plans of 2nd and 3rd floors of the Castle of 𝕾lammis'. Elphinstone has
misnumbered the floors, for the plan in fact shows the first and second floors.
It is unlikely that a plan of the ground (or first) floor would not have been
included. The plans are a mixture, accurate in parts but not in others. This
suggests that they may have been sketched between 20 and 24 February 1746,
when Cumberland was at the castle for one night on his march north from
Edinburgh to Aberdeen. The plans are correct as to the tower staircase,
the west wing, part of the Laigh or Latter Meat Hall, the north staircase, the
library, the Great Hall and the Chapel. They are incorrect in the jamb of the
Great Tower, the link staircase and the east wing. They seem to be accurate in
the low service wings.

Among the drawings in the Charter Room at Glamis is an uncatalogued
plan which may be a second survey by Elphinstone. Drawn in sepia ink, it is

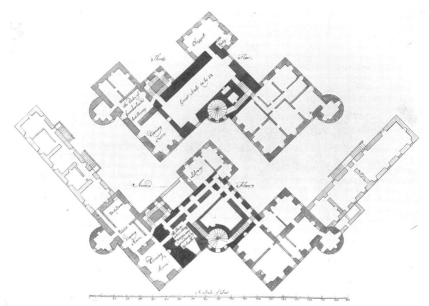

FIGURE 10.2   Plans of the second and third floors of Glamis drawn by John Elphinstone,
c. 1747.

unfinished, but it shows more accurately the arrangement of the east wing
and the staircase which was inserted around 1616 to link the main tower
staircase and the Laigh Hall. Like the published Elphinstone drawing, it
shows the tower stair at ground level. In the 1850s, another hand, probably
that of Thomas Liddel, sketched on it the proposal for a circular portico at the
base of the stair tower. Mercifully, this remained a proposal.

From the plans, it is clear that Elphinstone did not have access to the jamb
and the east wing of the castle. These parts contained the private apartments,
but it is unlikely that the family was in residence. Thomas, 8th Earl of
Strathmore, had married an English heiress from County Durham, and spent
much of his time on her English estates, so the private rooms may have been
locked. The castle had been used for housing prisoners of the rebels, and it is
unlikely that the Earl would have compromised himself by staying at Glamis
under those circumstances, for, if not very active in the Hanoverian interest,
he was positively inactive in the Rebel cause.

The west end of the Laigh Hall is described on the plan as 'The Room
where King Duncan was murdered by McBeath'. This must be one of the
earlier examples of the mistaken tradition. According to Fordoun, Duncan
was murdered at Bofnothgane (Pitgaveney) in Morayshire; Shakespeare,
perhaps less accurately, sets the scene at Inverness.

If Elphinstone is not being satirical in the dedicatory plate, he certainly gives way to humorous observation in the four views of the castle, and this humour together with the accuracy with which he depicts the building make these four drawings particularly enjoyable.

It is likely that, for the view of the castle to the south (K. Top. XLIX 23a 5; see Figure 10.1), Elphinstone made use of an existing drawing, either Slezer's or Winter's, and corrected some of the forced perspective used, which is at variance with that of the other drawings; but which of the older pictures he used is not clear. In Slezer – and in De Wet – a doorway is shown opening out of the back of the kitchen fireplace in the east wing, for which there is no structural evidence, and Elphinstone, like Winter, corrected this. On the other hand, he follows Slezer in the number and position of the armorial tablets on the link building and on the west face of the east wing. Winter, however, shows a continuous band, as do De Wet and, at a later period, James Moore. Elphinstone agrees with Slezer and Winter that the entrance door had a full entablature and was surmounted by an empanelled shield bearing a lion for Lyon and not the Royal Arms as at present. Although Winter shows a gable – as does Slezer – on the south front of the west wing, Elphinstone does not, and in this he is supported by Sandby. Also shown are four sundials, one on each of the great rounds and one on the southern angle of each of the wings.

On the terrace in front of the castle are four statues, probably of lead, and portraying in attitudes of exquisite discomfort four minor classical deities, and on the grass below the terrace are two of the four statues of the Stuart kings ordered by Patrick, 3rd Earl of Strathmore, from Arnold Quellin. The two shown are of James VI and I, and James VII and II; the other two, those of Charles I and Charles II, are out of the picture. The statues of James VI and I, and of Charles I, still survive at Glamis, but the others have disappeared. Also shown is Quellin's bust of Patrick, 3rd Earl, in its roundel above the entrance.[2]

As befits the main approach to the castle, all the figures shown in this picture are of the gentry, one might almost say of the nobility, so fine their clothes and dégagé their attitudes. In the left foreground, a man is admiring a large stone panel carved with the Strathmore arms. This has probably just been delivered, and clearly does not meet with the approval of his dog. In the centre, two women, one in riding dress and a jockey cap, are walking towards the castle, and to their left a man is being excessively fond of his dog. Seated on a stone roller, two gossips are exchanging the latest *on-dits*, and other well-dressed figures are enjoying the late afternoon sunshine.

A more prosaic note is struck in the view from the south-east (K. Top. XLIX 23a 6; see Figure 10.3). The castle is subordinate to the view of the

FIGURE 10.3   View of Glamis from the south-east by John Elphinstone, c. 1747.

garden and of the office wing which occupies much of the centre of the picture. This does not mean that the castle is not carefully observed. On both this and the previous drawing, Elphinstone shows the small window on the south wall of the east wing, which all other early drawings omit, and an attempt to suggest the difference between those parts of the elevation which were harled, and those where the stonework was left exposed. It is known that parts of Glamis were harled in 1701, and this may have been selective in its application. The garden shown is the one described as 'on the Angles' or 'little Groves of Espalieres', and some fruit trees are shown against the garden wall. In the wall of the office range is an arched recess with a stone shelf. It seems unduly large for a bee bole, but that is what it is, for on the shelf are three straw bee skeps. The figures are less elegant than those in front of the castle, and may even be poor relations. In addition to the two groups, there are two individual figures: one a gardener with his wheelbarrow, the other a surveyor at his plane table taking a prospect of the castle.

The view of the Castle of Glamis to the north-west (K. Top 28a 4; see Figure 10.4) shows a view that has completely changed today. The west wing and both office wings have been demolished, as has the staircase block – although the scar of this remains visible on the back of the Great Tower. Before the alterations of the eighteenth and nineteenth centuries, when a round was substituted for the square corner house on the north-west angle of

FIGURE 10.4   View of Glamis from the north-west by John Elphinstone, c. 1747.

the Tower, the north front was treated in a more formal manner than was usual in early seventeenth-century work. As Elphinstone has drawn it, Glamis shows a remarkable likeness in the near-symmetry of its upper works to the almost contemporary work at Crathes. There are two other elements of importance in this view. It shows quite clearly that the stone mullions and transoms of the chapel windows are original and not a nineteenth-century alteration. Equally clearly, it shows the two windows to the secret rooms. There are the two windows in the lower part of the Great Tower, which can be seen beyond the wall connecting the stair and chapel towers. These windows lit the passage within the thickness of the wall on the north side of the Laigh Hall. At some time subsequent to 1765, both the windows and the passage were blocked up and off, giving rise to the story of the secret room.

Apart from the well-dressed couple, all the figures in this drawing relate to the work of the house. Indoor servants stand in the doorways doing nothing in particular except for one, busier than his fellows, who is fetching a bucket of water. The great travelling chariot, drawn by four horses, with coachman, postilion and one mounted outrider, whose horse does not look under his full control, is preparing to mount, and another is bringing his horse from the stable. Another servant is practising his drives, which can hardly have been soothing for the horses, and a family group of a packman with his wife and child are leaving. In the foreground, an untidy heap of peats and logs for the castle fires has been dumped.

FIGURE 10.5   View of Glamis Castle from the north-east by John Elphinstone, c. 1747.

In the last picture of the series, the view of Castle Glamis from the north-east (K. Top. XLIX 23a 3; see Figure 10.5), there is more told about the building. The battered plinth of the Great Round is continued across the back of Earl Patrick's addition to the east wing, and a small window appears on the second floor of the west wing. This window does not appear on the plan, but is almost certain to have been there lighting a mural closet which has been overlooked. Where the views differ from the plan, examination of the building shows that the views are generally to be preferred.

The human interest is maintained: apart from a small party of gentry who seem to have left the castle by the wrong door, and are clearly hurrying away from the life of the Base Court, we are still with the servants. A man is drawing water from the well, and a maid with a bucket on her head is awaiting her turn. Another load of peats has been brought in by cart and is waiting to be added to the heap already on the ground, the outrider is making another and more determined attempt to mount, and no-one is paying the least attention to a ragged beggar and his child who are asking for alms. In the right-hand corner, shaded by a tree and previously hidden by the stable, the energetic bulling of a cow is taking place – Kirriemuir is, after all, only a few miles away.

What other drawings were included in the words 'Glammis etc' of the dedication is not clear. Probably the north-east prospect of Castle Lyon (K.

Top. L 62 303158) was included, and there may have been others of Castle Lyon, which was a Strathmore property which no longer survives. This drawing shows part of the formal gardens, a lawn bounded on the south by a raised terrace and on the west by a topiary garden. On the grass, a group of elegantly-dressed members of the quality are displaying themselves, while the working side of the garden is represented by a large stone roller and by a gardener leaning on his rake.

Why these drawings should have been dedicated to the Duke of Cumberland is not clear. He may have had, although this seems unlikely, a taste for the romantic and antique, which he shared with Elphinstone; the drawings of Doune and Stirling are also dedicated to him, and he may have commissioned them as a record of his campaign. He may also have been vastly taken with the splendours of Glamis, and felt that, should a grateful nation be so minded to offer him a Scottish estate, then that of the Earl of Strathmore would serve as well as any and better than most. If this were the case, the inclusion of Castle Lyon would need no explanation. On the other hand, Elphinstone may have seen such a dedication as a means of ingratiating himself with the Commander-in-Chief, and of furthering his own career. He either gave or sold the drawings to the Duke, in whose collection they remained until his death, when they passed to his nephew, George III, eventually to form part of the King's Library.

ACKNOWLEDGEMENTS

I am most grateful to the Map Library at the British Museum for giving me access to Elphinstone's original drawings, and to the staff of the Library and Museum of the Corps of the Royal Engineers at Chatham for confirmation of the details of John Elphinstone's career.

NOTES

1. Yolande O'Donoghue, *William Roy 1726–1790. Pioneer of the Ordnance Survey*, British Museum, 1977.
2. M. R. Apted, Arnold Quellin's Statues at Glamis Castle, *The Antiquaries' Journal*, 1984.

11

A Roger Morris–John Adam Episode in Astylar Palladianism

JOHN HARRIS

In the history of Scottish eighteenth-century architecture, a group of designs in the archives[1] of the Urquharts of Craigston and of Cromarty Castle poses questions that even here remain unanswered. However, so great is my admiration for Kitty Cruft and her heroic achievement at the National Monuments Record of Scotland that I offer my observations on them in tribute.

First, let me describe them.[2] One group (see Figures 11.2 and 11.3) comprises a basement plan for a house seventy feet square, linked by quadrant arcades to service wings flanking a courtyard, and with further walled courtyards extending the wings laterally. On one front, a segmental bay projects into the area.

This plan is closely related to a group of five drawings comprising two plans of ground and first floors, one of the roof, one of the turret on the roof, and two sections differing somewhat from each other. The house in this second group measures seventy feet square.

This is likewise the size of a third group comprising two variant first-floor plans which lack the segmental bay but possess an entrance-front elevation with the arcaded links, the offices and the walls of the outer courtyards.

These are all clearly for a country house, whereas the second group (see e.g. Figure 11.1) that appears to be in the same hand (irrespective of variations in the details of delineating the scale) is for a smaller building that could be for either a town house or a hunting lodge. These comprise a plan

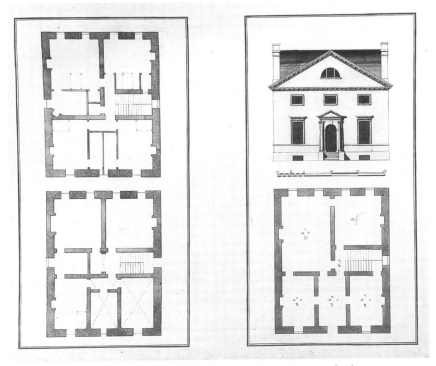

FIGURE 11.1   Mid-eighteenth-century design for a town house. Craigston Castle
Drawings.

FIGURE 11.2   Mid-eighteenth-century design for a Country House, entrance front.
Craigston Castle Drawings.

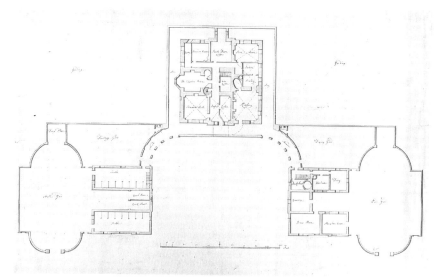

FIGURE 11.3 Mid-eighteenth-century design for a Country House, basement floor plan.
Craigston Castle Drawings.

and elevation, and three plans and an elevation drawn on one sheet and
repeated as a variant. Unlike the country-house designs, these are carefully
drawn within a border, almost as if intended for a printed pattern-book.

There is something distinctly idiosyncratic about these designs. They
breathe the spirit of English mainstream Neo-Palladianism and as astylar
essays remind us just a little of Roger Morris. Both groups are square
cube-like compositions, and of course Morris was the master of the Neo-
Palladian Cubist villa as at Whitton in Middlesex or Westcombe, Blackheath.
The most obvious idiosyncrasy is the square turret or cupola brought up
above the square central staircase well, lighting it with four Diocletian
windows and with the chimney shafts set at the angles. Morris was very fond
of these Diocletian turrets, but not combined with chimney shafts that add a
tiny piquant Vanbrughian touch to the design.

Naturally, any attribution depends on the approximate date of these
projects, and all that can be said on this matter is that Captain John Urquhart
of Craigston may have had ideas of rebuilding that castle in the 1740s, and in
1741 had bought back into the family Cromarty Castle. Therefore, in trying
to attach a name to these drawings, an architect in the 1740s needs to be
considered.

If we acknowledge a relationship to the Roger Morris style of cubic

North Front of The Right Hon.ble *LORD MILTON'S HOUSE*
in *EDINBURGH*.

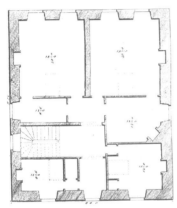

Bed Chamber Story.

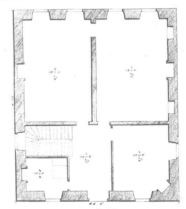

Principal Floor.

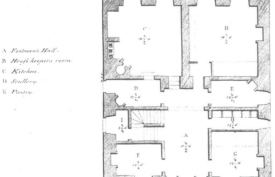

A *Footman's Hall*.
B *House keeper's room*.
C *Kitchen*.
D *Scullery*.
E *Pantry*.

F. *Second Table room*.
G. *Latter meat room*.
H. *Wine Cellar*.
I. *Cellar*.

Ground Story.

FIGURE 11.4   Elevation and plans of Milton House, Canongate, Edinburgh, from
Vitruvius Scoticus.

composition, there is also a family resemblance to Irish country houses with their long, extended lateral plans; but then there *is* a relationship between Scottish and Irish country houses.

There is another relationship: to the engraved work of William Halfpenny, as, for example, in his *A New and Compleat System of Architecture* (1749). This is not surprising, for Halfpenny and Roger's kinsman, Robert, were friends, as Halfpenny acknowledges in the preface to his book, when he thanks 'my ingenious friend Mr. Robert Morrice architect, to whom I communicated my designs'. In fact, when we turn to *The Modern Builder's Assistant* (1747) by William and John Halfpenny, Robert Morris and Timothy Lightholer, as in the *Compleat System* there are designs in a style familial to these Scottish ones, not least in the detail of three light windows grouped as one.

The utilitarian character of these designs, and in particular their astylism, can surely be read in the works of Sir John Vanbrugh for the Office of Ordnance. It is likewise for his associate and relative Sir Edward Lovett Pearce, another soldier, who introduced Neo-Palladianism to Ireland. Therefore it may be relevant that the next generation of Ordnance architects was no less than Roger Morris, who became Master Carpenter to the Office of Ordnance in 1734, a post which he owed to the 2nd Duke of Argyll, who was Master-General of the Ordnance from 1725 to 1740. Morris was closely involved with the family: with Colonel John Campbell (later 4th Duke) around 1725 at Combe Bank; for the 2nd Duke in 1731 at Adderbury; at Whitton Place for Lord Ilay (later 3rd Duke); and significantly at Inveraray Castle for this same 3rd Duke, where he is first mentioned in 1744.[3]

It is at this point perhaps that John Adam may come into the tale of these unidentified designs. As a young man in his twenties, through the 1740s, he was taking over his father's business, and, when William died in 1748, succeeded him as Master Mason to the Office of Ordnance. The link between Adam and Morris is first forged in August 1744 when early discussions about Inveraray were taking place. From this point on, Adam could have been exposed to the Morris Ordnance style, if not earlier as a learner in his craft. Of course, this is all hypothesis. Nevertheless, there is documentary evidence to associate Adam with John Urquhart. They were involved with the Free Stone Quarries at Bogneel's Town in May 1750, and Adam seems to have done work for him on a flat in Blackfriars Wynd, High Street, Edinburgh.[4]

There is another possibility, namely that this link into the Morris style and to Inveraray came about through Andrew Fletcher, Lord Milton, whose house in Canongate, Edinburgh, was designed by Adam sometime between 1745 and 1750 (see Figure 11.4). Fletcher was a key figure in the early negotiations for Inveraray, and his house bears an uncanny compositional relationship to the town-house scheme.[5]

I dare not speculate further in this tangled tale of late Morris and early John Adam.[6]

NOTES

1. First brought to my attention by Mr Harry Gordon Slade, who has written so well on the 'Craigston and Meldrum Estates, Carriacou 1769–1841' in *PSAS* 114 (1984), 481–537.
2. Kitty has given me guidance in a letter of 21 April 1989.
3. I am here indebted to Ian G. Lindsay and Mary Cosh, *Inverary and the Dukes of Argyll*, Edinburgh, 1973, in particular pp. 31–2.
4. Cf. the Cruft letter (note 2 above).
5. Cf. Lindsay and Cosh, op. cit., and *Vitruvius Scoticus*, plate 45. I did wonder if these town-house designs in the Urquhart archives had been intended for engraving, as single sheets in the matter of most of the *Vitruvius Scoticus* designs.
6. Finally, I must thank Ian Gow for his kind help and encouragement when I was failing a little in my obligations to Kitty.

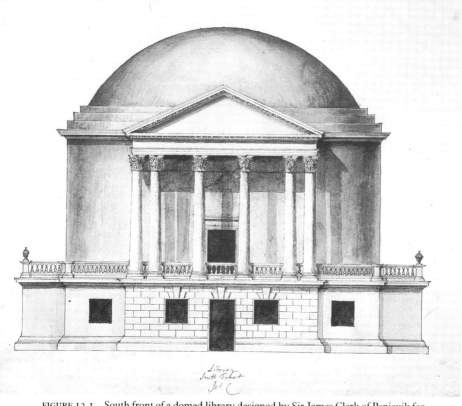

FIGURE 12.1   South front of a domed library designed by Sir James Clerk of Penicuik for Penicuik Estate (c. 1755–78).

12

A Bibliophile's Bagnio

Sir James Clerk's Pantheon for Penicuik

IAIN GORDON BROWN

John Dyer, sometime lawyer, clergyman, poet and itinerant painter, published 'The Ruins of Rome' in 1740. He had gone to Italy to follow the last-named of these callings and, fifteen years after his return, had produced the work which is not only an evocative picture of what Rome had meant to him, but also a fine and memorable encapsulation of many eighteenth-century attitudes to classical antiquity. Some of the ruined buildings of 'the Throne of Nations', glimpsed from the Palatine or Capitol, and the deliciously weed-grown townscape of the erstwhile 'great Queen of Earth', set Dyer musing upon the theme of decline and fall, on liberty, on vanity and human cruelty, and upon the conceit of Britain as the true heir of Imperial Rome. One building alone did Dyer select for scrutiny and emulation by the modern student of architecture 'advent'rous in the sacred search / Of ancient arts ...'; a structure of which 'yon venerable dome' survived intact, defying time and trumpeting the grandeur of a glorious golden age:

> Pantheon; plain and round; of this our World
> Majestick Emblem: With peculiar grace,
> Before its ample Orb, projected stands
> The many-pillar'd Portal; noblest work
> Of human skill: Here, curious Architect,
> If thou assay'st, ambitious, to surpass
> Palladius, Angelus, or British Jones;

On these fair Walls extend the certain Scale,
And turn th' instructive Compass: Careful mark
How far, in hidden Art, the noble Plain
Extends, and where the lovely Forms commence
Of flowing Sculpture; nor neglect to note
How range the taper Columns, and what Weight
Their leafy Brows sustain: Fair Corinth first
Boasted their Order, which Callimachus
(Reclining studious on Asopus' Banks
Beneath an Urn of some lamented Nymph)
Haply compos'd; the Urn with Foliage curl'd
Thinly conceal'd, the Chapiter inform'd.

Another fifteen years on, it was the Pantheon which a young artist, very assiduous in his pursuit of the ancient sources, singled out for particular praise. In his first letter to his mother from Rome, Robert Adam summed up perfectly the appeal of the great building to the Neo-Classical mind:

> What pleased me most of all was the Pantheon, of which the Greatness, and Simplicity of parts, fills the mind with extensive Thoughts, stamps upon you the Solemn, the Grave & Magestick, and seems to prevent all those Ideas of Gaity, or Frolick, which our modern buildings admitt of & inspire.[1]

Sir James Clerk of Penicuik, 3rd Baronet, was, like Dyer, trained in the law and also in painting; and he was, moreover, linked, by family marriage ties and by the architectural connection of their fathers, with Robert Adam. The latter, indeed, criticised the plans of Clerk's new house at Penicuik, built in the 1760s to the baronet's own design. It was as an accompaniment to this new house, in which (as Clerk put it) he had 'carried extravagance to the highest pitch',[2] that he designed at some unknown date, probably between 1755 and 1778, the building which forms the subject of this chapter.

Though this design, for a library and bathing establishment or bagnio combined, remained but an unrealised project, it is nevertheless of very considerable interest. It should be explained at this point that 'bagnio' is here used in its original, uncorrupted meaning of a steam bath or a hot and cold bathing establishment, a respectable meaning which it retained, in Scotland, at least until the early nineteenth century, by which time the word had long come, in English usage, to imply a house of ill-repute. Whereas Sir John and Sir James Clerk might have spoken with perfectly straight faces of building a 'bagnio', some of their English friends might have sniggered. The national distinction of usage apparently still survives in the minds of lexicographers:

Chambers Dictionary gives the bath-house as the first definition, with that of an oriental prison and a bawdy-house following; the *Concise Oxford Dictionary* and *Collins English Dictionary*, however, omit the first usage entirely, and go straight to prisons and brothels.

Clerk's project is one of the more remarkable of those many buildings, executed or simply fantasies of the drawing-board, which were products of the Neo-Classical passion for study or adaptation of the great original that was the Pantheon. For this bibliophile's bagnio, Clerk, as the 'curious Architect', followed Dyer's precepts to examine the original in all its details; and if he can hardly have expected to surpass the masters of Italy and England, then at least he could feel that in the Penicuik Pantheon he might have a building in which use and beauty were combined, where elegance and not immoderate expenditure might produce a worthy structure to do credit to the taste of the times while honouring the ancient models of perfection. His Pantheon is to be understood in the context of the Clerk family's moral and architectural tradition, and in the light of Pope's encomium of Burlington in which Sir James, and equally his father before him, had surely seen a standard worthy of emulation:

> You show us, Rome was glorious, not profuse
> And pompous buildings once were things of Use ...
> 'Tis Use alone that sanctifies Expence,
> And splendor borrows all her rays from Sense.[3]

In a perceptive study, William MacDonald has attempted to analyse the universality of the appeal of the Pantheon, both in physical form and in the realm of meaning: the Pantheon as structure and as symbol, as architectural design and as message. 'It speaks', MacDonald writes, 'of an even wider world than that of imperial Rome, and has left its stamp upon architecture more than any other building ... its progeny, in both shape and idea, are all about.'[4] In its role as inspirer of architects to imitate its form and meaning, its most notable characteristics have been its universality and its adaptability. The universality of its message is complemented by a form which allows infinite adaptation of some few or many of its physical characteristics. The Pantheon was seen as an 'icon of Rome's claims and mission'; but its 'all-encompassing imagery expressing immortality' meant that the building could be seen as meaningful in different ways at different times. Always it remained a symbol of Rome; and yet it was an inspiration to architects to adapt its form to fulfil new needs. 'Symbol and paradigm', the Pantheon has never been duplicated or copied exactly; 'each Pantheon-like building is, to a greater or lesser degree, a free interpretation'.[5]

Damie Stillman has discussed at some length the Neo-Classical variations
on the Pantheon theme, and has described the various ways in which
eighteenth- and early nineteenth-century architects modified or transformed
the original.[6] Yet, though two of Sir James Clerk's drawings for the Penicuik
Pantheon were published – albeit wrongly attributed to the 2nd Baronet – by
John Fleming as long ago as 1954,[7] no attention has been paid to them since,
by Stillman or anyone else. This is regrettable, for Clerk's Pantheon is fully as
worthy of study as anything described by Stillman either in his particular
article on 'The Pantheon Redecorated' or in his recent comprehensive study
of English Neo-Classical architecture.

The Pantheon theme was a recurrent one in the architectural exercises of
British Neo-Classicists, and elements of the original building can frequently
be detected in the Roman fantasies or among the visionary dreams, megalo-
maniac creations and unexecuted projects of the post-1750 architectural
generations. As an amateur designing a structure which was a modification of
the Pantheon form of a domed rotunda rising behind a trabeated portico,
Clerk was curiously in tune with what we may feel is one special quality of the
Roman original. For, in a way, the Pantheon is an amateur's building par
excellence.[8] It is a key structure in the history both of the amateur's
contribution to architectural achievement and of the relationship between
amateurs and professionals. The Pantheon exemplifies that fruitful type of
working relationship in which the former act not just as patrons but as men
who put a considerable amount of taste and thought into the design of a
building while nevertheless relying upon a professional to execute that design
and to handle the technical problems of construction. We do not consider
Hadrian the actual architect, as such, of the Pantheon; but we can accept that
the conception and moving spirit was almost certainly his.

Neo-Classical adaptations of the Pantheon might produce designs which in
their modification of the original theme retained yet a closeness of relation in
outward form which makes their derivation at once apparent.[9] Such are those
of the Pantheon's progeny which appear as isolated rotundas with attached
porticos: one thinks of Plaw's Belle Isle on Lake Windermere, or Jefferson's
library at the University of Virginia. Closely related, too, are those casinos,
mausolea and garden temples, such as those designs to be found among the
Adam drawings in the Soane Museum,[10] which (irrespective of their diminu-
tion in scale) easily betray their descent from the vast original. Less immediate
in their overt acknowledgement of their derivation are those interior features
of buildings which take the form of halls, saloons or domed circular spaces in
general, embedded in a larger complex of different shape. When considering
this last category of domed interior spaces, it seems only prudent not to
assume too readily a direct derivation from the Pantheon itself. The category

of eighteenth-century 'Pantheons' should perhaps be restricted to buildings which in their exterior appearance are modelled closely on the rotunda-cum-portico form, and which contain an interior domed space; this, rather than extending the class to include buildings which, regardless of allegiance to the original in matters of exterior form, just happen to incorporate a space which is – like the Pantheon – circular and domical.

The Pantheon is unique. Circular, domed rooms lit by *oculi*, however, were common in the architecture of the Roman baths, in *nymphaea* and in the garden architecture of the Roman world.[11] Though a building like Clerk's is certainly derived from the Pantheon, we should not forget the more general context of Pantheon-like structures in later Roman antiquity. The fact that many of these structures occur in thermal complexes, and that libraries were to be found in Roman bathing establishments, makes it a particularly happy choice of Clerk's to design a library and bath-house on the pattern of a circular, domed and top-lit room. The circular form for a library is also of significance in view of its inspiration. If the Roman Pantheon is a metaphor of the world-empire of Rome, the circle expressive of stability and permanence,[12] the Penicuik Pantheon is a metaphor of the whole world of learning, ancient and modern, science and art, encompassed in one building.

Since Palladio, architects had drawn inspiration from the vast remains of the Roman bath complexes, as indeed they had from the Pantheon. In the year that James Clerk came of age, Lord Burlington published Palladio's drawings of the ancient baths as *Fabbriche Antiche* (1730). Thus to Palladio's detailed investigations of the Pantheon were added complementary studies of the baths, the whole affording a corpus of material on which architectural students of Clerk's generation could let their imagination go to work. The influence of thermal architecture shown in the planning of the early Neo-Palladians was greatly strengthened by the more archaeological approach of the next, empiricist generation which had come to know the antiquities of Rome and the newly-discovered Campanian sites at first hand. For these younger contemporaries of James Clerk, the Pantheon appeared to be a part of one particular bath complex, and the assumption was that Pantheon-type structures were associated with bathing establishments in general. James Adam, for instance, could write to his sister Nelly of his projected publication on the baths, and in so doing make mention of the Pantheon as a part of the Baths of Agrippa.[13] Palladio's reconstructions of those same baths, along with those of Nero, Vespasian, Titus, Caracalla, Diocletian and Constantine, as published by Lord Burlington, showed great saucer-domed halls which indeed resembled the Pantheon. In his *Baths of the Romans Explained and Illustrated* of 1772, Charles Cameron further enshrined the notion that the

Pantheon, having served as a vestibule to the Baths of Agrippa, was a structure the like of which was to have been found in other thermal complexes.[14] What, then, could be more natural for Sir James Clerk to adopt as his model for a bath-house at a focal point of his park than the domed building which, allowing for its reduced scale, would look so much as if it had been taken from some learned archaeological reconstruction of an ancient bath? And how much more appropriate this seems, given the knowledge that Alexander Runciman's original scheme for the decoration of the new Penicuik House itself was to have been based in part upon the stucco reliefs in the Baths of Titus and the grotesque ornaments of other Roman ruins.[15]

Allusion has already been made to the presence of libraries as features of the Roman baths. Ancient evidence makes it clear that there were certainly books available in the Baths of Diocletian, and collections in other public baths, and that libraries were regarded as part of the general amenities of the bathing establishments. 'It is to be concluded, therefore, that the idle hours of the Roman citizen frequenting the thermae for sport and recreation could also fittingly be devoted to the pastime of reading.'[16] To a father and son as strongly imbued with antiquarianism as were Sir John and Sir James Clerk, the idea of setting up a library would have appealed as a Roman virtue. Julius Caesar had intended to establish a major library with Varro as general administrator of the public libraries of Rome; and Augustus, with Asinius Pollio to direct the project, achieved the Julian family ambition of founding libraries.[17] So Sir John Clerk, Baron of the Exchequer, had hoped to establish a library which would be a further manifestation of his belief in the concept of 'honestum otium'. His thoroughgoing pursuit of a Roman lifestyle was all-pervasive, and entered even into his leisure moments when shooting and fishing. Memoranda specify favourite Roman authors to be carried always in his pocket. Inscriptions, stumbled upon when out for a walk in the literary landscape of association created at Penicuik, would turn the mind to musing upon classical themes.[18] As an aspect of his cultivation of 'useful leisure', Sir John had envisaged a library and museum to be sited beside the High Pond and entered from the long walk which skirted the sloping ground descending to Blackpools Pond and the River North Esk.[19] To the details of this we shall return.

Seneca was the favourite classical author of Sir John Clerk, to whose influence and memory so much of Sir James's inspiration, in architecture and antiquarianism, was due. In accordance with Seneca's belief in frugality, the elder Clerk allowed himself very limited extravagance in building. 'Even for studies, where expenditure is most honourable, it is justifiable only so long as it is kept within bounds', wrote Seneca in *De tranquillitate animi* (ix 4); and Sir John's library design was modest indeed compared with his son's proposals. Small in scale and uninspiring in style, it could not be further removed from the Neo-Classical splendour envisaged by Sir James. The 2nd Baronet would have provided an attic storey to accommodate his collections of curiosities, thus translating into bricks and mortar his belief that those who had libraries of classical literature ought to form collections of antiquities – material remains of the past – which might illustrate the written word. In designing this little pavilion, Clerk will have imagined that he was keeping within the bounds of frugality, just as Seneca had advised, and so might remain true to the ideal of 'honestum otium' and avoid the slight of mere 'studiosa luxuria', the learned luxury which Seneca deplored (ix 5).

Inherited taste and filial piety apart, the 3rd Baronet, reading further in his Seneca, may have come upon the passage where the old Roman sneers at the pretensions of his own times when 'along with hot and cold baths a library is also provided as an embellishment to a great house' (ix 7). Sir James, less austere and more of a man of the world than his father, and also more willing to spend money on the arts, was able to make a virtue out of what Seneca had condemned and his father would have baulked at, and feel justified in at least planning his combined library and bagnio. In him there remained enough of the Clerk family canniness to want value for money, to insist that (in Pope's phrase) Use should sanctify Expence, and that profuseness should ever be tempered by economy, and to be attracted by the idea of one building doing the work of two. This duality of purpose was what, in Clerk's eyes, will have brought his projected building into line with what his contemporaries saw as one of the most attractive features of the ancient baths. In his Preface to *The Baths of the Romans*, Charles Cameron declared it his aim to consider 'what uses of pleasure, as well as convenience, the luxury of the times had appointed the Baths under the Roman Emperors'. The architects of the Enlightenment, borrowing from antiquity but putting the ancient forms to new uses, could take a less censorious view than did Seneca of increasing luxury that might carry with it its own obsolescence. Seneca observed: 'Thus does luxury find out something new in which to obliterate her own works. Formerly the Baths were few in number, and not much ornamented; for why should a thing of such little value be ornamented, which was invented for use and not for the purposes of delicacy?'[20] Clerk saw the eighteenth-century achievement as something that improved upon antiquity; and any building which offset mere extravagance or luxury with practical utility in another aspect – an almost too-elegant library made that much more commendable by the addition of a thoroughly functional bath; a semi-subterranean bath-house redeemed by having a superbly beautiful library-room upstairs – as a creditable modern achievement to bequeath to posterity. In the design for his

Pantheon, Clerk was able (in the words of the Adam brothers) to 'seize, with some degree of success, the beautiful spirit of antiquity, and to transfuse it, with novelty and variety'.[21]

The Clerks had a notable interest in medicine, amounting in certain members of the family to hypochondria. An aspect of these medical obsessions was an enthusiasm on the part of the 1st Baronet, shared by his son, for the beneficial effects of baths, especially cold bathing. An extensive correspondence with the leading authorities on the subject, Edward Baynard and Sir John Floyer, survives in the Clerk papers, together with the first Sir John's dissertation on the merits of bathing, and his lengthy diaries recording his use of cold baths.[22] This material affords an unexploited source of information which would enable us to add to existing knowledge of these matters as practised in Scotland.[23] James Clerk will certainly have been familiar with the Physicians' Hall in Edinburgh in which 'good pretty building' (as John Loveday reported)[24] there was below the library 'a Bagnio, & Rooms for Sweating'.

How then did Sir James's bibliophile's bagnio project take shape? In 1752–3, he added a new library to the old house of Newbiggin (i.e. the predecessor of the present 'Old' Penicuik House) together with a suite of rooms on the west side of the mansion. About these improvements his by then aged father seemed unenthusiastic, recording in his Memoirs that 'as there was no pressing occasion for these things, the work proceeded slowly'.[25] One senses that James was chafing at the bit, and while his father lived he was restricted in what he might do in the way of architectural enterprise. Baron Clerk died in 1755, and James came into his inheritance. Yet, a few of Sir John's ideas, as he had expressed them in his long poem 'The Country Seat', survived to exert some influence on Sir James's own building programme. In the actual decorative scheme for the staircases and halls of Sir James's grand new house, there is, for instance, surely some reflection of the Baron's notions of how a poetic palace should be frescoed with historical murals. Sir John, in 'The Country Seat', set great store by the presence of a library in a house, and in both the text itself and in the accompanying notes to the poem he went into some detail about the arrangements for heating such a room in order to avoid any risk of fire. His recommendation for a hypocaust below a library –

> Revive an antient Practice to conduct
> From a hot Bagnio 'mongst the cells aloft
> The tepid vapour in small tubes enclosed . . .

may have given his son an idea for juxtaposing the two distinct elements of his Pantheon building. Similarly, in the Baron's discourse on the lighting of

domes in a house, we may detect the germ of Sir James's idea of building a
domed structure with an *oculus*, thus making 'its Blazing Show resemble
Heaven'.

Isaac Ware's *Complete Body of Architecture* appeared in the year following
Baron Clerk's death. From this influential work, Sir James may have received
further ideas germane to the ultimate design of his Pantheon. As Plate 102
in Ware's book, there appears a 'temple with its dome, plain, elegant and
proportioned': a structure which

> in some retired part of the garden ... may burst upon the eye ... Its
> depth will give room for useful purposes, and in the centre may be a
> noble bath. The building will allow a hall before it, and a recess behind
> for dressing and undressing ... and the utility of this structure will be a
> consideration not less than its beauty.[26]

Ware's treatise probably afforded Clerk ideas on the siting of his projected
building. His Pantheon was to be at once a feature in the landscape and an
object of attraction in itself, a viewpoint from which to enjoy a prospect of the
park, and a useful asset to the gentleman's life. It was a building offering 'the
conveniences of repose' as well as being an 'edifice of shew'; and as such, as
Ware advised, it had to be carefully designed and sited.

Given the probable location for Clerk's Pantheon, which I believe to have
been intended for a site very much in the same area as the Baron's pavilion
already discussed – that is, to the south of the High Pond and overlooking
Blackpools Park (see Figure 12.2) – Ware's advice on the choice of ground
would be singularly appropriate. This was

> to fall upon a spot agreeable in itself, and commanding views where
> nature shews herself in all her wildness of luxuriant growth, in all her
> smiling graces; imbellished with landscapes, varied with wood and
> water, and profuse in all those rural elegances which compose the mind
> and settle it for contemplation. The repose of mind, content of heart,
> and quietness of soul we seek when we retire from bustle and from
> noise; the sweet moments of uninterrupted meditation, are not to be
> found in gloomy walks, or figured yew-trees: nature is the source of all,
> and it is in her we are to seek that unutterable pleasure.[27]

Ware's description happens to match well the topography of the Penicuik estate
to the south-west of the house: a long, gentle sweep of parkland to the river,
a lake behind and one to the left in front, wooded slopes beyond, and beyond
again the rugged open country and the hills. A location on the long terrace walk
nearer the new house I think unlikely: the full effect of the domed rotunda set
on its rusticated basement – most impressive when seen from a distance –

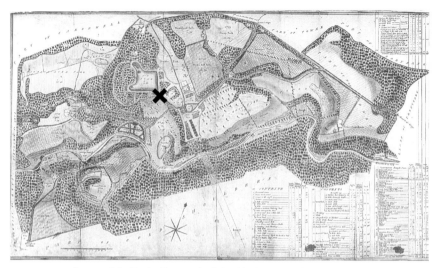

FIGURE 12.2   Survey of the Penicuik estate by John Ainslie, 1796, showing the site
probably selected by Sir James Clerk for his library.

would be lessened were it to have occupied a site where the eye would be
distracted by the house itself. We may remember the precept of Sir John
Clerk as expressed in 'The Country Seat':

> All Structures should a just proportion bear
> To that extent of Field on which they stand;
> It ill becomes a vast and noble Dome
> To be confin'd to straight and narrow Ground.

Whereas Sir John's projected library was to have had its principal front
facing north towards the High Pond and the Pentland Hills, Sir James's
Pantheon was to face the other way. Both buildings were evidently designed
to stand on sloping ground. We know this, in the case of the earlier project,
from the Baron's manuscript notes on his building: his 'Schem of Improvements' paper contains sketches of only the north elevation and the plan at the
entrance level which was to be reached from the terrace walk; but the notes
explain that a basement storey was designed for the south front, where the
ground would fall away. The plans and elevations of Sir James's Pantheon
show the south (principal) front (see Figure 12.1) with the Corinthian portico
raised on a basement, the balustrade of which is level with the terrace. The
section (see Figure 12.3) and plan show the basement floor containing the
bagnio and its associated rooms (waiting-room, dressing-room, and porter's
apartment) extending back only as far as the northern wall of the rotunda

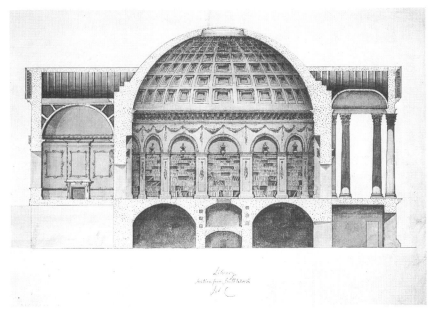

FIGURE 12.3   Cross-section of the domed library designed by Sir James Clerk of
Penicuik.

above. On the upper floor, where the ground level was higher, a 'consulting-room' extended north from the rotunda. The plan of a portico against a rotunda obviously echoes that of the Pantheon, albeit that the intermediate block of the original, located between portico and rotunda itself, is omitted. The consulting-room element of the plan presumably has for its authority the so-called Basilica of Neptune, which to eighteenth-century antiquaries appeared as part of a Pantheon complex though it was, in fact, quite separate.

The drawings do not furnish details of the workings of the hot and cold baths, though it would appear that the water supply was drawn from a reservoir to the north, almost certainly the High Pond. A bather entering by the basement door might enjoy the physical comforts of the bagnio before ascending by the passage and stair to the mental delights of the library above; or the reader, fatigued by study, might refresh himself by descending from the consulting-room to the bath.

Externally, the Penicuik dome has the three step-rings of the Pantheon dome. The pediment rises directly against these step-rings: a variant, of course, on the original theme, but one common enough (for instance) in the mausoleum and other designs of Robert Adam, or present rather earlier in Ambrose Phillips's designs for Montpellier, but not one introduced by

FIGURE 12.4   North front of the domed library designed by Sir James Clerk of Penicuik.

Burlington in his Tempietto at Chiswick or by Flitcroft in his Pantheon at
Stourhead, both of which adhere to the pattern of the Roman original.[28]
Internally, the dome displays seven concentric rows of coffers, two more than
the Pantheon itself, and from the section it appears that – however impractical
for the Midlothian climate – the rotunda was designed to be lit by an *oculus*.
The floor plan seems to show a grating which was presumably intended to
cover the central drain necessary in a hypaethral structure, though the section
indicates no obvious link between this and the bagnio below. The proportions
of the domed rotunda do not correspond to those of a scaled-down Pantheon,
as the height does not equal the fifty-foot diameter. But with the walls
articulated by twelve piers ornamented by festoon drops, with the heads of
the niches between those piers occupied by urns, and with an elegant running
festoon motif below the modillion cornice, Clerk had created a refined
Neo-Classical version of the ancient original. Two of the twelve arches were
to be allocated to the entrance and the door communicating with the
consulting-room; but the ten remaining ones contained book-presses ample
enough to accommodate a substantial library.

FIGURE 12.5   Detail of the garden front of Penicuik House.

The single most intriguing feature of the design is the fenestration of the
north front (see Figure 12.4). Here, the three windows intended to look out
over the High Pond take the form of arched aedicules, with festoons in the
pediments and balusters at the foot of each bay. Themselves highly decorative
and ornate, they provide the only refinements on the otherwise chaste and
austere northern elevation, where the unarticulated sweep of the rotunda wall
and the unornamented pediment are not enlivened by the presence of the
balustrated terrace. The supposition must be that Sir James particularly liked
these aedicules, for they closely resemble the triplet of windows which his
executant architect John Baxter introduced into the rear elevation of the new
Penicuik House (see Figure 12.5) in 1777–8 as replacements for the three
square-headed windows that had originally been built. It would seem that,
when the patron reluctantly accepted that his Pantheon would remain a paper
dream, he had determined to realise in another place this one feature of his
grand design, even at the expense of undoing work already completed.

A paper dream that is never translated into actuality cannot crumble and
decay and, ironically, can outlast the stone and lime of real estate buildings
and, in a way, survive even the fate of a great house. Sir James's Pantheon was
never built, and so remains forever a sparkling idea. One thinks again of John
Dyer and his vision of the transience of luxurious splendour:

Down fall their Parian Porches, Gilded Baths,
And roll before the Storm in clouds of dust . . .

And when reading 'The Ruins of Rome', it is difficult not to conjure up a vision of the Penicuik Pantheon, set in its classical landscape on the terrace above Blackpools Park –

Globose and huge,
Grey-mould'ring Temples swell, and wide o'ercast
The solitary Landskape, Hills and Woods,
And boundless Wilds. . . .

ACKNOWLEDGEMENTS

The drawings reproduced in this article are published by kind permission of Sir John Clerk of Penicuik, Bt, who has also permitted me to quote from his family papers deposited in the Scottish Record Office. For discussion of the drawings, I am indebted to Mr Ian Gow, Professor Alistair Rowan and Mr James Simpson.

NOTES

1. Scottish Record Office, Clerk of Penicuik Muniments, GD18/4765, 1 March 1755.
2. SRO, GD18/1758a.
3. 'Moral Essays': Epistle IV. ll. 23–4, 179–80. For an analysis of the Clerk architectural tradition from the first laird of Penicuik to the 3rd Baronet, see Iain Gordon Brown, 'Judges of Architectory: The Clerks of Pencuik no Amateurs', in *The Role of the Amateur Architect*, ed. Giles Worsley, London, 1994, pp. 43–51.
4. William L. MacDonald, *The Pantheon: Design, Meaning, and Progeny*, London, 1976, p. 11.
5. Ibid., pp. 114, 91–2, 94, 95.
6. Damie Stillman, 'The Pantheon Redecorated: Neoclassical Variations on an Antique Spatial and Decorative Theme', *Via*, 3 (1977), pp. 83–97; idem, *English Neo-classical Architecture*, 2 vols, London, 1988.
7. John Fleming, *Scottish Country Houses and Gardens*, London, 1954, p. 12.
8. On this theme, cf. MacDonald, pp. 12, 14.
9. On the adaptation of the Pantheon see, in general, Stillman, 'The Pantheon Redecorated', passim; and *English Neo-classical Architecture*, pp. 94, 322.
10. See, e.g., vol. 2: nos 23, 80 and 127; and several designs in vol. 9.
11. See J. B. Ward-Perkins, *Roman Imperial Architecture*, 2nd edn, Harmondsworth, 1981, pp. 57, 101–5, 166–8, 433–4; MacDonald, pp. 50, 58. On the influence of the architecture of the Roman baths on that of British public and domestic buildings, especially in matters of planning, see Sir John Summerson, *Architecture in Britain 1530–1830*, first integrated edn, Harmondsworth, 1970, p. 338; and Stillman, *English Neo-classical Architecture*, p. 36.

12. MacDonald, pp. 88, 132.
13. SRO, GD18/4863, 9 January 1760.
14. Charles Cameron, *The Baths of the Romans*, London, 1772, p. 43.
15. SRO, GD18/4680, Alexander Runciman to Sir James Clerk, 16 May 1770.
16. Clarence Eugene Boyd, *Public Libraries and Literary Culture in Ancient Rome*, Chicago, 1915, p. 63.
17. Ibid., pp. 1, 2, 48–9.
18. On Clerk and the Roman life, see Iain Gordon Brown, 'Sir John Clerk of Penicuik 1676–1755: Aspects of a Virtuoso Life', unpublished doctoral dissertation, Cambridge, 1980, esp. Chapter 7. From a concise account of the Clerk family's contributions to Scottish culture from generation to generation, see Iain Gordon Brown, *The Clerks of Penicuik: Portraits of Taste and Talent*, Edinburgh, 1987. For their antiquarianism, see Iain Gordon Brown, *The Hobby Horsical Antiquary*, Edinburgh, 1980, passim.
19. SRO, GD18/1483a/1 ('Schem of Improvements in the Baronie of Penicuik', 12 May 1741), p. 10.
20. Epistles, LXXXVI 8–9. The translation is Charles Cameron's, *The Baths of the Romans*, p. 13.
21. Robert and James Adam, *Works in Architecture*, no. 1, London, 1773, Preface, p. 6.
22. SRO, GD18/2133 (Baynard and Floyer correspondence); 2137 (bathing diaries); 2146 (dissertation on cold baths).
23. No attention was paid to the Clerk contribution to the subject by W. N. Boog Watson in 'Early Baths and Bagnios in Edinburgh', *Book of the Old Edinburgh Club*, XXXIV part 2 (1979), 57–67.
24. *Diary of a Tour in 1732 made by John Loveday of Caversham*, edited for the Roxburghe Club by J. E. T. Loveday, Edinburgh, 1890.
25. *Memoirs of the Life of Sir John Clerk of Penicuik*, edited by John M. Gray, Edinburgh, 1892, p. 228.
26. Isaac Ware, *A Complete Body of Architecture*, London, 1756, p. 647.
27. Ibid., pp. 636, 639–40; 644.
28. Adam domes: see, e.g., Soane Museum, vol. 2, nos 23, 127; vol. 9, passim; vol. 19, no. 143 (a design for the Earl of Coventry at Croome); vol. 38 (design for Lock Hospital Chapel, Grosvenor Place, London); vol. 51, no. 103 (Admiralty Screen, end pavilion design of 1759). On Phillips, see John Harris, *The Palladians*, London, 1981, p. 106.

FIGURE 13.1   Design for the south front of Walkinshaw by Robert Adam, c. 1791.

13

Robert Adam at Walkinshaw

FRANK ARNEIL WALKER

It might be a lovely place. Coiling through the moss, two Renfrewshire rivers – the Gryffe and the Black Cart – flow together a few miles short of their debouch into the Clyde. A line of swans moves slowly against the swollen stream. Some cattle idle away their day along the banks. A lark rises. But no birds sing; or so it seems within the torrential pall of sound that envelops the scene. From the west, waves of traffic noise roll across the fields from the M8 motorway. From the east, the booming roar of jetplanes landing or rising at Glasgow Airport intermittently engulfs the wide, flat countryside. Not riverside meadow-sweet but petrol and kerosene scent the air. Sound and smell subvert sight as the senses conspire to destroy the pastoral picture. The turbid rivers have a glaucous look. The grass is lank, dishevelled, bottle-strewn, here and there charred by illicit fires. The ground inclines abruptly, adjusting to uneven terracing, the lie of the land evidently contrived, less than natural. Two ruined stubs of walling, the arched edge of a basement vault, a black line of bitumen oozing out of the broken earth, betray a past beneath the green. These are the meagre vestiges of Robert Adam's Walkinshaw House, 'the only triangular Classical house in Britain'[1] (see Figures 13.1 and 13.2).

Demolition and neglect have afflicted Walkinshaw since it was demolished some seventy years ago. Almost certainly, the fabric had by then been hopelessly undermined by local pit workings[2] – just how catastrophically is evident in the ruined ashlar walls of the mansion's stables block still

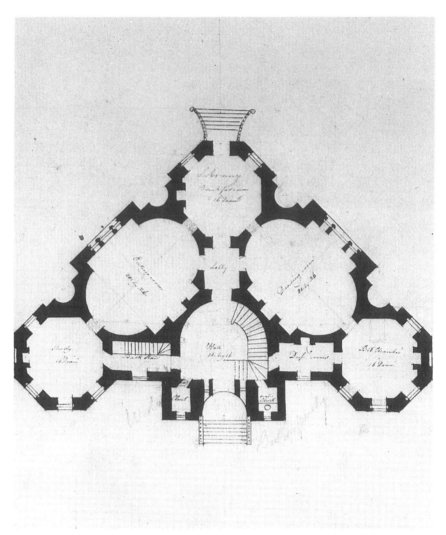

FIGURE 13.2   Design for the principal floor of Walkinshaw by Robert Adam, c. 1791.

precariously standing a little to the east, its crumbling arched screen and court separated by an overgrown walled garden from the mines and brickworks of Victorian encroachment. Ironically, these too are abandoned, compounding a prolonged disdain for the rural landscape. Indeed, since Walkinshaw's last occupant is recorded as undermanager at the nearby mine,[3] it seems likely that the house was already condemned to hard times, if not outright disrespect. Gracious living probably ceased at the start of the twentieth century when the then owner of the estate, John Charles Cunning-hame of Craigends, having married a certain Miss Pearson briefly ensconced by him at Walkinshaw,[4] preferred to abandon his Adam residence and begin married life at David Bryce's great Baronial house[5] a mile or two west at Houston.

Bryce's patron, Alexander Cunninghame of Craigends, had bought Walkinshaw in 1855. Even then, the property was in poor condition, the contributor to the *Second Statistical Account* noting a decade earlier that 'Walkingshaw [sic] House has not been regularly inhabited for some time' – indeed, not since the death of an earlier owner, Mr Boyd Alexander, in 1825 – 'and has gone much into disrepair'.[6] It was, however, 'thoroughly improved'[7] by its new owner, though whether this was done in the two years prior to the commissioning of the magnificent mansion at Houston is unclear. Certainly, estate and house had an ancient lineage and might well have seemed an attractive, honourable and no doubt economic proposition.

Walkinshaws of that Ilk had lived in this flat Renfrewshire countryside for centuries, the earliest mention of a house or 'mannor place'[8] being in 1532. In the 1680s, a Glasgow merchant named James Walkinshaw acquired the estate and altered the old house, making improvements to what was described as 'a very pretty dwelling ... having a naturall convenience of bringing vessels to it by watter'.[9] Almost a century later, around 1769–70, the estate was alienated by another James Walkinshaw and came into the hands of a Dr William Millar who, greatly enriched by a spell in Antigua, had returned to Scotland in search of a desirable demesne. Perhaps shared business ties with the West Indies had some bearing on the subsequent conveyance of Walkinshaw from the Millars to another Renfrewshire family, the prosperous and powerful McDowalls of Garthland and Castle Semple.[10] By 1791, the new owner, Day Hort McDowall (1753–1809),[11] had decided to build a new Walkinshaw House and had engaged Robert Adam to prepare designs.[12]

The McDowall presence in Renfrewshire dates from 1727. In that year, Colonel William McDowall (1677–1748), a younger son of Alexander McDowall of Garthland in Wigtownshire, returned to Scotland from a period of military service spent in the West Indies island of St Kitts. There he had married, acquiring, as a result, a substantial fortune through his widowed wife's inheritance from another Renfrewshire family, the Millikens of John-stone, who had done well out of the sugar trade. With this wealth, he established his household in some style in Glasgow, where he purchased the pretigious and architecturally precocious Shawfield Mansion (1711)[13] from Daniel Campbell. At the same time, he picked up the estate of Castle Semple, near Lochwinnoch, from Hugh, Lord Sempill,[14] at a bargain price, thereby securing for himself a pleasant and convenient country seat.

FIGURE 13.3   View of Castle Semple from the 1907 sale catalogue.

In Glasgow, McDowall set a high social profile, maintaining his lucrative West Indies interests through a prosperous partnership with Major James Milliken of Johnstone. Already elegantly housed in the city, he nevertheless began a building project intended to reinforce the classical grandeur of his home on the Trongait by building two identical three-storey tenement properties flanking the set-back forecourt of the Shawfield Mansion.[15] Since Colen Campbell's original conception for the house had aligned it on the axis of Stockwellgait opposite, this later aggrandisement served to intensify the impact of Palladian disposition on the urban form of Glasgow's Merchant City.

In Renfrewshire, McDowall lived the cultured laird's life of Scotland's new merchant aristocracy. Here, too, he built. In 1735 he tore down the old Park Castle on his estate, replacing it with a fine two-storey-and-basement pedimented mansion (1735–40)[16] which, though it did not boast a portico, was broadly Palladian in ambition, with niched and arcaded links leading to a double rank of outbuildings stepping forwards around a wide forecourt which looked south across Castle Semple Loch (see Figure 13.3).

On McDowall's death, his son William succeeded. The MP for Renfrewshire between 1768 and 1774, not only did he maintain his father's prominence in civic and business life but he was also 'a great improver in husbandry'[17] at Castle Semple. Moreover, he increased the family's landholdings by purchasing the Garthland estates from a cousin in Wigtownshire in 1760, acquiring the Garthland title on the latter's death in 1775. On the other hand, in Glasgow, where he had completed his father's tenement building project,[18] he disposed of the Shawfield Mansion, selling it in 1760 to John Glassford.

William McDowall (II) died in 1786 having fathered twelve children, the eldest of whom, yet another William (1749–1810), now continued the family line at Castle Semple and in Glasgow. He followed in his father's footsteps in parliamentary affairs, intermittently representing Renfrewshire, Ayrshire and the Glasgow Burghs. In 1793, he became Lord Lieutenant of Renfrewshire. For ten years or so 'he made great improvements on the Castlesemple grounds',[19] developed the burgeoning textile industry at Lochwinnoch and in 1788 laid out a model village there on a geometrically rigorous cross-plan.[20] About the same time, he must have contemplated a major facelift for his country home. At any rate, in the summer of 1791, Robert Adam was at Castle Semple to discuss possible architectural changes. Adam was already known to the family through William's younger brother James (1752–1808), who as Lord Provost of Glasgow (1790–1) was doubtless closely involved with the Trades Hall commission in Glassford Street and, as 'preses of the managers',[21] with the building of the Royal Infirmary. It proved a fortuitous visit for, along with the task of recasting the mansion at Castle Semple, Adam was also instructed by the third brother of the family, Day Hort McDowall (1753–1809), who was shortly to be married, to design a new house for him and his wife at Walkinshaw.[22]

Both the lochside location of William McDowall's mansion near Lochwinnoch and, more especially, the riparian mossland site of Walkinshaw seem to invoke an improbable affinity with the flat, canal-crossed landscape of the Veneto:[23] Palladian possibilities and precedents spring to mind. Adam, however, had left the classical purities of Shardeloes and Bowood a generation behind. No columned portico nor pilastered façade was therefore added to Castle Semple. Nor was the new Walkinshaw, despite its being 'beautifully situated at the confluence of the Gryfe and the Black Cart'[24] with every 'naturall convenience of bringing vessels to it by watter',[25] to be conceived as some latter-day Villa Malcontenta.

Instead, proposals for the reshaping of Castle Semple emerged with appropriately eponymous vigour in Adam's by now fashionable Castle Style[26] (see Figures 13.4 and 13.5). A large, arcaded, castellated drum projected from the centre of a rectangular block terminated by conically capped square end towers. Between drum and towers, the walls were surprisingly lavishly lit by tripartite windows, those to the ground storey retaining the familiar Venetian form. It was the typical hybrid conceit of Adam's late Romanticism: medieval allusion in machicolation, bartizan and hood moulding; closed classical control in symmetrical organisation. The whole idea was similar in strategy to the massing worked out in the 1777 schemes which he had

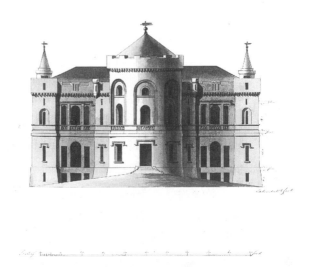

FIGURE 13.4   Design for the principal front of Castle Semple by Robert Adam, c. 1791.

FIGURE 13.5   Design for the principal floor of Castle Semple by Robert Adam, c. 1791.

produced for The Oaks in Surrey,[27] one of the Earl of Derby's seats, and in style to the Scottishness first adumbrated in the mansion which he built in 1771 for Baron Mure at Caldwell near Beith,[28] just over the hill from Castle Semple.

For Walkinshaw, however, Adam seems to have preferred a less allusive manner.[29] It may be that William McDowall's decision not to proceed with the recasting of Castle Semple in Castle Style idiom persuaded Adam to take a different line with his brother's commission. At any rate, an austerely classical design, neither Scottish nor indeed Italianate, emerged. Quite why Adam elected to use a triangle (see Figure 13.1) as the basis of the Walkinshaw plan[30] is another question altogether, but one which provokes some intriguing speculation.

Such a constraining perimeter geometry presents serious planning problems and cannot surely have been an arbitrary decision. Could the triangle be read as a 'delta', symbolic flattery of Adam's oddly-named patron, Day Hort McDowall? Strictly, such an appropriation should have entailed an equilateral configuration, while Adam's version is a right-angled isosceles plan. But it would have been naively and inconveniently formalist to hold, as it were, to the law of the letter. As Alistair Rowan has pointed out,[31] Adam's decision enables him to order the planning of the two shorter sides on an orthodox rectilinear matrix while, by introducing octagonal elements at all three corners, he can pick up a similar draughting discipline along the main front.

Rowan has also written[32] about the sources of Adam's geometrical preoccupation at Walkinshaw, tracing the evolution of the triangular plan from garden lodges and follies to villa designs by his late eighteenth-century contemporaries Carter, Carr and Nash. Earlier precedents by James Gibbs, Carlo Fontana and Johann Fischer von Erlach are also adduced to the genealogy. In his stunning book *Architecture in the Age of Reason*, Kaufmann, though not concerned to deal with Adam, notes similar explorations by Archer, Halfpenny, Laugier, d'Ixnard, Neufforge and, of course, Soane.[33] The provenance is rich, though its precise determination may remain ambiguous.

It is possible to speculate. The triangular plan of Longford Castle in Wiltshire, built in 1591 but reconstructed in 1717, had appeared in Colen Campbell's *Vitruvius Britannicus* and would almost certainly be known to Adam. John Carter's triangular design for Midford Castle, Somerset, published in *The Builder's Magazine* in the mid-1770s,[34] might form a conceptual link for, since Carter 'followed Adam's style in the interiors'[35] of several of his projects, some reciprocal relationship may be at work: Midford's castellated character, for example, could well have caught Adam's eye. Much more closely comparable to the formal lineaments of the Walkinshaw plan, however, is William Halfpenny's House No 31 which, in 1749, had been illustrated in his *New and Compleat System*.[36] Here, as at Longford and Midford, an equilateral triangle has its apices marked by drum towers, but, unlike the two castles, each of the three sides of the triangle is flanked by a discrete rectangular unit of accommodation. In effect, all seven elements of the composition – triangle, drums and rectangles – retain a detached architectonic integrity. While a progressive 'predilection for elementary geometry was perhaps the most conspicuous trait of architecture about 1800',[37] it is this strategy of individuated form *within* the grand geometrical conceit which characterises Adam's arrangement at Walkinshaw.

At Walkinshaw, the triangle fixes perimeter form rather than internal space and, while the disposition of the elements within this enclosing boundary is highly formalistic, it is still a remarkably compact and economical arrangement. And if the core of the plan is now no more than a small lobby, it is, nonetheless, an ingeniously efficient adjunct to the galleried stairway hall which rises three floors behind the main entrance façade. But it is the austere three-dimensional expression of the building in which 'the basic principle ruling composition . . . was the concept of independence',[38] which makes Day Hort McDowall's mansion all but unique in the Adam oeuvre. Octagonal corners, flanking blocks of rooms, even the twin towers of tiered closets which project on each side of the main entrance,[39] all are distinct and separate in a clear, articulated massing of the parts.

The splayed bulk of Walkinshaw's corner towers might seem like left-over bastions from Adam's Castle Style manner; but there are no bartizans, crow-steps or corbels. The subdivision of the fenestration in each of the pedimented blocks of rooms on the house's two shorter sides – its tripartite rhythm carried down into a basement thermal window[40] – lingers on from his earlier Italianate idiom; but there is little else left that is so overtly classical. Dim accents from the past endure, but there is now nothing either Romantic or Palladian in Adam's syntax. Walkinshaw is tough-minded, almost revolutionary Neo-Classicism.

In 1795, only a year or two after the completion of Walkinshaw, catastrophe befell the third generation of Renfrewshire McDowalls. At Castle Semple, William suddenly found himself on the brink of ruin as a result of the collapse of the firm of Alexander Houston & Co. In 'one of the greatest commercial disasters ever known in Glasgow',[41] he, his brother James and a third partner, Robert Houston Rae, all faced immense debts. For years, the Houston company had dominated Glasgow's sugar trade, but in the late 1780s they were extending credit in Grenada and St Vincent on a lavish scale, and, when in 1794 the Carib War broke out, the consequent loss of the Grenada crop proved to be 'the nudge needed to overturn what had become a fundamentally over-expanded concern'.[42] The crash was spectacular, virtually a national calamity in a time of general economic depression.[43]

FIGURE 13.6   Design for the side elevations at Walkinshaw by Robert Adam, c. 1791.

FIGURE 13.7   Photograph of Walkinshaw from *The Castles and Mansions of Renfrewshire and Buteshire*, 1889.

Sensing the danger, Glasgow's West Indies merchant community gave immediate financial support. Further loans were raised from private individuals and from banks against the security of William McDowall's estates.[44] The government issued Exchequer Bills. But nothing could stem the tide: the sale of land in St Kitts realised more capital[45] while legal procedures delayed the inevitable, but by about 1806 the unfortunate William McDowall of Garthland had been 'distressed and poinded'[46] and the sale of the Castle Semple estate forced through an appointed trustee.[47]

It was William's brother Day Hort who purchased Castle Semple, paying around £75,000[48] for its 527 acres.[49] In time, the McDowall creditors were paid,[50] but the family never recovered its former wealth. To save his brother, Day Hort had in turn overstretched himself and, faced with the necessity to cover his outlay at Castle Semple, could not sell Walkinshaw for a good enough price. Having made a will committing his Walkinshaw property as 'surety for my brother William McDowall, Esquire, of Garthland',[51] in 1809 he took his own life, drowning himself in a pond at Castle Semple.[52] James, 'the late Provost', William's partner, had already died in the West Indies, probably in the preceding year, 'perhaps by dissipation, or drinking, or from the great failure'.[53] And in the following year, 1810, William himself died suddenly, leaving the whisper that he, too, *'put hand* to himself'.[54] James's son, William IV (1770–1840), who succeeded to his uncle's title but not his riches, thought of building a new McDowall mansion at Barr, just south of Lochwinnoch. But, apart from the appearance of some freestone earmarked as 'pillars for the front of his intended mansion',[55] nothing was done. Brief but brilliant, the McDowall dynasty was at an end.

Castle Semple changed hands around 1810, this time passing from the family's control to one John Harvey who came, ironically, from Grenada in the West Indies.[56] It survived in progressively decaying condition until the mansion house was razed in the 1960s. Walkinshaw had already gone forty years before.[57]

NOTES

1. A. J. Rowan, Bossom Lectures, 3: 'Ideal Villas as Projected and Built', *Journal of the Royal Society of Arts* 122, September 1974, p. 697.
2. Renfrew District Libraries, 728.81 Pam.Pc, 1912.
3. Ibid.
4. Ibid.
5. V. Fiddes and A. Rowan, *David Bryce, 1803–1876*, exhibition catalogue, University of Edinburgh, Edinburgh, 1976, p. 118.
6. *The New Statistical Account of Scotland*, vol. VII, Renfrew-Argyle, Blackwood, Edinburgh, 1845, p. 19.
7. Renfrew District Libraries, op. cit.
8. Ibid.

9. A. H. Millar, *The Castles and Mansions of Renfrewshire and Buteshire*, Glasgow, 1889, no. 55.

10. For the McDowall family, see G. Crawford (G. Robertson), *A General Description of the Shire of Renfrew* ..., Paisley, 1710 (1818); A. Crawfurd, 'The Pedigree of the McDowalls of Garthland in Galloway, and Castlesempill in Renfrewshire', *Cairn of Lochwinyoch matters*, holograph, Lochwinnoch, 1827–54, vol. XXIX, 1841; and W. Hector, *Selections from the Judicial Records of Renfrewshire*, Cook, Paisley, 1878.

11. This unusual name 'Day Hort' is sometimes given as 'Dayhort'. Contemporary documents do, however, prefer the former.

12. A. Rowan, *Designs for Castles and Country Villas by Robert and James Adam*, Phaidon, Oxford, 1985, p. 92. Note that Rowan, following A. T. Bolton, *The Architecture of Robert and James Adam*, Country Life, London, 1922, locates Walkinshaw at 'Barrhead, Renfrewshire', when in fact the house lies to the north of Paisley, not the south, at NS 462669.

13. For the Shawfield Mansion, see C. Campbell, *Vitruvius Britannicus or The British Architects* ..., London, 1717, vol. II, p. 3; G. L. M. Goodfellow, 'Colen Campbell's Shawfield Mansion in Glasgow', *Journal of the Society of Architectural Historians*, October 1964, vol. XXIII, no. 3; and H. M. Colvin, 'A Scottish Origin for English Palladianism', *Architectural History*, 1974, vol. XVII.

14. A. Crawfurd, *Cairn of Lochwinyoch Matters*, op. cit., vol. XIX, 1837, pp. 79–86.

15. Strathclyde Regional Archives, B10/15/6733.

16. W. Semple, *The History of the Town and Parish of Paisley*, Paisley, 1782, p. 149: 'He demolished the Old Castle of Sempill in the year 1735; and built an elegant large modern house, being 60' long and 45' broad, three stories high, having rustic corners, being pavilion roofed, and a platform covered with lead 36' long, and 24' broad above, with a large cupola in the middle, crowned with three globes, viz. every one perpendicular above another'.

It is possible that McDowall's architect was John Craig (died c. 1745), who from 1735 was 'town's wright' in Glasgow. I am grateful to Dr James Macaulay for drawing my attention to accounts for timbers paid by William McDowall to John Craig in 1736 (Scottish Record Office, GD237/13a).

17. Crawfurd, op. cit., vol. XXIX, 1841, p. 18.

18. Strathclyde Regional Archives, B10/15/6733.

19. Crawfurd, op. cit., vol. XIX, 1837, p. 85.

20. Ibid., vol. XI, pp. 43–53. See also J. Ainslie's map of Renfrewshire, 1796, which clearly shows the cross and square plan of the village.

21. J. Denholm, *The History of the City of Glasgow* ..., Glasgow, 1804, pp. 201–3, where it is recorded that James McDowall and Robert Adam were among those present at the laying of the foundation-stone for the Trades Hall on 9 September 1791, and pp. 196–201, where again it is recorded that the provost, James McDowall, laid the foundation-stone of the Royal Infirmary on 18 May 1792, though this time the presence of the Adam brothers at the ceremony is not clear.

22. Rowan, op. cit., p. 92.

23. The similarities in this rather unexpected comparison are further underlined by the fact that William McDowall reclaimed around 400

acres of land from Castle Semple Loch by canalisation carried out in 1773–4 (Crawfurd, op. cit., vol. XXIX, pp. 18–19).

24. A. Millar, op. cit., no. 55.
25. Ibid.
26. For a brief note on the buildings of the Castle Semple estate, see F. A. Walker, *The South Clyde Estuary*, RIAS/Scottish Academic Press, Edinburgh, 1986, pp. 69–70.
27. Rowan, op. cit., pp. 104–5.
28. Ibid., pp. 94–7.
29. A pencil sketch in Adam's most vigorous Castle Style manner (National Monuments Record, RED/30/2; Soane Museum, vol. 74) purports to be a proposal for the front elevation of Walkinshaw. This is surely wrongly catalogued, and I am grateful to Professor Alistair Rowan for disabusing me of the temptation to speculate on this confusing ascription.
30. National Monuments Record, RE/340, RED/30/1, 3–9, RE/341.
31. Rowan, Bossom Lectures, op. cit., pp. 697–8.
32. Ibid., pp. 695–7.
33. E. Kaufmann, *Architecture in the Age of Reason*, Dover, New York, 1955, pp. 6, 29, 46, 52, 57, 144, 152, 213.
34. Ibid., pp. 49–50, fig. 38.
35. Ibid., p. 50.
36. Ibid., p. 29, fig. 22.
37. Ibid., p. 182.
38. Ibid., p. 188.
39. Note that the squat porch shown in photographs of Walkinshaw House (e.g. NMRS, RE/340), although appropriately cubic, is ill-related to the lines of the house itself and must be a later – probably mid-nineteenth-century – addition.
40. See NMRS, RED/30/3. Note, however, that photographs show what appears to be a canted bay window appearing at ground floor on the west elevation. Nineteenth-century OS maps do not corroborate this satisfactorily but do show considerable extensions developed on the other shorter, i.e. northern, side of the triangular plan. They also show that Walkinshaw stood 'among some full grown wood' (Crawford (Robertson), op. cit., p. 343).
41. *Minute Book of the Board of Green Cloth, 1809–1820*, Maclehose, Glasgow, 1891, p. 101.
42. T. M. Devine, 'Glasgow Merchants in Colonial Trade, 1770–1815', Ph.D. dissertation, University of Strathclyde, Glasgow, 1971, p. 47.
43. T. C. Smout, *A History of the Scottish People, 1560–1830*, Collins, London, 1971, p. 384, refers to 'the depression of 1793'.
44. McDowall of Castle Semple and Garthland Papers in the Scottish Record Office contain numerous Heritable Bonds and Dispositions in Security raised in the last years of the eighteenth century and the early years of the nineteenth. See, for example, SRO GD237/139(1), £5,000 – from Thistle Bank; SRO GD237/150, £5,000 – from John Hay, Banker in Edinburgh; SRO GD237/162/1, £1,000 – from Sir William Forbes & Co., Bankers in Edinburgh.
45. Crawfurd, op. cit., vol. XXIX, p. 40: 'Mrs. Napier of Milliken thinks the estates in St. Kitts were sold at the great failure. But she is not sure.'
46. Ibid., p. 41.

47. McDowall Papers, SRO, GD237/134: 'Analysis of Bill for vesting the Estates in Scotland of William McDowall, James McDowall and Robert Houston Rae Esq. and of Alexander Houston & Co. in Trustees with powers to sell recover and collect the same and apply the proceeds towards discharging their debts to the crown and other creditors', 1806, noted that Charles Selkrig, an Edinburgh accountant, 'shall have the power to sell the Estates . . .'.

48. Crawfurd, op. cit., vol. XXIX, p. 23, dates the sale 'about 1807'.

49. McDowall Papers, SRO, GD237/139/4, Castle Semple Estate advertisement for sale at Royal Exchange Coffeehouse, Edinburgh, 13 December 1808; this suggests that the sale was somewhat later than Crawfurd's guess.

50. *Minute Book of the Broad of Green Cloth, 1809–1820*, op. cit., p. 66.

51. Strathclyde Regional Archives, T-MJ 366, Deeds of Day Hort McDowall of Walkinshaw, Trust Deed in Settlement, registered 29 July 1809, written at Walkinshaw 12 April 1806.

52. Crawfurd, op. cit., vol. XXIX.

53. Ibid., p. 48.

54. Ibid., p. 43.

55. Ibid., p. 53.

56. Ibid., p. 41.

57. M. Binney, et al., *Lost Houses of Scotland*, SAVE, London, 1980, states that Walkinshaw House was demolished in 1920, as does Renfrew District Libraries, op. cit., n. 2 above.

FIGURE 14.1　Etching of 'Adam's Hut' in the grounds of Eldin House, Lasswade, by John Clerk of Eldin.

14

Robert Adam and John Clerk of Eldin

From Primitive Hut to Temple of Religion[1]

RICHARD EMERSON

John Clerk of Eldin, 1728–1812, the seventh son of Sir John Clerk of Penicuik, has a walk-on part in the story of the Scottish Enlightenment. His collaboration with James Hutton, the geologist, for whose third volume of *The Theory of the Earth* he prepared the illustrations, might have brought him centre stage had this volume not remained unpublished on Hutton's death. Fame, however, came in Clerk's lifetime as the author of the *Discourse on Naval Tactics*, which he published in 1782. His tactical theories, developed with model ships and communicated to friends in 1780, were said by Admiral Rodney himself to have led to his naval victory over the French at the Battle of Saints in April 1782.[2] But if the Battle of Saints was won playing on the ponds of Eldin, Clerk's modern reputation has rested solely on his work as an etcher. This chapter looks for the first time at his works as an architect and re-examines his relationship with his brother-in-law Robert Adam.[3]

Like the Adam brothers, Clerk was wet-nursed on architecture, his father and theirs having collaborated on building the tiny baroque Mavisbank in the 1720s, and in 1753 he married their sister Susannah. Ten years later, Clerk acquired land at Eldin, Lasswade.[4] Though small, the estate was founded on the Pendrich coalfield, which now underpinned Clerk's finances, enabling him to give up his business as a clothier in Edinburgh and, from 1769, to embark upon a programme of improvements at Eldin. The Expenditure Book,[5] which provides most of the evidence for Clerk's life between 1769 and 1786, shows that Clerk turned to his brother-in-law John Adam for architectural advice at Eldin, recording a payment to him on 9 August 1769. This may have been in connection with work on the house, recorded in the early months of 1769, and on the new stables, built that November, which formed a courtyard at the rear of the house with the new kitchen and chaise-house, built in January 1770.

Less certain is the date and authorship of Adam's Hut, a summer-house in the garden,[6] which Clerk laid out at Eldin (see Figure 14.1). There is no record, by that name, of its construction in the Expenditure Book, which is minute in its details (3d for opium in December 1779), but it may be identifiable with the gardener's cottage, built in 1773 and thatched in August of that year.[7] A further clue to its date is provided by its appearance in an undated etched view by Clerk, which hitherto provided the only record of its existence.

Clerk's interest in etching began by his own account in 1772 or 1773 and was, according to his son, Lord Eldin, abandoned in 1779.[8] The plate of Adam's Hut shows evidence of Clerk's not very successful attempt at aquatint. Other plates with similar tone-biting include views of Dalhousie and Castle Loch Orr, both of which he included in a second publication of etchings in February 1774.[9] It seems likely, therefore, that the plate of Adam's Hut was worked between 1772/3 and 1774. The date of the building of Adam's Hut itself must therefore lie between 1769, when Clerk began building at Eldin, and 1774, the latest likely date of the etched view, with 1773 being the more probable.

Clerk named the hut after his brother-in-law, and this may reflect Robert's help in its design. Three drawings of the hut – indicating incidentally that the etching reverses the actual view – and a plan, all in Robert Adam's hand, survive among the unidentified drawings in the Soane Museum.[10] Interestingly, the name contains a pun, which must have reflected a family joke, on Adam, the first architect. A similar amused reference to the concept of the primitive hut as the origin of architecture had formed the basis for the arms adopted by Robert Adam for his seal on the eve of his departure for Rome in 1754.[11] Unlike Adam, whose seal's Antique wigwams are derived from Perrault, Clerk was not motivated by archaeological atavism. His Hut, with its big inglenook chimney and turf roof, has its roots in the vernacular building traditions of Lowland Scotland rather than in the Garden of Eden, and its cousins, scarcely less picturesque, people his topographical drawings and etchings.[12]

The relationship between the two men in the late 1760s and early 1770s – the period of Clerk's first work in architecture – remains difficult to define. Robert, James and the two unmarried sisters had set up house in London, while John continued to run the Scottish end of William Adam & Co., and contact may not have been close. However, following John Adam's retirement from architecture in 1772, Robert and James Adam were obliged to maintain the offices in both Edinburgh and London. Thereafter, Robert returned annually to Scotland, when he must have seen more of his sister and her husband, John Clerk. The Expenditure Book contains few references to contacts with the absent London brothers: the first, in April 1772, is a commission to William Adam junior to buy two pairs of silk stockings. Robert Adam's name does not appear until 1774, in connection with a series of financial transactions between Clerk and William Adam & Co. which continue until 1784, including a payment of £148 10s in 1781 by James Adam relating to the supply of coal pitch from Clerk's mines.

As Robert Adam's career brought him increasingly home, the period of closest artistic contact between the two men begins. In January 1780, Clerk visited the Adams in London while promoting the treatise on Naval Warfare. In November 1782, Robert Adam wrote to Clerk from London promising to send details of an aquatint process which Clerk might find useful for the plates of his Naval Tactics. However, the plates had already been engraved commercially by Andrew Bell in August 1782, and he replied that he already knew the process.[13] Clerk, with his mind now occupied with Naval man-oeuvres and schemes for raising the Royal George, was no longer interested in print-making, although he continued to sell prints, some of them shaded, in sets through the printseller Thomas Phillip and the booksellers Gordon and Murray, as late as January 1784.[14] In 1786, at the instigation of the Earl of Buchan, Clerk presented a volume of his etchings to George III. Eight of the plates were soft-ground etchings 'shaded with Indian ink upon a print outline', and Buchan, in his accompanying letter, explains that these were 'tinted by Mr Robert Adam'.

The background against which this surprising collaboration should be seen is to be found in two family collections of drawings which fill out the bare framework of dates and places that otherwise document their friendship over the next decade: an album of Clerk drawings at Penicuik, and the Adam family drawings at Blair Adam. We may start with a small drawing, tucked into the Penicuik album, and folded as if sent in a letter[15] (see Figure 14.2). It shows a picturesque cottage set in a landscape, with a view of Edinburgh from the south-west in the background. Above this is a small plan of the cottage, inscribed 'Plan for the coloured hut and tower', and on the same sheet are the elevation of an alternative design for a hut, with its plan, and two further variants, one accompanied by a diminutive plan. These are incontrovertibly design drawings by Clerk and, like the other contents of the album, have parallels in Robert Adam's work of the 1780s. In particular, a small picturesque drawing, signed by Adam and dated 1780,[16] which is a version of

FIGURE 14.2   Design for a 'Hut' attributed to John Clerk of Eldin.

FIGURE 14.3   View of Barony House by John Clerk of Eldin, Lasswade.

a design for a hut at Dalquharran for Adam's niece, Mrs Kennedy of Dunure,[17] shares with Clerk's design for a coloured hut its irregular plan, rustic tree-trunk porch, small thatched dormers, little outshots and a round tower with a conical roof at one end.

Like Adam's summer-house or hut for Dalquharran, Clerk's designs for a hut were produced for a member of the family, his nephew, James Clerk, in about 1781. No further design drawings survive, but the alternative scheme for a cruciform hut can be closely matched at Barony House, Lasswade (see Figure 14.3), formerly Lasswade Cottage, where James Clerk lived from 1782[18] and where his son, George, later 6th Baronet, was born in 1787. Happily, not only the building itself but also Clerk's watercolour view of it survives.[19]

Barony House is a child of the Romantic movement's brief flirtation with Lasswade. This was not the mésalliance that it now appears: the Esk valley, before coal and council houses destroyed it, was considered one of Scotland's most romantic and picturesque scenes, the river threading between the villas and seats of Melville, Polton, Mavisbank, Oxenfoord, Hawthornden and Dalkeith, while Lasswade attracted Walter Scott, who took Barony House from 1796 to 1804, the Wordsworths, who took tea from Scott in 1803, and De Quincy, who took Man's Bush Cottage from 1840 until his death in 1859. The house, Lasswade Cottage, as Clerk and Scott knew it, began as a small group of eighteenth-century thatched cottages in an L-plan, part of a scatter

FIGURE 14.4   Oil painting of Midfield House, Lasswade, by Alexander Carse, 1807.

of cottages along the steep valley slopes, 'the marked irregularity of the ground preventing the usual convenience of street arrangement',[20] onto which Clerk had added, at right angles, a big thatched, bow-ended drawing-room wing: Neo-Classical, New Town elegance within, Arcady, complete with pantomime cows, if Clerk's view is to be believed, without.

The association with Walter Scott ensured Lasswade Cottage's survival, when, in the 1860s or 1870s, the first additions were made: never was a sheep more ludicrously vested in wolf's clothing as cottage idyll was inflated to baronial Barony House. Further additions in 1914 were also baronial, and, to judge what Clerk's cottage looked like in the long summers of the early 1800s, when beau monde and bellettrist flocked to Lasswade, one has to look to Midfield Cottage across the valley. Long vanished, Midfield was, however, recorded in three views by Alexander Carse in 1807[21] (see Figure 14.4), together with its occupants and staff. So similar is Midfield to Lasswade Cottage, with its big thatched, bow-ended drawing-room grafted onto a cot-town of farm cottages, that it must also be by Clerk.

If coincidence found the uncles designing Huts in the same year, a more deliberate joint exercise was their trip to Ayrshire in 1788, where both men drew Robert Adam's Castle at Culzean, repeated in 1789, when they travelled together to Aberdeenshire and Banffshire, visiting Cullen House, where Adam was preparing a scheme for a vast new house for Lord Findlater. A view of Cullen House, by Adam, now at Blair Adam, is inscribed on the verso: 'No. 100 Cullen Castle, From an outline of Mr Clerk's'.[22]

On the same tour, they must have visited the ruined Boyne Castle, Banffshire, another Findlater property, of which a drawing appears in the Clerk volume at Penicuik. They clearly also visited Baron Gordon at Cluny Castle, Aberdeenshire, for whom Adam produced a scheme in 1790, working in London from Clerk's sketches of the existing tower house. Clerk's drawings survive,[23] and versions of them are among the Adam office drawings in the Soane Museum, together with a similar view of Fyvie Castle, Aberdeenshire.[24] There is no documented Adam involvement with Fyvie, but William Gordon is known to have been carrying out extensive building works there in 1793, for which the architect is not known, and the evidence of the Clerk drawing may point to Adam's having been consulted on the 1789 tour.

Evidently compiled at the end of the 1780s, the Penicuik album also includes a view of Oxenfoord Castle, built to the designs of 'R. & J. Adam', from 1780. Another version is at Blair Adam,[25] together with other views of the house by Robert Adam. A view of the Castle, after Adam, was engraved in 1787, which may provide a date for the group.[26] Taken with the evidence above, this suggests that at this date the two men may habitually have sketched together. That they shared a common subject-matter is emphasised by the presence in the same Clerk album of a series of views of imaginary castles in landscapes, which closely resemble Robert Adam's picturesque castle drawings of the 1780s.[27] A Clerk drawing at Penicuik, noted 'J. Clerk after R. Adams',[28] illustrates the two-way traffic of this relationship.

Clerk's architectural career and his relationship with Robert Adam ends with a puzzle. In 1786, the old church of Lasswade, whose ruins still remain, was in a dilapidated condition, and the Presbytery minutes record that tradesmen were asked to inspect the state of the church.[29] On 30 October 1786, the tradesmen reported that repairs would cost £358 14s 10d,

> but a doubt occurred both to the Heritors and the Presbytery whether it would be most expedient to execute said repairs or build a new church. The Presbytery agreed to delay further consideration of this affair till some further meeting. In the meantime they appointed Messrs Young and Brunton (mason and wright) to deliberate on a plan for the new church and to consult with the committee of the Heritors.

Unfortunately, at this point, the Presbytery clerk, who has hitherto taken a detailed interest in matters architectural and financial, is replaced by a man of fervent religious mind, obsessed by the charisma of the presbytery's most dominant member, the Reverend Alexander 'Jupiter' Carlyle, according to Sir Walter Scott 'the grandest demi-god I ever saw'. Carlyle's oratory seems to have driven all thought of buildings from the clerk's mind. The Heritors' records too are lost,[30] except for an extract from the minutes for 1791, sent to Henry Dundas of Melville. Happily, this extract covers the weeks leading up to the decision to build a new church.

The first meeting recorded is that of 27 January 1791, when the Heritors again ask tradesmen to report on the condition of the church, a repeat of the exercise carried out in 1786. On 24 February 1791, at a meeting which was attended by John Clerk, as a heritor, 'The meeting desired Mr Baxter,[31] one of their number to report what sum would be sufficient

1. to repair the church in its present state,
2. to repair it with additions sufficient to accommodate 1,200 persons and
3. to prepare a plan and estimate of a new church sufficient to accommodate persons.'

At the meeting of 17 March 1791, Mr Paton (the Minister) reported that 'he had received a letter from Mr Baxter acquainting him that the state of his health would not permit him to undertake the business referred to him by the Heritors at last meeting'. This meeting, too, was attended by Clerk, in company with a number of Heritors, and at the next meeting, a week later,

Mr Clerk of Eldin produced a plan and scheme of a new church for the inspection and examination of the Heritors particularly applicable to the division of the church and the seats among the several Heritors and which plan and scheme were approved in most respects by the present meeting and have returned the plan to Mr Clerk with their ideas for further improvement and as the plan and scheme is in much forward-ness, the present meeting wish for a full meeting of the Heritors or persons to represent them that a Division of the Church agreable to the Heritors may be made before the plan be extended.

On 5 April 1791, the full meeting of eleven Heritors and their representa-tives took place, among them were Sir James Clerk of Penicuik, Mr Clerk of Mavisbank and Clerk of Eldin, but not Lord Advocate Dundas, the Heritor with the third highest valuation after Sir James Clerk and Mrs Gibson of Bogghall. In the vote, the majority 'declared themselves for a new church', with Clerk of Eldin abstaining. 'The meeting adjourned till this day fortnight that Mr Gibson might have an opportunity of inspecting the present church with tradesmen named by himself and reporting to the meeting the opinion of the repairs necessary and the expense on that day.' Though it is not recorded, a decision must also have been taken to send to Dundas a copy of the minutes together with a rough sketch of Clerk's plan of the new church, drawn on the back of the minutes. This plan, noted with dimensions, shows the allocation of seats: '12 lofts for Heritors 12 feet deep at the front to be divided agreeable to valuable'. Thus, on a Greek-cross plan, the principal Heritors have lofts with a wide frontage, while those with a lesser valuation have lofts with proportionately narrower fronts. With this plan, the extract of the minutes closes.

The surviving minutes would appear to suggest that the design of the new church was Clerk's, and obviously the Greek-cross plan, which ingeniously reconciles the competing claims of the Heritors while reflecting their precedence, is his. The Church as built has a Greek-cross plan (see Figure 14.5) but, and this is where the puzzle begins, so did a scheme of 1791 by Robert Adam. Adam's scheme was not built, but was it done on spec or commissioned, and, if commissioned, by whom? Certainly, it is not the plan and scheme which Clerk put forward in March and April 1791, for which he was credited and from the vote on which he abstained. The puzzle is not made easier by the embarrassment of clues which chance has cast up. Robert Adam's diary for this period survives[32] and, although it contains no reference to Lasswade Church, it shows that he dined with the Clerks at Eldin on 22 May 1791, on his way from London to Edinburgh. It is likely that they discussed the building of the new church and Clerk's 'plan and scheme', presented to the Heritors only six weeks earlier.

If this was the first that Adam had heard of the proposal to rebuild the church, it would provide the earliest date possible for his design, which in adopting a Greek-cross plan seems to indicate a familiarity with Clerk's and the Heritors' preference but, interestingly, does not incorporate Clerk's proposed arrangement of twelve lofts, providing fifteen instead. There remains, however, the possibility that Adam already knew of the proposal to rebuild and of the preferred plan, either from one of the heritors, among whom was Mrs Calderwood Durham of Polton, for whom Adam had prepared a scheme of additions and alterations in 1788, which, since it was in part carried out,[33] may have been building at this date, or from the overseeing Presbytery, dominated, as we have seen, by Alexander Carlyle, one of Robert Adam's oldest friends and a frequent correspondent.

It is, on the face of it, unlikely that the absentee Heritor, Henry Dundas, should have commissioned Adam to prepare a scheme for Lasswade Church;[34] for his new house, then building at Melville, he had preferred Adam's younger rival, James Playfair, also a Scots architect working in London. Dundas's position is interesting: virtually the most powerful man in Scotland, he had been engaged in a feud with Clerk of Eldin, who thought he

FIGURE 14.5   View of Lasswade Church in 1956.

had been treated shabbily over his bid for the Secretaryship of the Annexed
Estates, which was in Dundas's gift. Dundas was also Clerk's landlord,
owning the South Park at Eldin, which Clerk held on a lease and upon which
he had planted the greater part of his garden. Clerk, in turn, owned the rights
to the coal in Melville Park, which he estimated was worth the employment of
twenty colliers for twenty years. Dundas would only sell Clerk the small
South Park at Eldin in exchange for Clerk's surrendering his coal rights
under Dundas's parkland at Melville. This Clerk thought a poor bargain and

angrily refused to comply.[35] There was therefore a background of bad feeling between the two men, and it is worth examining the possibility, at least, that Dundas put forward a rival scheme to Clerk's, drawn up by his own architect, James Playfair, and to which Robert Adam's scheme is a riposte, perhaps commissioned by Clerk.

Coincidentally, James Playfair's account book for this period also survives[36] and records a visit to Melville in January 1791 in connection with building work at the house. At this time, the Heritors were exercising themselves over the state of the church. In March of the same year, Playfair corresponded with Henry Dundas concerning Melville, while the Heritors, of whom Dundas was one, albeit absent, were calling for a plan and estimate for a new church. However, while the account book is particular in detailing time spent on preparing drawings for Melville, from May to October 1791, there is no mention of Lasswade Church, the 'Temple of Religion' whose foundation-stone was laid by Sir James Clerk in April 1792.[37] This rules out Playfair.

Certainly, the church, which was described as the 'New Church' in the Presbytery minutes of 21 August 1792, an interest in building having re-turned to the minute books with the arrival of a new clerk, and which was demolished in 1956, was an extraordinary and Frenchily sophisticated Neo-Classical building which shares with Adam only its plan. If this is by Clerk and we have only his thatched cottages to compare it with, he was certainly a major architect *manqué*.

By the time the foundation-stone of the new church was laid, Robert Adam was dead, and death was probably much in Clerk's mind as he instructed his last work in architecture, adapting the remains of the abandoned medieval church to form the burial aisle of the Clerks of Eldin, in which, in 1812, he was buried.

NOTES

1. I am grateful to James Holloway, National Galleries of Scotland, for drawing my attention to the Clerk of Penicuik Album at Penicuik and for providing me with copies of Carse's views of Midfield in 1976, when this chapter had its inception.
2. Obituary: *Gentleman's Magazine*, London, 1812, part 2, p. 197. See also SRO, GD18/5486/8/1, which quotes Rodney: 'This country is more obliged to your friend Mr Clerk than to any one other individual in it. To him and to him alone belongs the merit of my manoeuvre of cutting the enemy's line upon 12th Aprile'.
3. The relationship between Clerk and the Adam family up to 1760 is covered in John Fleming, *Robert Adam and his Circle*, London, 1955, while the question of who influenced whom is examined in A. A. Tait, *Robert Adam and John Clerk of Eldin*, Master Drawings vol. XVI, no. 1, 1978. This, however, is written without reference to Clerk's Expenditure Book for the years 1769–86 in the National Library of Scotland, MS

102, which, if used, might have led him to different conclusions. Tait's subsequent book *The Landscape Garden in Scotland 1735–1835*, Edinburgh, 1980, also covers some of the same ground as this chapter, but again comes to a different view.

4. Tait (1980, p. 117) dates the acquisition of Eldin to 1776, while the NSA vol. 1, Edinburgh and London, 1845, states that the estate was apparently a gift from his father 'at an early period of his life'. J. G. Bertram, *Clerk of Eldin, Etchings and Drawings*, Exhibition Catalogue, Edinburgh, 1978, gives 1763. A letter from Clerk to Peggie Adam of 4 September 1763 is addressed from Pendrich, GD18/5486/4/1, and Clerk clearly owned the Pendrich coalfield in 1768, GD18/1113; moreover, since expenditure at Eldin is detailed in Clerk's earliest surviving accounts in 1769, acquisition by the late 1760s is certain. The house is not named on Lawrie's map of 1763.

5. NLS MS 102.

6. The Expenditure Book records payments to Peter Alexander for 'making the garden' in 1769: NLS MS 102.

7. NLS MS 102.

8. *A Series of Etchings chiefly of Views in Scotland* by John Clerk of Eldin Esq., Printed For the Bannatyne Club, Edinburgh, 1855, p. xviii. Clerk ordered his first etching materials, copper and paper, in September 1772. Turpentine, wax and more copper followed in October, and more copper in January 1773; no further expenditure on such materials is noted thereafter, which confirms his early dissatisfaction with the medium: NLS MS 102.

9. The other prints were 'St. Andrews, Lieth [*sic*], Cambuskenneth, Colledge near Dumfries, and Ravensheugh'. His first publication of a set of thirty-six unspecified small etchings had been supplied to the Edinburgh printseller Thomas Phillip at the end of November 1773. The sale of prints through commercial printsellers suggests that Clerk did not see himself as an amateur 'Sunday artist' as he has been described: Tait, 1978, p. 53.

10. Clerk, 1855, p. xviii. The notes to the plates are Clerk's own. I would not have found these drawings had Robert Wolterstoff not kindly pointed me in the direction of the Soane. Vol. 2, pp. 141, 143 and 144 may be identified as drawings of, or designs for Adam's Hut.

11. I am grateful to Dr Iain Gordon Brown for drawing my attention to the seal in discussion. Since then, he has explored further some of the ideas in this chapter. Iain Gordon Brown, 'Gentlemen or architects? Adam heraldry and its implications', *Architectural Heritage* 4: *Robert Adam*, Edinburgh, 1994, pp. 82–92; and idem, 'Atavism and ideas of architectural progress in Robert Adam's Vitruvian Seal', *Georgian Group Journal*, 1994, pp. 70–3. If this building is in fact the gardener's house of 1773, the name would contain a parallel pun on Adam, the first Gardener.

12. For a discussion of the building-type most frequently drawn by Clerk, see Ray Marshall, *The Ingleneuk Hearth in Scottish Buildings: A Preliminary Survey*, Vernacular Buildings 8, Dundee, 1984. This building-type, which shares many characteristics with Adam's Hut, was disappearing in Clerk's lifetime: 'The cottages were formerly very mean; the walls (built of mud and stone) would have been unable to sustain the ponderous roof of clay and divot, had they not been very low and well

propt up with very clumsy buttresses of unhewn stone. The inside was still more exceptionable. The lumm, or chimney, of dismal aspect, erected against ye end wall, by its unaccountable width, took up a great deal of the hut ... An additional light to that of the chimney, from a slit or bole in the wall, made up the whole architecture of the building. At present cottages are constructed of good mason work, seven or eight feet high in the walls and neatly thatched with straw ... they are generally built ... several of them together in a row.' George Robertson, *General view of Agriculture in the County of Midlothian*, Edinburgh, 1793.

13. NLS MS 102; this undermines Tait's conclusion (1978, p. 54) that 'the plates of "Naval Tactics" ... the style ... and the way they were engraved all seems to have emanated from Adam'.

14. NLS MS 102: 'Two compleat copies of my prints with the coloured and shadded [shaded] ones in addition at 52/6 = 5–5, 25% to be discounted to them as doolers when sold 1.6.3'. Sets were also sold to individuals, namely Mr George Fairholme of Greenhill and Commissioner Wharton.

15. Partly illustrated in Tait, *The Landscape Garden in Scotland*, pp. 177 and 117–8, where it is suggested that this is a design for Adam's Hut, to which he also gives the name Eldin Cottage.

16. *Catalogue of British Architectural Drawings and Watercolours 1660–1960*, Sotheby's, Thursday, 25 June 1981, Lot 7, illustrated. Copy in NMRS.

17. This drawing is clearly a version of one of four summer-house designs for Dalquharran at Blair Adam, BA 88, 89, 420 and 656, three drawn by Robert Adam and one, BA 89, in an amateur hand, noted as being Mrs Kennedy's copy. The similarity between BA 88, illustrated in Tait (1980), plate 67, and Clerk's design for a 'coloured hut', is noted, op. cit., p. 117; however, there is confusion over dating: Tait, op. cit., p. 108, states that BA 88 and 89 are dated 1789, and elsewhere, Tait (1978), no. 55, BA 420 is dated c. 1790. None of the drawings is in fact dated. If they are dateable to 1780, rather than 1789–90, the proposals must in fact relate to Dalquharran old house, for which Adam prepared a scheme of alterations in 1781.

18. 'Capt. Clerk' appears in the window-tax returns for the parish of Lasswade for the first time in 1782. This is James Clerk, an officer in the East India Company, third son of the 4th Baronet: SRO, E.326.1 and GD/18/6185.

19. A framed pen-and-wash drawing, neither signed nor dated but evidently by Clerk of Eldin, used to hang at Barony House; it is now at Penicuik, with a copy in NMRS.

20. *Old Statistical Account*, vol. 10, pp. 277–88.

21. Illustrated Lindsay Errington, Alexander Carse, National Galleries of Scotland, 1987, figs 4 and 5 and plate 2.

22. Drawing at Blair Adam (BA 154), illustrated in *Drawings from Blair Adam*, National Gallery, Department of Prints and Drawings, Catalogue 1983, no. 31. See also A. A. Tait, *Robert Adam at Home, 1728–1978*, Exhibition Catalogue, Edinburgh, 1978, no. 15, where the drawing is wrongly attributed to Clerk. Another version of this drawing, signed by Robert Adam on the original mount, was sold at Christie's, 20 June 1978, and was purchased by the National Galleries of Scotland in 1991. Interestingly, these drawings show Cullen House with a picturesque Baronial roofline which it did not then boast; see the view of Cullen

House from the north, drawn by Clerk on the same trip, now in the Penicuik Album, with copies at NMRS and NGS. One must assume that the bartizans and gables which in these drawings enrich the plain, earlier eighteenth-century additions to Cullen, are the product of Clerk's rather than Adam's imagination.

23. Two anonymous pen-and-wash views among the Adam drawings in the Soane Museum, vol. 1, nos 112 and 113, which it is here suggested are by or after Clerk, are illustrated in H. G. Slade, 'Cluny Castle, Aberdeenshire', *Proceedings of the Society of Antiquaries of Scotland*, vol. 111, plate 47. Related drawings are in the National Gallery of Scotland, Department of Prints and Drawings, and yet another which appeared on the art market in 1989 is in the writer's possession. A more finished drawing in the NGS, clearly part of the same group, is the original for Robertson's engraved view, which appeared in the *Edinburgh Magazine* in August 1790, confirming the probable 1789 date of the group as a whole. The engraving is illustrated in Slade, op. cit., plate 48.

24. Soane Museum, vol. 2, no. 26. See T. Clifford, R. Emerson and J. Holloway, *Treasures of Fyvie*, Edinburgh, 1985, Exhibition Catalogue, Fig. 5, for an illustration of this drawing, and pp. 15–16, where Adam's possible involvement in the late eighteenth-century alterations at Fyvie is discussed.

25. BA 407, illustrated in Tait, *Robert Adam at Home*, 1978, no. 17, where it is attributed to Robert Adam.

26. William Angus, *The Seats of the Nobility and Gentry*, 1787, illustrated in Tait (1980), plate 73 and pp. 111–12.

27. James Holloway and Lindsay Errington, *The Discovery of Scotland*, Edinburgh, 1978, Exhibition Catalogue, plate vi and p. 63. See also Tait (1980), p. 116. The pencilled title 'Castle of Eudolpho' must have been added after the publication of Mrs Radcliffe's novel in 1794.

28. Not seen but noted by Tait, *The Landscape Garden in Scotland*, p. 116, n. 57.

29. Presbytery Records CH2/424/17. This follows a similar exercise in 1774, when George Paterson and William Robertson, Architects, provided a report on the condition of the church so that the Presbytery might consider alternative plans and estimates for extensive repairs or for a new church. Although the Presbytery accepted Mr Paterson's plan to cut off the three arches from the west end of the church and take in a space from the east, and to employ Messrs Paterson and Young for the work, it appears not to have proceeded: GD/164/Box 40/286 (NMRS, noted by Ierne Grant).

30. The Heritors' Records for Lasswade for 1769–96 were noted as lost in 1820; CH2/424/17, p. 316. The surviving extract is to be found at GD51/5/632.

31. For John Baxter junior (d. 1798) and his father John Baxter, who had been builder and executant architect of Penicuik House, see Howard Colvin, *A Biographical Dictionary of British Architects*, 1978. Baxter lived at Mayshade, Lasswade, a villa built by his father in 1753, and was a Heritor. In 1786, plans and estimates for a new Manse at Lasswade designed by John Baxter and to be built by Robert Burns were approved by the Presbytery.

32. GD18/4968, published as Margaret H. B. Sanderson, 'Robert Adam's

Last Visit to Scotland, 1791', *Architectural History*, vol. 25, 1982. It should be noted that the visits on 5 and 15 July to the 'Lord President' do not refer to Henry Dundas as there suggested, since the Lord President of the Court of Session in 1791 was Ilay Campbell, Lord Succoth, who had succeeded Henry Dundas in 1789.

33. Not in David King, *The Complete Works of Robert James Adam*, London, 1991; demolished, but photos of Adam drawings and house before demolition are in NMRS.

34. Adam's scheme is in the Soane Museum, vol. 33, nos 79–83. Titled a new design for Lasswade Church, it is signed 'Robt Adam Architect' and dated 1791.

35. GD18/5756 and GD18/5486. The coal rights were finally sold to Robert, Lord Melville, in 1810 by Clerk's son Johnnie, later Lord Eldin: GD51/11/115.

36. National Library of Scotland, Adv. MS 33.5.25.

37. The draft of his speech survives: GD18/4106. Payments for the building of the church were noted in the Roslin Accounts for 1792 and 1794 by Ierne Grant, GD164/Box 79/832/5, and payments to Alexander Penny-cook for the erection of the gallery in 1802–4, GD164/Box 79/832/14. Recorded in 1956 by Kitty Cruft for the Scottish National Buildings Record, it is not clear how much the church was altered in the nineteenth century. Described as a 'neat church with a spire' in Piggot's *Directory*, 1825–6, the *New Statistical Account* records, in 1843, that 'during the last few years it has undergone extensive repairs and alterations which effect the highest credit on the liberality, taste and good judgement of the Heritors'. The collapse in a storm in 1866 of the tower of the medieval church, which had until then acted as a belfry for the new church, led to David MacGibbon's providing working drawings and estimates for a new belfry in the following year, GD51/11/150.

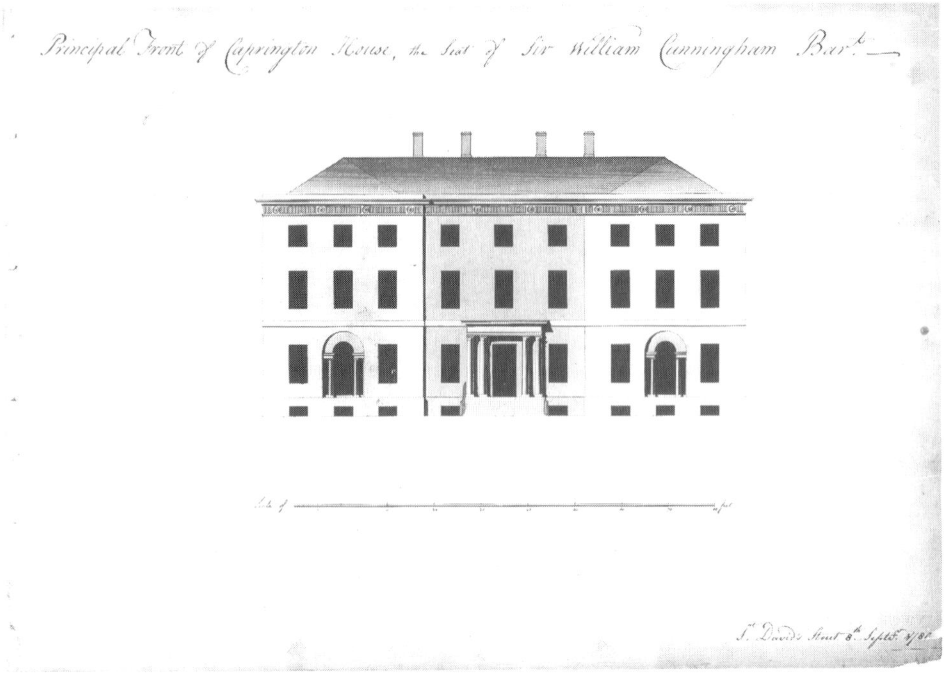

FIGURE 15.1   Design for the principal front of Caprington by David Henderson, 1780.

15

David (or John?) Henderson's Designs for Caprington Castle

IAN GOW

The recent discovery of a set of unexecuted designs[1] dated 1780 for classicising Caprington Castle (see Figures 15.1–3) allows a fresh insight into the artistic personality of David Henderson, who belongs to that band of apparently successful but still very obscure later eighteenth-century Scottish architects. The drawings were originally bound together between thick pink paper covers to form a presentation portfolio, and reflect well on their author's competence as a draughtsman. The two alternative elevations and five plans are spaciously laid out with broad margins, and the use of undiluted Indian ink for the windows gives them a clean-cut look. If this sophistication is borrowed, it says much for Henderson's taste and ambition that he should have modelled his style on Robert Adam. This is particularly noticeable in his treatment of the scale. Adam, in common with his father, William, had developed a technique whereby a design was presented to a future patron in the form of a trompe-l'oeil engraving which was possibly intended to flatter the client by anticipating that their house might feature in one of their published volumes devoted to distinguished architectural exemplars. Henderson's rounded hand with its curvaceous flourishes, however, lacks the discipline of the Adam office's copper-plate script, but it is through mimicking the address that these drawings can be pinned down to Henderson from the Edinburgh Street Directories.

At Caprington, Henderson was faced with the perennial problem of Scottish architecture which required the conversion of an ancient tower into a symmetrical country house. His solution by duplication offered little new to a long tradition established by Sir William Bruce, but the design is memorable on account of its highly inventive room shapes (see Figure 15.3). Henderson was sufficiently pleased with the oval bedchambers in the old tower to repeat the idea on two floors. If his handling of their entrances and placing of the windows lacks that skill through which Adam could easily and consistently maintain the internal symmetry of every room, they were commodious enough with their attached dressing-rooms, and workable. It is difficult not to feel, however, that the rather zany oval kitchen with its circular scullery and oven is a good idea stretched a little too far, but it is certainly evidence of a lively mind.

The elevations are of equal interest. The cheaper design (see Figure 15.1), with its elegantly-drawn fluted frieze and paterae, is a direct crib from Adam's Register House in Edinburgh, and this was a model that Henderson knew well because he was one of the contractors who built it. The alternative 'more Ornamented' (Fig. 15.2) elevation is individualistic in its almost Ledolcian severity and channelled rustication. It anticipates the façade of the Edinburgh Assembly Rooms which is firmly attributed to Henderson's son, John. The Caprington designs therefore raise the question of whether they are a joint effort.

John's brief career provides a further example of his father's ambition because, like Robert Adam, he had been sent to complete his architectural education in Rome. He has attracted the attention of later historians as a young man of promise through his quarrel while there with the young Soane over the patronage of the Earl-Bishop of Derry. Henderson junior is not listed in the Edinburgh Street Directories in his own right, although he was certainly active in the city during the early 1780s. It might be tempting to attribute the Caprington drawings to the younger man, were it not for the existence of a further set of designs dated 1767 by David Henderson which show the same distinctive rounded hand (see Figure 15.6).

The father's architectural career had developed from his initial experience as a practical mason, as Howard Colvin has shown.[2] The long explanations attached to the drawings for Mr Hunter's house show[3] that he was familiar with building techniques, and there is even a note of insistence in his concern for total architectural control over minor details. Henderson belonged to Sauchie, near Alloa, but a move to Edinburgh in the 1760s enabled him to take full advantage of the new opportunities that the capital then afforded. Mr Hunter's house was to be built in New Street, and this was an early experiment in urban innovation that paved the way to the New Town.

James Hunter was an influential patron to catch, and was to emerge as a leading figure through his partnership in Sir William Forbes's bank. The house design is distinguished by an arcaded portico at street level, and it bears the same channelled rustication as the 'more Ornamented' Caprington

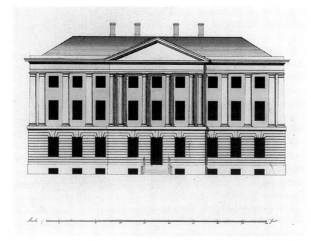

FIGURE 15.2   Design for the principal front of Caprington, 'more ornamented' by David
   Henderson, 1780.

drawing. The explanation reveals that the house was to be built to match Lord
Kames's adjoining house, and so it is possible that this had already been built
to Henderson's design. These drawings also show Henderson's concern with
presentation, and they are bound into a volume with marbled paper boards.
The designs are followed by a great many blank pages headed with the
following inscription:

> Instructions for the different undertakers to be employed and also an
> exact copy of their agreements to be inserted occasionally as the work
> advances.

Henderson won the competition in 1765 for the North Bridge that enabled
the Old Town of Edinburgh to expand, but he was unable to raise the
necessary security to execute his design. In 1768, he provided a plan for new
buildings for the College.[4] Civil engineering, however, continued to play a
prominent part in his activities at the Pease Bridge, Auldgirth Bridge and the
Borrowstounness Canal Company.

Of his executed buildings, Inverleith House of 1773 is relevant for the
Caprington design on account of the geometry of its plan. The villa has a
subtle elliptical bow containing the cantilevered stair on the entrance front,
and the curiosity of its pavilions being attached by oblique straight, rather
than concave, walls. Evidence from Robert Mylne's sketchbook and an
account by the Royal Commission on the Ancient and Historical Monuments
of Scotland reveals that curved ends have been eliminated from the Drawing-
Room and the first-floor Library through later vicissitudes.[5] The lugged

doorcase on the garden front recalls the attic windows of his design for
Mr Hunter's house. This fascination with unusual shapes makes his published proposals for a book of architecture particularly interesting and is
further evidence of his ambition.

If the list of works by Henderson senior is slowly lengthening, there
remains little documented work in his son's oeuvre. Some detail, however,
can be sketched in through an examination of the extensive surviving papers
of the Edinburgh Assembly Rooms,[6] his major work, and Kitty Cruft's recent
examination of the account book of Francis, 6th Earl of Wemyss, his most
important patron.[7] On 12 February 1782, he won the competition for the
Rooms. In both 1784 and 1785, he was paid £50 by the Earl 'for his trouble
for drawing plans for different buildings about Amisfield and for his advice'
and 'Mr John Henderson Architect in Edinr. for plans and advice in carrying
on my buildings at Amisfield'. It is possible that his success at the Assembly
Rooms, to which Lord Wemyss was a subscriber, brought him to the Earl's
notice, but it is interesting to see a payment to David Henderson in his
account book for 1783 for his assistance in arbitration with Charles Sanderson
at the Retreat, his house in Berwickshire. Sadly, no drawings by John
Henderson survive for either the Assembly Rooms or Amisfield.

If the Assembly Rooms brought John Henderson publicity among the
nobility and gentry, it was to prove a difficult task to execute. He had won the
competition with a plan for a restricted site near the Register Office. Although
it was effectively a public building in its scale, the Rooms were the
responsibility of a private body of subscribers. When the Register House site
fell through, the City offered a more prominent site in George Street, the
spine of Craig's New Town plan, bringing the necessity for a grand street
façade. During construction, the architect and the building committee made
the decision to turn the basement into a full storey. They argued that this
would give the possibility of a Supper Room beneath the Ballroom and that
the extra eight feet, added to the original nine, would make possible 'a more
elegant front to George Street'. Because of the need for an instant decision,
there was no possibility of assembling the subscribers to vote on this drastic
deviation, and they therefore found themselves saddled with an additional
charge of £500 as a *fait accompli*. Thus, almost from the outset, the building
was entangled in debts and recrimination. The architect's tragically early
death on 16 February 1786 left the work in confusion. His father was
appointed to continue the work, but the Assembly Rooms remained unfinished on his death about a year later.

The façade of the Rooms, which is so similar to the 'more Ornamented'
Caprington design, must therefore have been settled prior to the son's death.
They share other similarities. The Ladies and Gentlemen's Retiring Rooms in

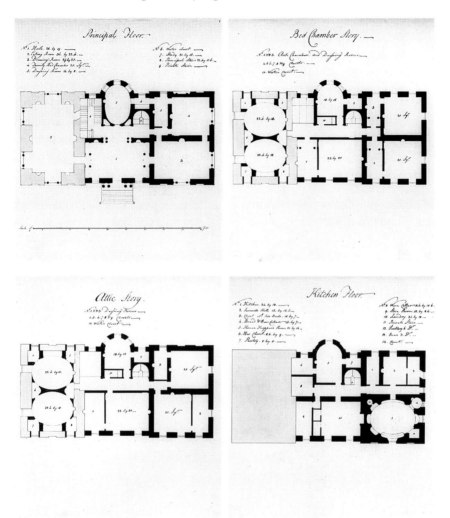

FIGURE 15.3 a–d   Designs for the principal floor, the bedchamber floor, the attic floor and
   the kitchen floor of Caprington by David Henderson, 1780.

the mezzanine storey of the Assembly Rooms were oval in form, and one has
survived. During David Henderson's supervision, there was a dispute with
the upholsterers because he had departed from his son's plan after orders for
the benches had been given. As a result, Young and Trotter found themselves
left with six sofas and a number of long seats and benches which not only did

not now fit the building but were unsaleable for any other purpose. To be so useless, there must have been a fairly substantial change in the room shapes.

Lord Wemyss's seat at Amisfield was of the utmost importance for Scottish architecture because it was designed in 1756 by Isaac Ware and thus represented the introduction of orthodox English Palladianism into Scotland. The Earl's deep interest in architecture, however, was accompanied by a dynamically restless patronage which makes it extremely difficult to unravel the individual responsibility of the galaxy of talented architects who succeeded each other both at Amisfield and subsequently at Gosford, a later enthusiasm. It is not clear if Ware's design was executed in its published form[8] (see Figure 15.4a), and he certainly does not seem to have supervised construction. It is therefore difficult to gauge the extent of Henderson's alterations from the scanty photographic record prepared hurriedly in 1925 when demolition was already under way.[9] The one interior photograph shows the same deep frieze of floral festoons in the 'Dining Room' as in the Ballroom of the Assembly Rooms, and Nisbet, the plasterer, was paid for work in both buildings. Henderson's drawing of the principal front of Amisfield was engraved for *Archaeologia Scotica*, vol. 1 (see Figure 15.4b), published in 1792; and the author on the article on Haddington, the Rev. Dr George Barclay of Middleton, recorded that 'that ingenious architect, Mr John Henderson, had adorned this essay with an elevation of the north front'. Comparison between this engraving and Ware's published design suggests that Henderson gave the house a more fashionable appearance by flattening or concealing Ware's hipped roofs behind a balustrade, excavating the basement and replacing the entrance steps with a magnificent carriage ramp. The surviving photographs show that Henderson's design was executed but that the engraving suppressed the florid Rococo tympanum carving. It is interesting to see channelled rustication on the front of the ramp.

Sadly, the engraved design for Amisfield has preserved no idiosyncrasies of draughtsmanship which would facilitate the attribution of any unidentified late eighteenth-century architectural drawings to John Henderson. He remains such a mysterious figure that any facts are welcome and, as an appropriate parting shot, he was made a member of the Royal Company of Archers on 11 May 1782, and displayed sufficient prowess to carry off two of the Company's trophies in 1783 and 1785.[10]

The new detailed knowledge of David Henderson's draughtsmanship, however, does permit a further attribution to his list of works. In The Royal Commission on the Ancient and Historical Monuments of Scotland's *Inventory of Peeblesshire*, 1967, an anonymous set of designs for the Whim was illustrated. As the name of this property suggests, its origins lie in a caprice of the Earl of Islay, later the 3rd Duke of Argyll who had purchased a tract

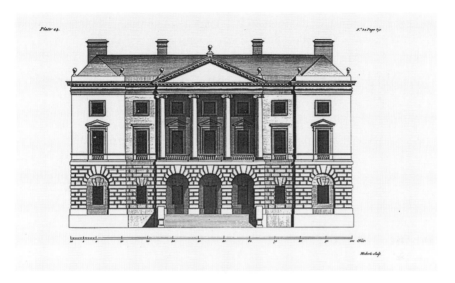

FIGURE 15.4 a–b   Isaac Ware's published design for Amisfield contrasted with John
Henderson's published design showing his alterations.

of peat-bog for an agricultural experiment. In 1730, he erected a modest
three-bay 'farm house' to which John Adam added a pavilion in 1759.
Recently, Mary Cosh, the authority on the Duke, has re-examined her
research files and concluded that the building was equipped with a pair of
single-storey pavilions, so that symmetry was maintained.

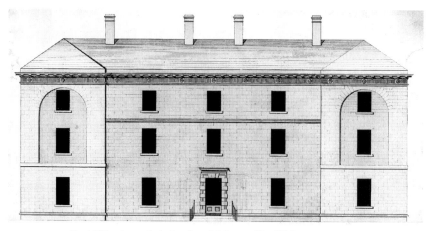

FIGURE 15.5   David Henderson's design for additions to The Whim, c. 1775.

In 1763, the estate was purchased by Sir James Montgomery of Stanhope. The designs for his additions[11] show how the five-bay building was built up with an additional storey to promote it to the dignity of a more conventional country house (see Figure 15.5). At the same time, an impressive stable block, fronting the offices on the entrance drive, was erected. The mode employed to effect these improvements is so similar to the Caprington designs with the fluted frieze and blind arcades that, taken along with the style of draughtsmanship, there can be no doubt that David Henderson was the architect. Additions to the inscriptions relating to Montgomery's promotion to Lord Chief Baron of the Exchequer in 1775 suggests that the design was in process of execution close to that date. Because the Caprington drawings reveal a greater degree of polish, the earlier date for the Whim designs seems likely. The careful delineation of the masonry courses on the elevation reflects the unusual way in which the building was extended. For the same reason, the plan did not, perhaps, give Henderson much scope for internal geometry, but it is very satisfactory to see a degree of ingenuity in the plan of the Kitchen with canted oval ovens recalling Caprington. As characteristic is the elaborate presentation of the preliminary and executed designs which are both bound in portfolios, one of which has the same pinky-mauve paper interleaved. The portfolios also contain a number of loose drawings. These include a design for a single-storeyed range of offices, and once again Henderson's fascination with shaped rooms is expressed in the plan with its oval cold bath and circular dairy, both of which have niches on the diagonals. A design for a lodge is inscribed 'Mr Henderson' on the back.

Finally, on purely visual grounds, Boquhan in Stirlingshire looks like a

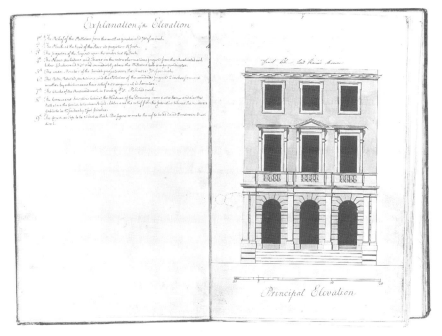

FIGURE 15.6   Bound volume of designs and specifications for Mr Hunter's house by David Henderson, 1767.

FIGURE 15.7   Photograph of Boquhan House, c. 1920, before demolition.

further Henderson commission in old photographs (see Figure 15.7) prior to its demolition and the erection of a modern house on the site. Happily, in the diary for 1790 written by its then owner, General John Fletcher Campbell, Henderson's name occurs. The diaries are by no means an easy read, but Mary Cosh's eagle eye picked up the name of Nisbet the plasterer. Henderson's name then meant little, but it seems interesting that Boquhan is a further instance of their collaboration:

> 'I passed Boquhan' says Nisbet the plasterer 'where I formerly wrought everything well' accosting me as I ranged about the new houses in George Square according to custom for weeks past after Walker's Lecture looking for a Lodging between 3 & 4 ... 'What, the fashion has changed since your Stucco of the Rooms there, the cornice and frieze are more weighty than what you now employ'. 'Sir it is true but we were under Mr Henderson's directions'.[12]

It would be very satisfactory if this group of Henderson designs were to trigger off a further string of attributions to an architect whose artistic personality is beginning to grow more distinct.

ACKNOWLEDGEMENTS

The author would particularly like to express his thanks to David MacLees, who brought the Caprington portfolio into NMRS for copying, and to Professor Alistair Rowan for his comments. He is also grateful to Robert Cuninghame Esq. of Caprington, James Hunter Blair and J. D. Lockie for their kind permission to examine and publish drawings in their care.

NOTES

1. A record drawing of Caprington dated 1829 shows that the Castle had been extended in Adam Castellated style by that date with a canted bay in the centre and the old tower duplicated on the right-hand side of the façade. The Castle was subsequently further embellished in troubadour style by Patrick Wilson. One of the lodges, however, was unusual, with the main gate supported by piers in the form of castellated archways with lodges connected by railings at the extremities, but this may have received machicolations from the same hand that extended the Castle before 1829. The National Monuments Record of Scotland holds photographic copies of these designs.
2. H. M. Colvin, *A Biographical Dictionary of British Architects, 1600–1840*, 1978.
3. NMRS holds photographic copies of these drawings.
4. Andrew Fraser, *The Building of Old College*, 1989, pp. 91–2.
5. The Scottish Record Office, Mylne Papers, SRO GD1/51/37, and The Royal Commission on the Ancient and Historical Monuments of Scotland, *Inventory of Edinburgh*, 1951.

6. The Scottish Record Office, GD1/377.
7. NMRS, Inventory of Private Collections no. 148, 1984.
8. Isaac Ware, *A Complete Body of Architecture*, 1768, plate 45.
9. The Royal Incorporation of Architects in Scotland Photographic Collection (deposited in NMRS): five photographs taken for George Sinclair, Architect, of Haddington during demolition in 1925.
10. James Balfour Paul, *The History of the Royal Company of Archers The Queen's Body-Guard in Scotland*, 1875.
11. The NMRS holds photographic copies of all of these designs for the Whim.
12. National Library of Scotland, Saltoun Papers MS 17762, Diary of General John Campbell Fletcher, 1790–1. See also I. G. Lindsay and Mary Cosh, *Inveraray and the Dukes of Argyll*, 1973, p. 365, n. 219(c).

FIGURE 16.1   Engraved view of Eglinton Castle as rebuilt to the designs of John Paterson, c. 1796, by R. Scott after J. McKinlay, from *The Scots Magazine*, 1 February, 1815.

16

'This Disagreeable Business'

John Paterson against the Earl of Eglinton

MARGARET H. B. SANDERSON

A few years after Robert Adam's death, his widowed sister, Mrs Mary Drysdale, packed off to London a box of drawings which she had rescued from the house of one of his clerks of works, Alexander Cairncross, in Edinburgh, where 'anybody that chused might break open the Box and take out any drawings they pleased'. She had long been suspicious, she remarked, of what 'that fellow Paterson' might be up to.[1]

John Paterson, Adam's clerk of works at the New College of Edinburgh and other sites between 1789 and 1791, appears from his correspondence with his chief to have been a reliable and resourceful assistant, who developed as keen an eye for the main chance as Adam himself. It was thanks to Paterson's making the most of influential contacts that the firm gained important late commissions in Edinburgh and Glasgow. However he may have acquired his ideas, Paterson assimilated the characteristic principles of the Adam style, becoming the main practitioner in the Adam Castle idiom in the early nineteenth century, with a flair for designing elegant interiors, particularly oval and circular rooms, reminiscent of his master. After a dispute with the Adams – he was perhaps inclined to overstep the limits of his subordinate role – he was replaced as clerk of works at the New College towards the end of 1791 while Robert Adam himself was on his last visit to Scotland.

The son of an experienced architect and builder, Paterson eventually established a considerable practice in Scotland and the north of England which lasted over forty years.[2] Yet, although he appears to have done

FIGURE 16.2   Vignette view of the seventeenth-century Eglinton Castle from John
Ainslie's volume of Estate Plans, c. 1790.

independent work in the north of Scotland before becoming Adam's manager
in 1789, and his work at Dundee Infirmary and the Glasgow Bridewell has
been dated 1794 and 1795 respectively, he apparently found the 1790s, after
his dismissal by the Adams, a difficult time.

Three bundles of legal papers in the muniments of the Earls of Eglinton,
deposited in the Scottish Record Office, throw some new light on the
circumstances surrounding his work at Eglinton Castle, Ayrshire, one of his
earlier and hitherto least-documented commissions.[3] In 1817, about thirteen
years after work was completed, Paterson sued the Earl for alleged outstanding fees for superintendence and for travelling expenses, amounting to over
£1,100. 'This disagreeable business', as the Earl called the dispute, dragged
on after his own death in 1819, going to arbitration in 1821. In 1829, only
three years before the architect's death, the arbiters found the Eglinton
Trustees liable to pay Paterson only £724 13s 1d.

The client, formerly Hugh Montgomerie of Coilsfield (1739–1819), had an
active military career behind him and three spells as MP for Ayrshire when in
1796 he succeeded his cousin as the 12th Earl of Eglinton. He inherited a
programme of improvement of the estates and policies begun by the 10th Earl
in mid-century. Vignettes in the beautiful estate plan-books drawn by the
land-surveyor John Ainslie around 1790 have preserved the appearance of the
outmoded castle, which the earls had long been hoping to modernise[4] (see
Figure 16.2). The ghost of the seventeenth-century building still lingers in
some of the drawings for a replacement prepared by John Baxter junior in
1775 (see Figure 16.3), which were not implemented although certain major
repairs may have been carried out.[5]

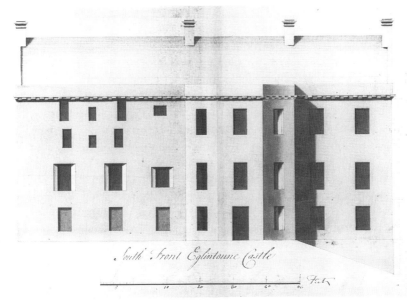

FIGURE 16.3   Unexecuted design for the South Front of Eglinton Castle by John Baxter, 1775.

One of the first things the 12th Earl did on succeeding was to ask his Edinburgh agent, Mr John Anderson, to find him a suitable architect to take on the work. On 23 November 1796, Anderson informed him that 'Paterson the Architect is in the North country but expected home every day, when I will send him West'. On 22 December, he followed this up with a second letter to the Earl:

> I have at length seen Paterson and find that he is busy compromising matters with his creditors so that he cannot undertake to set off sooner than this day se'night, but he promises to devote his whole time and attention to the business after he is once begun to it – I have agreed to this delay as I really believe that he is more capable for what you wish than any other person.

The Earl was in a hurry, however. On 23 December, before the agent's second letter had reached him, he sent a note to Anderson intimating that he had found an alternative to Paterson:

> I desired Laughlan to write to you that he has shown me a plan for our grand addition at Eglinton that I approve of much – I only want Russell [?the builder] now to look at it and consider it carefully. I imagine I will have no use for Paterson.

But if the Earl was in a hurry, Paterson was very anxious for the commission. Anderson's reference to creditors is significant of his circumstances. In fact, the agent later recalled that the architect 'was then in considerable difficulties ... In truth, he was then in real want'. When he heard that an alternative architect was in the offing, Paterson wrote to the agent on 26 December begging for the Earl's patience for a few more days, promising (rashly, as it turned out) 'to take the expenses of the journey on myself, and unless I have the happiness to make a design to please his Lordship I will never make a claim against him ... and in case I am so fortunate ... I am ready and will refer the amount of my payment to you and will be satisfied with your award'.

The Earl agreed to meet Paterson, who managed to travel west about the end of the year; neither party could subsequently remember the exact date. There is a clear impression that, while the agent had faith in the new architect's professional abilities, there were other things about him that he did not like. Anderson later recalled how he had sent Paterson out to Coilsfield, where the Earl was then living, at the same time warning his Lordship that,

> while I believed Mr Paterson to be very clever yet he was very apt to draw his employers into much more expensive undertakings than they ever intended. Paterson remained long with his Lordship and I believe succeeded in ingratiating himself into his Lordship's favour.

So well did client and architect agree that besides the work at Eglinton, begun in 1797, Paterson was asked to design a new house at Coilsfield, begun the following year.[6] The speed of the whole business concerning Eglinton may have been largely responsible for the later misunderstanding and distrust which clearly developed between client and architect. No written contract appears to have been drawn up and no formal written statement with regard to the latter's remuneration. Paterson admitted this later in the legal battle, although insisting that 'his agreement with the noble Defender was a *verbal* agreement', which among other things had fixed the rate for superintendence of the building at five per cent of the total cost. The estate factor insisted that Paterson's urgent letter of 26 December was 'the only writing of any kind on the subject of his remuneration'. The Earl and his agents continued to deny the existence of any mutual verbal agreement. The most the factor would ever admit was that 'I have certainly heard somewhere that Mr Paterson expected 5 p. cent on the total outlay for his troubles'. It is worth noting that Paterson once quoted his rate for superintendence as four per cent in connection with Abercairny and Taymouth.[7]

Paterson's plans for Eglinton Castle do not appear to have survived, or are hitherto untraced.[8] During the court case, the Earl's agent referred to plans having been drawn up soon after the first meeting between client and architect at the end of 1796. Others costing a total of £272 5s are said to have been paid for in 1798, 1800 and 1801. The intention appears to have been to create a Culzean-type reconstruction of the old Eglinton tower; 'grand addition' was how the Earl habitually described the project. The original idea of preserving the old tower was abandoned, however, and instead a new circular central tower was raised, to a height of 100 feet, with four corner towers seventy feet high (see Figure 16.1). Although all the wall-heads were provided with battlements in castle tradition, all windows were square-headed, although early engravings give conflicting impressions as to how narrow were those in the towers. The age of photography and the ruins themselves show these to have been narrow but by no means medieval-type 'slits'. The castle was provided with extensive 'offices', while the improved gardens were given elaborate hothouses and a gardener's house, all of which came within Paterson's responsibility.[9]

The legal process reveals something of the chronology of building operations. Paterson, who was employed between 1797 and 1804, claimed to have spent about six months of each year at the site, but this was disputed by local witnesses, who thought that four months a year was nearer the truth. In June 1798, James Murray, carpenter, arrived to begin work, possibly within the central tower. On 16 October 1799, the builder Adam Russell agreed to begin work on the east and west wings and the bridge over the River Lugton near the castle. The Irvine masons, Balfour and Wallace Balsillie, who were already subcontracted to work on the west wing, began raising the corner towers, the new stair and the kitchen court in January 1804. Between 1802 and 1808, work proceeded on the garden walls, hothouses and gardener's house. Other tradesmen included Robert Armstrong, plumber, and Robert Buchan, painter, from Edinburgh, William Douglas, plumber, and William Laing and Sons, smiths, from Glasgow, and the craftsman in marble Richard Westmacott of South Audley Street, London, who carved the chimneypieces, working from Paterson's drawings. He was also given plans of the rooms for which the marble chimneypieces were intended.

Between 1797 and 1803, Paterson was paid £1,272 for superintending the works. When in 1817, therefore, he raised an action for recovery of the unpaid balance of his superintendent's fees and travelling expenses, amounting to over £1,100, the Earl of Eglinton was astounded. It was strange, he remarked, that it had taken the architect so long to discover that 'this enormous sum' was outstanding, brushing aside the plea of 'delicacy of feeling' which Mr Paterson said had prevented him from asking for it sooner. In support of his claim, the pursuer drew up an account of those expenditures other than the main castle building, over which he had had control, on which he now claimed his five per cent superintendent's fee. In December 1818, the

Earl presented his 'Objections' to the articles of this account. The tone of this lengthy legal document, quoting as it does from letters between the Earl and his agents, betrays a distrust and even dislike between the parties which must have made personal relations very difficult during the building operations.[10]

The Earl's two main objections, presented on legal advice, were first, that the pursuer's account was 'wholly unvouched', that is, no tradesmen's receipted bills were produced to back it up, although Paterson was said to have had possession of these; and second, that no written contract or agreement could be produced in support of the architect's claim to remuneration of five per cent. The Earl insisted that in the absence of a contract he was entitled to believe that Paterson had been satisfied with the £1,272 he had already received.

He went on to question the amounts of certain tradesmen's bills cited in Paterson's account, having obtained statements from local workmen and others: £23,631 13s 10½d alleged to have been paid to the builders, joiners, plumbers and smiths; £1,200 for marble; £2,570 for painting. Besides, it was objected, some of the workmanship was not properly part of the building work over which the architect had personal supervision:

> The sumptuous marbles . . . can by no possible construction be included in a charge for Superintending the *building* of the Castle, And as to the charge of Commission by *an Architect* on . . . the *painting* the House, he might with equal propriety charge . . . on the sum expended at this time in furnishing of new the principal apartments in the Castle, for he had just as much to do with the one in his capacity of architect as the other.

Paterson's claim to have superintended the erection of the hothouses in the new garden was regarded as amounting almost to impertinence; one could not expect to charge the same for superintending 'a great Castle' as for the erection of hothouses. As for travelling expenses, where was the evidence for Mr Paterson's charge of 200 guineas? Lord Eglinton had always understood that, when an architect was paid a commission on the sum expended on building, the commission covered everything, the rule of 'the Trade' being that 'travelling expenses are in no case allowed unless there is a special agreement to that effect'. It was no answer to say that Mr Paterson constantly required to go back and forth; 'he was quite aware of the necessity before he undertook the business'. And, further objected the Earl, if Mr Paterson was thinking of referring the viability of his claim to practising architects for their opinion, 'such a remit at this distance of time is out of the question'.

The objections simply verbalised an unpleasant situation between the parties in which the Earl had already refused to pay bills to Russell the builder, complained that the architect's accounts were rendered in a manner which he could not understand, and had in other ways given his opinions on Mr Paterson's insufficiency. His dislike even provoked the Earl to insinuate that Paterson may have left his claim over all this time so that 'by change of servants' it would be difficult to find local witnesses to testify against him. In a letter to his agent in July 1818, now incorporated in the 'Objections', the Earl had declared: 'I had sufficient evidence to prove Mr Paterson's bad conduct which he was aware of'.

Some of this 'evidence', were it to be proved, would amount to very serious professional misconduct. In a pregnant turn of phrase, the Earl remarked that Paterson and Russell the builder 'understood one another thoroughly as to the building of the House'. He alleged that seasoned wood purchased by Anderson the Edinburgh agent and shipped to Irvine harbour

> was permitted to be carried off to other buildings in which Mr Russell was engaged, and unseasoned wood put into my House in its place ... The principal beam of the roof instead of being seasoned wood was taken from my own plantation and cut down the very day it was put up ... it shrunk and occasioned an immense quantity of iron to be introduced to support it, which I believe still remains to be seen ... Now, Mr Paterson was positively in the House at the time this took place. Besides I might mention many other Defects owing either to Carelessness or their understanding one another ...

Some of the doors, it was said, would scarcely open and were sunk from 'the partitions', and at that time (1818) people were employed in repairing them. A number of workmen corroborated the evidence about defects in the structure, including James Murray, the carpenter, who spoke of repairs to the roof and floor of the billiard room, saying that the roof was so bad that it would not surprise him were it to fall in, the wood being useless from the effects of dry rot. He said that the mason work had required annual repairs and that the saloon floor had had to be taken out completely and repaired. He corroborated the Earl's allegation that the seasoned wood specially purchased for the work had been taken away. Wallace Balsillie, the Irvine builder, swore that Paterson gave all orders to the workmen and contractors. Several contractors and suppliers, he said, were in the habit of paying Paterson a percentage for such preference: he knew for certain that this was so with Miller, marble-cutter in Glasgow, and Lang the locksmith, New Wynd, Glasgow. Balsillie, for good measure, remembered the Earl saying that 'that Paterson had led him into a great deal of expence which might have been saved'. Robert Strathdee, the factor, had the impression that Paterson had not often been at Eglinton but 'had one Sim under him in the Superintendence ... What he did at one time was often undone at another time'.

The following year, 1819, the Earl died with the business unfinished; the Trustees for the young 13th Earl, of later Tournament fame, took his place as defenders. In March 1820, the Lord Ordinary, in pronouncing Interlocutor in the case, called on Paterson to 'Condescend' on the facts which he alleged. In response, the architect made a case for his charging five per cent by citing an agreement for that rate made with the Earl as late as 1804 with regard to Coilsfield, the total expenditure on that house being calculated at £14,000 and the offices £3,400, and the fee for superintendence amounting to £870, plus £105 travelling expenses. This was to be paid in instalments: £500 on acceptance, £200 when the roof was on the house and offices, and £275 on completion of the work. Superintendence, it was agreed, was to include drawings for ornamental ceilings and marbles and the stationery needed to complete the measurement.[11] In support of his own claim for five per cent, he cited a case 'depending between the late Earl of Wemyss and the executors of Mr Robert Adam', relating to plans for Gosford. In a paper prepared for Lord Wemyss, it had been stated that Adam 'had a fix'd and determined rule by which he charged for all plans that he made in the course of his business. If he was merely to furnish plans and to take no charge of the buildings ... his charge was 1% of estimated value of the buildings ... If superintending he charged 5% on the price of the building.' This rate had been confirmed by Messrs Pepys, Cockerel, Smirke and Dance, to whom the matter had been referred, although they were of the opinion that it was difficult to apply in this case as the building had not been raised above the floor of the principal rooms at Adam's death.

In 1821, the case of Paterson v. the Eglinton Trustees was referred to arbiters, who referred the question of charge for superintendence to the architects Alexander Laing and Robert Reid. Laing, while modestly explaining that he had long 'in a considerable degree retired from business' and that 'Mr Reid must be a better judge', gave his opinion that payment might not be due on painting and the chimneypieces, as 'these articles are generally chosen and directed by the employers'. He considered that five per cent was a high charge for garden walls and glazier work (on the hothouses) 'of which there is a great quantity in these [Eglinton] gardens'. Robert Reid agreed that five per cent was 'generally' applicable to 'all the artificers' work of every description executed under [an architect's] direction and control', but that the amount would depend on his distance from the work; he should be paid both for the expense of travel and loss of time on other business.

The arbiters accepted Paterson's claim for five per cent. However, like the late Earl, they questioned the extent of his direction over some of the works listed in his claim. He replied in a set of 'Observations' in 1823.[12] If the late Earl's 'Objections' reveal *his* dissatisfaction with his architect, the latter's

'Observations' convey a distinct sense of *his* having been put upon by his late employer. His statements fill out the picture of his activities not only at Eglinton Castle but also on various other parts of the estate.

The arbiters had brushed aside his claim for having been asked to 'take soundings' in Ardrossan harbour, the Earl's great enterprise in the early years of the nineteenth century.[13] Paterson replied that his labours at Ardrossan had amounted to a good deal more than that:

> He has been able to lay his hand on a sketch of the original survey ...
> On this plan the Arbiters will find delineated the old Harbour of
> Saltcoats, the New Quay on the Ardrossan side of the Harbour with the
> line of division between Lord Eglinton's property and that of Mr Reid
> Cunningham. There is likewise a considerable part of the Town of
> Saltcoats laid down, ...

Reid Cunningham objected to the Earl's claiming part of the shore dues from vessels using the existing entry to the harbour, which necessitated a new survey by Paterson, done 'with great labour', in which a new entry was found 'near what are called "the old salt pans", with 10 feet of water close to the shore'. When the Earl saw this second survey, all idea of a harbour at Saltcoats had been abandoned. There followed

> a re-survey and frequent observations particularly in stormy weather,
> that the operations of the water might be better attended to ...
> The present [Ardrossan] harbour forming a natural breakwater, the
> Observer made a finished drawing of Docks, with the design for the
> town, – all of which were submitted by his Lordship to the late Mr
> Rennie, Engineer, who was pleased to approve of the whole.

With regard to the vexed question of travelling expenses, 'the Arbiters will easily believe it is now impossible for the Observer to produce vouchers of actual outlay by *Tavern bills etc*'. The late Mr Anderson, the agent, had agreed to pay him £30 per annum, although that sum hardly covered his expenses.

Other 'Observations' put on record various tasks for Lord Eglinton, for which Paterson's plans have not survived and which in some cases were unexecuted; it seems safe to assume that these plans would have been dated between 1797 and 1804.[14]

1. Plan of a spire for Sourlie Mains farm: 'erected with timber under the Observer's own directions to try the effect, before the expence of Stone was entered into'.
2. Plans for alterations to the house of the late Mrs Mason in Eaglesham village, for its conversion to an inn. This work was completed.

3. Plan and superintendence of an Ice House at Eglinton, built under Paterson's direction.

4. Plan of a Stone Bridge over the River Lugton behind the Castle.

5. Plans for a castellated tower proposed to be built on Castlehill, Ardrossan. According to Paterson, Lord Eglinton passed these plans on to Lord Blaney.

6. Plans for a new manse at Eaglesham, in connection with which Paterson travelled from Edinburgh to meet with the local Presbytery and Mr Strathdee, the factor.

7. A survey of the village of Dreghorn, near Irvine, with plans for a proposed new crescent, squares and market place (those for the market on three separate sheets). These plans occasioned 'many meetings' at Dreghorn with Lord Eglinton and his factor; they were not implemented.

8. Drawings in connection with repairs to the Eglinton burial vault and the Earl's seat in Kilwinning church; this was accompanied by a report on the 'insufficiency of the works before the repairs were taken out of the hands of the contractors'.

9. Drawings of farm offices at Eglinton, 'and lining out the foundations in a field west of the Stable offices'.

The architect concluded forcefully:

> Mr Strathdee as well as Messrs McEwing and Ferrier can give the Arbiters very correct ideas of the vexatious trouble given Mr Paterson by his Lordship in the Conducting of his works at Eglinton by sending for Mr Paterson for the merest trifle to the prejudice of his other employments as if Mr Paterson had been rather a resident Inspector, as Architect of the building ... not confined to his own profession ... but employed in other Works – such as lining out pieces of made water, leveling the Banks, assisting him in forming the general lines of his approaches through the Parks – Opening up his close clumps of trees into open grove – and in short in everything he found his advantage in, particularly in the line of the Canal, which Mr Paterson proved the practicability of, before Mr Rennie was called as Engineer.

In the Arbiters' reply to this outburst, a reply which included evidence taken from workmen, the only additional facts about Paterson's work are contained in Strathdee's recollection that he had heard the Earl speak to the architect 'about a Temple or Tea Room at the end of the Walk leading to Kilwinning', when the Earl asked for a plan.[15] In 1826, the Arbiters finally referred the whole matter to an oversman. In 1829, only three years before his death, Paterson's claim to his five per cent was acknowledged, but doubts about individual articles in his account reduced the Trustees' liability to just over £700.

The new Eglinton Castle generally received rather brief descriptions from early nineteenth-century travellers.[16] By the time Millar came to publish his *Castles and Mansions of Ayrshire* in 1885, he was not certain of the identity of the architect: 'there is a tradition that the name of the architect was Paterson'. Perhaps the problems surrounding the building of the Castle had been forgotten.

A nineteenth-century traveller in the north of England, whose journal has survived, wrote glowingly of a visit to Brancepeth Castle, Durham, which in 1818–19 had been given the grand addition of a new tower by John Paterson for its owner Matthew Russell.[17] The visit revived old memories for the traveller of 'John Patterson, a Scotch Architect, an old family friend of ours whom my Father took out of the Abbey of Holy-Rood, introduced to Lord Eglinton and others and so he got into Noble practice and realised a fortune'.

The writer went on to remark:

> How often when I used to get a snug dinner from the old Gentleman in his elegant retreat at Greenhill, and in his flat in Buccleugh Place in 1830: 1: 4:[18] have I heard him recount his doings about this structure [Brancepeth] which was the Magnum Opus of his Career!

Paterson had rehearsed, characteristically, how the Russell family had asked him to suggest a plan for the Castle's restoration, only to be 'astonished' nine months later when he returned with an elaborate series of working plans for every part of the structure. The 'delighted' client had agreed at once to his terms: '£500 per annum for three quarters of his time, to which was added the run of a very hospitable house'.

> Whilst cosily discussing his undeniable old Port or delicious claret, and hearing him prose about the jolly doings of Mr Russell and him, I had no idea of ever seeing this Alhambra of fancy, but now, it had all the greater attractions for me from these recollections.

The picture of John Paterson, garrulous to the end, is a lively one; better to remember the successes than an occasional 'disagreeable' episode. Yet, the 12th Earl of Eglinton had been one of his early patrons on the road to success. The diarist's reference to Paterson's early introduction to the Earl suggests that they had met before Anderson brought Paterson to Ayrshire to design the new Castle. Eglinton, sadly, was broken up in the twentieth century, the contents sold in 1925 and the building thereafter unroofed and demolished. Although today its surviving corner tower forms the romantic focal point

FIGURE 16.4   Eglinton Castle from the air after demolition, 1984.

of a country park (see Figure 16.4), no evidence of Mr Paterson's alleged 'insufficiency' remains.

NOTES

1. Clerk of Penicuik Muniments (SRO): GD18/5549/21.
2. H. Colvin, *Biographical Dictionary of British Architects*, 1978, pp. 623–4.
3. Eglinton Muniments (SRO): GD/3, Additional, Paterson papers, Bundles 1–3. I am most grateful to the Earl of Eglinton and Winton who some years ago gave me permission to examine documents in his family muniments in preparing articles of local and general historical interest.
4. Register House Plans series (SRO): RHP 3.
5. Royal Commission on the Ancient and Historical Monuments of Scotland; National Monuments Record of Scotland: AYD/69/3; 39/8; 39/9; 39/6/CN. Ayr Sheriff Court records (SRO), Register of Improvements to Entailed Estates: SC/6/72/1.
6. Colvin, 1978, p. 624; Coilsfield was demolished in 1971.
7. Ibid., pp. 623–4.
8. So far I have checked only the plans collections of the Scottish Record Office and the National Monuments Record of Scotland for surviving Eglinton castle plans of the Paterson period.
9. Documentation on Eglinton gardens during Paterson's superintendence will be found in GD3 Paterson papers, Bundle 2, no. 15. In Bundle 1,

no. 7, it was claimed that the gardener's house, which had cost almost £1,000 to build, was uninhabitable in 1806.

10. 'Objections' by the Earl: GD3 Paterson papers, Bundle 1, no. 5.

11. The Coilsfield agreement appears to have been restrospective, as the house was begun in 1798. Documentation on the agreement is in GD3 Paterson papers, Bundle 1, no. 7.

12. 'Observations' by Paterson: GD3 Paterson papers, Bundle 2, no. 9.

13. Ardrossan Harbour was founded in 1806. Grand designs for the adjacent town, including a canal linking the harbour to Glasgow, which involved the services of Rennie and Telford, ran out of funds by 1815 when work came to a standstill. Operations were resumed in 1833 and completed on a reduced scale. Documentation on the expenditure on the harbour will be found in Eglinton Muniments: GD3, Section 4, industrial and commercial papers. Information relates more to the operation of the harbour than building.

14. There is no trace of any of these plans in the Register House Plans series in the Scottish Record Office.

15. GD3 Paterson papers, Bundle 2, no. 14.

16. J. C. Nattes, *Scotia Depicta*, 1804; Frances H. Groome, *Ordnance Gazeteer of Scotland*, vol. 3 (1883), 554; A. H. Millar, *Castles and Mansions of Ayrshire*, 1885.

17. I am grateful to Ian Gow of the National Monuments Record of Scotland for drawing my attention to this source.

18. Paterson died in 1832.

'The New Square Style'

Robert Smirke's Scottish Houses

J. MORDAUNT CROOK

In May 1818, Joseph Farington noted in his diary:

> Robert Smirke ... spoke of his excursions to Scotland and of the time they took him as being inconvenient. Every time he goes he refuses offers of commissions, but he has now many works in hand in that country: viz. for the Marquis of Queensbury, Lord Blantyre, Lord Weymss, Mr. Balfour, Mr. James Drummond ... and others.[1]

Smirke was certainly busy. For Queensbury, he had just completed Kinmount; for Blantyre he was already planning Erskine; for Wemyss he was working on a scheme to Neo-Classicise Gosford; for Balfour he was rebuilding Whittinghame; and for Drummond he was romanticising Strathallan. Was he also still dreaming of transmogrifying Broomhall? Presumably not. But in September 1815 the same diarist did notice that Smirke had been busy in 'the neighbourhood of Kelso',[2] no doubt extending Newton Don. In June 1816, the architect was again observed returning from Scotland, this time after a month's absence, having covered 1,100 miles.[3] The new County Buildings at Perth were clearly proving a taxing operation. And that key commission had triggered two more in its immediate vicinity: Kinfauns and Cultoquhey. Ten commissions in twenty years – and all this just a sideshow to the biggest architectural practice in London. No wonder Farington noted in November 1815 that young Smirke – newly appointed, with Nash and Soane, Attached Architect to the Office of Works – looked 'ill, worn and out of condition'.[4]

Apart from that pipe-dream project for Lord Elgin, this group of Scottish commissions grew out of a network of patronage built up by the Smirke family among Tory politicians and landowners during the period of the Napoleonic War. James Drummond was Tory MP for Perthshire before becoming 8th Viscount Strathallan: he was one of the twenty-two 'stalwarts' who voted in the House of Lords against even the third reading of the Great Reform Bill. The laird of Kinfauns, Francis, 14th Lord Gray (1765–1842) was a leading Tory Representative Peer. Both he and Drummond sat on the committee which in 1814 chose Smirke as architect of Perth's new County Buildings.[5] Anthony Maxtone of Cultoquhey was their close neighbour. Blantyre – distantly related to Gray – was also a Representative Peer, albeit briefly, between bouts of military service. Another professional Tory – MP this time for Roxburghshire – was Sir Alexander Don, Baronet (1799–1826), the very 'model of a cavalier'[6] and a long-standing confidant of Sir Walter Scott.[7] His property at Newton Don eventually passed into the hands of the Balfour family, for whom Smirke had already rebuilt Whittinghame. That estate, in turn, had ancient links with the families of Douglas and Charteris: we shake the genealogical kaleidoscope, and Smirke emerges as architect to Lord Queensbury at Kinmount and Lord Wemyss at Gosford.[8] Whittinghame was built on a fortune made in India; so, before the money ran low, was Cultoquhey. The fortunes of Broomhall and Gosford rose – and fell – with the prosperity of coal. But in the final analysis, the building of all these houses in the euphoric years after Waterloo reflects, to a greater or lesser degree, the protected prosperity of land.

Smirke's designs for Broomhall[9] and Gosford[10] – Doric frontispieces to houses by Harrison and Adam – remain hypotheses, preserved only as presentation perspectives. Cultoquhey, near Crieff (1822–5), is not an important house: its vestigial Tudor detailing betrays the fact that here was a client who had already lost most of his fortune.[11] Newton Don, Berwickshire (1813–18), is in some ways an unsatisfactory composition: Robert Adam's unfinished segmental bays are hardly enhanced by Smirke's uncompromising fenestration.[12] Its strength is its garden, wooded and well-watered, stretching down to the banks of the Eden.[13] That leaves five: a clever piece of castellation (Strathallan); a mixed Tudor mansion (Erskine); two Neo-Classical seats of Greco-cubic formation (Kinmount and Whittinghame); and a Picturesque castle (Kinfauns) in a setting which approaches the sublime.

To the old house at Strathallan, Smirke added, in 1817–18, a symmetrical frontispiece with a deep *porte-cochère*, battlements and corner turrets (see Figure 17.1). At the same time, he clothed both lateral fronts with a varied medley of battlements, turrets and Gothic windows. Today, pleasantly weathered and creeper-covered, the castle's riverside aspect compensates for its meagre mouldings, even for its awkwardness of form. It is still – in the

FIGURE 17.1   Strathallan Castle, designed by Sir Robert Smirke, photo c. 1900.

language of the day – a 'fine mixed-Baronial castle'; and it still looks out over 'a veritable arborous sea'.[14] Inside, Smirke added veined marble chimneypieces, ribbed ceilings and arcaded panelling. The plain staircase follows the four sides of the staircase hall of the old house.

Erskine House, Renfrewshire (1818–28; see Figure 17.2) has survived less happily. Built of locally quarried stone on the site of a medieval castle, it still overlooks the Clyde; but its ambience is much changed. 'The prevailing style', it was noted, is 'that known as Tudor'.[15] 'Mixed Gothic' would be equally apt: Jacobean gables and pinnacles; windows pointed or square labelled; and a pierced balustrade with no clear historical ancestry. It was a style that Smirke developed later on at Sir Robert Peel's house, Drayton Manor, Staffordshire (1831–5). At Erskine, the plan assumes a solid 'E' formation, entered axially by a large *porte-cochère* and vestibule leading directly into a gallery decorated with moulded ribs rising from the floor to form a vaulted ceiling. 'The splendid irregularity of the style,' it was claimed, 'has been seldom displayed, in modern times, to greater advantage ... and particularly when seen from the water its effect is rich and striking ... The vestibule, hall and gallery open from one into the other with folding doors; and the whole of their extent can be seen at once from the entrance, presenting a splendid perspective of 196ft.'[16] Alas, building had scarcely been completed when Blantyre was slain in the Brussels insurrection of 1830. Since then, proximity to a busy ferry, and long use as a hospital, has taken its toll of Erskine House.

Kinmount, Dumfriesshire (1812) and Whittinghame, East Lothian (1817–19) are architecturally more interesting. Both belong – along with two English houses, Eden Hall, Cumberland (1821; demolished 1934) and Normanby

FIGURE 17.2   Erskine House, from A. H. Millar's *Castles and Mansions of Renfrewshire and Buteshire*, 1889.

Park, Lincolnshire (1821) – to a distinctive subgroup: a Greco-cubic quartet, designed according to Smirke's own version of Neo-Classical theory. That theory justifies a brief digression.

What Smirke most admired in Greek architecture was its economy of form, its rationality, its 'primal simplicity'. 'An excess of ornament', he believed, 'is in all cases a symptom of a vulgar or degenerate taste'. As he saw it, all classicism since the Greeks had been degenerate: Roman had corrupted Greek, and Renaissance had corrupted Roman. Palladio's scholarship had merely resulted in a sculptural, '*basso-relievo* style'; and the eighteenth century's rediscovery of Greece held out some promise of reform only if it guaranteed a new rationality of design, a compositional revolution based on Laugier's reductive principle of 'apparent utility'. Every member, every detail, must echo its primitive function. For instance, 'an architrave ... when broken ... is no longer an architrave ... [and] the well instructed eye ... will not tolerate an affectation of *infirmity*'. Any portico should 'appear to be either actually useful or not evidently otherwise': hence the symbolic utility of a columned *porte-cochère*. Balustrading, he considered, was but 'a vulgar expedient', useful only for prowling cats; a niche was just 'a monstrous conceit'; and rustication 'an old and incorrigible impostor'. The use of all such Renaissance 'frippery', Smirke concluded, involved 'something approaching to moral turpitude'.[17]

The result of such thinking was a method of composition applicable to Grecian or Gothic, but particularly appropriate to the economy and austerity of the Greek Revival. Its technique involved the elimination of adventitious ornament and a formal reliance on geometrical units. C. R. Cockerell

FIGURE 17.3   Kinmount House after alterations to the skyline c. 1897.

despised this rejection of Renaissance apparatus, and dismissed Smirke's fondness for layered, overlapping planes as thoroughly 'vicious'.[18] Pugin christened it 'the New Square style'.[19] But Smirke's calculated understatement, his reductive logic and his cool rectangularity merit more than a second look. As an approach to composition, of course, it was by no means unique: its ancestry is French; its adoption widespread in Neo-Classical Europe. Farington noted, for example, Dance's comment that James Wyatt's houses looked like 'mere blocks of stone'.[20] But in Smirke's hands, Neo-Classical reticence was carried to dogmatic lengths. Here indeed, in Cockerell's phrase, is 'the severity and . . . squareness peculiar to the Greek'.[21]

Kinmount is a good example. Its composition comprises a series of cubes, rising in pyramidal mass. Like Normanby and Eden Hall, it has a blocky, broken silhouette. But at Kinmount, this device is complicated by the addition of a central tower and massive *porte-cochère*. 'A degree of boldness and originality', Neale observed, 'is . . . exhibited in the design of the exterior . . . The elevation is modern . . . but when viewed in some points, it has the aspect and solidity of an ancient castle, towering above a most luxuriant wood'.[22] Indeed it does; and the effect is achieved with extraordinary economy of means. The balanced masses of grey sandstone are pierced by windows bare of ornament except for an occasional overarch. Inside, the ground floor rooms are arranged symmetrically around a central hall which rises the full height of the tower, past gilded balcony and coffered arch, to a shallow glazed dome. The single-return staircase, also top-lit, is situated to the side of the hall. Later additions – superfluous balustrades and a whole battery of urns (c. 1897)[23] (see

FIGURE 17.4   Smirke's perspective sketch for the entrance front of Whittinghame, 1817.

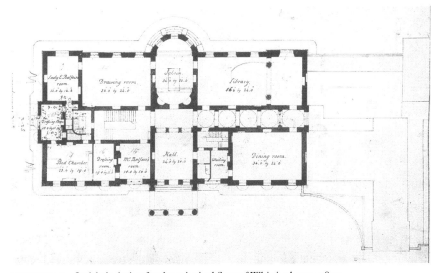

FIGURE 17.5   Smirke's design for the principal floor of Whittinghame, 1817.

Figure 17.3) – have spoilt the elemental qualities of the composition. Even so, Kinmount still embodies Smirke's conception of Picturesque Classicism.

At Kinmount, young William Burn had been employed as Clerk of Works.[24] At Whittinghame, he again had a role to play, but this time as an agent of stylistic change. Having inherited a fortune made in India by his father, James Balfour of Balbirnie bought Whittinghame from the Hays in 1817. In rebuilding the house and improving the estate, 'he spent and circulated in one year more money ... than many do in ten'.[25] Smirke's original scheme[26] (see Figures 17.4 and 17.5) – completed in 1819 – expands his favourite axial formula. The main hall, entered from a *porte-cochère* of four

Doric columns, meets at right angles a saucer-domed corridor which neatly
bisects the house and provides access both to the main reception rooms along
the garden front and to the staircase – laterally-placed, single-return-flight,
vertiginously steep. These rooms are 'square' indeed: as chaste and rectilinear
as the exterior.

Lacking the vertical thrust of Kinmount's pyramidal form, Whittinghame's
external arrangement of complementary cubes seems emphatically, even
ponderously horizontal. But the predominant lines of the central block and
terminal bays – three- and two-storey respectively – are boldly balanced by
the chunky blocking of both side elevations and the garden front's segmental
bow. Understated it may be; boring it is not. Solid, grave and uncomprom-
isingly severe, Whittinghame takes a style better suited, perhaps, to public
building and coldly translates it into a stern domestic idiom. Too coldly
perhaps, and too stern: within less than a decade, Burn had been called back
to soften Smirke's austerity, adding balustrades to the elevations and aggrand-
ising the western wing into a second library and Doric service pavilion (1827).[27]
Neo-Classical dogma was beginning to crumble. In 1871, the garden setting
was Italianised with steps and terracing. And in 1899–1902, Smirke's purist
conception was compromised still further. Prime Minister Balfour turned the
porte-cochère into a vestibule, replaced glazing-bars with plate glass, and
dressed up study and dining-room with florid Jacobean mouldings.[28]

Kinfauns Castle, Perthshire (1820–6; see Figure 18.4),[29] was the biggest
of Smirke's Scottish commissions, and its site cried out for architectural
histrionics. Standing high above Perth, on the steep slopes which separate
Kinnoull from the valley of the Tay, its situation dictated the plan: two main
fronts, facing south and east, tied together by the squarest of keeps, behind
which offices cluster round small open courts. Alone therefore among
Smirke's castles, Kinfauns is asymmetrical; and this asymmetry is multiplied
by the syncopation of its silhouette. Equally irregular are its details: outside,
the fenestration is clearly that of a classicist, but the forms employed are
simplified Romanesque, Gothic or Tudor; inside, ceilings and doors, panelling and plasterwork, are all as much Tudor as Gothic.[30]

T. F. Dibdin, bibliophile and gossip, arrived one dark night and left us a
memorable description:

> lamps, lofty ceilings ... marble sculpture, pictures, bronzes ... one of
> the most elegantly furnished tables in Scotland ... my Lord Gray's
> 'batterie de cuisine' was 'de toute force' ... The noble owner ... is a
> great lover of Mechanics ... We had not sat down half an hour at the
> dinner table, when a singular clock over the sideboard struck up, in a
> trumpet step, a very animated martial air. I thought a band of soldiers

was about to enter ... The Billiard Room is my Lord's 'workshop' ...
here is everything to excite surprise and elicit admiration. How hard
you can hit – how heavily you weigh – how swiftly you walk –
electrifying machines in all shapes ... clocks, watches, guns, swords,
musical instruments ... [And] the kitchen ... [contains] the best grouse
soup in Scotland ... [According to Lady Gray] every part and parcel of
the building, the furniture, and the ornaments is *paid for*.[31] What an
honourable inheritance! ... How rich and how *rare*! The particular
charm of the interior is the gaiety and cheerfulness of the whole. There
is no gloom. Light and warmth are everywhere. But then, what a
neighbourhood! What a river to look down upon, with its green banks
and wooded heights ... the nice care and exact finish of the pleasure
grounds – the gates and lodges in stone, all in the best taste I have
anywhere seen ...[32]

At Kinfauns, Smirke made no attempt to recreate a past architectural style.
Instead, he set out to turn the associations of 'olden time' into three
dimensions, designing pictorially within the categories of the Sublime and the
Picturesque. The critics approved: 'exceedingly well-suited to its elevated site
and to the grandeur of the surrounding scenery';[33] 'nature combined with the
embellishments of art';[34] 'cliffs and wooded hills ... variegated trees and
clumps ... placed as if by the hand of a Claude ... within the enclosure of
Kinfauns, there is nothing to alter, nothing to be removed. It is in every way
perfect';[35] 'The pointed and mullioned windows and the heavily moulded
doorways were evidently constructed at a time when the adaptation of the
Gothic style to domestic architecture was imperfectly understood; and though
the wide experience of our own day might condemn many of the details as
incongruous or inelegant, the most severe critic must admit the general effect
of the lordly pile to be magnificent ... The grandeur of Sir Robert Smirke's
ideas, both as to magnitude and proportion, is well exemplified at Kinfauns
Castle.'[36]

Quite so. This is scenographic design, not archaeological replication. All
Smirke's Scottish houses, but particularly Kinmount, Whittinghame and
Kinfauns, convey a similar compositional message: here was a man who knew
about volume; here was an architect who understood mass.

NOTES
1. *Diary of Joseph Farington*, British Museum Print Room typescript,
   p. 7,382, 9 May 1818, ed. K. Cave, XV (1984), 5, 198.
2. Ibid., p. 6,765, 23 September 1815, ed. K. Cave, XIII (1984), 4,710.
3. Ibid., p. 6,933, 21 May 1816, ed. K. Cave, XIV (1984), 4,839.
4. Ibid., p. 6,973, 8 November 1815, ed. K. Cave, XVIII (1984), 4,731.

5. Minutes of the Committee for Perth County Buildings (Perth County Records).
6. J. G. Lockhart, *Memories of Sir Walter Scott*, 1845, p. 371. His son, the actor Sir William Henry Don, took part in the Eglinton Tournament (*DNB*).
7. 'Much connected with the turf, but ... few could speak better in public ... He had tact, wit, power of sarcasm, and that indefinable something which marks a gentleman ... and as he had a taste for literature and the fine arts, there were few more pleasant companions' (Sir Walter Scott, *Journal*, 1891 edn, p. 175).
8. Smirke's patrons at Kinmount and Gosford both inherited from 'Old Q', Wordsworth's 'Degenerate Douglas', who died – 'like the setting sun' – in 1810.
9. J. Mordaunt Crook, 'Broomhall Fife', *Country Life*, cxlii (29 January 1970), 242–6. Smirke's Doric columns were used instead for both county buildings (Broomhall Mss.).
10. Wemyss MSS, Gosford; NMRS ELD/54/16–17.
11. Maxstone was financially helped by his brother-in-law Robert Graham: he bequeathed what remained of Lord Lynedock's estates at Balgowan and Lynedock to Maxtone's son James, who thereupon assumed the name of Maxtone-Graham. Sold in 1955, Cultoquhey is now a hotel. See *New Statistical Account of Scotland*, Edinburgh, 1845; S. Korner, *Rambles Round Crieff*, 1865, 88–9; C. Aspinall-Oglander, *Freshly Remembered*, 1956, p. 291. There is a paper model of the preceding house in SRO, RHP, 49259.
12. Adam's plans (Soane Museum, xxxi/51–5; Newton Don MSS) were prepared c. 1790 for the 5th Baronet. Smirke's design for a double Doric lodge is watermarked 1813 (RIBA J.11/96–7).
13. 'A remarkably pretty cheerful place – fine single trees, scattered over a beautiful sloping lawn, all unfinished (Sir A. having more taste, I fancy, than cash), but meant to be in the English style, kept neat about the doors, with walks and shrubbery' (Lady Louisa Stuart, 1800, quoted in J. Fleming, *Scottish Country Houses and Gardens*, 1954, p. 121). See also J. Haig, *Topographical and Historical Account of ... Kelso*, 1825, p. 145; J. Rutherford, *Border Handbook*, 1849, p. 66; C. B. Balfour in *Berwickshire Naturalists' Field CLub*, xiv (1892–3), 296; A. A. Tait, *The Landscape Garden in Scotland*, Edinburgh, 1980.
14. T. Hunter, *Woods and Estates of Perthshire*, 1883, p. 316. The estate was sold in 1910 by Drummond's descendant, the 6th Earl of Perth, for £127,000 (*Complete Peerage*, xii) to the Roberts family.
15. A. H. Millar, *Castles and Mansions of Renfrewshire and Buteshire*, Glasgow, 1889, p. 26, pl. ext. For interiors, see *The Princess Louise Scottish Hospital ... at Erskine House*, 1917. For a plan by C. R. Cockerell, see *Architectural History* xiv (1971), fig. 12b.
16. Quoted in *New Statistical Account of Scotland*, 1845, vii, 515. Blantyre's rental income in 1818 was £2074 6s 8d. p.a. See G. Robertson, *A General Description of the Shire of Renfrew* (1818), p. 388.
17. RIBA MS Box 6 (c. 1810 onwards). See J. Mordaunt Crook, 'Sir Robert Smirke: a Centenary Florilegium', *Architectural Review* cxiii, 1967, pp. 208–10.
18. C. R. Cockerell, *Diaries*, 12 April 1822, cited in D. Watkin, *Life and*

Work of C. R. Cockerell, 1974, p. 72, referring to the Union Club and Royal College of Physicians, Trafalgar Square (1822–7).

19. A. W. Pugin, *Contrasts* (1836), Frontispiece, referring to the Inner Temple Library and Parliament Chambers (1819; 1827–8).
20. *Diary of Joseph Farington*, op. cit., forthcoming index volume.
21. Cockerell, *Diaries*, January 1824; cited in Watkin, *Cockerell*, p. 76, referring to Smirke's St George's Brandon Hill, Bristol (1823).
22. J. P. Neale, *Seats*, First Series, vii (1823), pl. ext.
23. Added by Edward Brook of Halton Mills and Hoddam Castle, Yorkshire, who purchased the estate from the Douglas Family (*Trans. Dumfriesshire and Galloway Natural History and Antiquarian Society*, 1897, p. 87).
24. Ex. inf. Anne Riches.
25. J. Martine, *Reminiscences of the County of Haddington*, 1894, p. 42. James Dorward of Haddington built the house of pale Culalo freestone ferried from Burntisland to Dunbar, and thence carted to the site. The grounds were laid out by W. S. Gilpin. Cultivation of the garden, stretching to Whittinghame Water, was later improved by William Rintoul (ibid.; *New Statistical Account of Scotland*, ii, 65; P. Harris, *Life in a Scottish Country House: The Story of A. J. Balfour and Whittinghame House*, Whittinghame, 1989, pp. 30, 79).
26. Plans: RIBA J.11/26 (1–6); Whittinghame Estate Office MSS.
27. Plans: NMRS ELD/106 (ex RIBA).
28. Sir Robert Lorimer, Lawrence Turner and Eustace Balfour – the Prime Minister's younger brother – supplied designs (Whittinghame Estate Office MSS, SRO). See also Lady Frances Balfour, *Ne Obliviscaris*, 1930, i, pp. 305–7 (pl. ext.) and ii, p. 437; J. Small, *Castles and Mansions of the Lothians*, 1883, p. 11; A. G. Bradby, *Gateway of Scotland*, 1912, p. 320. The elaborate dining-room Arts and Crafts chimneypiece by Alexander Fisher (1900) is now in the V&A. After serving first as a wartime refugee centre, then as a school, Whittinghame has now been converted into flats.
29. Lord Gray succeeded in 1807, and set to work immediately on the garden buildings; Smirke's drawings (Darnoway House, Morayshire; NMRS PTD/64) are variously dated 1813 (farmhouse) to 1831 (offices); but the bulk of the castle was built between 1820 and 1826 (West Lodge; sculpture by Cochrane).
30. For example, 'The Picture Gallery' (eighty-two by twenty-five feet: illustration, J. P. Neale, *Seats*, second series, IV, 1829).
31. The cost of construction was £31,253 5s 5½d, including Smirke's fee of 'say £1,200'; in 1829 the final account, including fittings etc., came to £41,664 2s 5d (accounts, Abercairny and Seaforth MSS, SRO; copies in NMRS; quoted in R. Speake, *Kinfauns Castle*, 1982, p. 12).
32. T. F. Dibdin, *Tour in the Northern Counties of England and in Scotland*, ii (1838), 935–43. Gray was President of the Society of Antiquaries, a Fellow of the Royal Society, and 'perhaps the most liberal patron of science and the fine arts now alive' (G. Penney, *Traditions of Perth*, 1836, p. 277). For his library, sold at Sotheby's on 23 May 1932, see G. P. Johnstone, *Catalogue of the Books in the Library of Kinfauns Castle*, Edinburgh, 1928.
33. T. Hunter, *Woods and Estates of Perthshire*, 1883, p. 483.

34. W. Marshall, *Historic Scenes in Perthshire*, 1880, p. 111.
35. [A. Fullarton, publ.], *Select Views in Perthshire*, 1844, p. 28.
36. A. H. Millar, *Castles and Mansions*, 1890, pp. 109–10 (pl. ext.). See also *New Statistical Account of Scotland*, 1845, X, 1,207, 1,215. The interior – notably the staircase – was altered for Sir Donald Currie in 1910–11 by William Flockhart and F. W. Deas, as were the outbuildings, by Lorimer, in 1926–8. Kinfauns was bought in 1933 from the Earl of Moray by the Cooperative Holdings Association, and was until recently the property of Manchester Corporation.

18

J. P. Neale and the *Views* of Scotland

JAMES MACAULAY

For anyone interested in the history of the British country house, there are certain indispensable printed sources among which must be numbered John Preston Neale's *Views of the Seats of the Noblemen and Gentlemen in England and Wales, Scotland and Ireland*.

Neale (1780–1847) started his working life as a post office clerk but became a topographical artist. His first published work, with John Varley, the artist, appeared when he was only sixteen; but it was the *Views of the Seats* that made his enduring reputation. The first series of six volumes was published annually from 1818 onwards and was followed by the second series of five volumes, although Neale intended six, which began in 1824 and continued until 1829 with a break of a year in 1827 'to enable me to collect Views of all the finest Mansions not yet included in my work'.[1] Altogether, the eleven volumes contain just over 700 views, of which almost one tenth are of Scottish houses. Over half of these appeared in volume six, published in 1823, with the remainder scattered throughout all five volumes in the second series.

In March 1981, a bound collection of the original drawings for the Scottish *Seats* appeared for sale in London. An inscription stated that they had been presented by the artist to Francis Gray, Lord Gray of Kinfauns Castle in Perthshire. Of the seventy-six drawings, all, save for fifteen, are signed and dated by Neale, and of these only the drawing of Crathes Castle, dated 1824, was not published. The published views do, however, include interiors of

FIGURE 18.1   Engraved view of Gask from Neale's *Views of the Seats of the Noblemen and Gentlemen in England and Wales, Scotland and Ireland.*

Culzean Castle, Ayrshire, and of Kinfauns Castle, although the original drawings are not among those in the bound volume.[2]

The dates of the drawings span the years 1817 to 1830. In 1817, there is just one house, Dalmeny in West Lothian, the first example of the Tudor revival in Scotland, followed in the next year by Castle Forbes, Aberdeenshire, the first Baronial essay by Archibald Simpson.[3] In 1819, Duff House, Banffshire, begun in 1735 by William Adam, and Balbirnie House, Fife, a skilful interpretation of the Greek revival by Richard Crichton, were drawn. Thereafter, the number of drawings in each year multiplied until 1829, after which there are only three dated drawings. In 1820, there were four including Dalguise and Gask (see Figure 18.1), both in Perthshire; in the next year, the total of five included three Perthshire mansions. In addition to the dated and signed drawings by Neale, the fifteen others by an unknown hand or hands include four other Perthshire country houses. As might be expected, three fifths of the total of seventy-six houses are new works of the early nineteenth century, with the majority of the remainder being divided between the eighteenth and seventeenth centuries.

The appearance in 1981 of the portfolio containing Neale's Scottish drawings was significant when assessed alongside the discovery in 1976 at Ardblair Castle, Perthshire, of two sets of early nineteenth-century diaries by the brothers John and Charles Steuart of Dalguise.[4] The link had been succintly summarised by Neale himself in his address at the commencement of volume one of the *Views* in 1824: 'To J. Steuart, Esq., of Dalguise House, *1818* Perthshire ... I am likewise greatly indebted ... for many beautiful Scotch views ...'.

John Steuart, who was born at Ardblair Castle, inherited the financially encumbered estate of Dalguise in 1822 on the death of his father, who left his younger son a settlement of £2,000. Through their mother, the brothers were related to the Oliphants of Gask, a notable Perthshire family. Their cousin, Laurence Oliphant, married Henrietta, the daughter of Margaret Graham (heiress of Orchill) and the architect James Gillespie, who took the additional surname of Graham in 1825. The Grahams of Orchill and the Steuarts of Dalguise were also related to one another. It is not surprising, therefore, that Neale's *Views* contain twenty-two Perthshire houses, a far larger number than from any other Scottish county.

Either by inclination or through contact with Gillespie Graham, the Steuart brothers both displayed an early appreciation of architecture. It was with something approaching family pride that Charles Steuart recorded jubilantly in January 1822 that 'Neale's Views has Gask in it'.[4] Four years earlier, when he was still only fifteen, he noted that 'The Cathedral [of Dunkeld] is under repairs at present. The windows are opened as they originally were and I think it will soon be a very handsome building.' He was also interested in art, and in the spring of 1821 in Edinburgh he 'went to the Exhibition of Pictures. I have taken a ticket for the season [at] 5/- ... I think that the picture of the Earl of Kintore's Gamekeeper and pony by Raeburn is one of the best in the Exhibition.' Doubtless, his artistic taste and that of his elder brother would have been improved by their close friendship with the portrait painter John Watson, later Sir John Watson Gordon and third president of the Royal Scottish Academy. Watson rented accommodation to the brothers in 1822 at '22 Frederick St. very uncomfortable as yet Mr. Watson retains a few rooms for his painting in'. Both brothers trained in Edinburgh as lawyers.

The diaries reveal that the social life of the landed gentry was much the same in the early nineteenth century as it is today, and with many of the same cares and worries. Not only were owners of estates entertained while on long visits to one another's houses, but they also formed a close-knit circle in Edinburgh. A typical diary entry in January 1819 states that, with other guests, 'Mr. and Mrs. Gillespie and Orchil dined here at Holyrood House ... Walter Scott lately presented Mr. Gillespie with a complete Set of his poems in 10 vols.'

Charles Steuart's diaries span the years 1820 to 1825. Thereafter, he went to Gibraltar, where he contracted a fever and died in the autumn of 1828. The

FIGURE 18.2   Neale's engraved view of Rossie Priory.

diaries of John Steuart begin in the same year and continue to 1828 when he
left Scotland to take up an appointment as a sheriff at the Cape of Good Hope.
Unfortunately, neither set of diaries reveals how the connection between John
Steuart and Neale began. The first reference occurs in May 1820: 'Wrote out
description of Grandtully for Neale's Views in England, Scotld. and Ireland'.
Grandtully Castle, a late sixteenth-century tower some ten miles to the
north-west of Dalguise, was a seat of the Stewarts of Grandtully and Murthly.
Not only were they neighbours of the Steuarts of Dalguise, but Gillespie
Graham had close enough connections that in 1829 he was engaged to design
new Murthly Castle as a Jacobean extravaganza.[5]

   As there is no diary for 1821, it is only from 1822 that the full involvement
of John Steuart with Neale's ambitious enterprise is gradually revealed.
Living for much of the time in Edinburgh, Steuart was fortunate, since the
capital (then as now) was the fountainhead of country-house patronage, so
that he could make contact easily with some of Scotland's most eminent
architectural practitioners who seem to have been happy, including the
publicity-shy William Burn, to supply drawings from which the views could
be worked by engravers to the format and standard required for publication.
Thus, on 7 January 1822, Steuart 'Called for Dickson and got Rossie Castle
[see Figure 18.2] and Scone'. One can understand that the Dicksons would
have Rossie Castle material, being the nephews of the architect Richard
Crichton who had died in 1817; but for the Dicksons to have material for
Scone Palace, designed by the English architect William Atkinson, seems

FIGURE 18.3   Neale's engraved view of Penicuik House.

odd. A month later, Steuart visited 'Burn, Architect, who promised to give me Views of Dundas, Salton, etc', paid another call in the spring 'and sent him View of Ardgowan' which Burn would alter early in the next decade. Strangely enough, considering Steuart's close friendship with Gillespie Graham, he wrote to another friend when inquiring about Ross Priory, the Gothic mansion designed by Gillespie Graham in 1810 on the eastern shore of Loch Lomond.[6] However, another two years would pass before the owner received his view of Ross Priory. It was also in 1824 that Steuart recorded several visits to Thomas Hamilton, then the doyen of Edinburgh architects.

Owners and friends of owners of houses were also approached. In January 1822, Steuart 'Wrote to Mr. Dundas with description of Dundas Castle [extended a few years before by William Burn] and about View', and on the same day he met 'F[rancis] Grant, who promised to enquire about a View and Desn. of Kilgraston', although it was five years later that James Grant wrote: 'Mr Gibb [presumably Robert Gibb, a foundation associate of the Royal Scottish Academy in 1826] is to paint views of Kilgraston for engravings for the book you are to give it the honour of a place in very soon'. Also in January 1822, Steuart called on Clerk Maxwell, having earlier 'Sent a Number of Neale' when it was agreed to make a site visit to Penicuik House in East Lothian (see Figure 18.3), the eighteenth-century Palladian mansion owned by Clerk Maxwell's relatives. Steuart was not so certain 'about Coul House, which I think I shall not send to Neale'. One owner who had her own opinions was the Countess of Moray. When returning the drawing of

Donibristle, Fife, she added to the accompanying letter, 'To prevent Mistakes, Lady M. thinks it best to mention, that it is not wished to have any road or path in the foreground of the Drawing, as it is thought to have a bad effect on the landscape, and there is in fact *no road* in the Situation in which it is placed in the Drawing'.[7] Of course, as the series of Views progressed, it was inevitable that unsolicited proposals should arrive. Thus, Lady Sinclair wrote to Steuart at 7 Abercromby Place, Edinburgh, on 30 May 1827 that

> in case Mr. Neale's publication ... should not be provided with a view of Rosedoe House, on the banks of Loch Lomond, it has occurred to her that it may perhaps be desirable to obtain one and she encloses a sketch which was lately taken by Miss Catherine Sinclair from a part of the grounds, – though the drawing has been rather rubbed in travelling she thinks the outline may still be sufficiently obvious.[8]

However, another owner in that same year had become so irritated that he penned a curt note to Steuart: 'As there is no chance of our meeting soon I should feel obliged if you would return me, at your convenience, the View of Fingask, and the Description of the Same which I sent you last year'.[9]

It would seem that John Steuart acted as Neale's agent in Scotland, being responsible for the collection of the drawings as well as the accompanying description, and for their preparation for publication. Not only were John Watson's services employed, but so too were those of the engraver William Kay, who was paid early in January for the view of Dalguise which Neale had signed and dated in 1820. When it appeared in print in 1822, Steuart noted with some satisfaction: 'I received the number of Neale contg. Dalguise which looks well'. In that same year, Steuart 'Sent Kay's two views in frames to Mr. Grant of Kilgraston', and in 1823 was given 'directions about the views of Donibristle, Darnaway, Arniston, Dalkeith, Newbattle and Dalhousie'. Probably the finest of the Edinburgh engravers was W. H. Lizars, so it is strange to read that Steuart 'Desired Kay to copy Lizar's View of Ardgowan' which was later sent to William Burn. Other artists whose talents were utilised included Alexander Nasmyth, who was asked 'to do a view of Drummond Castle', and in 1825 'Mr. Crawford' (presumably Edward Crawford) was sent 'to make a sketch for Neale' of Dalkeith House, one of the unsigned drawings in the bound volume. David Octavius Hill was consulted 'about views of Ochtertyre and Brechin', for which he was paid £1. The Neale drawing of Brechin Castle is dated 1821, but the Ochtertyre drawing is anonymous. Hill is mentioned again as 'painting a view of Lude for Mrs. Robertson'.

An amateur artist who was of much use to Steuart is first mentioned towards the end of March 1822, when Steuart 'Called for J.A.S. who came to town last night. He has done a beautiful View of Taymouth from the east (across the river) for Lady Breadalbane.' Two years later, Mrs Oliphant of Gask wrote to Charles Steuart that '[Laurence] will be very happy if your Brother will send him the book with the View of Gask done by Mr. Stewart Murthly'.[10] The artist was John Archibald Stewart, the heir to the Grandtully and Murthly estates. An enthusiastic antiquarian, he once presented Charles Steuart with some engravings including one of York Minster. Once he had succeeded to the family baronetcy, and in order to distinguish him from his brothers, he is referred to in contemporary correspondence as 'The Baronet'. It was under his direction that the new Murthly Castle was begun in 1829, although building work progressed for only three years before being halted. Yet, as early as February 1820, John Steuart recorded: 'Waited on Gillespie with JAS and talked over business of addition of Murthly etc'.

Stewart of Murthly's younger brother George was also involved in the collection of material for Neale. In June 1822, he wrote: 'I have been prevented from writing by many occurrences but principally, because I hoped to be again at Murthly where all the papers connected with Neale are at present. Until I go there I can neither send you more information on that subject, nor Crathes which is written out.'[11] Despite the last phrase, he was writing again two months later: 'You mention your expectation of receiving the description of Crathes, and others from me; but I thought we had agreed to suspend all proceedings for Neale until your arrival in Perthshire ... Do not fail to bring all the contents of your Portfolio that we may study the interest of Mr Neale at large.'[12]

Throughout the summer of 1822, Steuart was occupied daily in compiling material for Neale, a task which demanded the occasional excursion from Edinburgh, including a week-long tour in the company of Gillespie Graham to Berwickshire with stays at Duns Castle, remodelled by Gillespie Graham from 1818 onwards,[13] and other houses, after which Steuart jotted down notes 'to serve as a Memorandum for Neale or the Travellers Guide'. In early July, he was off to Dumfriesshire 'and took a distant view of Murraythwaite House from the east'. As might be expected, the most frequent journeys were to and from Perthshire, and it was during one of these that he 'called at Kinfauns and saw Lord and Lady Gray: we examined the new Chateau wc. is on an admirable plan'. Another visitor was just as laudatory:

> Mr. Smirke has, I think, been very successful in combining all the elegance of Gothick Architecture, with the simplicity which is always requisite in a moderate sized mansion, indeed, as Lady Gray says, one of the advantages of the new house will be that there are none of the rooms too large for two persons to live in with comfort[14] (see Figure 18.4).

FIGURE 18.4   Neale's engraved view of Kinfauns Castle.

The most celebrated new mansion in Scotland was Abbotsford, which it would have been unthinkable to have omitted. In 1827, Steuart met 'Sir Walter Scott in Shandwick Place to whom I shewed the sketches for Neale. We walked along streets together, and he told me various interesting anecdotes and invited me to go to Abbotsford at Christmas.' Two months afterwards, Steuart 'Wrote to Neale, of giving £10 to Gibb for the use of this view of Abbotsford Hall'. Less than a month before his encounter with the famous author, Steuart had 'received a few lines from Lord Gray respecting Blore's Views of Abbotsford', a venture which remained unfulfilled.

In the exchanges of correspondence between Steuart and Neale, it was inevitable that there would be misunderstandings and mischances. In his first surviving letter, Neale, writing from Kenneth Street, Blackfriars, apologised for omitting a letter of thanks and continued:

> I beg now to acquaint you that the two Drawings of Grandtully and Murthly were returned to your friend Mr. Steuart [sic] when that Gentleman was in London. I am happy to find that you have already so many Drawings. I am now beginning to be very anxious for them. I am very glad to hear that you are about to get Dalkeith and Abbotsford be assured that I shall not mind a few pounds to obtain *correct* sketches of these places large *pencil* sketches will quite answer my purposes.[15]

Two years later, one of the Stewart brothers wrote to John Steuart explaining 'that as the view of Ochertyre is lost, unless G.G. [*sic*] has it, you should write to Sir P. Murray and request him to send you the original drawing for transmission to Neale, and you can assure him of its safety. Pray what have you done with regard to descriptions of Dalkeith, Dalhousie etc.'[16] That there was some urgency was outlined by Neale some weeks later. 'I have placed several of the Scotch Drawings in the hands of the Engravers ... I very much want the remaining descriptions, I should like you to send me as soon as possible the accounts of Blythswood, Lee Place, Wishaw, Darnaway Castle, as these are all fine mansions.'[17] Yet, within a few months, Neale announced: 'I have determined upon suspending my publication on the completion of the present Volume, 6 months, not only on acct. of the great depreciation of my property, but also to give me an opportunity of collecting Views of *all* the Mansions worthy of notice.'[18] A year later, Steuart made an extract of a letter to Neale. 'A long time ago you empowered me to go to the extent of £9 or 10 on your account in collecting views. The expenses I have paid from first to last, connected with the drawings have been very considerable, but of course I say nothing of them, and only refer to the small account I have kept since I was so authorised', which totalled £6 2s 6d.

As has already been noted, the ultimate recipient of the original drawings for the Scottish views was Lord Gray. The first mention of his interest in the enterprise was early in 1826. 'With regard to the views, he is anxious that some little history of the old castle, a description of the pictures should be made to accompany them.'[19] Three months later, Lord Gray informed Steuart in a postscript that 'Gibb is making a beautiful painting of the Gallery from the entrance end'.[20] Undoubtedly, Lord Gray was desirous of having his new seat given prominence in Neale's publication. 'We must get something settled about our drawings for Mr. Neal [*sic*]. I am rather inclined to favour your idea', he wrote to Steuart, 'and if we could get a good drawing executed with Smirke's own pictural Elevation put in I should be happy in that case to have a drawing also of the back part of the Castle being done and along with the Gallery inserted in the Views of Gentm. Seats etc.'[21] Once the drawings were finished, Steuart received a missive from Lord Gray: 'I yesterday sent two cases by common Perth Carrier containing the View of this place by Williams [presumably John Francis Williams], and under it a Small View of the back of the House. In a separate box you will find the View of the Gallery by Gibb.'[22] While Lord Gray was reconciled to the fact that it might not be possible 'to get proper drawings executed in Edinr. from these pictures', he would only allow them to be forewarded to London provided 'that none of them were to be soiled or damaged'.[23] Evidently, the drawings were made in Edinburgh, and Lord Gray asked for a sight of them prior to their despatch to

FIGURE 18.5   Neale's engraved view of the Gallery at Kinfauns Castle after an oil painting
   by Robert Gibb, 1827.

London, from where in November Neale sent a reassurance about their
care.[24] Even so, Lord Gray was still being finicky. 'I don't care so much about
the drawing of the Gallery and I hope he [Neale] will make good engravings
from them all'[25] (see Figure 18.5). As late as the summer of 1827, Lord Gray
was still critical of the engraving of the gallery at Kinfauns Castle. 'The large
Vase is not in proper perspective and the ceiling is badly executed.'[26]
Happily, when the volume containing the description and views did arrive,
Lord Gray was delighted. 'They are really very nice particularly the general
view which is sweetly done and the acct. is freer from error than I
expected.'[27] It had already been suggested to Steuart by George Stewart of
Murthly that Neale 'should dedicate his Vol. to Lord Gray – who might be of
more use to him than even the Duke of Buccleuch'.[28] It should be no
surprise, therefore, that the entire body of drawings, with the exception of the
drawing of Dundas Castle, which Neale presented to Steuart, was donated to
Lord Gray and 'most respectfully inscribed by John Preston Neale'.[29]

NOTES

1. J. P. Neale to J. Steuart, Bennett St, Blackfriars, 4 January 1827, SRO,
   GD38/2/72.
2. The drawings are now in the J. Pierpont Morgan Library, New York.

They were made available to the author in London by courtesy of Mr Frederick Koch.

3. James Macaulay, *The Gothic Revival, 1745–1845*, 1975, pp. 205–89, 319–20.
4. The diaries are among the Blair Oliphant MSS. The author acknowledges the kindness of Mr L. Blair Oliphant in giving permission for the extracts to be published for the first time.
5. Macaulay, op. cit., pp. 247–9.
6. Ibid., p. 234.
7. Lady Moray to J. Steuart, 17 August 1826, SRO, GD38/2/71.
8. Lady Sinclair to J. Steuart, 7 Abercromby Place, 30 May 1827, SRO, GD38/2/72.
9. P. Murray Threipland to J. Steuart, Fingask Castle, 2 February 1827, SRO, GD38/2/72.
10. Mrs Oliphant of Gask to C. Steuart, 10 January 1824, SRO, GD38/2/69.
11. G. Stewart to J. Steuart, Logie Almond, 3 June 1822, SRO, GD38/2/67.
12. G. Stewart to J. Steuart, Murthly, 5 August 1822, SRO, GD38/2/69.
13. Macaulay, op. cit., pp. 241–3.
14. Lord Charles Murray to the Duchess of Atholl, Megginch Castle, 3 October 1823. John, 7th Duke of Atholl, *Chronicles of the Atholl and Tullibardine Families*, vol. 4 (1908), p. 347.
15. J. P. Neale to J. Steuart, Kenneth St, Blackfriars, 21 October 1824, SRO, GD38/2/69.
16. G. Stewart to J. Steuart, Murthly, 10 March 1826, SRO, GD38/2/71.
17. J. P. Neale to J. Steuart, Bennett St, Blackfriars, 27 April 1826, SRO, GD38/2/71.
18. Ditto, 28 November 1826, SRO, GD38/2/71.
19. J. Richardson to J. Steuart, 10 January 1826, SRO, GD38/2/71.
20. Lord Gray to J. Steuart, Kinfauns Castle, 24 April 1826, SRO, GD38/2/71.
21. Lord Gray to J. Steuart, New Club, 29 June 1826, SRO, GD38/2/71.
22. Lord Gray to J. Steuart, Kinfauns Castle, 22 September 1826, SRO, GD38/2/71.
23. Lord Gray to J. Steuart, Kinfauns Castle, 17 October 1826, SRO, GD38/2/71.
24. J. P. Neale to J. Steuart, Bennett St, Blackfriars, 28 November 1826, SRO, GD38/2/71.
25. Lord Gray to J. Steuart, Kinfauns Castle, 14 January 1827, SRO, GD38/2/72.
26. Lord Gray to J. Steuart, Seafield Baths, 16 August 1827, SRO, GD38/2/73.
27. Lord Gray to J. Steuart, Kinfauns Castle, 15 October 1827, SRO, GD38/2/73.
28. G. Stewart to J. Steuart, Murthly, 4 April 1827, SRO, GD38/2/72.
29. J. P. Neale to J. Steuart, Bennett St, Blackfriars, 13 December 1827, SRO, GD38/2/73.

FIGURE 19.1 Watercolour view of Craigievar by R. W. Billings, prepared for the
engraver of the plate in his *Baronial and Ecclesiastical Architecture of Scotland*, 1848,
after John Smith of Aberdeen's conservative repairs in 1826.

19

John Smith and Craigievar Castle

WILLIAM A. BROGDEN

I first came to know the work of John Smith (1781–1852) in 1972 when preparing plans to restore his Easter Skene House near Dunecht in Aberdeenshire, and I recall very vividly a forthright and characteristic Kitty Cruft warning not to 'trick it out in London fashion'. The owners had assumed that the house was by William Smith and built in about 1870, in the worst possible Victorian taste, and therefore fair game for improvement. We all soon realised that it was in fact an early exercise in the 'Old Scotch Style', and was a building of considerable internal logic and merit.

The owners' initial confusion and contempt is not unusual, whether with respect to houses in Baronial style of the nineteenth or twentieth centuries, or the originals themselves. Scots Baronial is still seen as something of a joke by too many, and by others who ought to know better, and despite the recent fashion for 'restoring' them, the sixteenth- and seventeenth-century tower houses of the north-east are often treated in a very cavalier, if romantic, manner.

John Smith was essentially a provincial builder, and remained so all his life – but what a province to build in! His time coincided with the extraordinary growth of the town of Aberdeen and an equally phenomenal burst of activity in the country. In parallel with his work in King Street, the Castlegate and Union Street, he built up a goodly country practice beginning interestingly with an essay in the Castle style. At Castle Forbes, near Alford, Aberdeenshire, he succeeded Archibald Simpson, who apparently through inexperience had contrived to undermine the ancient castle his employer had

FIGURE 19.2   Cluny Castle, designed by John Smith c. 1820.

determined to keep as the core of his new house. Smith's job was to finish
the house, by then well under way. As a design, Castle Forbes, although
asymmetrical, picturesque and made of granite, is still vaguely English, or
perhaps Welsh, in character.

   At some time before 1820, at nearby Cluny Castle, Smith became involved
in a very different project (see Figure 19.2). Cluny was a small 'Z'-plan tower
house built between 1600 and 1604. Smith was briefed by a very rich Colonel
John Gordon to transform it into a modern mansion house in the best Castle
style, and Smith succeeded very admirably in producing a marvellously
Brobdingnagian effort in gleaming white granite, almost a caricature of a
castle. By antiquarians, sad at the loss of a genuine tower house, by those who
can see the charm of Robert Adam's more modest scheme, and by those who
see the whole enterprise of building modern houses in the style of castles as
folly, Smith has been blamed for his design. But, if Cluny Castle is viewed

dispassionately, it really is a splendid affair. It is a picturesque assembly of sixteenth-century stylistic elements mostly English. The Scots Baronial style follows on in the 1820s and 1830s.

Considering how many well-made, splendid and perhaps dotty houses were built in the Baronial style once it had been perfected, it is curious to note that the style was not always welcome; and, especially among professionals, it could bring forth contempt. To them it constituted nothing less than an architectural and national affront. For them the national was Britain, which, if viewed as a whole, was incredibly rich in excellent building from past ages, and these almost exclusively English prototypes they were happy to adapt to modern use, whereas Scottish castles smacked too much of the rude, gaunt and perhaps too well-remembered past.

One of John Smith's students was Robert Kerr, founder of the Architectural Association, Professor at University College London, and author of *The Gentleman's House*. And while Kerr was not so disgusted with Scottish architecture as his countryman James Fergusson, he still placed 'Scottish Baronial' at the bottom of styles appropriate for houses for gentlemen. He declared that the style was only appropriate for Scottish scenery: 'the beautiful heather braes of Loch Lomond, or the fir woods and birch-covered banks of the Dee',[1] and even at its best he would only allow its effect to be 'quaint but not graceful; noble by association with ideas of power, but that power of an obsolete order';[2] and even the 'goodly Castle of Balmoral' by John and William Smith, which Kerr characterised as an 'Elizabethan Manor-house', would be 'an eyesore to every passer-by' if built in Hampshire.

Even now in the north-east of Scotland there is, at best, an ambivalence about Scots Baronial, and a prevailing inclination to tear away the Victorian extensions and to get back to the old keep is very much a part of the recent fashion for the real thing – a sixteenth-century tower house, warmed by an Aga stove, and awash with modern plumbing.

No building better defines the type, nor more clearly identifies the ideal, than Craigievar Castle, between Alford and Lumphanan. It was too remote for Francis Grose to find, but it has been celebrated since by Billings and by MacGibbon and Ross, and is much loved by all who see it. Its setting, while remote, is yet civilised by woodland, shelter belts and good agriculture. It is very much the tower – plain, small, squarish in plan rising to seemingly extra-ordinary height, finishing with turrets, ogee-shaped roofs and cap-houses. Internally it is cosy yet grand, and with the addition of electricity would make the beau-ideal of the castle-hunting would-be restorer.

Yet the Craigievar we see, we owe to John Smith. Whatever 'horrors' he may have been perpetrating for Colonel Gordon at Cluny, Smith recognised that Craigievar was 'one of the finest specimens of architecture in this

FIGURE 19.3   Billings's watercolour view of Craigievar, 1848, showing Smith's new roof
and alterations to the fenestration.

country of the age and style in which it is built',[3] and well worth keeping.
Smith's art conceals itself, and, although he made significant changes, yet
they are not apparent (see Figures 19.1 and 19.3–5). His recommendations to
Sir John Forbes remain valid and form a set of principles about restoration of
old buildings. The first of these is programmatic and unstated: Forbes did not
employ Smith to make Craigievar into a modern mansion house, as Smith had
already built a new house for the family near Aberdeen. The guiding
principles were the building itself and modesty. Although the roof is entirely
by Smith, its form is generally as he found it, and his adjustments in height
here and there and the slight alterations in form are just that – adjustment and
slight alteration. Of more significance are the new windows: these are much
bigger than the originals, and they are now sash and case, whereas the house
would have been built with windows of a late medieval pattern, probably
fixed leaded lights and wooden shutters (see Figures 19.6–7). For all that, one

FIGURE 19.4   Billings's view of the Hall at Craigievar, 1848.

FIGURE 19.5   Billings's view of a bedroom at Craigievar, 1848.

FIGURE 19.6   Photograph of the hall at Craigievar, c. 1900, showing Smith's 1826 sash
windows.

FIGURE 19.7   Photograph of the hall at Craigievar, c. 1900, as furnished after 1826 to
serve as the dining-room, with an antiquarian set of high chairs made up to suit the
early table and the necessary footstools underneath.

still hardly notices the change, and that is probably because Smith retained a simplicity in his treatment, and the form and material for the enlarged jambs and cills derive from the originals and new granite quarried nearby – unlike Cluny, where the windows were 'perfected'; that is, the best sixteenth-century models were chosen. Therefore they add significantly to the elaboration of that design. Similarly, Smith held back on his treatment of the exterior walls, recommending that they be simply repointed and 'rough cast with best pre-pared Scotch lime to match the colour of the granite mouldings; which will greatly improve the appearance of the Building as well as preserve the walls'.[4] At Cluny, he had recased the whole building in fine ashlar, as, to judge from his engravings in the *Baronial and Ecclesiastical Antiquities of Scotland*, R. W. Billings would have had Smith do at Craigievar as well.

The architect as custodian and repairer of old buildings is an honourable tradition, if a less spectacular one than rebuilding in the current fashion. It is an approach which absolutely relies on an enlightened and modest client, and they are as rare as enlightened and modest architects, especially in early and mid-nineteenth-century Aberdeenshire. Smith was clearly capable of it, and perhaps his son and successor, William, was rather less capable in that regard; but William Kelly, who carried on the family firm from the turn of the nineteenth century, best exemplifies these traits, and for clients such as the Douglases of Tilquhillie (near Banchory in Kincardineshire), or the Pearsons at Birse (also in Kincardineshire), or at Castle Fraser, Aberdeenshire, he showed that castles, and more humble buildings, too, could be renewed and made modern and comfortable, but remain essentially themselves.

It is to that ideal that contemporary restorers should look, and cool their romantic ardour somewhat, getting the details right, using the right materials, humouring and thereby honouring the old building.

NOTES

1. Robert Kerr, *The Gentleman's House*, 1871 edn reprinted 1972, p. 377.
2. Ibid.
3. John Smith to Sir John Forbes, Baronet of Craigievar, 16 November 1824: SRO 90250/41/3/32.
4. Ibid.

FIGURE 20.1   View of Monymusk from the west, c. 1878.

20

A Neo-Baronial Monymusk Not Built By William Burn

ALISTAIR ROWAN

T he House of Monymusk, set in ample Aberdeenshire pastures by the broad waters of the Don, offers a classic example of a Scottish landed-family home which has developed over the years. An L-shaped tower house of four storeys (see Figure 20.1), harled with the soft, rounded corners so typical of the north-east, it has gained, over the centuries, two long low wings, running south as a suite of reception rooms and east to provide extensions to the kitchens and domestic offices. In the later Victorian period, these wings, which were built by the amateur architect Alexander Jaffrey in 1719, were spruced up, punctuated as it were by a few judicious accents in hard grey granite, to increase the picturesqueness of the composition and to take a little of the bland look off the early Georgian additions. Parts of the interior were modernised by the Edinburgh firm of decorators, John Taylor and Son, about the same time, and then in 1937 the Baronial hall in the old tower house was redecorated and 'restored'.

The House of Monymusk could not be called great architecture; perhaps, properly considered, it is not, in a self-conscious sense, architecture at all. It is just a big, plain Scottish house; the home to a branch of the Forbes family from 1549 until early in the eighteenth century, when it was purchased by Sir Francis Grant, a Senator of the College of Justice, and the founder of the present family of Grant of Monymusk. Like many an old family place, the house is full of interest, with its own quiet charm, and a spirit that is much greater than the sum of its parts. Yet there is one period in this unassuming history when Moneymusk could at least be described as having teetered on the brink of becoming architecture. In 1837, its then owner, Robert Grant, made plans to embark on a radical rebuild, and contacted William Burn – then perhaps the premier country-house architect in Britain – to help him develop his ideas. A memorandum, two sets of plans, a specification for the new building and a number of letters survive to chart the course of this brief episode of the building's history. Nothing ever came of these proposals, for Burn's ideas were doomed to rise like a bubble to the surface of his client's consciousness, there to burst and be lost from view. Though his Monymusk was not to be, its story is worth recording both for the evidence that it offers of what was thought of as desirable in early Victorian Scotland and as an example of how the architect liked to handle a job.

Robert Grant was the youngest son of Sir Archibald Grant, fourth baronet of Monymusk. He had three elder brothers, Archibald, James and Isaac, none of whom was married. Indeed Archibald, the eldest, died before his father, but both James and Isaac inherited the baronetcy, in 1820 and in 1859, though they do not appear to have lived in the house. It was Robert who demonstrated much the most managerial energy and who ran the estate. About 1820, he had employed John Smith of Aberdeen to rebuild the school in Monymusk village and then a group of houses on either side of the church. Twenty years later, he added a range of new offices in a faintly Elizabethan style to the old home farm, this time to the designs of James Milne and Peter Anderson, local builders who had worked on the estate before. Undoubtedly, his great ambition was to rebuild or at any rate substantially to remodel the house. He does not appear to have considered any architect other than Burn, who was by the 1830s well established, a sound man and in a sense the obvious conventional choice for the extensive alterations which his client had in mind. As there is no copy of any introductory letter among the other building papers preserved at the house, we may perhaps assume that Grant opened negotiations by calling at Burn's office, at 131 George Street, Edinburgh, and requesting him to make a survey of the old house.

Work began in earnest in the summer of 1837 when one of Burn's clerks, a Mr Bell, spent eight days, including his travel to and from Monymusk, making plans of the house and grounds. When Bell left to return to Edinburgh on 7 August, he took with him a memorandum prepared by the proprietor, entitled 'Note Regarding the proposed additions to the House of Monymusk for Mr. Burn's consideration & opinion'. The 'note' is an unusual document, as it sets out, in written form, first the client's instructions and then his views as to his own requirements. Surprisingly, it also seems to imply that, for a job of this size, Burn did not consider it essential to visit the property itself. This was a job which could be done at one remove through the assistance of a trusted senior man. Robert Grant's note refers to a choice of plans; it is not clear whether these are sketches of ideas by himself or whether Burn had jotted down some generic type-plans for his client to consider in Edinburgh. On balance, the first alternative seems the more probable.

> Note regarding the proposed addition to the house of Monymusk for Mr. Burn's consideration & opinion.
>
> Under the impression that on examining the plans of the house & Grounds, Mr. Burn will see the advantage if not necessity of removing the whole of the South or Drawing room wing, Mr. Grant would suggest that the line of the West wall of the new building should not be more than 4 or 5 feet further west than the outside of the present line of building and that the remainder of the width required should be gained by extending the building to the East of present front of the House. By this arrangement any alteration in the present Dining room would be unnecessary & the Flower garden would not be cut up, neither would the lime walk require to be removed.
>
> Plan No. 1 appears to Mr. Grant the most suitable for the arrangement of the Drawingroom floor. Perhaps the Library might be improved by being a little longer. As regards the arrangements of the Ground Floor, Mr. Grant would wish a grand Entrance & Staircase, a small business room (under the Library) and a Bed Room, Dining Room & Watercloset and if feasible a passage communication from the Bed room & Business Room to the Servants apartments without the necessity of crossing the Entrance or Staircase – the Small Ante Room to be so altered as to improve the communication from the Drawing Room and Library to the Dining Room. The floor above the Drawingroom to be divided into Bedrooms with Dressing Rooms to each & to have a water closet. A water closet to be placed in or near the situation of the present highest water closet so as to accommodate the upper bedrooms.
>
> The roof of the East wing to be removed, the walls to be raised & pedimented windows let into the roof and the upper floors of that wing divided into three or four Servants Bed Rooms in such a manner as Mr. Burn may consider best. The connection to these bedrooms to be by the continuation of the present small stair at the east end of that wing.

Here, in a condensed form, is the perfect early Victorian list of requirements. Communication between different parts of the building is important; so too is status, for Robert Grant requires a 'grand Entrance & Staircase' and wishes this to be arranged in such a way as to be available for use independently of the routes used by his servants. The location of the business room

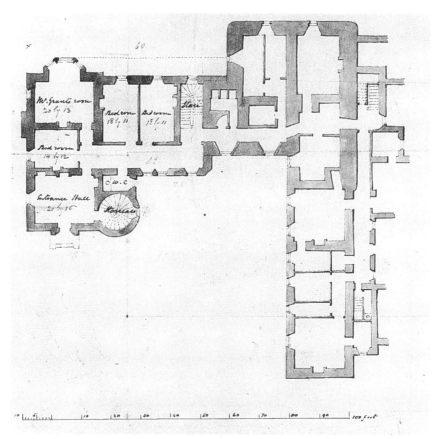

FIGURE 20.2   William Burn's design for additions to Monymusk, 1838. Proposed plan
for the ground floor.

on the ground floor aims at a further segregation between the genteel areas
of the house and its working parts, while the concern to have lavatories
conveniently placed on each floor well illustrates the improved standards of
sanitation expected in the early Victorian period. The 'Note' also provides a
salutary reminder that quite modest considerations can at times assume an
unexpected consequence in the minds of people who commission architectural designs. The Grants intended to continue living at Monymusk while
their new extension was being built, so the uninterrupted use of the dining-
room was important for them, as were seemingly the lime walk and even the
flower garden.

While Burn was normally not dilatory in dealing with his clients' needs,
Robert Grant was to be disappointed in his expectations of prompt service.

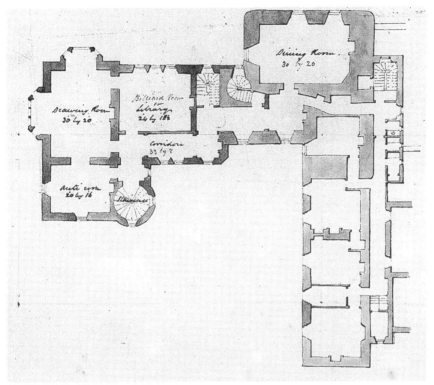

FIGURE 20.3   William Burn's design for additions to Monymusk, 1838. Plan of the
principal floor.

The summer passed, and it was not until well into November that anything
more was heard of his plans to extend the house. 'I have for the last two
months been anxiously looking for the arrival of the sketches which you
promised to send me', he writes on 18 November. 'I must again call your
attention to the memorandum which I sent to you by Mr. Bell on the 7th of
August and beg that you will favour me with a reply as soon as possible.' This
letter stirred the office into action, for Burn's first drawings were ready by 11
January 1838 and were sent to his client on 24 January with a letter offering to
attend to any alterations or improvements he might suggest. In accordance
with his usual office practice, Burn sent the Grants a set of miniature floor
plans, drawn out to a scale of one sixteenth of an inch to one foot, showing the
layout he proposed and marking the new work in red and the existing work in
grey. He included four plans for the ground floor, the principal floor (for, like
many Scottish houses and most tower houses, family life at Monymusk was

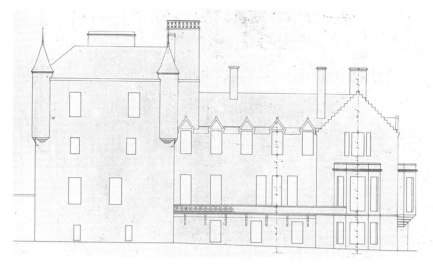

FIGURE 20.4   William Burn's working drawing for the west front of the additions to
Monymusk, 1838.

carried out at first-floor level), the bedroom floor and the attics. An attractive
monochrome perspective sketch, showing the new wing and entrance in
relation to the older parts of the house, completed the design proposals at this
stage (see Figures 20.2 and 20.3). Burn reported that the working plans were
then 'all in pencil' and that the elevations would be finished in the week. He
hoped to send all the drawings to Monymusk 'before the middle of February'.

Burn's plan skilfully met the requirements of Robert Grant's note. What he
proposed was a compact wing extending south from the tower of the old
house and widening on the east side to accommodate a rectangular entrance
hall off which an ample spiral stair led directly to the main floor level. Mr
Grant's business room, the bedrooms, lavatory and servants' passage were
all neatly accommodated behind the hall, just as the note required, while, on
the floor above, a sequence of anteroom, drawing-room and library were to
connect, via a dog-leg corridor, with the main floor of the tower house where
the great hall was retained as the principal dining-room. Like many of the
principal rooms devised by Burn's practice, the drawing-room promised to be
a space of great charm, located with an eye to maximum exposure to the sun,
at the south-west corner of the house, and lit by spacious bay-windows (one
was to be an oriel) overlooking the gardens and the lime avenue. In a manner
which was to become a hallmark of the houses of Burn's junior partner, David
Bryce, the drawing-room and library beside it were to be connected by a
cantilevered balcony which ran across the west elevation of the house and
linked the new work with the dining-room in the great hall. The potential of

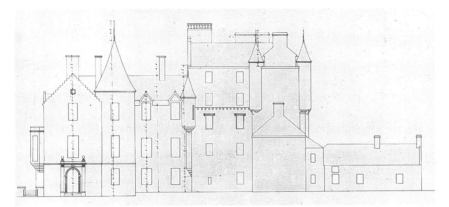

FIGURE 20.5   William Burn's working drawing for additions to the entrance front and
tower house of Monymusk, 1838.

such an arrangement for special moments on a warm summer evening, with
the windows of all the principal rooms thrown open, can readily be imagined.

The Grants were delighted with these proposals: 'I duly received your note
together with the sketch of the house with the alterations and additions which
you propose', Grant wrote on 2 February. 'Both the elevation and the plans
which you have sent exceed Mrs. Grant's and my own expectations in point of
appearance and arrangement and I hope when you make your calculation of the
probable expense of the *whole* building it may be found to be within the sum
which I stated to you.' He hoped that Burn would be able to send the working
plans, elevations and specifications by the middle of the month and in the
meantime, to speed things along, wondered whether he could 'furnish any local
information from tradesmen or others' which might help Burn to calculate the
cost. He then added, as a helpful aside, that in Aberdeenshire masons worked
at twenty-two shillings and carpenters at eighteen shillings per foot.

It seems possible that Grant may have sent Burn a further letter, of which
no copy now survives, discussing the stages to be followed to get contractors
on to the site, for the architect's next letter, written on 9 February 1838, is full
of advice on these matters. As it provides a detailed and quite particular
description of Burn's way of working with his contractors, it is worth quoting
in full.

> My Dear Sir,
> I have completed the plans and specification of your house [see Figures
> 20.4 and 20.5] this evening and given orders that they be sent to you
> next week. On the ground floor you will observe I have gained an
> additional small room at end of passage next the Entrance Hall.
>   I think it quite unnecessary to send you a Clerk of Works to assist in

obtaining estimates as all you have to do is send to a few respectable tradesmen, and give each the use of the plans and specifications for *three* days and if you can get three Estimates for *each* department of the works I should think you would have enough. But certainly four for the mason, and four for the carpenter and joiner work, would be amply sufficient. If again a mason and carpenter would measure the plans at same time together (which I always insist on) estimates would be got in half the time, and as the plumber, plasterer and slater departments can be measured by each in a few hours, I never give to these parties the plans and specifications, but desire them to examine and measure their works while the plans are in the hands of the masons & carpenters, and by adopting the same course and *restricting peremptorily* the use of the plans & specification to three days and nights to *each pair* of contractors (a mason and carpenter) you will have no difficulty in getting thro' this preliminary part of the business. But you must be decided with the tradesmen in enforcing the regulations I have suggested.

I start in the morning by mail for Grantham but from the urgency of several matters here I shall return direct on getting my business done, and hope to be back in eight or ten days, when I shall attend to any communication I may recieve from you.

I am, my dear Sir,
    Yours faithfully,
        William Burn

It is no doubt the procedures envisaged in this letter which provide the immediate explanation of why Burn's additions were never built. The architect's 'Specification of the Work' – a standard nineteenth-century building document of seventeen closely-written pages – makes it clear that Burn expected the estimates to cover five sections; the mason work and excavations; the carpentry, joinery, glazing, ironmongery and smith work; the plumber work; the slater work; and 'the plasterwork including the deafening'. Burn left it 'in the power of the Proprietor to employ any of the contracting parties for one or all of these departments', but it is quite clear that, though as a professional architect he thought it would be easy to procure a variety of estimates, Robert Grant in rural Aberdeenshire viewed the whole business differently. While Burn is businesslike, if perhaps a little too insistent on the limited access which he usually permitted to his plans, he appears curiously impractical in his failure to make any suggestion as to a list of competent tradesmen whom his client might approach. Perhaps he relied too much on an impression that, as Grant had worked with architects and builders before, he would know what to do. Left to his own devices, however, his client could not really cope, and failed to carry his intentions through to their proper conclusion. So far from compelling competing masons and carpenters to measure the plans together within the limited timespan of three days, and to liaise with other tradesmen at the same time, he was at a loss to know how to proceed. The weather at the beginning of the year had been unusually severe, with deep snow that lay for a long time. Rather than put himself to the trouble of procuring a variety of estimates – even from Milne or Anderson, who had worked for him only a few years before – or of searching out different tradesmen, he fell back on a single surveyor, James Scott of Chapel of Garioch, to calculate a price for the house.

The earlier estimate made by Scott of Burn's sketch plan had been within the Grants' budget at £1,776. Now, with the finished design, the price had risen to £2,927 3s 8d, or almost fifty per cent more than his client's maximum figure. 'There is some difference in the First Estimate of the sketch and this one of the Working Plans & Specifications', Scott wrote disarmingly on 9 March 1838. 'I have stated all expenses I think there will be incurred about the building. I went over all the Plans minutely. The only part I forgot to take the measurement of is what is paved. I have stated it as in the first estimate but I think the pavement will be considerably less as pavement in the present entrance hall could be used which I have not calculated.' The estimate even included £186 18s 10d for papering and painting the interior, though Scott could not 'be sure of the price of Flock wallpaper or the sizes'!

What Robert Grant was sure of was that he could not afford the house. Indeed, the estimated cost was so far beyond his intentions that he seems immediately to have given up the possibility of executing even a part of the design. It is rarely easy to acknowledge financial constraints openly, and in the uncongenial task of putting his architect off we may detect a little duplicity. Grant wrote to Burn the next day. He does not complain that the finished design is beyond his means, for, had he done so, Burn would have been bound to have requested a sight of the estimates he had received and to have offered to make economies. It was easier and less embarrassing to shift the blame:

> Your letter of the 9th Februray together with the plans and specifica-
> tions for the proposed addition reached me about the 20th Ult and so far
> as I am capable of judging everything appears to be as clear and distinct
> as could possibly be wished. I regret however to say that the unpre-
> cedented severity and length of the winter and the great depth of snow
> on the ground since the middle of January, which at this moment is
> scarcely half gone, has rendered the woods totally inaccessible and pre-
> cluded the possibility of preparing a single tree. Under these unfortunate
> and unforseen circumstances I consider it prudent and advisable to

postpone my intention of building for another season; besides which I am convinced that many arrangements could be made in the Autumn both as regards the cutting down and the preparing the timber as well as the quarrying and preparing for the mason work which would prove advantageous to the building and which would also make a very material saving in the expenses. Although it has become necessary and almost unavoidable for me to defer this operation for a time I trust you will believe that I am both ready and anxious to repay the expense which you have incurred as well as to settle your professional charges the amount of which I beg you will take the trouble of stating. When the proper time arrives for proceeding with the work, I trust you will send me a Clerk of Works who may be depended upon.

On 28 March, Burn sent in his bill. He charged £14 8s 0d for the expenses of Mr Bell for 'eight days times going to Monymusk, making plans and surveys of the house and ground' and 100 guineas for his own sketch plans, working drawings and specification. Robert Grant paid the account promptly on 7 April, adding in his covering letter:

when it is in my power to proceed with the work I trust I may calculate upon your assistance in enabling me to bring it to a successful termination. Had the plans been completed in September as you promised there would have been no difficulty in proceeding with the building. But the delay of five months which took place coupled with the extreem severity of the Spring occasioned obstacles which could only be overcome at a great additional expense and which, as I before stated, induced me to postpone the undertaking.

Did Burn believe this letter? Or did he and his young partner David Bryce recognise the symptoms of a commission that had already gone cold? The summer of 1838 came and went. Not a tree was felled, no quarry was opened, nor any attempt made to prepare stone for building in the following year. And so it is Burn who, on 9 April 1838, has the last word in the story of the unbuilt additions to the House of Monymusk. When it came to shifting the blame, he was more than a match for his client:

My dear Sir,
I thank you for your letter of the 7th and enclosure for which I send a stamped receipt. So far as I am personally concerned, the delay in your proceedings has been so far provided for, having obtained a situation for the person I had secured for Clerk of Works, and the only regret I feel arises from the disappointment I have occasioned to several persons, having expressly stated my promise to you in excuse for postponing

their plans, and Mrs Raeburn's house I was unable to attend to at all from that circumstance – but it cannot be helped & I have only again to express my obligation to you and am, my dear Sir,

Yours ever faithfully,
Wm. Burn

FIGURE 21.1   Engraved view of Dunrobin after a drawing by the Duchess-Countess of Sutherland published in *Scotland Illustrated*, 1838.

21

The Duchess-Countess of Sutherland and Dunrobin Castle

JOHN GIFFORD

In June 1766, the Earl and Countess of Sutherland both died of fever at Bath, where they had gone to shake off the depression occasioned by the death of their elder daughter a few months before. Their surviving daughter, the one-year-old Elizabeth, then inherited her father's earldom and vast estates in Sutherland.[1] The new Countess's tutors or guardians placed her in the care of her maternal grandmother, Lady Alva, who immediately extracted from them the wherewithal to acquire a chariot whose vermilion wheels made a fine contrast to its dark red body ornamented with gilded coronets.[2] In 1771, the tutors agreed to buy Lady Alva a larger house in Edinburgh's new and fashionable George Square and purchase £550 worth of furniture for it from Young and Trotter.[3] Lady Alva did not neglect the education of her granddaughter, who was taught English first by William Robertson, Principal of Edinburgh University, and then in 1776 by Samuel Joseph Pratt (the poet and playwright 'Courtney Melmoth'), who found at their first meeting that she 'recited Milton and the Spectator with a skill that required little aid from tutorage'.[4] In the autumn of 1779, Lady Alva took her to London, where they remained until the summer of 1782 when the Countess visited, apparently for the first time, Dunrobin Castle, the ancestral seat in Sutherland.[5]

Dunrobin Castle in 1782 was a harled L-plan house built in the 1640s along the north and west sides of a courtyard, quite unpretentious except for round conical-roofed towers at the west corners and an ogee-topped stairtower in the inner angle with the small thirteenth- or fourteenth-century keep which

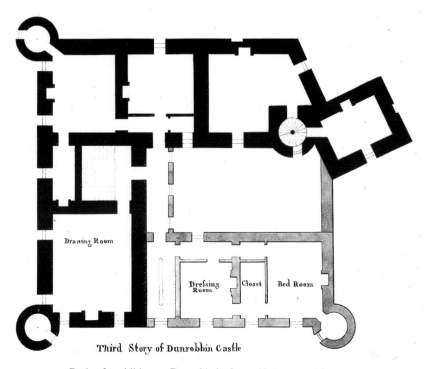

Drawing Room

Dressing Room   Closet   Bed Room

Third Story of Dunrobbin Castle

FIGURE 21.2   Design for additions to Dunrobin by James McLeran, 1786.

projected from the north range's south-east corner. In 1768, the Countess's tutors, informed that the house 'in many parts received Water in the Winter time', had authorised the expenditure of a maximum of £70 on the roof,[6] but, by the time of the Countess's visit, further work was needed, the factor complaining that:

> at this hour there is not a shour of rain but runs over the whole house and I am sorry to tell you that the dining room the only finishd room in the house ... is much damaged ... it is absoloutly necessary that no time should be lost in giving some directions about the roof to preserve the house ... for surely Lady Suth[erlan]d will never allow the old Castle to tumble to the ground.[7]

In November 1782, on her return from Dunrobin, the Countess informed her tutors that she had 'ordered a Sketch of the intended Repairs with an Estimate of the Expence thereof to be made out and sent her ...'.[8] As a result, the mason James Anderson and the architect-wright James Boog were employed over the next five years to make extensive repairs.[9]

The Countess spent the next two years in Edinburgh and London, where in 1785 she married George Granville, Viscount Trentham, son of Earl Gower and heir to a huge English fortune. A son George was born the next year, and the couple spent the early part of 1787 in Italy, where the Countess made conscientious notes in her diary on the buildings they visited.[10] At the end of July 1787, they arrived at Dunrobin, where they stayed until the middle of October.[11] Almost three months' experience of married life in that house and the expectation of an increasing family were probably sufficient reason for Earl Gower (as Lord Trentham had become in 1786 when his father was made Marquess of Stafford) to extend the house by building a corridor addition on the courtyard front of the west range and by erecting a south range containing a new kitchen and bedrooms (see Figure 21.2). James McLeran was employed as architect and contractor.[12] For the new south range, he designed a plain harled block rather weakly dressed up with a crenellated parapet along its south front. A round tower at its south-east corner balanced the seventeenth-century south-west tower, but with the embellishment of small Gothic windows. Such castellated and Gothic hints were eschewed on the west range's new courtyard façade, where McLeran superimposed segmental-arched, round-headed and bullseye windows. Work was completed in 1790.[13] By then, the Countess was living in Paris, where her husband had been appointed ambassador, and it was not until 1793 that she inspected the restored and enlarged Dunrobin Castle, apparently with approval, for General Grant of Ballindalloch wrote to her:

> I am happy to find that you was pleased upon your arrival with the alterations which had been made in the antiquated Castle, which is now as good a house as you could wish in that part of the world, for the reception of the Natives, and the few Foreigners who find their way into that terrestial Paradise . . .[14]

At the beginning of 1803, Lord Gower inherited the Northamptonshire and Lancashire estates of his maternal uncle, the 3rd Duke of Bridgwater, together with canal property worth £75,000 a year. On the death of his father later that year, he became Marquess of Stafford and the owner of another large English estate. After a few years reorganising the administration and raising the profitability of this inheritance, Lord Stafford devoted much of his time and wealth to the 'improvement' of his wife's lands in Sutherland, revolutionising that county's economy by the building of harbours, roads and bridges, the introduction of large-scale sheep-farming, the clearance of tenants from the inland straths to new coastal villages, and attempts to establish coal-mining and manufacturing industries. In 1833 he was created Duke of Sutherland (his wife entitling herself the Duchess-Countess of

Sutherland), and it was estimated that by the time of his death in the same year he had spent £60,000 on these works.[15]

Alterations to Dunrobin Castle between 1803 and 1833 were surprisingly modest. The Countess and her husband seem to have regarded the house more as a holiday cottage and private retreat than as a symbol of their power and wealth, of which in any case the local inhabitants needed no reminder. Perhaps because they saw the house in this way, those alterations which were made between 1803 and the Duke's death were from their own designs or those of their elder son, Lord Gower, whose severe deafness rendered him unfit for public life,[16] although execution was superintended by an estate architect, first George Alexander and then, after 1823, Alexander Coupar.

The first improvement at Dunrobin to which Lord Stafford, his wife and son gave their collective attention was the making of a walled garden between the castle and the sea to the south, this garden being divided into two unequal parts by a drive from the shore. The design was produced in 1804 by the eighteen-year-old Lord Gower and approved by his parents, the Countess assuring him that 'the plan is thought to be particularly well drawn'.[17] At the entrance to the drive was placed a pair of squat round towers, very martial in appearance, with deep parapets carried on double tiers of corbelling. These were probably built by 1805, when the Countess included them in a drawing (later engraved) of Dunrobin from the sea.[18] The whole work seems to have been completed in 1808, when the Countess wrote from Dunrobin to her husband:

> the greatest improvement is the restoration of the garden wall to what it was in the time I suppose of its original foundation – you remember the entrance I told you of from the sea ... it has a very fine & really a grand effect, George [Lord Gower] was charmed with it ...[19]

Just east of the garden was and is a square pavilion built in 1732. In 1805, the Countess proposed to fit it up as a gardener's house, replacing the slated pyramidal roof with a shallow-pitch tiled roof hidden by a corbelled and battlemented parapet.[20] Despite receiving her husband's agreement, she then drew back from the alteration, displaying a thriftiness which was to recur in her later approach to work at Dunrobin: 'The estimate for executing the proposed alteration in the Pavillion amounting to £220. I think it better to let the Pavillion remain as it is ...'.[21] A few years later, however, castellated lodges very similar in appearance to the design for the pavilion were provided at the end of the north drive.[22]

Much more ambitious than the garden walls and suggested remodelling of the pavilion was the proposal in 1811 to provide Dunrobin with the stables it had lacked since a fire in 1790. It is clear that Lord Gower produced a design for a stable range and equally clear that his parents or at least his father did not hesitate to correct and improve this architectural essay. On 2 September, his mother wrote to him:

> I have always forgot to say how pretty we thought the last drawing you sent Eliz[abe]th [Lady Elizabeth Leveson-Gower] which we take to be an idea of the new stables you mention – however this may be, L[or]d S[tafford] looked at it this ev[enin]g & said he thought it would do very well for stables to be built across as it were from the Laundry to the larder, making a kind of Court, but that he would make the doors of the stable fronting the avenue, to prevent the smell, & have arches instead of windows & make one side a remise for carriages ... This would be a very handsome thing & he supposed w[oul]d cost £1000 – & if the coal [the Brora coalworks] turns out well he will do it ...[23]

The Countess's accompanying sketch of Lord Stafford's reworking of their son's scheme shows a round-headed arch flanked by drum towers with arcaded ranges on either side. Lord Stafford would have placed this block just north of the castle astride the end of the north avenue, from which it would have appeared a Baronial fortification worthy of Romantic imagination but quite disproportionate to the homely castle behind. In the event, stables of a more conventional classical type were built at the avenue's far end in 1813–15, probably designed by George Alexander.[24]

Inside Dunrobin Castle, the Countess had the dining-room redecorated according to her instructions and sketches in 1817–18, a sideboard recess being formed and a new cornice introduced.[25] In passing on her orders to the factor, James Loch, the Commissioner for the Stafford and Sutherland estates, wrote of the cornice: 'It is to have *no carving* about it *whatever*. It is to be coloured a yellowish white and the Walls a drab colour like the Stafford out of livery coats.'[26] In 1823, the dining room received a further improvement by the introduction of plate-glass windows, as had already happened in the drawing-room. These were offered by Lord Gower as a gift, which his mother accepted with a characteristic disclaimer of extravagance: 'I am very willing to accept of the present of windows for the dining room. it will be a great improvement & plate glass at the manufactory near the Albion mills is now very cheap ...'[27] Her son's further suggestion that the charter-room in the medieval keep might be fitted up as a dressing-room or bachelor bedroom was received with less enthusiasm by the Countess, who was conscious of the historical association of the castle with *her* earldom: 'I cannot quite make up my mind as yet *on the sudden* to renovating the Charter room. It is the only *old* thing we have left. It might now do for a dressing room with a temporary carpet, Glass, & dressing table ...'[28]

In 1833, Lord Stafford was created Duke of Sutherland but died less than six months later. Almost immediately, his widow, now the Duchess-Countess of Sutherland, wrote to her son, the second Duke: 'I will do the addition to Dunrobin according to the plan you may chuse'.[29] However, within a year her son had been displaced as her principal architectural adviser by the sculptor Richard Westmacott. On 16 November 1834, she informed James Loch: 'Mr Westmacot thinks the whole of the new building ought to be rough stone not polished excepting the borders (sills) of the windows, & the windows to the front view to be as much *slits* as possible'.[30] This 'new building' was to be a castellated north wing containing a new kitchen, enabling the kitchen in the south range to be converted into a bedroom and dressing-room for the Duke, with another good bedroom and dressing-room on the first floor, the Duchess-Countess reserving the second floor for her own occupation. The general outline of the scheme was agreed by the Duke in April 1835, when he wrote to his mother: 'I think y[ou]r little sketch of the addition for Dunrobin extremely pretty & that it w[oul]d be a great improvement, as I said yesterday, to have the Kitchen as proposed – & to make an apartment of the Kitchen'.[31]

In the autumn of 1835, Westmacott, visited Dunrobin and the architectural form of the addition began to take shape. On 5 September, the Duchess-Countess explained her ideas to her son, stressing their practicality and, since she intended to pay for the work out of her own income, cheapness:

> Mr Westmacott is quite engoué with this house which he regards as a rare & curious specimen of the 12.th Century, & almost *unique*. he wishes to improve it without altering the existing House, & has been instilling his ideas into Cooper's mind, & making plans which we may consider when we meet – My favourite one & the only one I c[oul]d afford to execute is by throwing the Kitchin out of doors to obtain a good Bedroom & dressing room with perhaps adding a small sitting room at the end of the present Kitchin – this c[oul]d be your appar[tmen]t if you liked it ... the place of the new Kitchin w[oul]d be to go out behind out of the present window of the servants' hall into a short Corridor leading to a Tower, the upper parts of which w[oul]d be à plein pied with the present house, a Kitchin on a vaulted foundation, which w[oul]d contain the servants hall below & the Kitchin offices, sculleries &c. en suite – behind the Tuffa ... This w[oul]d interfere with nothing & I could undertake it and Cooper thinks it w[oul]d not cost more than £1500.[32]

The Duchess-Countess wrote again the next day, still full of enthusiasm:

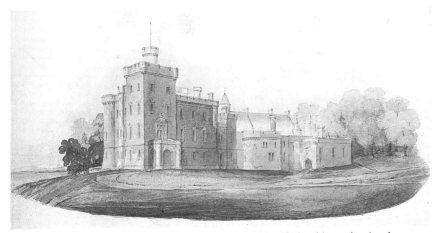

FIGURE 21.3   Design for additions to Dunrobin by an unidentified architect, showing the
Duchess-Countess of Sutherland's kitchen-wing.

> M.ʳ Westmacot's plan is so much admired, & w[oul]d be so convenient
> & has been so well digested, & he instructing Cooper & to send him the
> working details that I am tempted to set about it directly ... M.ʳ Gunn
> [the factor] says he can have it built & roofed in by the time I come next
> year & they say it will not cost me more than 1500.£ which I shall easily
> manage out of my income, & in doing it, I think I shall have much
> added to my own convenience as well as to that of future Inhabitants.[33]

In the same letter, she reported Westmacott's proposal for an eastern
extension of the south range, 'which w[oul]d look magnificent' but 'must be
carried up from below, otherwise it might not be secure, & though a beautiful
thing, the doing it w[oul]d be tedious & so expensive', and so, she concluded,
'I therefore leave that to you, & shall confine myself to these Kitchin
offices.'[34] Three days later, she announced to James Loch her determination
to proceed with the scheme whatever his view as to its advisability, but careful
again to clear herself of extravagance:

> M.ʳˢ Loch will assist me in staking out my new Kitchin & Offices which
> I am going to build out of my income, not consulting *you* only her. It
> will cost probably something within 1500£ & be a great ease to the
> house & I get the old Kitchin by this for an appartment.[35]

The next day, she told her son: 'I am more than ever coiffé with my Kitchin &
wish you had been here to have partaken in the amusement of it'.[36] This letter
crossed with his written the same day to her in which, despite the expression

of general approval, a certain wariness as to what his mother might be up to can be detected:

> I shall much like to see the plans for Dunrobin. I think your idea of the Kitchen very good & that a very agreeable apartment might be made of the old one. Till I see W's plans of course I cannot give an opinion, further than that I think your idea very good.[37]

More enthusiastic was his wife's letter the next day:

> We are much pleased with the ideas for Dunrobin & your little sketches are very picturesque – Westmacott must be full of feeling for architecture judging by the great beauty of his architectural drawings, & I have heard great assistance to Lady Pembroke at Wilton.[38]

Four days later, the Duchess-Countess seems to have been moved by thrift and the advice of Alexander Coupar, the estate architect, to consider amending Westmacott's scheme by omitting the arch through which the drive from the shore would have been brought past the north end of the new kitchen to the front of the castle. She explained to her son: 'Cooper desires the addition to be built without the arch which is merely for picturesque effect & w[oul]d cost 4 or 500£ he says – if so I shall do the rest, & that can be added if expedient afterwards ...'.[39] On 16 September, James Loch wrote in some alarm from Dunrobin to the Duke:

> Gunn says that Cooper & Bunby have prevailed on her [the Duchess-Countess] to alter Westmacotts plan & to spoil it. This I will endeavour to explain to her. Cooper says M.[r] W[estmacot]t is no architect, which is very conceited in him. Westmacott writes to the Duchess, not to permit Cooper to alter any thing as he has no taste, which is quite true.[40]

The threat was quickly averted, and two days later the Duchess-Countess wrote to the Duke: 'Cooper & Leslie with Mr Loch & myself had a consultation about the building yesterday adhering to Mr Westmacott's plans arch & all ...'.[41] The next day she sent the Duke a plan of the proposed building, writing: 'I hope you will like it – if not I will let it go no farther, but I am much coiffé with it myself'.[42]

Work on the foundations of the kitchen wing began in October[43] after the Duchess-Countess's return to London, where she was kept informed of progress by letters from James Loch. Westmacott, also back in London, made a wooden model of the new building, which was sent to Coupar at Dunrobin.[44] One matter of concern was how and what Westmacott should be paid. In August, the Duchess-Countess had asked her son: 'What can I do as to M.[r] Westmacot? He is not a regular architect but does as much as any could do as a friend'.[45] Now a possible answer suggested itself, and she again consulted the Duke:

> He [Westmacott] was praising a new fine Book of the Alhambra which he said was too dear for him £30. I do not know if it w[oul]d do to give it him, least he sh[oul]d think I took it as a hint. What do you think? or have you any notion of what might be agreable & proper.[46]

A mild winter enabled the building work to proceed quickly, and, at the end of January 1836, James Loch wrote to the Duke from Dunrobin: 'I think you will be very much pleased with Westmacotts Kitchin &c at Dunrobin. They are plain, Massive, and in excessive good *fortress* Taste. They will give much Convenience – in every way.'[47] However, it is clear that details still had to be decided, since, two months later, the Aberdeen architect-contractor William Leslie visited the Duchess-Countess in London to show her drawings which she pronounced 'in very good taste excellent gothick Cats' heads, handsome plain architecture. I have ordered copies in small when all is settled which is to be by M[r] Westmacot's advice to whom I have just sent him.'[48]

The Duchess-Countess was again at Dunrobin in the summer of 1836, when she found the 'new building extremely pretty indeed & pictoresque', although a little apprehensive that 'the beauty of the new building may not make people think less well of the old'.[49] Westmacott's archway was again a subject of contention, Coupar having apparently produced an alternative design which the Duchess-Countess seemed disposed to adopt. On 15 July, Loch told the Duke:

> Westmacott writes to me in despair, saying that Couper is ruining the whole design. The fact is, he is the most conceited fellow ever was, tho an excellent tradesman – I have eternal difficulties with him. both Westmacot & I have written to your Mother begging of her to adhere to his plan. I have even sent Westmacotts private letter of despair. could you say a few words teling her to adhere. Westmacotts Gateway was simple & massive Couper has presumed to make an alteration that Westmacott says is frightful.[50]

Perhaps in direct response to this appeal, the Duke wrote to his mother the next day stating firmly:

> I was certainly struck with the drawing by Cooper of the gateway marked N[o] 1 which you sent thro' me to West[macot]t as being very commonplace & not good – I sh[oul]d think it very necessary for you to keep Cooper to the designs you give him, & not let him in points of taste alter Westmacotts. They are very fond of putting in some of their own taste, & it is very lucky that you are there to keep him in order.[51]

The Duchess-Countess replied defensively: 'I shall take care with Mr Westmacots help of the gate way. It is not yet begun.'[52]

By August, the Duchess-Countess was able to consider how to arrange the new rooms to be made from the old kitchen in the south range. She assured her son that the addition of the new kitchen wing and the fitting-up of these rooms would make 'the House quite enough for what is required in this part of the world where you do not wish to collect all the Ross & Caithness gentry, but fill it mostly with one's own Family & Visitors ...'.[53] She returned to London for the winter, and there she ordered grates and furniture for the enlarged Dunrobin in March 1837.[54] With the finishing of the alterations in sight, she seems to have found it necessary to remind her son that the castle was intended for family holidays and that 'There will be no room for governesses but enough for maids'.[55] When she arrived at Dunrobin in July, she found the work almost completed, and enthused over the addition in a letter to the Duke: 'The offices are excellent – They look beautiful & *in harmony* with the rest – tell Mr Westmacot if you see him'.[56] Rather more cautious a note was struck a week later in a letter from James Loch, perhaps mindful of being the grandson of William Adam and the nephew of John, Robert and James Adam:

> The Addition to the Castle is ... well conceived and executed – a critic might have wished the more Castellated mullions carried more generally over the whole, but their absence suits better the plainness of the old building. Its general and picturesque effect is quite good, its details are less so. Shewing that the person was a painter and not an Architect.'[57]

The Duchess-Countess of Sutherland died within two years of the completion of this remodelling and enlargement of her 'antiquated castle'. Five years later, her son began the huge additions which almost entirely hid from public gaze both his mother's work and the medieval tower which that work was intended to complement.

NOTES

1. Robert Douglas, *The Peerage of Scotland*, 2nd edn., rev. John Philip Wood, Edinburgh, 1813, p. 585.
2. National Library of Scotland, Dep. 313/725, minutes of the tutors of Elizabeth, Countess of Sutherland, 11 December 1766; NLS, Dep. 313/722, account of George McFarquhar, 6 September 1766.
3. NLS, Dep. 313/725, minutes of the tutors of Elizabeth, Countess of Sutherland, 17 December 1771 and 11 March 1773.
4. William Fraser, *The Sutherland Book*, i, Edinburgh, 1892, p. 465.
5. Ibid., i, p. 467.
6. NLS, Dep. 313/725, minutes of the tutors of Elizabeth, Countess of Sutherland, 2 December 1767 and 18 March 1768.

7. NLS, Dep. 313/1113, Lieutenant-Colonel James Sutherland to Alexander Mackenzie, CS, 1 June 1782.
8. NLS, Dep. 313/725, minutes of the tutors of Elizabeth, Countess of Sutherland, 16 November 1782.
9. NLS, Dep. 313/1622–3, factor's accounts, 1782–7.
10. Fraser, op. cit., i, pp. 468–72. The Countess's Journal is in NLS, Dep. 314/14.
11. Fraser, op. cit., i, p. 473.
12. NLS, Dep. 313/1623, factor's accounts, 1788–90. Photographs of McLeran's plans and elevations are in the National Monuments Record of Scotland.
13. NLS, Dep. 313/1623, factor's accounts, 1790.
14. Quoted in Fraser, op. cit., i, p. 480n.
15. *Dictionary of National Biography*, ed. Sidney Lee, xi, London, 1909, pp. 1025–6.
16. Lord Ronald Gower, *My Reminiscences*, new edn, London, 1895, p. 64.
17. NLS, Dep. 313/725, f. 24, Elizabeth, Marchioness of Stafford, to George, Earl Gower, 1 November 1804.
18. The drawing is in NLS, Dep. 314/15. The engraving was published in *Views in Orkney and the North-Eastern Coast of Scotland.*
19. NLS, Dep. 313/747, Elizabeth, Marchioness of Stafford, to George Granville, second Marquess of Stafford, 26 July 1808.
20. NLS, Dep. 313/746, idem to idem, 15 July 1805.
21. NLS, Dep. 313/746, idem to idem, 30 July 1805.
22. NLS, Dep. 313/747, idem to idem, 8 July 1810.
23. NLS, Dep. 313/754, Elizabeth, Marchioness of Stafford, to George, Earl Gower, 2 September 1811.
24. NLS, Dep. 313/1629–30, factor's accounts, 1813–15.
25. NLS, Dep. 313/1136, James Loch to Francis Suther, 31 August, 27 September and 18 October 1817; NLS, Dep. 313/1145, James Loch to Elizabeth, Marchioness of Stafford, 11 August 1818.
26. NLS, Dep. 313/1136, James Loch to Francis Suther, 31 August 1817.
27. NLS, Dep. 313/757, f. 13, Elizabeth, Marchioness of Stafford, to George, Earl Gower, 19 September 1823.
28. Ibid.
29. NLS, Dep. 313/761, f. 36, Elizabeth, Duchess-Countess of Sutherland, to George, second Duke of Sutherland, 24 October 1833.
30. Scottish Record Office, GD268/230/24, Elizabeth, Duchess-Countess of Sutherland, to James Loch, 16 November 1834.
31. NLS, Dep. 313/831, George, second Duke of Sutherland, to Elizabeth, Duchess-Countess of Sutherland, 10 April 1835.
32. NLS, Dep. 313/763, Elizabeth, Duchess-Countess of Sutherland, to George, second Duke of Sutherland, 5 September 1835.
33. NLS, Dep. 313/763, idem to idem, 6 September 1835.
34. Ibid.
35. SRO, GD268/230/41, Elizabeth, Duchess-Countess of Sutherland, to James Loch, 8 September 1835.
36. NLS, Dep. 313/763, Elizabeth, Duchess-Countess of Sutherland, to George, second Duke of Sutherland, 9 September 1835.
37. NLS, Dep. 313/831, George, second Duke of Sutherland, to Elizabeth, Duchess-Countess of Sutherland, 9 September 1835.

38. NLS, Dep. 313/831, Harriet, Duchess of Sutherland, to Elizabeth, Duchess-Countess of Sutherland, 10 September 1835.
39. NLS, Dep. 313/763, Elizabeth, Duchess-Countess of Sutherland, to George, second Duke of Sutherland, 14 September 1835.
40. NLS, Dep. 313/1160, James Loch to George, second Duke of Sutherland, 16 September 1835.
41. NLS, Dep. 313/763, Elizabeth, Duchess-Countess of Sutherland, to George, second Duke of Sutherland, 18 September 1835.
42. NLS, Dep. 313/763, idem to idem, 19 September 1835.
43. NLS, Dep. 313/1152, James Loch to Elizabeth, Duchess-Countess of Sutherland, 25 October 1835.
44. NLS, Dep. 313/763, Elizabeth, Duchess-Countess of Sutherland, to George, second Duke of Sutherland, 2 and 3 November 1835; SRO, GD/268/230/30 and 27, Elizabeth, Duchess-Countess of Sutherland, to James Loch, 5 and 9 November 1835.
45. NLS, Dep. 313/763, Elizabeth, Duchess-Countess of Sutherland, to George, second Duke of Sutherland, 7 August 1835.
46. NLS, Dep. 313/763, idem to idem, 2 November 1835. The book was presumably John Frederick Lewis's *Sketches and Drawings of the Alhambra*.
47. NLS, Dep. 313/1161, James Loch to George, second Duke of Sutherland, 22 January 1836.
48. NLS, Dep. 313/764, Elizabeth, Duchess-Countess of Sutherland, to George, second Duke of Sutherland, 25 March 1836.
49. NLS, Dep. 313/764, idem to idem, 6 and 11 July 1836.
50. NLS, Dep. 313/1161, James Loch to George, second Duke of Sutherland, 15 July 1836.
51. NLS, Dep. 313/830, George, second Duke of Sutherland, to Elizabeth, Duchess-Countess of Sutherland, 16 July 1836.
52. NLS, Dep. 313/764, Elizabeth, Duchess-Countess of Sutherland, to George, second Duke of Sutherland, 17 July 1836.
53. NLS, Dep. 313/764, idem to idem, 13 August 1836.
54. NLS, Dep. 313/765, idem to idem, 16 March 1837.
55. Ibid.
56. NLS, Dep. 313/765, idem to idem, 17 July 1837.
57. NLS, Dep. 313/1162, James Loch to George, second Duke of Sutherland, 24 July 1837.

22

Relugas and the Dick Lauder Family

JOE ROCK

Anyone strolling in the southern suburbs of Edinburgh could be forgiven for wondering about the origin of the name 'Relugas Road', and be still further puzzled on discovering that it translates roughly from the Gaelic as 'shieling of the swift stream'. There are no streams that could be described as swift within a five-mile radius. The clue to the name lies in the name of the suburb: Grange, called after the sixteenth-century tower house which stood in this once open landscape.

The Grange came to the Lauder family when Sir Andrew Lauder, 5th Baronet, married his cousin Isobel, daughter of William Dick of Grange. The family seat, however, was at Fountainhall, a charming late sixteenth-century house, south-west of Pencaitland near Edinburgh, and which still stands today, relatively unchanged. This house had been purchased by John Lauder, merchant and burgess of Edinburgh (created Baronet on 25 January 1690), in 1685.

Thus it was from Fountainhall at 6 a.m. on Monday, 3 August 1801, that Thomas Dick Lauder (1784–1848) aged 16, two friends and a sheepdog pup named Bawtie set off on a pedestrian tour of the Highlands. The young gentlemen wore blue cashmere jackets, dark nankeen trousers and gaiters. On their backs they carried japanned tin boxes designed to carry fish. Into these they had stuffed their clothing and, according to Thomas's account, in order not to look silly carrying fishing boxes, they each took a fishing rod as a walking stick. This caused problems later while walking on a Sunday, because they then appeared to be off fishing and consequently had to avoid church-going crowds. By 6:30 p.m. they were in Perth, having crossed the Firth of Forth by ferry from Leith. On the second day, they reached Dunkeld, where, after breakfast the following day, they were shown the Hermitage and pleasure grounds by the Duke's gardener.

This may not have been Thomas's first direct acquaintance with the Duke's pleasure grounds, but the sense of terror and delight in all things natural expressed in his journal was never to leave him.

> Having crossed the ferry the Gardener led us through a great part of the pleasure Grounds belonging to the Duke of Athol, where we saw a great number of very fine trees; he afterwards conducted us through the Gardens, which though they were pretty extensive, have yet very little worth seeing about them except a conical Mount which stands in a corner of them, most part of which is artificial, having been raised by James, Duke of Atholl about the year 1730. It is called Stanley Hill. It has walks cut circuitously to the top of it where several antique canon of different sizes, and fashions, are planted, which occasionally fire a Feu de Joye. ... Our conductor now led us to the door of Ossian's hall, or what is very often known by the appellation of the Hermitage; on this side it presents no very remarkable appearance. On unlocking the Door, a fine painting of the Bard presented itself. While we were admiring this, it (to appearance) of its own accord, flew back and discovered the entrance into the hall; this seeming piece of enchantment, was per-formed by our Conductor, who effected it by pulling a rope. On entering the Hall (which is entirely impanelled with mirrors, having that side opposite to the cascade, made of one entire window) we were astonished with the volume of water that poured over the opposite high rock, the noise stunned, and the mirrors, reflecting the water on all sides of us, and giving it the appearance of falling in different directions, amazed us. This really seemed the effect of enchantment ...[1]

On Sunday, 9 August 1801, they arrived on the doorstep of Relugas House near Forres, to be welcomed by Charlotte Cuming, only daughter of George Cuming of Relugas, ws (1746–1804). Seven years later, Thomas Dick Lauder would marry Charlotte at Relugas, and it is his beautifully handwritten and illustrated account of the pedestrian tour just quoted which is still a prized family possession. Eight miles south-west of Forres, this large rambling house, which is so important for an understanding of the Picturesque movement in Scotland, is the unlikely origin of the obscure street-name in Edinburgh.[2]

The 'Pedestrian Tour', written up in 1803, gives some indication of the independence which Thomas had achieved, living alone with his father, Sir Andrew Lauder Dick[3] (d. 1820), 6th Baronet, at Fountainhall, punctuated only by visits from his father's august legal colleagues including the scholarly Lord Fountainhall, his uncle. His mother, Lady Elizabeth Broun, died three years after his birth, and his only sister died as an infant.

The 'Pedestrian Tour' is also a remarkable record of the sixteen-year-old's precocious skills as an antiquarian, with historical diversions along the way carefully cross-referenced to manuscript or published source material. This is a skill that he was later to develop in a more romantic spirit, publishing *Lochindhu* in 1825 and *The Wolf of Badenoch* in 1827, where fact and fiction are carefully interwoven.

In dedicating the 'Pedestrian Tour' to his father, Thomas does not mention the highly accomplished watercolour illustrations. They are signed by Thomas, but they clearly indicate that he had been a pupil of Hugh William Williams (1773–1829), and indeed some of the brushwork suggests that Williams may have assisted in their production.

Hugh Williams, known as 'Grecian Williams' after his highly-acclaimed 1822 Exhibition of his topographical views of Greece, remains relatively unknown for his views of Scottish landscape. He had begun his professional career in Glasgow, where he established a drawing academy before settling in Edinburgh around 1797, and his watercolours of the mid-1790s helped to form Picturesque taste in Scotland. He was a close and long-standing friend of Thomas, and on the basis of the 'Pedestrian Tour' it is probably safe to assume that many of Lauder's early ideas on the Picturesque developed in conversations with Williams, who in his lifetime was well regarded as a man of taste.[4]

Thomas served for a short time in the army prior to his marriage to the heiress of Relugas,[5] and there is no doubt that the release from some of his financial constraints allowed him to devote more time to writing and thinking. He published papers on chemistry, natural history and meteorology, and wrote for Blackwood's Magazine where, much to his amusement, his contributions were mistaken for those of Walter Scott. He was a man of enormous gifts, if rather full of a sense of his own importance, and he had an opinion on most subjects. Henry, Lord Cockburn (1779–1854), another close friend, said of him that he could have 'made his way in the world as a player or a ballad-singer, or a street fiddler, or a geologist, or a civil engineer, or a surveyor and easily or eminently, as an artist or a lawyer'.

Sir Thomas was appointed Secretary of the Board of Manufactures and, after spending much time developing the Trustees Academy into an art school, he was appointed Secretary to the Royal Institution for the Fine Arts. He continued publishing, and spent his final long illness dictating papers on the rivers of Scotland which appeared in Tait's Magazine from 1847 to 1849.

Among his many accomplishments, he considered himself a poet, and his longest work is the informative 'Relugas', hidden in a handsomely-bound manuscript in the family possession.[6] Begun in 1813, it records the visits to Relugas of special friends including Hugh Williams, the Rev. John Thomson of Duddingston, James Brodie of Brodie and Dr John Gordon, the brilliant anatomist who delivered a course of lectures at the University in Edinburgh when only twenty-one and who died in 1818 aged twenty-three.[7] While strolling together on the Relugas estate, Gordon annotated Lauder's copy of John Lightfoot's *Flora Scotica* (1777) with information on the habitat of plants. However, it is in the illuminating and very detailed 'Notes', apparently begun in 1820 when the poem itself was complete, and in the 'Pedestrian Tour', that most is to be discovered about Relugas House and Lauder's experiments there with garden design.

The first watercolour in the 'Pedestrian Tour' gives us the only known impression of the original Relugas House, a simple tower house shown standing on the slopes of a vitrified fort between the River Findhorn and its tributary, the 'swift stream', the Divie. The oldest part, and probably the house in the watercolour, is said to have been dated 1785, although there were Cumings of Relugas long before that. Thomas states in the 'Pedestrian Tour' that a 'plan of enlargement' was in hand in 1801, and that this was executed is confirmed by a number of sources, including Mrs Stewart Smith, who states that Thomas and his cousin, Charlotte Cuming, were married at Relugas in 1808, 'which had just been enlarged and beautified'.[8] The architect and extent of this work is unknown, but it is likely that George Cumming designed the alterations himself.

The 'Notes' reveal that 'Mr Alexander Wilson from Berwickshire was the person who carried out all the agricultural improvements for Mr. Cuming and who has ever since superintended the property'.[9] Before his death in 1804, George Cuming had done much else to improve the estate, building the bridge over the Divie below Relugas House, and planting trees:

> Once was Relugas wild and bleak, and drear,
> Till thou with judgement and with taste began
> With nature for thy guide, these woods to rear
> Which now the western breezes gently fan . . .[10]

Thus Lauder built upon the foundations laid by his father-in-law and was able to develop his Picturesque ideas in a mature landscape. So successful was he that Relugas became a focal point for the Picturesque movement in Scotland. In fact, he had some difficulty getting started on work at Relugas himself, occasioned by the mismanagement, 'not to give it any harsher appellation', of his father-in-law's partner and man of business after his death, Mr John Wauchope. He appears to have concentrated his early efforts in building up the estate to about 1,000 acres, and, as the notes to stanza 12 state, he also indulged in some earthworks:

> The house of Relugas did not always stand on a lovely level green. The front of it was choked by an enormous lumpish hill, rising close to it. This was part of the promontory to the south west which had been so frequently pared and cut, that it had all the formality of an artificial mount. The public road ran close behind it, so that it was impossible to remove it without laying the place open to every passenger. But after the grand new Parliamentary road was carried through the property in 1810, I cut it entirely away and carried it out to the north of the house, increasing the space in that direction.

It was not until his father's death in 1820, when he became the 7th Baronet, that he was capable of the major alterations to Relugas that his lifestyle now required. The house, so far from Sir Thomas's real element, Edinburgh society, had to grow to accommodate as much of that society as he could draw north, and the additions developed in proportion to the number of visitors that the house was required to accommodate.

No drawings for any work at Relugas have yet appeared, and the architect of the major additions undertaken by Sir Thomas is unknown. Sir Thomas himself, no doubt, had a great influence on the work. Unexpectedly, the Grange in Edinburgh provides the date for the work at Relugas. The Lauder family made little use of the Grange, and it had been let for a long period previous to August 1830, when William Henry Playfair (1790–1858), one of the leading architects in Edinburgh, was asked to produce plans for enlargement. These alterations, suitably modest for a family whose motto reads 'ut migraturus habita' (dwell as if about to depart), provided little more than a new entrance, a dining-room and a drawing-room.[11] Lauder and his architect would no doubt have been delighted at MacGibbon and Ross's comment in 1892 that 'the old portions and the new are so blended together that at first sight one hardly knows where the old work ends and the new begins'.[12]

The works were estimated at £3,343 7s 4d in December 1830, and in January the following year Sir Thomas complained that a new house in the fashionable Moray Place at the west end of the city would have cost him less. The clue to the date of the work at Relugas was noted by Mrs Stewart Smith in 1898: 'Above the front portal are the sculptured arms of the Dick Lauder and Cumin families, supported by the white lions, with the date of the re-construction, 1827'.[13] The author was not aware that the alterations to

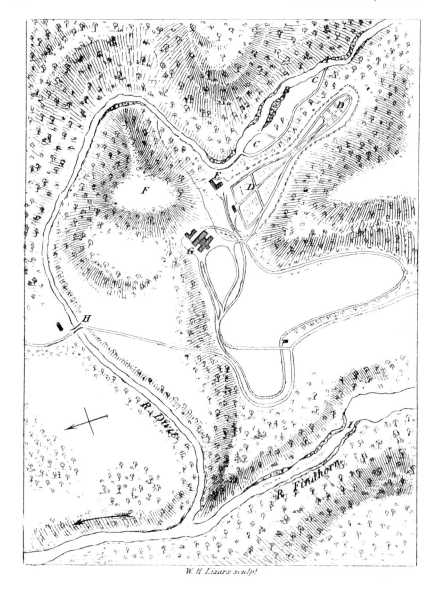

W. H. Lizars sculp.!

A, Macrae's Loun. B Otter's rock. C. C. Mill Island.
D. D. Garden. E. Stables. F. Doune. G. The House.
H. The Bridge of Divie. I. Randolph's Bridge.

FIGURE 22.1 Plan of Relugas by Sir Thomas Dick Lauder, published in his *An Account of the Great Floods*, 1830.

the Grange were not planned until 1830, and it is most likely that this achievement of arms was removed from Relugas when the family sold the house in 1847.[14]

The *New Statistical Account* of 1845 offers further information:

> The house of Relugas was considerably enlarged and improved about fourteen years ago [1830], by an addition consisting of a very handsome suite of apartments, 96 feet in length, with an arched vestibule projecting from the centre.[15]

The *porte-cochère* alluded to here is perhaps a clue to the architect. It is of unusual proportions, perhaps not surprisingly, in view of the number of guests welcomed under its protection, and it attracted attention in later published descriptions.[16] It is similar in scale to that designed by W. H. Playfair at Drumbanagher House in Northern Ireland and built in 1829–30. Playfair also designed Dunphail House, the next house along the River Findhorn from Relugas, for Major Cuming-Bruce in 1829,[7] and, as we have seen, he produced drawings for the Grange in 1830, which were made between visits to Drumbanagher. Playfair is the most likely architect of the 1827 additions to Relugas.

Elizabeth Grant of Rothiemurchus, who visited Relugas in 1809 but wrote of her experience much later, provides a description of the occupants which is worthy of repetition:

> Mr. & Mrs. Lauder were little more than children themselves, in manner at least; really young in years and gifted with almost bewildering animal spirits, they did keep up a racket at Relugas! It was one eternal carnival: up late, a plentiful Scotch breakfast, out all day, a dinner of many courses, mumming all evening and a supper at the end to please the old lady ... Sir Thomas, with all his frivolity, was a very accomplished man; his taste is excellent, as all his improvements showed; no walks could have been better conducted, no trees better placed, no views better chosen, and his refinement was carried all through, to the colours of the furniture and the arrangement of it ...[18]

It was this accomplishment which drew so many visitors north, with the added promise of entertainment and the culinary skills of the 'old lady', Mrs Cuming:

> The gooseberry, humble fruit! – her power obeys,
> And yields a juice which that of Spain defies.[19]

Henry, Lord Cockburn (1779–1854), took a party north each year which, by 1824, had become known as the Findhorn Club, such was its size and regularity. Indeed, in June 1824 he hired the entire Caledonian Coach from Edinburgh to Inverness to transport himself and his party.[20]

One visitor whom Sir Thomas could not entice north was Sir Walter Scott, to whom he wrote long and detailed letters on history and books. In an extraordinary letter written in 1824, he describes two chairs he had made, which were still in the vestibule at the Grange in 1898:[21]

> I have had two of them executed here for my vestibule, and the arms emblazoned on them in the true tinctures and metals and their effect really exceeds my most sanguine expectations. I was led to design this sort of chair from my Cabinet maker having sent me a set of sketches of the wretched armorial chairs usually made for halls, which are mean in the extreme. The idea occurred to me of giving the chair somewhat the appearance of the shield and helmet as erected in the chapel previous to a tilting match; and although it was impossible to combine the trophy, as accurately as placed, with the form which a chair must of necessity assume, yet I think I have in some degree succeeded, + I do not despair to see the idea improved upon. The front feet of my chairs are made to represent the buts of two tilting lances. Those behind are of the same form, but are carried quite through the chair, and elevated to the length of 11 feet, all the height that the vestibule of my cottage will admit of, though perhaps they would be better were there room to make them somewhat higher. They are terminated with real lance heads of iron, + have the proper red silken pennons attached to them, with the crest and motto done in silver on them. The seat, legs and lances, are all made of black bog oak, or the wood stained black. The shields are cut out of Sycamore, + the carved helmet and crest are (to use carpenters language) planted on, and the whole is painted and gilded, and silvered properly, according to the heraldic bearings. The moment I had conceived the idea of these chairs, the armoury at Abbotsford crossed my mind, and I bethought me, how noble would be the effect of a few of these chairs placed in two rows down the sides of the grand hall of arms, and I resolved to take the liberty of sending you a sketch of one.[22]

After the hospitality of the house, it was the landscape at Relugas which was the great attraction. It was the product of minimal interference in the eighteenth century and carefully-controlled improvements in the nineteenth. The Rev. William Leslie, in 1823, noted:

> All this impressive scenery is to the highest advantage exhibited at Relucas; the Baronet, at no light cost, having formed trim walks in the most classic pastoral taste along the precipitous rock; yet everywhere so

obviously safe, that the most conceitedly affected Miss, could make no pretence of apprehension.[23]

In 1842, Sir Thomas, by then an established authority on Picturesque taste, edited a reprint of Sir Uvedale Price, *An Essay on the Picturesque* (London, 1794), into which he inserted his own comments. There can be little doubt that he was referring to his own work at Relugas when he said:

> I have seen a secluded ravine, so wild, with fallen rocky fragments tossed down all over the bottom, and so overgrown with weeds and brambles . . . so that it became almost impossible to scramble through it without the imminent risk of grazing the shins, if not of breaking a leg; whilst in other parts, there were swamps which were almost impassable. What was to be done in such a case as this? At the expence of much gunpowder, a smooth gravel walk with regular and equidistant edges, would have been constructed by a disciple of the smoothing and shaving style of gardening, whilst those of the opposite school might have said 'let it not be touched at all'. The plan followed was different from either. Covered drains at a very considerable expense were put into all the boggy places, so that the ground was not only rendered perfectly firm, but the grassy surface was improved in quality, and thus it was left untouched and natural looking, whilst all appearance of art was hid below the ground. Then as to the stony parts – the smaller fragments were removed irregularly, and thrown aside in such a manner as to leave a naturally winding passage among the larger masses, the great, deep, and dangerous holes were filled up with fragments of stone, and so the weeds were allowed to rise among them, in such a manner, as to give the whole the perfect effect of accident . . . Had the work been so ill done as that the art employed had been permitted to have exposed itself, the whole of the sentiment of wild and savage loneliness with which this ravine, that led to nothing, was filled, would have fled.[24]

Previously, in the same publication, he had noted that:

> whilst untaught Nature, or the accurate imitation of an untaught Nature, should be permitted wildly to luxuriate everywhere throughout the extended grounds, those more immediately connected with the house should be formed by Nature which has yielded herself somewhat to the rules of art, so as to be in harmony with the formality of architecture . . .

Sir Thomas appears to have taken his cue from Henry Home, Lord Kames (1696–1782), an enthusiastic improver who in his *Elements of Criticism*

(Edinburgh, 1763) wrote that regularity was required in that part of the garden which was adjacent to the dwelling house, but, in proportion to the distance from the house, the regularity ought to be less considered. The gardens at Relugas were thus not very original for their date, but they were regarded as the most striking of their kind, combining cultivated areas around the house with skilfully-managed 'nature' nearby, in the ravines of the Divie. Writing in 1830, Sir Thomas described his beloved Relugas:

> Entering the Relugas property from the Dunphail march, a branch of the pleasure-walks led down the left bank of the Divie, for above two miles, quite to the point of its junction with the Findhorn ... The rocks and recesses of the woodland banks, and the little grassy slopes were covered in a wild way with many thousand shrubs, of all kinds, especially with laurels, rhododendrons, azaleas, lilacs, and a profusion of roses ... whilst the rocks were covered with the different saxifrages, hung with all sorts of creepers and enamelled with a variety of garden flowers, all growing artlessly, as if sown by the hand of Nature ... On the Mill Island itself, the greatest care was lavished, the peaceful mill-stream, the lawny grass glades, the winding walks, and the rocky ridges, having been adorned with all that was most rare, till it was converted into a spot of delightful retirement. At its lower extremity the mill-stream returned into the river over a broken cascade, crossed by picturesque bridges, where a little rustic Doric temple, partly constructed of masonry and partly of unpeeled spruce trees, occupied an isolated rock.[25]

On 29 July 1829, he had written to Sir Walter Scott that he was superintending the thinning of some old trunks of wood.[26] He can hardly have begun before disaster struck. The Relugas estate was devastated by the floods which swept through Morayshire on 3 and 4 August 1829, destroying an enormous amount of property. One of the first parts of the carefully devised landscape to be swept away was the small thatched temple described above and which appears in a delightful portrait of Thomas's son, John Dick Lauder (1813–1876), 8th Baronet (see Figure 22.4), still in the family collection. It was in this temple that Sir Thomas sheltered from a sultry shower on his return from church on the morning of Sunday, 2 August.

Lauder's description of the flood still makes terrifying reading, not least because of the author's apparent lack of concern for his own safety. Nearly thirty years after standing in the Hermitage at Dunkeld in awe of the thundering waters of the Bran, his fear is tempered only by his delight in the force of nature:

FIGURE 22.2   Sir Thomas Dick Lauder's sketch of Relugas before the Great Flood of 1829.

FIGURE 22.3   Sir Thomas Dick Lauder's view of Relugas after the Great Flood of 1829.

FIGURE 22.4   Portrait of John Dick Lauder aged fifteen, by Donald Alexander.

> At the bridge over the Divie, to the north of the house, the river
> bounding out from the rocky glen behind the Doune, was fearful. The
> arch is 24 feet high, and its span from rock to rock is 60 feet. The flood
> filled up more than two thirds of its height, being above 16 feet up
> within it ... As we stood on the bridge, we were distinctly sensible of a
> continued tremulous motion, besides which we felt as if its fabric
> received sudden blows, at irregular intervals. It required nerve to stand
> in its centre, and look over its upper parapet ...

Sir Thomas published two etchings of the scene below the house, showing
it before and after the flood, which speak louder than words about the force of
the water[27] (see Figures 22.2 and 22.3).

Elizabeth Grant gave the education of his children as the reason for the
family quitting Relugas for Edinburgh in 1831, and no doubt this had some
bearing on the decision. However, 1829 also saw the death of old Mrs

FIGURE 22.5   Pencil drawing of Relugas by Thomas North Dick-Lauder, 1896. Private
collection.

Cuming, the very heart of the convivial spirit which abounded in the house.
There were few reasons left to stay at Relugas.

The house, as we have seen, was sold shortly before the death of Sir Thomas
in 1848, and it remained much as it appears in the drawing of 1896 (see Figure
22.5), made by Thomas North Dick Lauder (1846–1919), 9th Baronet, who
was apparently employed by *Country Life* magazine as an illustrator. It was
eventually demolished in 1957, having been uninhabited for a number of
years, and replaced by a modern house.

NOTES

1. For another delightful and complete account of the Hermitage at
   Dunkeld, see David Irwin, 'A "Picturesque" Experience: The Hermitage at Dunkeld', *Connoisseur*, vol. 187, no. 753, November 1974, pp.
   196–201.
2. MSS in family collection, 'Account of a Pedestrian Tour through part of
   the Highlands and Hebrides of Scotland, performed in the Autumn
   of 1801 by Messrs Leslie and Lauder'. A Mr Macpherson was also of the
   party, but he remained at Invereshie when the others went north.

3. The family name reversed, on the death of Sir Andrew in 1830, to Dick Lauder. See J. Stewart Smith, *The Grange of St. Giles*, Edinburgh, 1898, p. 310.

4. See Sir Thomas Dick Lauder, *Scottish Rivers*, Edinburgh, 1874, p. 26. This refers to the friendship between Dick Lauder, Williams and the Rev. John Thomson of Duddingston.

5. The *Dictionary of National Biography* states that Lauder was in the 79th Regiment (Cameron Highlanders), but in his 'Notes' to his poem 'Relugas', Lauder refers to Col. James Maitland, a brother officer in the 26th Regiment.

6. MSS in family collection, 'Miscellanies in Prose and Verse' by Sir Thomas Dick Lauder.

7. The 'Notes' to the poem give perhaps the best biographical account of John Gordon.

8. J. Stewart Smith, op. cit.

9. George Cuming had been a close friend of Sir Robert Gordon of Gordonstoun, further along the River Findhorn, and the family had probably learned from Sir Robert that it was difficult to get a gardener to come north. William Miller, gardener at Holyrood Palace, sent Sir Robert at least two young men in 1765 and 1767 with the comment that 'they all want to push southwards'. (See Edinburgh University Library, MSS Laing Add 6, in Laing: Mixed Papers III, Letters to Sir Robert Gordon from William Miller.)

10. MSS in family collection, 'Miscellanies in Prose and Verse', Notes to the poem Relugas, by Sir Thomas Dick Lauder.

11. Lady Dick Lauder had wanted to extend the tower upwards by one floor, but Playfair felt that this would be unsafe. See Edinburgh University Library MSS, Playfair Letter Books, vol. IV, Letters from W. H. Playfair to Sir Thomas Dick Lauder, dated 15 November and 29 December 1830.

12. MacGibbon and Ross (eds), *The Castellated and Domestic Architecture of Scotland*, Edinburgh, 1892, vol. V, pp. 289–93. Mrs J. Stewart Smith, op. cit., p. 357, reproduces a drawing by Sir Thomas Dick Lauder dated 22 January 1825, showing the Grange before the alteration.

13. Stewart Smith, op. cit.

14. J. and W. Watson, *Morayshire Described: being a guide to visitors ...*, Elgin, 1868, p. 119.

15. *New Statistical Account for Scotland*, 1845, vol. XIII, pp. 185–6.

16. J. and W. Watson, op. cit.

17. George Bain, *The River Findhorn*, Nairn, 1911.

18. Lady Strachey (ed.), *Memoirs of a Highland Lady*, London, 1898, p. 98. Elizabeth Grant of Rothiemurchus also gives a description of Relugas, which is in a section of her memoirs dated 1809: 'It had been a common small Scotch House, but an Italian front had been thrown before the old building, an Italian tower had been raised over the offices, and with neatly kept grounds, it was about the prettiest place ever lived in'. However, as she began writing her memoirs in 1845, the alterations which she describes are probably not those made before 1808, but more likely those made later by Sir Thomas.

19. Op. cit. 'Relugas', a poem by Sir Thomas Dick Lauder. A portrait of Mrs Cuming and three of her grandchildren, painted by Donald

Alexander in the drawing-room at Relugas in 1826, was offered for sale at Christie's in Edinburgh on 22 November 1988 (and subsequently), Lot 593 (illustrated in colour).

20. National Library of Scotland, MSS 3909, f. 66–67v, letter from Sir Thomas Dick Lauder to Sir Walter Scott, dated June 1824.
21. Stewart Smith, op. cit., p. 328.
22. National Library of Scotland, MSS 3909, f. 65v–66v, letter from Sir Thomas Dick Lauder to Sir Walter Scott, dated 1 June 1824.
23. Rev. William Leslie, *A Manual of the antiquities, distinguished buildings and natural curiosities of Moray*, Elgin, 1823, p. 79.
24. Sir Thomas Dick Lauder (ed.), *Sir Uvedale Price on the Picturesque, with an Essay on the origin of taste and much original matter*, Edinburgh and London, 1842.
25. Sir Thomas Dick Lauder, *An Account of the Great Floods of August 1829, in the Province of Moray and adjoining Districts*, Edinburgh, 1830.
26. National Library of Scotland, MSS 3909, f. 207, Letter from Sir Thomas Dick Lauder to Sir Walter Scott, dated 29 July 1829.
27. Lauder, op. cit., plates XXVI and XXVII, pp. 98–9.

FIGURE 23.1   View of the Gothic Fountain at Falkland c. 1970, designed by Alexander
Roos, with Falkland Palace beyond.

23

Introducing Alexander Roos

HOWARD COLVIN

To a Scottish architectual historian, the name of Alexander Roos is likely to mean one building only: the Gothic fountain which embellishes the town centre of Falkland in Fife (see Figure 23.1). A spired octagon on a sturdy rectangular base, it dispenses water through two lions' masks, while four more lions stationed at the corners hold up heraldic shields. It was a gift to the town by Mr Tyndall Bruce of Falkland House, but was not fully completed until after his death in 1855. Born Onesiphorus Tyndall, he was a member of a well-known family of Bristol merchants in which his curious Christian name (meaning appropriately 'one who brings profit') was hereditary.[1] He was a barrister by profession, but in 1828 his marriage to Margaret Bruce, the niece and heiress of John Bruce of Nuthill, converted him into a Scottish landowner with a large estate in Fife.[2] Between 1839 and 1844, Onesiphorus Tyndall Bruce replaced the old house of Nuthill with the new House of Falkland designed for him by William Burn, but for the interior decoration and for the design of the formal garden he turned to a young man called Alexander Roos.

Roos is a Germanic name, and Thieme and Becker list a score of artists and craftsmen under it, all German, Austrian, Dutch or Scandinavian. However, Alexander Roos was born in Italy, for he gave that country as his native land in the English census of 1851,[3] and he was generally regarded in England as Italian by birth. Moreover, in a volume of drawings by Roos in the Royal Institute of British Architects' collection, there is a sketch of an Italian house or villa inscribed 'Orti di Sallustio' and accompanied by some sentimental verses which imply that this was the author's birthplace. 'Orti di Sallustio' or 'Horti Sallustiani' was the name of the area in Rome between the Quirinal Hill and the Aurelian Walls to the north. In the early nineteenth century, it was occupied by gardens and villas, in one of which Roos was presumably born. This would fit in with the late Edward Croft-Murray's suggestion that he might have been the son of Karl Roos (1776–1836), a German cabinet-maker established in Rome.[4]

In 1851, Alexander Roos was forty-one years old, so he would have been born in or about 1810. Whatever his parentage, there is abundant evidence that as a young man he made a diligent study of architectural antiquities at Rome, Pompeii, Paestum, Agrigento and elsewhere in Italy. In the volume at the RIBA, there are elegant drawings of an Etruscan tomb at Corneto dated 1829 and many careful copies of painted decoration at Pompeii, some dated 1833. By 1835, however, Roos was in England working for J. H. Galton at Hadzor House in Worcestershire.[5] Hadzor had recently been remodelled by Matthew Habershon, and Roos's role here appears to have been mainly that of an interior decorator. One room decorated in the Pompeian style remains as evidence of his ability to make practical use of his archaeological studies.

J. H. Galton, a member of a wealthy family of bankers, was a man of taste whom the German connoisseur Dr G. F. Waagen described as 'an earnest lover of art' when he visited Hadzor in 1850. In addition to a notable collection of paintings, Galton possessed sculpture by Thorwaldsen, Finelli, Gibson, Gott and R. J. Wyatt.[6] How he came to employ Roos we do not know, but, as he was often in Italy and died there in 1867, he may well have come across him in that country. It is not unlikely that Galton first employed Roos as an itinerant antiquarian draughtsman. This is certainly suggested by the fact that in 1844, when Galton visited Syria, Roos declined an invitation to accompany him owing to his developing architectural practice in England.[7]

From references to Galton in Roos's letters to Tyndall Bruce, it seems probable that it was to the former that he owed his introduction to the latter. At Falkland, Tyndall Bruce's first choice of architect had been C. R. Cockerell. Having failed to persuade Bruce to make Falkland Palace habitable, Cockerell made designs for a new house in a curious semi-Elizabethan style which, for one reason or another, did not satisfy his client, who in the end employed William Burn as his architect.[8] Roos was brought in to design the formal garden and to advise on the interior decoration, which was carried out by D. R. Hay and Co. of Edinburgh. The garden is illustrated in McIntosh's *Book of the Garden*, where it is stated that 'the design and arrangement of the surrounding grounds and flower garden were committed to M. Rous [*sic*], an Italian architect and landscape gardener of rising

FIGURE 23.2   Bird's-eye view of Falkland House, designed by William Burn and showing
Roos's parterres, from Charles McIntosh's *The Book of the Garden*, 1853.

eminence' (see Figure 23.2).[9] The interior decoration appears to have been
mainly in a seventeenth-century style appropriate to the architecture of the
house, but its remodelling by R. W. Schultz for the Marquess of Bute makes
it difficult to distinguish the Neo-Jacobean of the 1840s from the idiosyncratic
Arts and Crafts of the 1890s.[10]

Roos's connection with Tyndall Bruce continued until the latter's death
in 1855. The architect's initial involvement with the house and garden was
followed in 1849 by a commission to design a 'Temple of Decision' and in
1853 the fountain which Bruce presented to the burgh of Falkland. The
temple was to be of the Doric order, and a sketch by Roos agrees with the
existing Doric temple on Green Hill in the Falkland policies. The finishing
touches to this building are set out in an undated 'Memorandum of works
proposed to be done at Falkland' in Roos's hand: this includes repairs to a
'New Bridge in the Pleasure Garden', the planting of rhododendrons in the
Plantations, and various other minor repairs and alterations.[11]

Twenty-five letters from Roos to Tyndall Bruce survive.[12] They extend in
date from 1843 to 1855 and provide a running commentary on the growth of
his architectural practice. It is evident that several of Roos's clients were

FIGURE 23.3   Roos's watercolour design for painted decoration on the Drawing Room
ceiling at Auldbar Castle. The splashes of distemper disfiguring the design presumably
occurred during execution.

Tyndall Bruce's friends, and that Roos owed his employment in Scotland
largely to the latter's introductions. Already in 1843 he was carrying out
extensive alterations at Auldbar Castle in Angus for Patrick Chalmers, a laird
of antiquarian interests who wanted to give his house a more picturesque
character than it had received at the hands of a previous architect (perhaps
Archibald Elliott), who had added a symmetrical castellated front in about
1800. In July 1843, Robert Millar, 'mason and builder in Brechin', and
others, contracted to make numerous alterations and additions 'to the House
of Auldbar, consisting of a Vestibule and Drawing Room (see Figure 23.3),
Tower, Entrance Hall, new Court of Kitchen, and Offices', and a 'new
Garden Terrace Wall', 'all conform to Plans and sections prepared by
Alexander Roos Esqr., Architect in London'.[13] The Gothic Lodge at Auldbar,
illustrated in the Edinburgh *Building Chronicle* for 1854 as the design of
'Signor Roos', must have been added some years later.

   In October 1843, it was through Tyndall Bruce that Roos was invited to go
to Gask in Perthshire to design a 'Terrace and Garden' contemplated by Mr
Oliphant of that Ilk, and at the same time he was engaged in 'gardening and
planting' for R. B. Wardlaw Ramsay at Whitehill House, Lasswade, Midlothian. This, like Falkland, was a house of which Burn was the architect, and
Roos acknowledged Burn's helpfulness towards him. There was, he said, 'no
feeling of rivalry or professional jealousy' between them. On the contrary,

Burn 'recommends me everywhere for the improvement of [the] gardens and grounds of houses' which he was building. One of these was Revesby Abbey in Lincolnshire. Other English houses where Roos was employed as an interior decorator or as a garden designer were Drayton in Northamptonshire (garden 1844, interior of Great Hall decorated a few years later),[14] and Tyntesfield, Somerset (garden 1849–50).[15] In March 1845, he was back from an unnamed country house near Buxton, in May 1848 from Ireland, and in May 1849 from Inverness-shire. Roos's practice was, however, by no means confined to gardening and decorating. One of his earliest works in England was the remodelling in an Italianate style of Bedgebury near Goudhurst in Kent for General Viscount Beresford, who had bought the estate in 1836. The transformation was already in progress in 1838,[16] and in 1840 Colbran's *New Guide to Tunbridge Wells* spoke enthusiastically of the new 'Palladian' front, of the flower garden 'laid out in the Italian style', and of the elegant interiors. 'The architectural proportions and embellishments, inside and out, are from the designs of Alexander Roos, Esq., a young Italian artist of great taste and judgement, by whom, also, the ceilings of the principal rooms are painted'. When General Beresford's stepson and heir, Alexander Beresford Hope, newly imbued with the ideals of the Cambridge Camden Society, decided to apply them to the neighbouring church at Kilndown, recently erected to the designs of Salvin, Roos was one of the architects involved in converting this characteristic wide-naved box of 1839 into a richly-decorated interior, complete with all the apparatus of the new ecclesiology.[17] Beresford Hope's elder brother Henry Thomas Hope was the owner of the Deepdene in Surrey, the country house built by their connoisseur father Thomas Hope (d. 1831). Between 1836 and 1841, Henry Thomas Hope had the Deepdene remodelled in the Italianate style, and the existence in the Yale Center for British Art of a plan of the house made by Roos in 1841 strongly suggests that he was involved.[18] Another early client was Sir William Middleton of Shrubland Park, Suffolk, where in 1841 Roos designed an authentically Italianate lodge at the Ipswich entrance to the park some years before Barry's involvement in the house itself.[19] In February 1845, Roos informed Tyndall Bruce that he was about to begin two new buildings, 'one in the Italian and the other in the Gothic style'. A reference to Lord Ellenborough identifies the latter as Southam Delabere in Gloucestershire, where Roos must have been responsible for some of the Neo-Norman and Gothic additions to the Tudor manor-house which, to modern taste, by no means improved it.[20]

Already an architect, a decorator and a garden designer, Roos in 1851 embarked on a new career as an urban developer on the Bute estate in South Wales. His patron Tyndall Bruce had been the 'dearest and most intimate friend' of the second Marquess of Bute, and after the latter's early death in

1848 he was one of the two trustees who managed the estate on behalf of the infant heir.[21] The development of Cardiff into a major industrial city and port, already under way in 1845, was their joint responsibility, and, on Tyndall Bruce's recommendation, Roos was appointed architect to the Bute estate. Here he quickly gained the confidence both of Bruce's co-trustee John Boyle and of the Dowager Lady Bute, who considered him 'very agreeable and gentlemanlike as well as clever in his profession'.[22] A letter to Bruce dated 15 April 1851 shows him setting out a street in St John's parish, building detached villas 'near the Toll Gate on the Newport Road', and taking stock of Lady Bute's schemes for an almshouse and for a 'Museum to collect the Pictures of the late Marquess of Bute'. In Cathays Park, he was involved in laying out the shrubberies and an arboretum with a fountain, and in establishing a bowling green. Two years later, he was 'very busy making plans for new Squares and Terraces' and superintending the construction of a main sewer, or *cloaca ex agro Cardiffii*, as he facetiously called it. He was also designing (gratis) the Sailors' Home which Bute munificence bestowed on the rapidly expanding town. Roos's original sketch design among Tyndall Bruce's papers shows a substantial building of Jacobean character with entrance hall and administrative offices at one end of a double row of 'cabins', and kitchen and dining-hall at the other.[23] By 1855, the Sailors' Home was nearly finished, a church (All Saints) had been begun to Roos's designs, and he was starting work on a terrace of houses about 300 feet long next to a street named after Tyndall. Tyndall Bruce's death the same year deprives us of further letters from his architectural protégé, and as soon as the 3rd Marquess of Bute came of age in 1868 he dismissed Roos and gave his architectural patronage to John Prichard of Llandaff and William Burges.[24] This seems to have marked the end of Roos's career as an architect. He died in London on 30 June 1881, leaving an estate valued at the then substantial sum of £27,663. The principal beneficiary of his will was his 'dear and valued friend' Edward Sayer of Oak Lodge, Finchley, but he also left £5,000 to his sister 'Emilia Roos, widow Bonin, residing in Rome', £200 to his 'kind landlady' at 38 Pulteney Street, and £100 to the rector of St James, Piccadilly, for distribution to the poor.[25]

Such, then, was the career of Alexander Roos, so far as it can at present be reconstructed. Largely sustained by the patronage of Onesiphorus Tyndall Bruce, his practice extended to every part of the British Isles, and comprised landscape gardening as well as architecture and interior decoration. Nothing he designed was of major importance, but the participation of an Italian-born architect in the Italian revival of the 1830s and early 1840s is of obvious interest. As the designer of formal gardens with parterres and balustraded terraces, Roos was (with W. A. Nesfield) one of the pioneers of the Victorian flower-garden. As a Gothic architect, despite his early association with Beresford Hope, he inevitably suffers from comparison with his successors at Cardiff, Prichard and Burges. Even by the standards of the 1850s, his churches at Cardiff and Streatham were buildings of little distinction.[26] But at least the fountain at Falkland remains to his credit as a worthy memorial, both to the munificence of Onesiphorus Tyndall Bruce and to the talented young architect whose career he did so much to foster.

NOTES

1. The death of Onesiphorus Tyndall, merchant, at Bristol, is recorded in the *Gentleman's Magazine* for 1753, p. 200.
2. J. Bateman, *The Great Landowners of Great Britain* (1879), credits Bruce's son with 7,058 acres in Fife and a rent-roll of over £11,000.
3. Microfilm in Westminster City Library, return under 38 Great Pulteney Street, London, where Roos lived in lodgings.
4. Edward Croft-Murray, *Decorative Painting in England 1537–1837*, vol. 2 (1970), p. 271. The RIBA *Drawings Catalogue* mistakenly locates 'Orti di Sallustio' in Turin.
5. See Croft-Murray, op. cit. I have not examined the Galton papers in the Reference Library at Birmingham, but the catalogue mentions a specification for stables with a cancelled building agreement dated 1843 which is witnessed by Roos.
6. G. F. Waagen, *Treasures of Art in Great Britain*, vol. 3 (1854), pp. 220–6. See also *Joseph Gott Sculptor*, Exhibition Catalogue, Leeds, 1972, p. 52.
7. Letters to O. Tyndall Bruce in Scottish Record Office, GD152/53/4, Bundle 27/11.
8. For Cockerell's design, see David Watkin, *C. R. Cockerell*, 1974, pp. 192, 252, plate 93. There are nine letters from Cockerell to O. T. Bruce about this commission in SRO, GD152/53/1, dating from 1828 to 1835.
9. C. McIntosh, *The Book of the Garden*, vol. 1 (1853), pp. 618–19. The inner parterres on either side of the principal fountain were planted with scarlet geraniums, verbenas and similar showy plants, while the outer ones at the angles were laid out in coloured sand. In a letter of 12 May 1844 to Tyndall Bruce, Roos advocates the use for gardening purposes of 'brickdust, Mineral Coal, Copper Ore, various kinds of Shells, Chalk, Colored Marbles, broken in small particles, quartz, Iron Ore, Glass, and particularly the remains of a Glass casting which is thrown away at the manufacture, Sands, *puzzolana*, and in fact any sort of mineral or coloured marble which you can procure in your neighbourhood' (SRO, GD152/53/4, Bundle 27/9).
10. For the latter, see Gavin Stamp, *Robert Weir Schultz and his work for the Marquess of Bute*, 1981, pp. 24–31.
11. SRO, GD152/204/1/6/4. Roos's sketch is in his letter of 11 May 1849 (GD152/53/5/10/3).
12. They are to be found in SRO, GD152/53/4, 5, 6, 7, 196 and 198. I am greatly indebted to Miss Ierne Grant, who catalogued the Tyndall Bruce papers, for directing me to Roos's letters and for much other assistance.

13. National Library of Scotland, Chalmers of Auldbar papers, MS 15436, f. 57. Letters from Roos are in MS 15421, ff. 18–56, drawings in MS 15437. There are further drawings, including some by Roos, in the National Monuments Record of Scotland. Auldbar was demolished in 1964.

14. On 12 May 1844, Roos wrote to Tyndall Bruce from Drayton to say that he was 'laying [out] the Gardens and new Buildings'. For his redecoration of the Great Hall, see John Cornforth in *Country Life*, 27 May 1965, p. 1289.

15. See Roos's letters of 11 May 1849 and 15 February 1850.

16. C. Greenwood, *Epitome of County History: Kent*, 1838, p. 230.

17. J. Newman, *West Kent and the Weald*, Buildings of England, 1976, p. 353. See also I. Law, *The Book of the Beresford Hopes*, 1925.

18. The plan is illustrated by G. B. Waywell, *The Lever and Hope Sculptures*, Monumenta Artis Romanae XVI, Berlin, 1986, fig. 8.

19. C. Hussey, 'Shrubland Park, Suffolk', *Country Life*, 19 November 1953, p. 1657.

20. N. Kingsley, *The Country Houses of Gloucestershire*, 1, Cheltenham, 1989, pp. 167–9.

21. John Davies, *Cardiff and the Marquess of Bute*, Cardiff, 1981, p. 45.

22. GD152/53/6, bundle 13.

23. The drawing is SRO, GD152/198/18/8. See also *Builder* 1853, p. 470, 1856, p. 21. The Sailors' Home has been demolished.

24. J. Mordaunt Crook, 'Patron Extraordinary: John, 3rd Marquess of Bute (1847–1900)', in *Victorian South Wales*, Victorian Society's Seventh Conference Report, 1969.

25. Will in Principal Probate Registry, Somerset House, London.

26. Besides All Saints, Cardiff, Roos was involved in completing St Andrew's Church to his own designs after those of John Prichard proved too expensive (*Builder* 1863, p. 210), but in 1869 work on his own St Margaret's, Roath, was suspended in order that it might be completed to new designs by Prichard that satisfied the 3rd Marquess's exacting taste (see Eastlake, *Gothic Revival*, ed. Crook, 1970, p. 139). For his Immanual Church at Streatham, Surrey, built in 1853–4 at the expense of Tyndall Bruce's friend Andrew Hamilton, and remodelled by Benjamin Ferrey in 1864–5, see Roos's letter of 2 June 1853 to Bruce and a lithograph of the original design in GD152/66.

24

The Scottish Houses of William Leiper

JOHN R. HUME

More than twenty-five years ago, I first encountered the National Monuments Record of Scotland, and Miss Catherine Cruft. As a young lecturer trying to piece together the jigsaw of Scotland's fractured industrial past, I had come to Melville Street to seek photographs. With Miss Cruft's guidance, I ploughed through the Record, boxful by boxful, finding images, ideas and information that have remained with me. That state-of-knowledge overview was immensely important in helping me to create a framework of reference for looking at industrial buildings. Since then, I have had much cause to be grateful to Miss Cruft for help and advice.

In choosing to write a summary overview of William Leiper's houses, I pay tribute to one aspect of the NMRS and Miss Cruft's contribution to it: the way in which it can be used in surveying the general character of a building-type, or the work of a particular architect. No-one would claim that the NMRS is exhaustive, but tantalising gaps can be as stimulating as finding long-sought gems.

William Leiper appealed as an architect about whom surprisingly little had been published.[1] One of his buildings, Templeton's Carpet Factory in Glasgow, has become world-renowned, featuring on one of the architectural stamps issued in 1990, and his churches in Glasgow have become well-known through such books as *Glasgow at a Glance* and *The Architecture of Glasgow*,[2] as has his only major commercial building, the Sun Insurance building in West George Street, where he had his office from 1894.[3] His houses have until recently received much less attention, and this article aims to summarise the basic details of them in a socio-economic framework.

William Leiper was born in Glasgow on 21 May 1839, son of a writing master and teacher of arithmetic.[4] He was brought up in Garnethill and Partick,[5] and was educated at home and at the High School of Glasgow. He served an apprenticeship as an architect with the Glasgow firm of Boucher and Cousland between 1855 and 1861, and then moved to London, where he worked with the well-known Greek Revival architects, J. L. Pearson and William White. He returned to Scotland to join the practice of Andrew Heiton in Perth, a practitioner of the Scottish Baronial style. He strongly influenced Heiton's own work, introducing him to the Early French style.[6] After serving as draughtsman for Heiton in the building of a Dublin church, Leiper returned to Glasgow, where he joined the practice of Campbell Douglas and Stevenson.

With this broad-based experience of both Scottish and English architecture, Leiper joined Robert Grieve Melvin to form the firm of Melvin and Leiper. Their first commission was the competition of Stirling's Library in Miller Street, probably designed by J. Moyr Smith,[7] whose executant architect, James Smith, had died. While in partnership with Melvin, Leiper designed Dumbarton Burgh Hall and Academy, Dowanhill Church in Glasgow and his first two houses, Kirktonhill, Dumbarton, and The Elms, Arbroath. The houses and burgh hall were in a French Gothic style influenced by the work of William Burges, a friend of Leiper's,[8] and Dowanhill was partly inspired by J. L. Pearson's designs. The partnership with Melvin broke up in 1867, and Leiper began to specialise in house design. In 1871, he moved to a house built for himself in Helensburgh, named Terpersie after a castle in his ancestral Aberdeenshire. He lived there for the rest of his life, with only a short intermission. Leiper never married, but stained-glass monograms and portraits of Mary Queen of Scots and Darnley in Terpersie hint at a broken romance.

Apart from houses, discussed below, Leiper continued to design churches and public buildings. Partick Burgh Halls (1872) incorporates the first example of Beaux Arts detailing in Glasgow.[9] His churches in Brechin, Lanark and Whiteinch were modest affairs, but his Queen's Park Church was elaborate and refined. He entered competitions for Woodlands United Presbyterian Church (1874) and Hillhead Established Church (1875) but was unsuccessful, though elements of his designs were incorporated in the churches built.[10] Leiper's disappointment was a factor in his departure for Paris, in 1878 to study painting, but the collapse of the 1870s building boom in that year was probably a more powerful reason. In 1881, he was attracted back to Scotland by a commission to design the interiors of the circular

Russian Imperial Yacht, *Livadia*, ordered from John Elder and Co. of Govan, said to have been the first such commission from a recognised architect.[11]

Thereafter, he combined a successful practice in house design and alteration with commissions for a variety of other buildings. He was responsible for the major churches of Hyndland and St James's, Kilmacolm and a minor Catholic Apostolic church in Govanhill, Glasgow. He designed small schools in Helensburgh[12] and Garelochhead, and the William Black Memorial Lighthouse on Mull.[13] His finest works of this period are probably Templeton's Carpet Factory and the Sun Insurance Office in Glasgow. The former is the most dazzling factory building of its period, and the latter won a silver medal at the Paris Exhibition of 1900. It was one of the first modern office blocks in Glasgow. Leiper took W. Hunter McNab into partnership in 1896, and retired in 1909, though the partnership nominally continued until 1911. His last building was probably a private Roman Catholic Chapel at Glendaruel, built in 1912,[14] and his last commission was organising the mural decoration of the Banqueting Hall in Glasgow City Chambers by a group of Glasgow artists, a scheme completed in 1915. William Leiper died at his home, Terpersie, on 27 May 1916, and was buried in the family lair in Sighthill Cemetery, Glasgow.[15]

Leiper was a competent painter both of landscapes and of architectural subjects, and always emphasised the artistic in his designs. His particular architect friends were similarly inclined. They included Alexander Thomson, J. L. Pearson, William Burges and John Honeyman. He was also friendly with several Scottish painters of repute, notably William McTaggart. Leiper ran his practice along the lines of a studio, and several of his apprentices made names as artistic architects, including James Salmon the Younger, A. N. Prentice, Leonard Rome Guthrie and J. Steel Maitland, his last apprentice.[16] He worked, like Lorimer, with noted craftsmen and craft firms in both London and Scotland, including Daniel Cottier, Guthrie and Co., W. B. Simpson, J. and G. Mossman, Birnie Rhind and McCulloch and Co.[17] His local reputation as a man of broad cultural interests is confirmed by an obituary which described him as landscape painter, rose-grower, member and office-bearer in St Columba's Church, Helensburgh, in which he was superintendent of the Sunday School and convener of the music committee.[18] More broadly, his professional abilities were recognised by his election as FRIBA in 1881, when he was proposed by Honeyman, Pearson and Burges,[19] and by his election as associate of the Royal Scottish Academy in 1891 and full member in 1896. He was a regular exhibitor at RSA exhibitions.

Leiper's concern for the artistic is evident in all his buildings, even minor ones. His interest in landscape is clear in the siting of his houses, with the plan carefully adapted to the setting and exposure, and with gardens designed

FIGURE 24.1   Cornhill House, near Biggar, from the south-west, designed by William
Leiper in French Gothic with Renaissance details.

to enhance the architecture. In his early houses, variety of roof forms was a
dominant feature, and though this becomes less obvious in later houses it
remains a characteristic of his style. So too is variation in the disposition of
windows and their design, and in wall construction. Carved details and
leaded and stained glass are effectively used in the spirit of the Gothic, which
was his earliest enthusiasm.

The nature and timing of Leiper's house commissions was clearly influenced by the Victorian and Edwardian trade cycles, with their succession
of booms and slumps. The boom of the mid-1860s, associated with the
American Civil War, allowed him to build his most elaborate houses, and the
early 1870s' prosperity linked to the Franco-Prussian War gave him another
window of opportunity. Though the 1880s were not a notable period of
prosperity, the cost of building materials fell and real incomes rose,[20] giving
Leiper a chance to design for less obviously wealthy clients. The later 1890s'
boom once again gave Leiper scope for more opulent designs, and though the
mid-1900s were not so prosperous there was still enough money around to
allow him to go on designing houses until the end of his active career.

It has not so far proved possible to identify the occupations of all of Leiper's
clients.[21] Some may, indeed, have been gentlemen in the Victorian sense of
men of wealth without particular occupation. Of those who can be identified,
most were industrialists or merchants, including two shipbuilders, a ship-

FIGURE 24.2   Cairndhu, Helensburgh, from the south-west, designed by Leiper in
François I style.

owner, three men in the textile trade (including one of the Templetons
who commissioned the carpet factory), two grocers, a distiller, a painter, a
cornflour maker, an oil merchant and a flour miller. All these men were
notable in their own industries and trades. The flour miller was the Lord
Provost of Glasgow. Professional and semi-professional clients included an
advocate, a surgeon, two estate factors and a stockbroker. Two were women,
a hotelier and a lady, probably a widow. This spectrum indicates that while
designing largely for the nouveau riche of the period, he received commissions from the more prominent and distinguished members of his potential
client group.

What his clients received varied widely in style and scale. Leiper worked in
French Gothic and Renaissance, Baronial, Greek Revival, Jacobean/Flemish
and a variety of Arts and Crafts styles, sometimes mixing them to a
remarkable extent. The following is a summary analysis of his principal styles
and the periods during which he used them. His first houses, Kirktonhill,
The Elms and Ranochlea, are in early French Gothic of the 'muscular variety'
of a type fashionable in the 1850s and used by Pearson, Burges and John
Prichard.[22] French Gothic details are also found in Leiper's extension to
Wheatpark. At Cornhill (see Figure 24.1) similar early French predominates,
but there are some Renaissance details in the tower, and in Cairndhu and
Balgray the style is François I Renaissance. Cairndhu (see Figure 24.2) has

FIGURE 24.3   Dalmore, Helensburgh, from the south-west, designed by Leiper in the
Scots Baronial style.

remarkable Anglo-Japanese interiors. The strong roof shapes of these houses
are carried through to the lodges, especially at Cornhill and The Elms. The
roof tower at Ranochlea has a similar profile to that of the Eagle Wharf
warehouses in London designed by Richard Norman Shaw.[23]

The next style adopted by Leiper was Scots Baronial. This had already
been developed on a grand scale by William Burn, David Bryce,[24] Charles
Kinnear of Peddie and Kinnear, and by Brown and Wardrop. Leiper's
Baronial, though using some motifs favoured by other Scottish architects,
especially Bryce, was also influenced by his London experience.[25] His
baronial details are invariably refined variants of genuine Scots domestic
features, mainly of the sixteenth and seventeenth centuries, and some
apparently based on his own investigations.[26] His early houses in this style
were Colearn and Dalmore (1869–73; see Figure 24.3) where the Baronial
exteriors contrast with Aesthetic Movement and Anglo-Japanese details.
There was then a gap of nearly ten years until Ruthven Tower, his most
refined baronial house, which was closely followed by Kinlochmoidart,
an enlarged Dalmore. In the late 1890s and early 1900s, in a period of
fin-de-siècle nostalgia, Leiper designed major extensions to Knockderry
Castle, Ballimore and Glendaruel, and built Auchenbothie and Viewfield.
The banqueting hall in Knockderry Castle is probably his grandest interior.

FIGURE 24.4   Morar Lodge (now Drumadoon), Helensburgh, from the south-west. The centre gable is an addition.

In his earlier Baronial houses, Leiper copied the tower house and lower seventeenth-century house composition found, for example, at Crathes and Fordyce Castles; his later ones have Baronial features applied to less academic forms. Auchenbothie and the minor The Croft, both at Kilmacolm, were the only houses he designed to be completely harled, though he built policy buildings in this style at Piersland, Auchenbothie and Viewfield. Leiper also used Baronial features in Red Tower and Morar Lodge, in stable blocks at Redholm and Piersland, and in a number of lodges, Scots Renaissance details in Deroran[27] and seventeenth-century material in Morar Lodge[28] (see Figure 24.4). The Baronial was Leiper's longest-running style.

According to his partner, W. Hunter McNab, Leiper designed several Greek Revival houses, but the only one yet identified is Bonnyton of about 1871, during his most eclectic period. Superficially similar to an Alexander Thomson house, it differs in treatment of details.[29] Another 'one-off' house is Castlepark which, with its decorated barge boards, has affinities to Boucher and Cousland's double villas of 1859 in Pollokshields[30] but is in other respects rather Japanese/American in style.

Most of Leiper's houses are, however, in a number of styles inspired by French and English vernacular revival styles which may be loosely grouped as Arts and Crafts. Without going into excessive subdivision, seven types and subtypes may be identified. The earliest are two houses built about 1870, Lindsaylands and Redholm. There is French vernacular influence in these, which may also have been inspired by the work of George Devey in the 1850s and of the circle of William White.[31] His own Terpersie, and Queensberry at Kilmacolm, have some features in common with this pair but are much simpler. The bold polygonal bay with gablets which dominates Lindsaylands and Redholm appears in a different guise at Knockderry House.

Leiper's second Arts and Crafts style is found in a group of seven houses, all in the west, the earliest of which dates from about 1883. Their ancestry may clearly be traced to Wealden houses of traditional type, reinterpreted by George Devey in the 1850s, and by Richard Norman Shaw and Devey's pupil Eden Nesfield between 1860 and 1880.[32] Four of the Leiper houses in this style, Tordarroch, Brantwoode, Tighnabruaich and Ard Luss, are basically on an L-plan; the other three, Dorlecote, Aros and Ganavan, are on a compact rectangular plan. The garden front of Deroran (see above) is also in this style. All except Tighnabruaich have tile-hanging on the upper storey, as favoured by Devey and Shaw, and most have some half-timbering, spectacularly Brantwoode. These houses were described in the Appendix as 'later' Arts and Crafts.

Piersland is on its own as a large house with the upper storey fully half-timbered in a Devey/Shaw style,[33] and Leiper's last houses, the three known as Rockbank, Ard Choille and Polkemmet, combine half-timbering (Rockbank) and plain rendering. The use of render in houses of this type was favoured by Lorimer and Voysey.[34] The plans of these houses are, however, similar to the Tordarroch (Polkemmet and Ard Choille) and Dorlecote (Rockbank) types.[35]

To one side of the mainstream of Leiper's Arts and Crafts houses are two, Knockderry House and Uplands, which seem to have been inspired by Richard Norman Shaw's remodelling of Cragside in Northumberland, though both are very much smaller. Knockderry House is, like Cragside, a reworking of a smaller house. The dramatic hillside setting of Uplands strongly evokes Cragside, which also influenced James Sellars's Keil at Campbeltown and John Honeyman's The Cliff, Wemyss Bay.[36]

While Leiper was evolving his Devey-Shaw-Nesfield style, he was also experimenting with a Jacobean-Flemish style. The three houses of this type were all built or extended in 1890–1. Moredun is the plainest, impressive in its vast expanses of polished ashlar. The 1891 extension to Clarendon is reminiscent of Richard Norman Shaw's Dawpool and Adcote, and incorporates Flemish stepped gables.[37] These appear exuberantly in Kelly House, which appears from photographs[38] to have been a richly-detailed but rather

FIGURE 24.5   Deroran (now Endrick Lodge), Stirling, from the east.

undisciplined building. It is revealing that his partner McNab claimed that Kelly was Leiper's favourite among his own works.

The last of Leiper's distinctive styles was to be found in a major addition to Glenkin, a minor addition to 19 East Montrose Street, both in Helensburgh, and in Westbreak, Kilmacolm. These were all characterised by 'coolie hat' roofs to corner towers or turrets.[39]

Deroran (see Figure 24.5) is in an intriguing mixture of styles. As already mentioned, it has some Scots Renaissance features, but the rest of the entrance front is somewhat in the manner of Lutyens. The garden front is, more typically for Leiper, elaborately tile-hung.

Allusion has been made to Leiper's interiors. The earlier houses had Aesthetic Movement decoration; in the houses of his middle period, Neo-Jacobean predominated. In all the houses where much original work survives, the quality of interior work is outstanding. Even where the interiors are in a plain Arts and Crafts style, as at Tighnabruaich and Ard Choille, the timber used (Kauri Pine) is carefully chosen and beautifully worked.

Leiper was certainly influenced by his immediate predecessors and contemporaries, but he put his own stamp on his designs, which in turn influenced his pupils and their contemporaries. In house-building, W. Hunter McNab,

A. N. Paterson, A. N. Prentice, Robert Wemyss, James Miller and Robert
Lorimer all clearly drew from Leiper.[40] McNab in his RIBA obituary used the
term 'Leiperian' twice, about two very different buildings, Moredun and
Tighnabruaich. Drawing from these allusions and developing the concept,
one could identify Picturesque massing, eclectic and refined detailing and
careful use of materials as essential elements in his designs: virtues equally
applicable to Gothic, Baronial and Arts and Crafts buildings.

Picturesque asymmetry is of the essence of Leiper's designs, a quality
derived from his background in the Gothic Revival. His asymmetry never,
however, results in loss of control of the balance necessary to effective
composition, though the surviving photographs suggest that he came peril-
ously near to failure in Kelly. It is, however, on his use of materials and on the
refinement of details that much of the effect of Leiper's houses depends.
Careful choice of stone, good slates, tiles, timber work and lead details are all
characteristic, and there is nothing thin or mean about his buildings. His
sense of colour was particularly good, and there is a warmth about many of
his houses that suits the frequently dull weather of the west coast of Scotland.
He often used red or pink sandstones, sometimes contrasting them with grey
rubble. He generally used snecked rubble, with a stugged surface, sometimes
with slanting joints. Where he used moulded or carved stonework, the
execution was always vigorous, reflecting the quality of the craftsmen he
employed. The window mullions and transoms in his Baronial houses were
more rounded in section than normal, a distinctive feature, and his mouldings
were generously proportioned.

Leiper used both slates and tiles for roofs, favouring light-coloured slates
and terracotta tiles, which he also used in the Sussex manner for vertical
faces. His external timber work was generally bold and simple, as was his use
of lead for finials and rainwater heads. His wrought-iron finials, often topped
with dated pennons, were, however, more ornate.

In their commentary on Leiper's house, Terpersie, Greig and Clarkson
suggest that he had little interest in windows,[41] but this is not borne out by
scrutiny of his other houses. Bow, oriel, Gothic, Arts and Crafts, stone and
timber mullions and transoms abound. Within these glazing frames, Leiper
was particularly imaginative, using both stained and plain leaded glass. In
his earlier houses, he used Aesthetic Movement glass comparable to that
employed by Philip Webb in his Red House at Bexleyheath, with portrait
heads. He then moved on to Anglo-Japanese treatments as favoured by the
Glasgow school of artists, including Daniel Cottier (Cairndhu).[42] At Knockderry Castle, the glass was by Guthrie and Co., Glasgow.[43] In his later
houses, he frequently used clear leaded glass, with distinctive geometrical
patterns.

Leiper was, like James Miller, a 'clients' architect' in the sense of being willing to design in a range of styles, unlike Alexander Thomson, whose houses are almost all Greek Revival, or Charles Rennie Mackintosh, who built exclusively in his Early Modern Movement style. Leiper's houses, on the whole, lack the single-theme vision of either of these architects. Instead, like his contemporaries in England, his designs were imbued with an Arts and Crafts love of variety of texture, colour, detail, of advancing and retreating planes, and of complex structures. Leiper's houses all repay repeated viewing and study, revealing him as an architect of remarkable sensitivity and thought. His sophisticated architecture of allusion and incident, made unfashionable by the Modern movement, had much to offer clients at the time, and still has a powerful appeal.

ACKNOWLEDGEMENTS

A synthetic, synoptic article like this must be based on a wide range of sources, as well as on extensive fieldwork. The author would like to thank particularly his friend and colleague, David Walker, whose notes on Leiper were a first-class introduction, and who commented on a draft of this article; Anne Riches, who provided a transcript of Leiper's RIBA nomination; Deborah Mays for advice and comments, and for typing the manuscript; Bernadette Goslin and Fiona Sinclair for help with houses in west Dunbartonshire; Ian Gow and Simon Green of the RCAHMS for information and support; Graham Hopner, Local Studies Librarian, Dumbarton District for access to Dean of Guild records; Lesley Couperwhite of the Watt Library, Greenock for photographs of Kelly House; and Rosalind Wood of the Mitchell Library, Glasgow. He is much indebted to Mrs Burges, Mr Craig, Mrs Gray, Mr de Haan, Mrs Leech, Miss MacDougall, Mrs MacGregor, Mrs McLintock, Mr and Mrs Parker, Mrs Stott and Mr and Mrs White for giving access to and information on Leiper buildings in their ownership.

NOTES

1. Apart from contemporary references, including obituaries, Frank Worsdall's 'Victorian Architect: William Leiper RSA 1839–1916', *Scottish Field*, June 1966, is the only published general account. An undergraduate thesis, 'William Leiper', by Thomas Greig and Alastair G. Clarkson of the Mackintosh School of Architecture (1978–9), builds on these sources, supplemented by selective fieldwork. David Walker's unpublished notes on Leiper are summarised in Andor Gomme and David Walker, *The Architecture of Glasgow* (1st edn, 1968, 2nd edn 1978), p. 294. My own note on Leiper in the Hyndland Parish Church Magazine, June 1987, was based partly on Dr Walker's notes.
2. A. M. Doak and Andrew McLaren Young (eds), *Glasgow at a Glance* (1st edn, 1965); Gomme and Walker, op. cit.

3. Frank Worsdall, *Victorian City*, 1982, p. 63.
4. Biographical section based largely on David Walker's notes, RIBA Fellowship papers (courtesy of Anne Riches), and obituaries in *Glasgow Herald*, *Journal of the Royal Institute of British Architects*, and *Helensburgh and Garelochhead Times*.
5. Renfrew Street (where he was born); Meadowbank Place, Partick; Annfield Terrace, Partick; and Dalhousie Street, Garnethill. He lived at 6 Annfield Terrace (now Banavie Road) from 1861–70, apart from his time in London (Post Office Directories).
6. Information courtesy of David Walker.
7. Information courtesy of David Walker.
8. According to W. H. McNab in the RIBA obituary. A clear source for Dumbarton Burgh Hall is Deane and Woodward's University Museum, Oxford; see C. L. Eastlake, *A History of the Gothic Revival*, 1872, plate facing p. 282.
9. Information courtesy of David Walker.
10. The Woodlands spire closely resembles that of Dowanhill, and Leiper is said to have selected as the prototype for Hillhead the Sainte Chapelle in Paris. Certainly, Leiper used related spirelets in his Lanark and Brechin churches.
11. His departure and return were recorded in *The Baillie*, 20 February 1878 and 1880.
12. Hermitage Primary School, drawing dated May 1893 in Helensburgh Dean of Guild drawings, Dumbarton Public Library.
13. William Black Memorial to a novelist; see D. B. Hague, 'Scottish Lights', in Lizbeth M. Thoms, *Scottish Archaeological Forum 8*, 1977, pp. 86–7.
14. Local tradition has it that 'the architect' came out of retirement to design the chapel as a memorial to Harrison Cripps's first wife, who committed suicide.
15. The family monument was designed by Leiper; he had no memorial of his own. I am indebted to Aonghus MacKechnie for this.
16. A. Stuart Gray, *Edwardian Architecture*, 1985, pp. 182, 294, 316; information from David Walker.
17. See below for Cottier and Guthrie and Co. Mossmans did the sculpture for Partick Burgh Hall, William Birnie Rhind for the Sun Insurance Building and McCulloch and Co for Camphill and Hyndland churches.
18. Obituary in *Helensburgh and Garelochhead Times*, 31 May 1916.
19. Fellowship papers, RIBA.
20. B. R. Mitchell and P. Deane, *Abstract of British Historical Statistics*, 1962, chapters 9 and 12. The cost of building materials fell steadily from 1882 to 1888.
21. These occupations are derived mainly from directories.
22. See e.g. Burges's Knightshayes of 1869, illustrated in Eastlake, op. cit., facing p. 356; and Prichard's Ettington Park of 1858–63, illustrated in Mark Girouard, *The Victorian Country House*, 1979, p. 58.
23. Andrew Saint, *Richard Norman Shaw*, 1976, pp. 29–30.
24. Valerie Fiddes and Alistair Rowan, *David Bryce 1803–1876*, 1976.
25. David Walker has drawn the London links to my attention.
26. Leiper published a sketch of Allardyce Castle in the *Edinburgh Architectural Association Sketchbook*, 1875–6. Many of his Baronial and

Renaissance details can be traced to surviving buildings of the sixteenth and seventeenth centuries, though some, such as the Maybole and Craignethan Castle details, were used earlier by David Bryce.

27. The tower at Deroran has detail derived from the Palace at Stirling Castle.

28. The chimney gable is from the Old College of Glasgow, a late seventeenth-century building.

29. Gomme and Walker, op. cit., pp. 130–6.

30. Castlepark is illustrated in *Historic Buildings of Clydesdale*, 1987, p. 43, and the Boucher and Cousland double villas in Frank Worsdall, *The City that Disappeared*, 1981, p. 35.

31. Jill Allibone, *George Devey, Architect, 1830–1886*, 1991, p. 33, Ashour Lodge; information from David Walker.

32. Ibid., pp. 29, 31, 47; Andrew Saint, op. cit., see chapters 2 and 3 and pp. 160–1. Leiper's contemporary, John McKean Brydon, with whom he worked at Campbell Douglas and Stevenson, had also worked with Shaw; see A. Stuart Gray, op. cit., p. 126.

33. Saint, op. cit., p. 68, Merrist Wood (1876–7).

34. Robert Lorimer was also using this plain style at about the same time; see Peter Savage, *Lorimer and the Edinburgh Craft Designers*, 1980, chapter 3; John Brandon-Jones et al., *C. F. A. Voysey, Architect and Designer 1857–1941*, 1978, pp. 53–4, Vodin, Pyrford Common.

35. Helensburgh Dean of Guild plans.

36. I am indebted to David Walker for reference to the Sellars and Honeyman houses.

37. Leiper's stepped gable treatment at Clarendon and Kelly House is preceded by Andrew Heiton's use of this motif at Castleroy, Dundee (1869 onwards) in a neo-perpendicular context. I am grateful to David Walker for this reference.

38. Photographs in Watt Library, Greenock, show the north and south elevations of a U-plan building.

39. Greig and Clarkson, op. cit., pp. 61–2.

40. See e.g. McNab's Beneffry of 1910, Springkell Avenue, Pollokshields: Elizabeth Williamson, Anne Riches and Malcolm Higgs, *The Buildings of Scotland: Glasgow*, 1990, p. 380; Prentice's The Retreat, Lakenheath, Suffolk: Clive Aslet, *The Last Country Houses*, 1982, plate viii, p. 64. Savage, op. cit., illustrates Lorimer buildings with bellcast polygonal roofs, rooftop animals and engaged towers with dormers, in all of which Leiper preceded him. See also Deborah Mays, 'Lorimer in Perspective', *RIBA Journal*, December 1990, pp. 34–9.

41. Greig and Clarkson, op. cit., p. 34.

42. Ibid., p. 26.

43. Ibid., p. 63.

25

The Country Houses, Larger Villas and Related Hotel Designs of Sir John James Burnet

DAVID M. WALKER

The domestic work of Sir John James Burnet was overshadowed in his own day by his great public and commercial masterworks and has remained so ever since. Although many of his houses are little known and some may not appeal to present-day tastes, the domestic side of his practice was as many-faceted as any other. It ranged from the mid-Victorian Baronial of Edinbarnet, and most probably also Killean, at the outset of his career to the Cubist houses of The Haven, Newbury, Berkshire, and Le Chateau at Silver End, Essex, designed, with his approval, by his partner Thomas Tait and their senior assistant Frederick MacManus at its close.

Tait and MacManus's work lies beyond the scope of this chapter, which is limited to houses built or altered before the First World War. Born in Glasgow on 31 March 1857, the son, and from 1871 the pupil, of John Burnet senior (1814–1901), John James Burnet completed his architectural education in Paris in 1875–7 at the Ecole des Beaux Arts under the supervision of Jean-Louis Pascal and Henri-Paul Nenot at the former's atelier and as a part-time assistant in the office of François Rolland.[1] He had not been home many months when, on 2 October 1878, the City of Glasgow Bank failed with losses of £6,000,000. It was an unlimited company, and every stockholder was liable to the full extent of his means. A chain of secondary bankruptcies drew into difficulty many people unconnected with the bank, and housebuilding in the west of Scotland remained flat for several years.

The elder Burnet had one major domestic commission in hand at the time,

Killean in Kintyre. Like other early works in which he undoubtedly had a hand, it is not listed in the younger Burnet's Royal Institute of British Architects nomination form of 1896, but the story of his houses may be said to begin there. Its building history is seemingly fairly well documented. The client was James Macalister Hall, a native of Campbeltown who had made a fortune as a merchant and shipowner in India. He had bought the estate of Tangy in 1870 and enlarged it by the purchase of that of Killean in July 1873. By August of the same year, he had obtained approval for the enlargement of the house to designs by the elder Burnet, but, just as the work was approaching completion in March 1875, all but the new billiard-room and porch were burned down. In July 1875, shortly before the eighteen-year-old younger Burnet enrolled at the Ecole, operations were about to be commenced for the erection of 'a magnificent new mansion house'. The designs were exhibited at the Royal Scottish Academy of 1876, but in more recent sale brochures Killean is reported as having been completed in the early 1880s, quite some years after Burnet had returned from the Ecole.[2]

The new house was built on a different site from the old, reusing its teak porch which had been made for Hall in the workshops of the shipbuilders Denny of Dumbarton, later to be important clients of the younger Burnet. Whether construction of the house was delayed, whether the younger Burnet had a hand in it before leaving for Paris or influenced its design from there, or whether a Burnet Son and Campbell drainage plan dated 1891 relates to work at that date, we seem unlikely to know now. All that can be said is that its simplicity of massing is very different from the elder Burnet's Kilmahew, Arden and Auchendennan, the elevations of which were cut up into a multiplicity of motifs, and that it has significant points in common with later houses which Burnet acknowledged as his own.

At Killean, the main house was roughly square on plan, two storeys high without basement or attics. A low wing ending in a game-larder pavilion projected from the entrance front to form a two-sided forecourt. It screened off a further L-plan single-storey and attic wing with which it formed a kitchen court, the south end of which was an addition of 1910. The elevations were distinguished by a number of subtleties characteristics of Burnet's early years. The main entrance was contained within a two-storey pavilion, the walls of which were built with a batter. From within its crenellated parapet rose a high French pavilion roof. A short straight link broached into a circular conical-roofed turret – a device we will meet again later – connected it to a conical-roofed drum tower on battered base courses which was balanced by a crowstepped gable on the end elevation. On the garden front, the main element was a strong, simple, Tudorish square tower of three storeys, the composition being neatly balanced by a broad Jacobethan canted bay on the

left and by a tall slim towerlet and a low service wing on the right. The larger
windows were mullioned and transomed with small-paned glazing which may
have been part of a later refitting of the house. The detailing was simple but
sophisticated, a cantilevered balcony and stepped crenellations with water
spouts at the main tower, broken pediment apices at the gables, and finely
profiled stacks punctuating the skyline, rounded at the angles and with very
deep battered copes. Apart from the canted bay corbelled to the square,
similar to that at Auchendennan but rather less tall, little of the elder Burnet's
Baronial idiom remained in evidence at Killean. Of the interior, not much can
now be said. Except perhaps for the hall, with its convex-angled lozenge-
shaped gallery of slim balusters, it has been refitted and in part Georgianised.

Balmaghie, Kirkcudbright, now cut down to a bungalow, was even less like
the elder Burnet's work than Killean. This massive and severely cubic
whinstone house of three tall storeys with a steep French roof was more like
an overgrown suburban mansion than a country house, similar to the plainer
French chateau designs of the period. Its Killean-type chimney stacks and tile
roof ridges indicate a date in the later 1870s or early 1880s, but the house has
not yet been securely dated, and the son's contribution to it can only be
guessed. The ground-floor plan does not seem to have been particularly
imaginative, being divided by a spinal hall corridor lit by the large three-light
window of the stair at the far end, but the principal floor may have had more
interest. While the batter of the ground-floor walls was a device that the elder
Burnet had adopted at Kilmahew in 1865, the elevations had a simplicity and
clarity not found in any of his other domestic designs. The probability must
be that the younger Burnet ruthlessly simplified a scheme of his father's,
perhaps to cut costs on a design which had proved too expensive. The early
Gothic porch was not characteristic of either the father or the son, being quite
different from the former's *porte-cochères*; but the dramatically-placed stacks,
the perforated tile ridges, the arch-braced bargeboards of the dormers,
the discs over the first-floor windows, the half-drum bow window of the
drawing-room, and above all the ruthlessly disciplined logic of the whole
suggest the son rather than the father.[3]

At Edinbarnet, Dunbartonshire, where the client was a banker, Walter
McKenzie of Cardovan, the younger Burnet's authorship is clearly established, since he exhibited it as his own work as late as 1907 and cited it in his
RIBA nomination form of 1896, albeit with the date 1890. At first sight, its
rather contrived asymmetry might seem to have nothing at all in common
with Balmaghie, but in certain respects its general arrangement was developed from it, the main block being approximately square on plan divided
by spinal corridors, and of three storeys and attics high with the principal
apartments at first-floor level. Edinbarnet differed in having a projecting

FIGURE 25.1   Deanston House, Doune, Perthshire, 1881–2.

asymmetrically sited frontal wing at the north-west. It contained an entrance
hall with a marble stair reaching almost to first-floor level, bypassing the
ground-floor hall-corridor arrangement of Balmaghie. This was not in itself a
new idea, stairhall entrances being a common feature in David Bryce's houses
and in turn of the elder Burnet's larger houses: what was completely new was
its incorporation into a substantial wing with mezzanines providing cloakroom and service accommodation at the lower level and a male preserve with
a billiard-room, well insulated from the remainder of the house, at an upper
level intermediate between the first and second floors of the main block. It
was an arrangement which was in differing and more sophisticated forms to
be a recurring feature of Burnet's subsequent Baronial houses.

Stylistically, Edinbarnet was closer in style to his father's work than
Killean, even if much simplified. As first built, its asymmetical elevations had
no dominant element but were interestingly varied. The most unusual details
were the conical-roofed north-west angle turret, clasped in chimneyheads and
broached from a square base at the wallhead as at Killean, and those of the
severely geometrical semi-circular arched porch which projected, again
asymmetrically, from the west gable of the frontal entrance wing. It had
deeply shadowed bargeboards and eaves contrasting with the crowstepped
gables and plain wallheads of the remainder. Throughout the design, the
fenestration was random, single lights, two lights and three lights, some with

transoms and some without, their asymmetry balanced up here and there by ornamental panels. The dormers had the same arch-braced and tied barge-boards as Balmaghie, but the chimneyheads were very severe with no copes and only a chamfer at the top, an early instance of Burnet treatments to come. On the east elevation, a stair to the garden with elaborately circled wrought-iron work spanned a sunk area and marked the end of the hall corridor at principal floor level. It was an unorthodox design, but everything about it had a certain logic and, as at Balmaghie, the studied avoidance of towers and turrets introduced solely for picturesque effect was doubtless a consciously Beaux Arts response to the Baronial of the elder Burnet's generation.

The internal finishes of Edinbarnet were surprisingly simple. The most memorable feature was the two-arched screen between the inner staircase vestibule and the main corridor. This had porthole balustrading and a Byzantinising capital at its central column. The handrail of the inner vestibule ended in a beast's head, the earliest known example of a detail which was to be characteristic. The principal rooms had little more than well-detailed Renaissance chimneypieces with timber surrounds, the drawing-room being the most handsome with a clever ceiling ribbed out into geometrical patterns, plain now but once lined out in gold. The billiard-room, currently dismantled, had an arched ceiling, marble chimneypiece and redwood panelling with an enriched frieze. The gardens were of considerable magnificence, the huge conservatory having an arched central transept foreshadowing the design of Burnet's Edinburgh International Exhibition of 1886.

In 1889, Edinbarnet was fire-damaged. In the course of its rebuilding in 1890, it was aggrandised, and something of the clarity of the original concept was lost. The gables of the south-west corner were built up as a crenellated tower, probably to emulate that of Killean, and the porch was embellished with American Romanesque columns of H. H. Richardson inspiration with short red sandstone shafts and elaborate capitals of interlaced foliage.[4]

Very different was the enlargement in 1881 of the modest two-storey-and-basement late Georgian mansion of Deanston, which had originally been built for a former owner of the works, John Smith. As at Killean and Balmaghie, the father may still have had some input into the design. Built for the new owners of the works, the Finlays, it was to be the only major domestic design in which the classical detailing which the younger Burnet had been taught at the Ecole was fully applied. A three-storey block with a bold drum frontage was added to the right and a further block comprising a tall square tower of five stages flanked by a further bow-ended wing added to the left, the latter extending into a single-storey winter garden. The left-hand wing repeated the fenestration pattern of the tower at Killean, an arrangement which may have derived from Alexander Thomson's Grecian Building on Glasgow's

Sauchiehall Street or possibly from William Henry Playfair's Belmont House at Corstorphine. Picturesquely stepped though the composition was, the probability must be that the original intention was to raise the Smith house to three storeys in conformity with the new work to produce a fully unified elevation. Low-pitched broad-eaved roofs and tall chimneyheads with double corniced tops crowned the composition, which, despite its asymmetry, had a Beaux Arts gravitas not to be found in any other of his domestic designs. Within, Burnet retained Smith's domed stairhall, but the new principal rooms had an impressive Beaux Arts seriousness with the Michelangelesque architectural and sculptural detail which was to be characteristic of his Classical and Baroque architecture down to the early years of the twentieth century.

Very different in scale and concept from both Deanston and Edinbarnet was Kilneiss at Moniaive, one of the most original houses of its date in the United Kingdom. Although again not mentioned in the younger Burnet's nomination form, the character of the design puts his sole authorship beyond all doubt. It was built in 1884 by a neighbour of the Burnets at Dowanhill, Andrew Paterson, a wealthy muslin manufacturer, as a wedding present for his son, the painter James Paterson, whose time in Paris in the studios of Jacquesson de la Chevreuse and Jean-Paul Laurens had crossed with Burnet's; another son, Alexander Nisbet Paterson, was then also in Paris at the Atelier Pascal on the younger Burnet's advice.

As Burnet found Kilneiss, it was a single-storey-and-attic cottage house of earlier nineteenth-century date with a detached outbuilding. He more than doubled the size of the house by adding a long back wing at right angles. This had a broad-eaved half-timbered upper floor with dormer gablets, and extended over the left-hand half of the original cottage, with an orielled gable cantilevered out asymmetrically over a new semi-circular bow as the principal feature of the remodelled frontage. To the right, its roof was swept down over a new rectangular bay, above which was a tall Godwinesque dormer of six lights. This roofed over the area between the bow and the rectangular bay as a verandah enclosed by a dwarf wall. Within the verandah, that favourite Burnet feature, a circular window with intersecting astragals forming a square central pane, made an early appearance. As first built, the half-timber was exposed, Franco-German rather than English Arts and Crafts, its asymmetrical geometry dictated by purely structural considerations; but the effect was not liked and was subsequently harled over. At the rear, the back wing terminated in a short crowstepped-gabled projecting wing of very unorthodox design containing a rear stair lit by an arched window of Norman Shaw derivation. The main entrance was on the flank of the new addition, a two-bay timber porch with simple but very original woodwork set on a dwarf wall. It was integrated into a conservatory running out at right angles as the corridor link to the outbuilding which Burnet rebuilt as Paterson's studio. Its frontal gable was built out as an inglenook with tiny windows on its splayed angles, and the rear gable cut out to form a huge studio window with a trapezoidal top sheltered by deeply shadowed eaves. The interior was very simply treated. The principal rooms were made interesting by alcove areas and plain Beaux Arts chimneypieces, and the main stair enclosed by arcaded screenwork of alternately square and turned shafts. Like that at the back, the main stair has a Shavian window. It does not show externally, being enclosed by the conservatory, an arrangement found at Baronald and Chesters a few years later. The studio was the most interesting apartment in the house with its arched inglenook, timber corbelled wallplates and lined roof with exposed tie beams. Stylistically, the origins of the design were diverse, including Godwin's houses at Bedford Park, Shaw, nineteenth-century French timber construction and in certain details perhaps contemporary American shingle-style houses such as those by John Calvin Stevens.[6]

The idea of a conservatory link to a large and otherwise detached apartment reappears at Auchterarder House, lavishly refitted in 1886–7 for the locomotive builder, James Reid, to house his art collection. As the younger Burnet found it, Auchterarder was a sizeable but rather undemonstrative red sandstone Neo-Jacobean house designed by William Burn in 1834 for Captain James Hunter, richer than most, with strapwork balustrades over the ground-floor bays and some elaborately patterned ceilings. At the main entrance, Burnet added a massive arched *porte-cochère* with attached Roman Doric columns and enclosed the forecourt with a balustrade. The *porte-cochère* was integrated in design with a three-bay winter garden, a much richer version of the Deanston model, which linked to an immensely grand billiard-room, the counterpart of the studio at Kilneiss. As at Kilneiss, the billiard-room was distinguished by a broad inglenook projection on the gable towards the entrance front, but the Auchterarder version was altogether more elaborate with a columned window on the south-east flank and a shallow canted bay with a garden door at the gable fronting the garden terrace, all with parapets continuing Burn's strapwork. Rich though the external detailing was, it hardly prepared the visitor for the grandeur within. Burn's ceilings and chimneypieces were generally respected, but the principal apartments were enriched with magnificent woodwork, the sculptural detail design and execution of which was in the hands of William Sherriff. Rich wainscot, scrolled broken pediment doorcases with pedimented sopra-porte panels and new dadoes were added in the hall, and splendid wrought-iron work with the familiar beast's-head terminals to the handrails was substituted for Burn's balusters at the stair. Similar enrichment took place in the principal rooms,

FIGURE 25.2   Auchterarder House, Perthshire, Billiard Room, 1886.

but the major expenditure was reserved for the winter garden and billiard-room. The winter garden had banded tile work as at Alloa Baths a few years later, and was a Roman spectacle worthy of Alma Tadema, with a three-bay screen of columns set in Burnet's characteristic broad architrave, a wellhead area with three lions' heads spouting water into a basin and a circular pool with a central jet, all superbly executed in marble and set in a floor of tesserae. The marble columns had Richardsonian capitals of interwoven foliage similar in character to J. M. MacLaren's sculptural detail at Palace Court, Bayswater a year or two later. Equally grand was the billiard-room itself, of great hall proportions, with an open Neo-Jacobean timber roof from which hung three openwork metal lights of quite incredible richness and elaboration. Its chimneybreast was of great width, characteristically curved back into the wall at the ends, and enclosed the inglenook within which the dado was equally characteristically swept up in swan-neck profiles at the chimneypiece.[7]

Burnet's commission for Auchterarder, in which he had to develop a Scots

Renaissance style which would answer Burn's, had far-reaching conse-
quences. It set the style for his own Alloa Baths,[8] for his partner John A.
Campbell's Ewing Gilmour Institute at Alexandria,[9] for his own Pathological
Institute at Glasgow Western Infirmary[10] and for a number of his station and
tenement designs. In the hands of pupils, followers and imitators, it spread
throughout the land.

Corrienessan, a finely-sited villa built in 1886–7 for Robert Kennedy on the
edge of the northern shore of Loch Ard, is markedly American in inspiration,
being a shingle-style house in plan and profile. Like Burnet's lodge at
Auchterarder, it had a big piended roof punctuated by a raking chimney stack
at its south-western angle, but the entrance gablet was crowstepped and the
porch had become an American-style verandah wrapped round the angle. The
first floor was reduced to narrow swept dormer window bands, the larger
dormer windows rising above their eaves line with half-timbered gables.
Only the material differed significantly from contemporary American practice,
although the half-timbered gables were more in the Richard Norman Shaw
idiom of Cragside, even if in a minor key. The interior is planned around a
galleried hall and lined with wainscot.[11]

Nunholm, Dowanhill, Glasgow, was a rather larger house reconstructed in
a similar idiom from a mid-Victorian villa for a neighbour of the elder Burnet,
Dr William Smart, a wealthy textile merchant and Glasgow's first professor of
political economy. Regrettably, it has been completely demolished, though
the design is partly recorded in a drawing, plan and photograph which Burnet
sent to *The British Architect* in July 1888. As first built, the house seems to
have been of two storeys and basement with a single-storey kitchen and
service outshot running along the rear, the back garden rising steeply behind.
Burnet enlarged the front of the house by adding a tower and a conservatory,
the former to provide a larger drawing-room. At the rear, the house was
enlarged by banking the garden level to form a sunken service passage, its
retaining wall and a dwarf colonnade bearing a half-timbered extension
constructed over the old service accommodation and the passage to provide a
new billiard-room with stairs to the garden, an adjacent study and two further
bedrooms. The plan shows that the remainder of the original building was
largely reconstructed to match the new work with a consistently topless
treatment of the chimneys on the Edinbarnet model. The half-timber work
was rather more elaborate than at Corrienessan, with some pargeting at the
plasterwork, and balustrading of the stairs to the garden of an Anglo-Japanese
pattern. The stone-built tower was characteristically severe in treatment
without stringcourses of any kind, only battered pilaster buttresses, gar-
goyles, stepped crenellations and a pierced raking chimneybreast, the roof
behind it being swept through it into the half-timbered quarter-octagon of its

stair. The profile finds parallels in Burnet's smaller church designs, while the motif of the roof sweeping through an arch pierced in a chimneyhead is also to be found at University Gardens in Glasgow. The tower formed an enlargement of the original drawing-room to an L-plan, the most remarkable domestic apartment ever built by Burnet. One cannot do better now than quote *The British Architect*:

> It is square on plan and covered with a dome of solid concrete, which is supported off the angles of the room by short corbelled out columns; the span is 14 feet and height from floor to crown, 26 feet. One side is occupied by an open timber stair conducting to the study, from the landing of which a bird's eye view of the whole room can be obtained. On the other side is [an arched] screen separating the drawing room from the conservatory, filled with clear glass with bands of blue-green, while the centre of the arch is occupied by a figure of an angel with outstretched wings designed and executed by Stephen Adam. The central part of the screen below is recessed back [into the conservatory] forming a niche about 8 feet high for the reception of a statue.

The main feature of the room was a gigantic chimneypiece and triptych-like overmantel set in an architrave frame with a square-stepped top. It enclosed a band of tilework and three tile pictures, the central with a figure panel, set in elegant Early Renaissance spindle balusters. The whole rose up the wall to a height of about sixteen feet. To quote *The British Architect* again:

> The woodwork is stained a dark reddish brown. The tiles in the overmantel are in bands of gold and amber, those inside the mantel being of dark blue and ivory. In the jambs of the fireplace, which are of white marble, are inserted two copper bas reliefs, the Christ and St John, by Donatello, reproduced from casts of the originals by a process of electrotyping by William Shireffs [*sic*], modeller. A similar panel of St Cecilia is framed on the upper part of the overmantel.

Both the chimneypiece and the glazed screen anticipated the style which George Walton was to make his own a few years later. The fourth side of the room opened into the original single-storeyed section of the drawing-room, the boudoir above having an oriel from which activities in the drawing-room could be observed. The dome and walls were decorated in warm reds and yellows.[12]

Burnet's competition design for the Clyde Yacht Club at Hunter's Quay shows where the Corrienessan-Nunholm idiom might have led had the right clients been found: at Hunter's Quay, an equally Shavian but rather more conventional neo-Tudor half-timbered design by Thomas Lennox Watson, brother of the naval architect George Lennox Watson, was selected. Burnet's design was in fact a good deal more adventurous in some of its features than anything Shaw had attempted, the whole emphasis of the design, as at Corrienessan, being on sundecks with sheltered areas recessed into the façade. Equally novel was the unmistakably shingle-style canted open porch in the angle of the clubhouse and its screenwell. The whole design suggests subscription to *The American Architect*, which may well have been arranged by Burnet's American cousins.[13]

In 1888, the timber merchant James Kennedy commissioned Burnet to carry out a remodelling as lavish as that for Smart at Nunholm. His house, 'The Chesters' (now known as Chesters) at Bearsden, was a generously-planned two-storey three-bay villa of vaguely Italianate character which he had built only eight years earlier. It was already large enough for Kennedy's requirements, and Burnet did not alter the exterior beyond adding, or perhaps remodelling, a columned porch in the re-entrant angle of the eastern elevation, and projecting the dining-room into a boldly circled bow on the west elevation. The eaves detail appears to have been restyled by Burnet, which, together with the absence of earlier woodwork within the house, suggests that he may have been called in to reinstate the house after a bad fire, although no record of one is known. A long L-plan service wing ran from the rear of the house, fronted for the whole of its length by a lean-to conservatory, the southern end of which, as at Nunholm and Baronald, was integrated into the planning of the house.

Internally, Burnet clad the hall corridor which ran through the house from east to west in wainscot divided into narrow strips by thin mouldings as at the Edinbarnet vestibule, the main features being the chimneypiece of rich antique Renaissance woodwork with twisted Corinthian columns and the deeply-moulded architrave frames of the doors, the panels of which have the same narrow proportions. Opening off the hall towards the rear of the house is the stair, a dog-leg entered through the timber arches which screen it. Its design is of some complexity, with a rail of elegantly serpentine profile and square balusters interpersed with very slim twisted ones.

All the principal rooms were very individually treated. The morning room has stepped-top door architraves reminiscent in profile of the Nunholm chimneypiece, a boldly detailed chimneypiece with decorative metal panels divided off by consoles, and an oblong mirror overmantel. The L-plan drawing-room is the richest room in the house. It has a deeply-coved ceiling, the coves being ribbed and the fields compartmented into squares of stencilled daisies. The walls have a rich dado, breaking into full wainscot on the west wall where Burnet's characteristic swan-necks frame a stepped architrave chimneypiece with a bolection moulded green marble slip and a

FIGURE 25.3   Nunholme, Dowanhill, Glasgow. 1887.

bevelled mirror overmantel. Flanking it on the right is a deep alcove with a
cove lit by the familiar circular window favoured by Burnet. The dining-room
is simpler but distinctively detailed, with a semi-elliptical chimneybreast of
low relief ornament sheltering a wide architraved chimneypiece with a mirror
overmantel. A low oblong bevelled mirror is integrated into the dado over the
sideboard and a pelmet cornice into the bow. The former billiard-room in the
north-east corner rivalled the drawing-room in splendour, the main feature
being the inglenook which projected into the conservatory, twin windows
flanking the chimneypiece offering views into it. A door with oval and
rectangle glazing leads into the white marble lavatory, lined out in green and
lit by some rather advanced pictorial glasswork of a type which was to grace
the pages of *The Studio* a year or two later.[14]

In 1889–92, Burnet designed two large Baronial houses in a turreted Scots
seventeenth-century style which had some details in common with his work at
Auchterarder. Quite different in style from the severely unturreted Edinbarnet and from the houses of Bryce and his followers, they probably owed
something to Leiper. The earlier of these was Baronald (now the Cartland
Bridge Hotel) near Lanark, built for Allan Farie of Farme Castle, Ruther-
glen. It was the largest, though not the most elaborate, house he ever built,

a massively picturesque pile in dark reddish brown sandstone constrasted
with buff dressings, ingeniously planned and full of original ideas. In his
nomination form, Burnet gives its date as 1889, although it was still under
construction in January 1891. The design date may in fact be slightly earlier.
The internal detailing is not quite so developed in style as that at Chesters,
even if the exterior is almost Edwardian in character and totally different in
style from the unturreted mid-Victorian Edinbarnet. More significantly, it is
noticeable that the shingle-style features which were incorporated into his
house designs of the later 1880s are entirely absent, suggesting that the main
lines of the design were settled in the middle years of the decade.

The design of the house is, as at Nunholm and in a lesser degree Chesters,
an exploration of the possibilities of integrating the winter garden into the
plan. It is built into a slope with the entrance at the higher end, so that the
house is entered at main floor level, obviating the necessity of entrance stairs
as at Edinbarnet. The frontal wing has mezzanine floors and is more closely
integrated into the house than at Edinbarnet, forming part of a three-quarter
quadrangle of linked tower-house-like blocks enclosing a central stairhall,
an altogether novel concept with no known precedent in Scottish country-
house planning. All the principal rooms were well out of sight of the entrance
front, where the quadrangle of building around the stairhall was completed
by a lean-to winter garden, enclosing the stairhall window to half its height.
Several rooms at different levels enjoyed views into it. The originality of the
concept was carried into the details: the circular windowed bow of the
cloakroom forming the base column of the oriel; the square angle piers whose
sculptured tops rose above the eaves of the winter garden; and the garderobe-
like corbelled splay in the angle of the oriel on the north-west elevation which
was in fact the plate safe of the dining room. The same originality of detail
characterised the interior, which still retains some of its original furniture and
family portraits. The vestibule has an inner screen of octagonal columns with
Richardsonian capitals, similar to those in the winter garden at Auchterarder
but of timber, framing a screen of etched glass. The inner vestibule leads to
the spacious hall-staircase, which has a Celtic Romanesque chimneypiece of
dwarf columns bearing a massive block entablature with circles of interlaced
work. The dog-leg stair has a turned baluster rail which returns through an
arcade of two unequal arches, one semi-circular, one semi-elliptical, borne on
an elaborate early Renaissance newel baluster column. Its tall three-light
window with elaborately tinctured transoms of monogrammed cartouches is
of clear glass leaded into Renaissance patterns affording views into the winter
garden. As in several other Burnet houses, the dining-room has a timber-
beamed ceiling. Its planning is somewhat unusual, the north-western oriel
with the plate safe forming a deep serving-area recess, the glazing being of

leaded glass in Renaissance patterns to prevent the servants looking into the garden. The dado is of wainscot, rising higher in swan-neck profiles at the doors and windows as at Auchterarder. Inset into it is an elaborate Renaissance surround to the black marble chimneypiece, still with its original red tiles and copper canopy. The drawing-room has a similar wainscot dado treatment but has a lighter and richer touch, with gilt strapwork lunettes over the doors and a geometrically ribbed ceiling on the Edinbarnet model extending into the circular corner tower. A feature of all the windows in the principal apartments is the elaborate Renaissance glasswork above the transoms.

The second of these turreted baronial houses, Garmoyle at Dumbarton, built in 1892 for the shipbuilder Lt-Col. John M. Denny, followed two lesser commissions there for another of the partners in Denny and Co., Walter Brock. These comprised the reconstruction of Bellfield, a plain mid-Victorian villa which had been burned in 1883, and the enlargement in 1890 of Levenford, a medium-sized and very well-designed Scots Baronial house which had been built for James Denny to designs by J. T. Rochead in 1853. The work there comprised what was virtually a new house back-to-back with the old and externally almost indistinguishable from it, only the half-timbered porch betraying Burnet's hand. It provided a new dining-room very similar to that at Baronald, a library and a study, all with particularly fine early Renaissance chimneypieces, those in the dining-room and the study introducing the elaborate arcaded or balustered semi-elliptical overmantels which were to feature in his houses of the later 1890s.[17] At Garmoyle, Burnet adopted the same Arts-and-Crafts rubble masonry technique as at Levenford, where Rochead's occasional raked joints had been made a more consistent pattern. Although their materials made them superficially different in appearance, Garmoyle was an updated version of Baronald. It was built into a bank in exactly the same way, the garden front was essentially similar but reduced to three storeys, and the entrance was in a projecting wing with mezzanines. But the main block was reduced not only in height but also in plan from a near-square to an L by the omission of the central stairhall and the winter garden (the fashion for which had abruptly passed), the stair being relocated in a drum tower linking the main block to the entrance wing on the east side. The composition was more extended, the service court being not only elevated to main-floor level as part of the total composition but also raised a floor adjacent to the main block to make up some of the bedroom accommodation lost by the overall reduction in height. The roof of the service wing was swept low down in an unbroken plane and returned across the gable of the entrance wing to form a wide canted porch integrated with the screen wall of the service court, very much as in the Clyde Yacht Club design. Other details, notably the two-storeyed south-western angle turret, the fine boat-shaped dormer head pediments and the balusters of the wallhead balustrades, widely spaced in Scots seventeenth-century fashion as at Auchterarder, antici-pated Lorimer's work in the same vein. More advanced in style than Leiper's houses of that vintage, its simple and robust Scots forms set the pattern for the future. Only the apices of the gable were still old-fashioned, having pedimented tops like those at Edinbarnet. On its interior, no comment can be made, as the house has been a Carmelite convent since 1934.[18]

In 1893–4 Burnet made a number of designs for the 12th Duke of Hamilton's Arran estate. His additions to Dougarie (or Dubhghuradh) Lodge, comprising mainly a broad square tower with a rectangular bay and an inglenook, were not built, probably because of the death of the Duke in 1895,[19] but something of its robust spirit was echoed in a delightful small house at Lamlash, Dalgorm, which, with its more diminutive neighbour, Rose Cottage, the nurse's house, was built in 1899–1900. All that was built at Dougarie itself was the fine boathouse with boldly bellcast bargeboards. At the same date, 1894, Burnet made a design for a new hotel at Lochranza which echoed the style of his Clyde Yacht Club design in a minor key, but this was doomed to be reduced to a reconstruction of the existing hotel.[20]

In 1895–8, Burnet had a number of commissions in Kintyre, where Macalister Hall had remained a particularly faithful client, commissioning a remarkable terrace of cantilevered verandah cottages at Killean known as the Dolls' Houses, and the library and museum at Campbeltown.[21] In the same town, William McKinnon, Hall's partner in McKinnon and Co. and the British India line, commissioned the small-scale and very domestic Campbel-town Cottage Hospital on the Southend Road in 1895,[22] since alas altered and spoiled, and a Mr William Brown the fine villa of Rothmar, built concurrently with the library in 1897 and, it is said, by the same contractor, W. H. White. Rothmar was not a particularly large house and rather low in proportion, but it was expensively built of the local salmon-pink Killellan stone, and its elevated site overlooking Campbeltown Loch gave it a commanding appear-ance. Its main block was L-shaped on plan, the rear arm extending into a set-back breakfast-room and service wing. The entrance was at the rear, a cloistral verandah in the re-entrant with a column at the outer angle. Such cloistral features were a favourite theme of Burnet's in the 1890s, notably at Campbeltown Library and the Gardner Memorial Church at Brechin, both with cantilevered roofs and low enclosing walls. The main elevation drew inspiration from Alexander Thomson's Busby House: the composition was essentially the same but in reverse, a broad-eaved rectangular main block with a peristyled cylindrical bow at one end balanced by a gable-fronted wing attached to the other. Burnet made the design his own, with the massive

FIGURE 25.4   Baronald, Lanark, 1890.

stone-built terrace on which the house stood, the segmental pediment at the
eaves over the bow, the piended form of the roof and the tall wide-corniced
stacks which punctuated the composition. Internally, the most remarkable
feature was the planning of the coved drawing-room, the bow being
asymmetrically placed as a continuation of one wall of the room and formed
into a deep apsidal alcove by partitioning off part of the opposite side of the
room as a garden vestibule.[23] The concept of deep alcoves in the drawing-
room was to be developed further in Burnet's next major house, Carronvale,
Larbert, reconstructed and much enlarged in the same year, 1897, for George
Sheriff.

Prior to Burnet's reconstruction, Carronvale had been a harled Georgian
house, the main element of which was an early nineteenth-century two-storey
three-bay front with an anta pilastered doorpiece and flanking ground-floor
windows with long elegant consoles. Burnet retained it as the central section
of the enlarged south frontage of his two-storey quadrangle, the western third
of which was infilled with cloakroom and lavatory accommodation. The
principal rooms were ranged along the south and west, the dining-room at the
south-east corner, the drawing-room at the south-west, and a large, bowed
billiard-room at the centre of the west front. On the east was a recessed
service court. The elevations were stylishly detailed, harled with generous
stone dressings under a low-pitched broad-eaved roof, red-tiled as at
Garmoyle. The south front was enriched by handsome canted bays with

curvaceous woodwork, and a double-arched early Italian Renaissance loggia graced the service wing. The east and west elevations were clapsed by oblong pyramid-roofed towers flanking the main elevation and forming alcoves to the dining and drawing-rooms, but were otherwise made asymmetrical, the drawing-room having a single-storey outshot not answered on the east side. A glazed verandah, supported on square stone piers with sculptured tops which rise above the glazing as at the Baronald conservatory, enclosed the bow of the billiard-room on the west side and returned round the north-west angle on to the north elevation, plain but punctuated by the same tall boldly corniced stacks as at Rothmar. Within the verandah, the walls were lined with a dado of tilework.

The interiors, which still survive virtually intact although redecorated for educational purposes, ranked next to those of Finlaystone as Burnet's richest domestic work. The entrance vestibule is entered asymmetrically by a glazed internal porch of spindle-balustered early Renaissance screenwork. It has a marble floor, a plain but bold marble chimneypiece with an overmantel of stepped Doric columns, and an inner entrance screen of spindle balusters and Renaissance woodcarving. This opens into the oblong central hall from which the stair rises behind a colonnade of square timber columns into a spacious stairhall with a coved ceiling on cherub consoles, the whole being lit by four lights of splendid free Renaissance leaded glass. The former study has a magnificent chimneypiece of antique Delft tiles set in a timber architrave frame of exaggerated proportions, and the former dining-room has a rather Philip Webb-like timber overmantel of three diamond panels set in spindle balusters. The drawing-room is remarkable for its stepped alcoves which enabled different activities to take place within the room: the southern is deeper and trabeated and was doubtless intended to accommodate a grand piano, the northern is shallower and more contained within its semi-elliptical arch so that at first sight the room appears L-shaped. The chimneypiece reflected Burnet's interest in the work of Norman Shaw, and is of unparalleled opulence, with Roman Doric columns of black and white marble framing the hearth and bearing a semi-elliptically bowed entablature. Its mantelshelf is an Ionic marble colonnade which bears a semi-elliptical chimneybreast, part of a deep frieze of excellent early Renaissance plasterwork with strapwork cartouches and putti which extends right round the room. The former billiard-room is an equally brilliant performance if quieter in treatment, its most remarkable feature being the ceiling, a great oval determined by the curvature of the bow where the cornice becomes a pelmet.[24]

Although not built anew, Finlaystone, remodelled in 1898–1903 for G. J. Kidston of the Clyde Shipping Company, was in many ways Burnet's finest domestic achievement, with interiors of a grandeur unmatched in any of his other houses. The Baroque classicism employed there was determined by the handsome early Georgian house already on the site. Built in 1746 for William, 12th Earl of Glencairn, to designs by John Douglas,[25] its Gibbsian detailing happily coincided in spirit with his own interpretation at that date. As Burnet found it, Finlaystone was a three-storey seven-bay astylar block with a piended and platformed roof, the centre three bays being slightly advanced on the east front. To the south, a service tower and a single-storey Romanesque wing had been added in 1872 for Colonel Carrick-Buchanan,[26] and to the north a three-storey bow had been added to the dining and drawing-rooms overlooking the Clyde at the top of a precipitous embankment. Beneath lay a walled garden.

Externally, Burnet added a single-storey block with a boldly rusticated central portico along the east front, and, in order to make the bedroom accommodation more spacious with high coved ceilings, he raised the top storey by inserting a deep fleur-de-lys frieze, broken by a segmental pediment of the Rothmar type crowning the boldly sculptured Kidston coat of arms at the centre of the east front. He also added a bay window to the west front and constructed a balustraded terrace punctuated by huge piers with grotesque urns along the north front. This ended in a fine bower with a pavement of tesserae, designed to take a canvas awning.

Burnet's interior work is of impressive quality. The low entrance hall has a semi-elliptically bowed grey marble chimneypiece of simple design, its grey marble theme being also picked up in the design of the floor. At ground-floor level, the new canted bay provided the dining-room with a serving recess. Its ceiling is compartmented by stained timber beams as at Baronald, Levenford and Carronvale. The billiard-room, projected into the frontal addition, has a truly impressive plaster ceiling of built-up trabeation, anticipating that of his King's Library at the British Museum.

The stair rises from the entrance hall and retains its magnificent mid-eighteenth-century balustrade of alternately straight and twisted shafts much repaired and probably extended by Burnet. Two huge pink marble Roman Doric columns, monoliths with black bases and capitals, rise up the narrow stairwell through two storeys, the handrail terminating in a magnificently carved griffin circling one of them. The walls are clad in gilt canvas. At the first-floor landing, where the capitals and entablature of the Doric columns make a dramatic appearance, the stairwell opens out into a fine ante-room which Burnet formed from a bedroom, its main feature a magnificent Baroque doorcase with cherub's heads which leads to the drawing-room.

The first-floor drawing-room is the finest apartment in the house. The ceiling is a very subtle elegant design, coved and elaborately compartmented with graceful lunettes and a beautiful consoled pendant in the bow; the cornice has a gilded cavetto running behind hollow consoles; and the chimneypiece is of white marble, finely sculptured and bearing a huge segmentally pedimented mirror overmantel with Michelangelesque supporting figures of Dawn and Even.

The drawing-room opens into the library, the bowed central room on the west front. This was also remodelled by Burnet, though less radically, the magnificent black marble rococo chimneypiece being retained. Beyond it, in the south-west corner of the main block, Burnet retained Douglas's study with its simple pine panelling.[27]

Three relatively minor commissions compared with Finlaystone and Carronvale were the Manager's House at Camelon, Falkirk, designed for J. C. Jeffrey Smith in November 1898,[28] the manse at the McLaren Memorial Church at Stenhousemuir, Larbert, built on to the gable of the church hall in 1905,[29] and Ledcameroch at Kilwinning designed for Mr and Mrs Robert Craig King and exhibited at the Royal Scottish Academy in 1886 though not built until 1898, by which date the design must have been completely revised.[30] Although quite different in design, all three were simply-detailed harled houses, that at Stenhousemuir having a small half-timbered element to answer the porch of the church. Ledcameroch was much the most sophisticated of them, neatly composed and extending into a long stable-block pierced by a gabled pend arch. Although now much altered externally as Melvin House, some fine interior work remains, notably the drawing-room chimneypiece, a simplified version of that at Carronvale.

Elements from all three of these houses were exploited to still greater effect at the Marine Hotel at Elie, where stone dressings were all but avoided. Rebuilt in stages from 1904 after the previous Burnet hotel of 1889 and 1900 had been destroyed by fire, it was a subtly-balanced asymmetrical composition of two storeys and an attic between four-storey gabled end pavilions, identical only at their slightly corbelled top floors with simplified segment-headed Venetians and Ernest Newton-school pediment gables with timber cornices. Tall corniced stacks of the Carronvale-Rothmar type punctuated the roof line, giving the whole an excellent profile as seen from the beach. The principal rooms were magnificently spacious and airy, with typically Burnetian coved ceilings of great elegance, and opened out into a long sunroom along the centre of the south frontage, an early addition to the original concept. The stair was a fine one, with superbly carved beasts at the ends of the rails. The Marine was a masterpiece of its genre, and its closure and eventual demolition after a bad fire has been a particularly sad loss.[31]

In 1900, Burnet was called in by Mark Bannatyne to update Windsor House at the west end of Kirklee (then Windsor) Terrace in Glasgow, a tall

FIGURE 25.5   Rothmar, Campbeltown, Argyll, 1897.

two-storey basement-and-attic mid-Victorian mansion, originally with elaborately bargeboarded gables. Burnet added an elegant glazed canopy with fine
wrought-iron cantilever brackets to the original doorpiece, built a tall square
tower of four storeys which repeated the features of that at Nunholm on
a grander scale at the north end of the house, and extended the rear into a
two-storey billiard-room wing. The interior of the main part of the house was
refitted in the same opulent high-art style as Nunholm with fine woodwork
and bas-reliefs, probably by Sheriff. The semi-elliptically arched billiard-
room is more in the idiom of Carronvale and Ledcameroch in having a
characteristic semi-elliptical chimneybreast with a deep frieze of strapwork.[32]

   In the years before the First World War, large-scale domestic commissions
were markedly fewer, at least partly because Burnet was spending the greater
part of his time in London, where an office had been established in 1905 to
supervise the building of the Edward VII Galleries at the British Museum.
Such domestic work as there was mainly comprised alterations, a conservatory with sculptured piers of the Baronald-Carronvale type at Craig House,
Ayrshire, for Pollok Morris in 1902,[33] new interiors at Rachan, Biggar, in
1904,[34] considerable internal reorganisation of the interior of Castlecraig,
Peeblesshire, for James Mann after he bought the estate in 1905,[35] and the
partial remodelling of Trochrague, Girvan, for George Todd, carried out in
stages between 1910 and 1923, where the top-floor windows were given
pedimented dormer heads like those of Bargany House nearby and a new
asymmetrical tower of squat proportions with a Windsor House-type parapet

was built.[36] But two major commissions remained, Fairnilee near Selkirk for
A. F. Roberts, in 1904–6, and the restoration of Duart Castle, Mull, for Sir
Fitzroy MacLean in 1911–16.

Fairnilee was Burnet's most completely realised domestic project, a great
formal garden, stables, gardener's lodge and cottages forming integral parts
of the total concept. In designing it, Burnet took his north-west/south-east
orientation from the late sixteenth-century house of the Kers and its garden.
Roberts had selected as the site for the new house the higher ground immediately to the north-east of the old. Burnet reroofed its surviving north-western
end as a generator house and linked the two houses together with a high wall
pierced by a magnificent set of gates. These form the entrance to the park
from the garden rather than the entrance to the house itself. A long formal
approach was constructed on a high masonry terrace along the north-eastern
margin of the garden, guarded at its south-eastern end by a segmentally
arched gateway in a screen wall with a balustraded parapet and a gardener's
house of similar character to Dalgorm. Arrival at the forecourt of the house at
the far end is marked by an ogee-roofed pavilion linked to the house by the
screen wall of a sunk court, infilled by an oriel led business-room in the 1930s.

Although the plan is reversed and rather more complex, biaxial with the
stair in a different location on the entrance front, Fairnilee is essentially a
harled and more vigorously detailed Garmoyle, the only substantial new
element being the substitution of a two-storeyed porch with a Baroque
Roman Doric aedicule doorpiece flanked by obelisks for Garmoyle's informal
shingle-style one. The interior was not one of Burnet's more elaborate
programmes, more a reflection of changing tastes than lack of money, but was
generously planned in terms of circulation space, so much so that it has not
survived without alteration. The porch and vestibule led diagonally to a
spacious wainscoted hall staircase, similar in arrangement to that at Carronvale in that it rose into an even more spacious upper hall with an arched
ceiling. At ground-floor level a spindle-balustered screen opened into an
inner hall forming an anteroom between the dining-room and the drawing-
room, and at half-landing level a further screen opened into an anteroom
over the vestibule. The principal rooms had refined ceilings, woodwork and
architraved chimneypieces. The most ambitious was the dining-room, which
was similar in style and arrangement to those at Baronald, Levenford and
Garmoyle, with a beamed ceiling, a serving recess in the oriel and a semi-
elliptical chimney-breast.[37]

Duart Castle, a thirteenth-century castle of enceinte with a late fourteenth-
century tower house and sixteenth- and seventeenth-century buildings
around three sides of its court, had been bought back by Sir Fitzroy in 1911.
It had fallen into ruin only in the 1740s and, although the parapet of the tower

and all the roofs had gone, it was otherwise fairly complete. In preparing his scheme for its restoration, Burnet had the advantage of a survey prepared by J. L. Peddie and R. Campbell for the National Art Survey in 1901, but he had this thoroughly checked and redrawn by Alexander MacGibbon before submitting his sketch scheme in September 1911. This was referred to the Royal Commission on the Ancient and Historical Monuments of Scotland, and one of the commissioners, Dr Thomas Ross, and the commission's architect, Frederick Lightly MacGibbon (the son of Ross's former partner, David MacGibbon) visited the castle in November, Fred preparing a further sketch scheme to demonstrate how Burnet's might be modified. It was probably on their advice that the intended porch enclosing the ancient entrance – a modification of a later entrance tower which had been demolished – was omitted from the final project. The final working drawings are not all dated, but the instructions on them show that the south-east range was tackled first, then the north-east range and finally the tower, for which the working drawings are dated June 1912.

Forming Duart into an early twentieth-century family seat proved a difficult task, as the original floor-to-ceiling heights were rather low in the courtyard ranges and the tower house was quite unconnected with the remainder. The vaults and two of the cross walls of the south-east range had to be taken out and the gun platform at the north angle roofed over as the present Ship Room (it was originally to have been a winter garden) to provide the necessary link between the dining-room in the north-eastern range and the hall of the tower house, which Burnet made into the drawing-room, slapping its south-eastern wall out into a large rectangular window recess to provide it with sufficient light.

Apart from some rationalisation of the very wasted doorways of the cellarage of the south-east range, where a bold seventeenth-century-style entrance door was provided, the elevations were otherwise largely respected, so that Duart looked very much as it did in the Board of Ordnance view of 1748 except that the rooflines were rather higher and the corbelling of the parapet of the tower had been omitted. Because of the outbreak of war, the interior of the castle was never quite completed as intended. The dining-room never received its wainscot, but good stone chimneypieces were provided, most notably that in the hall.[38]

Burnet's last sizeable domestic commission in Scotland was Letham Hill, Dhuhill Drive, Helensburgh, built for the Misses Wylie of Wylie and Lochhead in 1914, a harled T-plan house with half-timber at the upper level, its most prominent feature being a large mullioned bay lighting the stair. Although the Glasgow practice was by that date in the day-to-day care of Burnet's partner Norman Aitken Dick, details such as the Anglo-Japanese timber parapet of the canted bay on the garden front, a late echo of the balustrading of the perron at Nunholm, the tenoned bargeboards and the balustrading of the stair show that Burnet was still very much in command even if now in the Glasgow office for only about one week each month. Only in the smaller details is Dick's hand more apparent.[39]

Burnet suffered severely from eczema after the First World War and, although his hand was still clearly discernible in several of the large public and commercial commissions, he was thereafter content to leave such domestic work as there was in the hands of his partners, Thomas Smith Tait in London and Norman Dick in Glasgow. But the houses he either built or had a hand in over the preceding forty years are of extraordinary variety, challenging Godwin, Shaw, Leiper and Lorimer at their own game. Most importantly, he was, with James Marjoribanks MacLaren and their older contemporary in Dundee, John Murray Robertson, one of the few Scottish architects to be significantly influenced by contemporary American domestic design, at Corrienessan adopting the concept as well as the details of the Shingle Style more wholeheartedly than either of them. But whatever the style he was working in, Burnet's buildings are always stamped with his own distinctive personality. Direct precedents are never to be found. His was an original as well as a receptive mind, always evolving the design logically from the inside outwards as a solution to the programme set by the client rather than adapting any preconceived concept. He took in the principles which lay behind the designs which interested him and implemented them in his own way, never afraid of the unorthodox if it represented the logical solution to a planning or structural problem. Although discounted by Hermann Muthesius and largely neglected by subsequent critics, his domestic work constituted one of the most remarkable episodes in late nineteenth- and early twentieth-century design.

ACKNOWLEDGEMENTS

The work of Sir John Burnet has been a particular interest of the writer's for forty years. For general family and personal, information he has been indebted to the late Edith Burnet Hughes, Sir John's niece, and James John Burnet, his great nephew; to Sir John's former assistants the late Alfred G. Lochhead and the late John Watson and to the late Professor W. J. Smith; and for information from Sir John's dossier at the Ecole des Beaux Arts to Mr Richard Chafee.

At various times the writer has also been indebted to the owners or management of the buildings referred to in the text, particularly at Deanston, Auchterarder, Elie, Camelon, Fairnilee, Finlaystone, Edinbarnet, Killean,

Chesters, Cartland Bridge Hotel, Letham Hill, Duart and Corrienessan; and in the final preparation of the text to his former colleagues at Historic Scotland, particularly John Gifford; Rebecca Barker; Anne Riches; Aonghus MacKechnie; Dr Deborah Mays; Judith Anderson; Gillian Haggart; and Bernadette Goslin. Ian Gow, Rob Close, Professor Frank Walker, Michael Moss, Colin D. McKellar, Ailsa Tanner, The Fine Art Society and especially Michael Davis were helpful with a number of queries, while Professor James Dunbar-Nasmith was of particular assistance in respect of Duart. Finally, the writer is indebted to his former secretary, Mrs C. C. Marshall, who deciphered an appalling series of manuscripts, and to Professor Alastair Rowan, for tactful guidance on the reduction of an over-long typescript.

NOTES

1. Although since found to be inaccurate in some details, the most comprehensive account of Burnet's career is still my chapter on Burnet in Alastair Service's *Edwardian Architecture and its Origins*, London, 1975. More accurate details on his early life will be found in 'Scotland and Paris' in John Frew (ed.), *Scotland and Europe: Architecture and Design 1850–1940*, St Andrews, 1991, but there is still considerable confusion as to his years at the Ecole: his Royal Institute of British Architects nomination statement (November 1896) gives these as 1872–6, the records of the Ecole (per Richard Chafee) 1875–7. The principal contemporary sources for his life and work are the memoirs by A. N. Paterson, T. S. Tait and D. Theodore Fyfe in *The Journal of The Royal Institute of British Architects*, 2 June and 18 July 1938; *The Baillie*, 7 April 1886, 6 May 1914, 4 May 1921; *The Builders' Journal*, 9 October 1901; *The Architects' Journal*, 27 June 1923 (H. S. Goodhart Rendel); and E. J. Burrows and Co., *Modern Architectural Art*, parts I and II (Cheltenham n.d., c. 1923). See also the chapter on Burnet in Leonard Eaton, *American Architecture Comes of Age*, Cambridge, Mass., and London, 1973, and *The Royal Incorporation of Architects in Scotland Quarterly*, nos 84 (1951) and 94 (1953).
2. *Campbeltown Courier*, 19 July 1873 (purchase); 9 August 1873, additions to old house; 6 March 1875 (fire); 3 July 1875 (work about to begin, architect and contractors) per the present owner Mr David Atteg, courtesy Michael Davis; sale brochures Knight Frank and Rutley, 1979, and Langley Taylor, 1990.
3. *Building News*, 16 May 1890, article on John Burnet senior; survey plan and photographs held by A. Curtis Wolffe.
4. Royal Institute of British Architects nomination form, candidate's statement, November 1896; Royal Scottish Academy Exhibition Catalogue 1885; Edinburgh Architectural Association Exhibition Catalogue 1907; information from Mrs Heather Carrick and Mrs Elizabeth MacRobert, Edinbarnet Nursing Home; unpublished thesis, University of Strathclyde, per Professor Frank Walker.
5. *Builders' Journal*, 9 October 1901, obituary of John Burnet senior.
6. Ailsa Tanner and Anne Paterson Wallace, *James Paterson Moniaive and following family traditions*, Milngavie, 1983. The more Scottish-styled

rear wing may have been designed by A. N. Paterson, who exhibited designs for an addition at Kilneiss at the Royal Scottish Academy in 1894. For illustration, see P. Nuttgens, *Mackintosh and his contemporaries*, London, 1988, p. 34–5.

7. RIBA nomination form, candidate's statement; *The Journal of Decorative Art* vol. IX, July 1889, p. 110, courtesy Mr John Gifford; *JRIBA* 12 September 1938, note on p. 993.

8. A. Koch (ed.), *Academy Architecture*, London, 1897 (1); *Architect*, 16 May 1902.

9. *British Architect*, 28 June 1889; *Architect*, 7 February 1907.

10. A. Koch (ed.), *Academy Architecture*, 1894 (1); *Builder*, 19 May 1894.

11. Royal Scottish Academy Exhibition Catalogue 1887; personal information, the late W. Drysdale to the late A. G. Lochhead, June 1957; further information from the present owner, R. G. Lawson, December 1993. Kennedy was a civil engineer who had constructed the railway line to Aberfoyle. The house was an enlarged version of the manager's office of Burnet's Edinburgh International Exhibition of 1886, and may have incorporated material from it.

12. Royal Scottish Academy Exhibition Catalogue 1887; *British Architect*, 6 July 1888.

13. *British Architect*, 9 September 1890.

14. RIBA nomination form, candidate's statement. Mary McHugh, *Chesters House*, privately circulated, Glasgow 1985.

15. RIBA nomination form, candidate's statement; *British Architect*, 30 January and 6 February 1891.

16. Donald MacLeod, *Dumbarton Ancient and Modern*, Glasgow and Dumbarton, 1893, p. xli.

17. RIBA nomination form, candidate's statement; Donald MacLeod, op. cit.

18. RIBA nomination form, candidate's statement; *JRIBA*, 12 September 1938, note on p. 993; Donald MacLeod, op. cit.

19. A. Koch (ed.), *Academy Architecture*, 1894.

20. A. Koch (ed.), *Academy Architecture*, 1894.

21. A. Koch, *Academy Architecture*, 1899 (1); R. E. Millar, *Campbeltown Museum and Library* (Open University Project Report), Campbeltown, 1981.

22. *Builder*, 28 November 1896; *Cambeltown and District Cottage Hospital*, Dundee, 1933.

23. A. Koch (ed.), *Academy Architecture*, 1898.

24. *Builders' Journal*, 9 October 1901; *Building News*, 3 April 1903.

25. Plans at house, none quite as built; H. M. Colvin, *Dictionary of British Architects 1600–1840*, London, 1978, p. 272, quoting SRO GD/39/6/Box 3.

26. Plans at house, copy dated 4 March 1878 by A. McG. Mitchell of plans dated 1872 addressed 150 St Vincent Street, Glasgow (probably Kennedy and Dalglish).

27. *Architect*, 19 August 1904, 30 May 1906.

28. Plans at house, dated November 1898.

29. *The Parish Church of Stenhouse and Carron 1900–1975*, Falkirk, 1975; for church and hall, see *Architect*, 11 April 1902.

30. Royal Scottish Academy Exhibition Catalogue 1886; *Architects' Journal*,

27 June 1923; *JRIBA*, 18 July 1938; Michael Davis, *Castles and Mansions of Ayrshire*, Ardrishaig, 1991, p. 327.

31. *Architects' Journal*, 27 June 1923; *JRIBA*, 18 July 1938; information from management at hotel, 1965; original hotel illustrated, *Dundee Advertiser*, 14 June 1889.

32. Glasgow Dean of Guild plans 1/7741, Strathclyde Regional Archives.

33. Kilmarnock District Committee Minutes, Strathclyde Regional Archives CO3/12/3/35, 25 July 1902 per Rob Close; Michael Davis, *Castles and Mansions of Ayrshire*, Ardrishaig, 1991, p. 214.

34. Royal Scottish Academy Exhibition Catalogue 1904.

35. *Royal Commission on the Ancient and Historical Monuments of Scotland: Peeblesshire*, Edinburgh, 1967, no. 563.

36. *Architects' Journal*, 27 June 1923; *JRIBA*, 18 July 1938; Michael Davis, *Castles and Mansions of Ayrshire*, Ardrishaig, 1991, p. 394.

37. J. Nicoll, *Domestic Architecture in Scotland*, Aberdeen, 1908, plates 5–9; information from the present owner, Stephen Dean. The commission had originally been given to Lorimer, who had produced a scheme for restoring and enlarging the old house. Roberts, a Selkirk mill-owner, preferred a new house on the present site and instructed Lorimer to demolish the old house. Lorimer demurred and was dismissed.

38. *Building News*, 11 December 1916; *Royal Commission on the Ancient and Historical Monuments of Scotland: Argyll*, vol. 3, *Mull, Tiree, Coll and Northern Argyll*, Edinburgh, 1980, no. 339; D. Breeze (ed.), *Studies in Scottish Antiquity*, Edinburgh, 1984, p. 434; information from Sir Lachlan Maclean and Professor James Dunbar-Nasmith.

39. Plans at house.

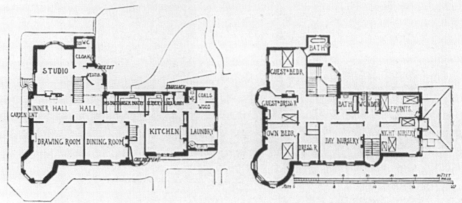

FIGURE 26.1   Perspective view of the garden front of the Longcroft, Helensburgh, with plans of the principal and bedroom floor, from *Academy Architecture*, vol. 1 (1903), p. 68. Designed by the architect, A. N. Paterson for his own residence.

26

The Architect's House and the Search for a 'National Style'

ANNE RICHES

In 1895, Alexander Paterson gave the Presidential address to the Glasgow Association of Architects on the subject of *Style, Individuality and Tradition*.[1] He confronted a burning issue among his contemporaries, the development of a 'national' architecture, and in 1900[2] he was able to give a practical demonstration of his ideas in the designs for his own house in Helensburgh. The Longcroft illustrated one aspect of the domestic architectural revolution in Scotland recognised by Hermann Muthesius.[3] As a consequence of his Beaux Arts training, Paterson saw this style evolving from a more general European form. To achieve it, he proposed that individuality had to be tempered by the local materials and the traditions of the country, a view very much in line with Lethaby's insistence on a return to first principles for every commission. What was the starting point for a Scottish style? Defining Scottishness, he propounded that the Scots were

> cautious yet pushing; logical, humorous and imaginative, yet parsi-
> monious or at least averse to lavish display; enthusiastic especially in its
> [Scottish] hero-worship, yet in matters of everyday life undemonstrative
> – such are some of the outstanding qualities of the people which did and
> still should find an echo in its architecture.[4]

Pursuing the form of a national style, he recommended the study of Renaissance architecture and in particular 'our national Scottish development of that style'. For example, he predictably pointed to Heriots, Drumlanrig,

Falkland and, with what must have been considerable regret, the Old College buildings of Glasgow University (demolished in his life-time), and he also followed James MacLaren in drawing attention to late seventeenth- and eighteenth-century smaller domestic buildings. All these buildings he suggested should be

> studied in breadth and dignity, largeness of scale, simplicity of composition, and interesting skyline, concentration of ornament and that of varied and fanciful character. I would have the spirit of such work translated and made use of in carrying out, with all modern resources, the different architectural problems of our day. I would have the typical mouldings and ornaments preserved, but refined and corrected when need were by reference to their prototypes, with such characteristic features as the traditional construction of the skew in corbie steps and the stone corbelling, with the accompanying transition from square to octagonal or circular forms in plan, made use of when occasion offered. It would accordingly be necessary, and above all things desirable, that the style should be studied, not as independent and self-centred (which it never was) but as the national phase of what is common to many countries. Hence with our examination of Scottish work, we should combine the French and English which so strongly influenced it, the Italian from which the first influence sprang and through this last, the Roman and Greek prototypes of them all.[5]

All this he proposed with the picturesque warning that style should not simply be applied, 'decking as it were a kilted Highlander with a Roman scarf. ... Correct rendering of a past style, applied with thought to the solution of a modern problem may be uninteresting (though there is no reason why it should be) but it will never be dull'.[6]

Alexander Nisbet Paterson (1862–1947) was brought up in the 'gently luxurious style of the prosperous business families of the day'.[7] His father was a successful manufacturer and prominent churchman whose active encouragement of his son's career helped to establish a flourishing practice. Alexander was no stranger to the Clyde estuary: although raised in Glasgow, childhood summers had been spent around Rhu and Cove. In 1893, while Alexander was still living at home, the family moved permanently from St John's Terrace, Hillhead, to Torwood House, Rhu, and Alexander travelled daily to Glasgow. When he married in 1897, his father made over The Turret, one of a group of four houses in Helensburgh which he had financed some years before, as a way of introducing his son professionally to the town. The Paterson family were no strangers to the artistic world: in 1877, the artist brother James went to the Beaux Arts and spent six years in Paris.[8] In 1883,

Alexander followed and spent three years in the ateliers of J. L. Pascal (architecture) and M. Galland (decoration).[9] The family friendship with the Burnets influenced the choice of Pascal, formerly mentor of J. J. Burnet. In 1884, J. J. Burnet undertook the commission from Alexander Paterson senior for the alterations and additions to Kilneiss[10] at Moniaive, as a wedding present for James, in a manner influenced by Shaw and the American shingle style. This house must have been well-known to young Alexander. Returning in 1886 from the Beaux Arts, it was natural that Alexander should spend three years in the Burnet office,[11] and his time there corresponded with John A. Campbell, also a student of Pascal's, becoming a partner and the firm undertaking a number of domestic commissions and relatively small-scale buildings including the Shaw/shingle-style Corrienessan at Loch Ard and the late English Gothic Glasgow University Union building (the MacIntyre building). The range of influences to which Paterson was exposed was clearly expressed in the Presidential lecture: 'in individuality working through style', he suggested, 'lies the whole interest of architecture', and masters of the art were Peruzzi, Wren and, of contemporaries, Shaw.[12] Burnet's interest in the Baronial was also crucial to Paterson's development of a national style.

During a period in London with R. W. Edis and Sir Aston Webb, he met R. Phene Spiers, who proposed him for associate membership of the RIBA.[13] Spiers had a wide circle and entertained liberally, and it is probable that Paterson met Lethaby and Weir Shultz among others at his evening gatherings. His developing ideas, while in no way so radical as Lethaby's, had much sympathy for Lethaby's idea that 'Architecture is building which is made to carry a story and convey a message' propounded in *Architecture, Mysticism and Myth*.[14] In 1892, Paterson returned to Glasgow and set up in practice. In 1896, he was able to take time from the practice and, as the RIBA Godwin Bursar, travel to the USA to study works of modern architecture. Once again the Burnet connection stood him in good stead, and it is probable that he met Charles McKim, among others. From his visit came a paper delivered at the RIBA in 1898 entitled *A study of domestic architecture in the Eastern states of America with special reference to questions of plan, construction, heating drainage etc.*,[15] a practical analysis of the workings of American houses and the conditions which led to their form. This experience also entered his 'national' architectural equation.

By 1900, Paterson was professionally established and living in Helensburgh. Since the arrival of the railway (c. 1860), Helensburgh had provided the possibility for the Glasgow middle classes to reject the comfortable urban terraces of the West End for a chance to create their private estates, albeit of a diminutive scale. By the turn of the century, it had developed along the waterfront and up the eastern slopes in a grid plan; to the west, the more picturesque concentric arcs formed by the Sutherland Crescents reached up the hill. From the 1860s, small-scale villas in good-sized plots were the housing currency. By the end of the century, rather more substantial houses appeared on the higher slopes and, following the arrival of the West Highland Railway and Helensburgh Upper Station in 1894, further sites became available. Development north of the new line did not begin until the turn of the century, and a less contrived layout emerged for which a number of the most influential contemporary architects designed fashionable and individual houses, creating the type of estate and house in the country described by Hermann Muthesius in his intuitive study *Das Englische Haus* (which despite the title included Scottish houses):

> Country houses large and small are scattered over the whole landscape; some are surrounded by parks that extend far into the fields, other more modest dwelling houses sufficing for the needs of the middle-classes are clustered together in estates. They lie fresh and trim amid the natural greenery. And together with this garden-like landscape they reflect the well-being of the country, the comfortable life-style of a people that has remained close to nature, for whom a fresh breath of country air blowing across the field is worth more than the refinements of an artificial city.[16]

The new breed of houses which so interested Muthesius was heralded at Helensburgh by M. H. Baillie Scott's White House of 1899–1900, its simplicity offering a sharp contrast to William Leiper's exuberant Red Tower of 1900. The most strikingly inventive house was Mackintosh's Hill House (1902–4), but Paterson's Longcroft was, in a quieter way, an equally interesting composition, drawing on some similar sources but reflecting different training, experience and interpretation.

Paterson acquired, from the Colquhoun Trust, one of the most attractive plots in Upper Helensburgh, offering not only spectacular views over the Clyde but also the picturesque drop down to the Glennan Burn at the western boundary. Even by the 1919 Ordnance Survey, the Longcroft (see Figure 26.1) stood on its own, remaining effectively a house in the country. Paterson's wife, Maggie Hamilton, daughter of the sculptor Whitelaw Hamilton and herself a talented painter of still-life subjects, designer and embroideress, played a vital part in the decoration and created marvellous embroidered panels for strategic locations. The house required a studio to fulfil Alexander's professional needs, and the family needed spacious living areas, day and night nurseries for Alistair and Viola and room for two resident domestic staff. It was to be a comfortable, middle-class Edwardian establishment. The site in part dictated the plan; to enjoy the views, the main reception rooms were placed on the south. His studio needed to be furthest from the daily activity of the family. To provide an entrance that would serve both, the logical solution was the traditional L-plan adopted in tower houses and many smaller Scottish vernacular houses and by some of his contemporaries on the east coast. The internal circulation illustrates clearly how house-planning had developed in the nineteenth century, culminating with freely assembled layouts that refused to fit into any formal classification, a trend which William Burn began. The Longcroft has a functional layout developed for convenient living, and it benefited from the small scale, which removed the need for extensive corridors. The debt to the tower house is clearest in the overall plan, with the bold angle turret at the south-west and a squat entrance turret also housing the stair, traditionally in the re-entrant angle. At the Longcroft, there was no separation of the public and family rooms: this was a solid, middle-class house, and they were one and the same thing; however, privacy was maintained, and none of them overlooked the drive and entrance court onto which the service range backed. There is a clear logic in the overall plan and the internal layout at all levels (including the basement, which was equipped with ducting for underfloor heating), typical, as he had suggested in his lecture, of the Scots.

The simplicity of plan is reflected in the exterior appearance: the house is traditionally harled with good grey freestone dressings to the prominent, chunky south-west turret, to the angled entrance turret and to all the main openings. As befitted the parsimonious Scot, ornament is rationed. It is used to the greatest effect in the stylised hoodmould over the door, which is completed by charming carved portraits of the children forming the label stops.[17] Paterson had acquired a love of sculpture during his Parisian days, and it appears again in the escutcheon over the door embracing the symbols of his and Maggie's work, architecture, painting and embroidery, and their initials in a thoroughly traditional manner. Flanking the carving, there is a motto of the rhyming type so popular at the time (see James MacLaren) but again rooted in the past. It reads: 'A HOUSE THAT GOD DOTH OVERSEE – IS GROUNDED AND WATCHED AS WELL CAN BE – SALVE BENE DICITE'. There is another carved panel over the door leading from the inner hall onto the balcony which leads to the garden terrace, and here is a quotation from Psalmody: 'LAETUS SORTE ME', flanked by flowers in pots. All other decoration is found in functional details, particularly the boldly-carved mouldings; those in the decoratively-shaped west gable with its solid apex stack owe their origin to smaller eighteenth-century buildings of which the Dutch gable house at William Street, Greenock, is an example. The only frivolity in the entire building is the mock dovecot in the gable head apparently punched into the chimney flues. On the south elevation, the dormer heads of the first-floor

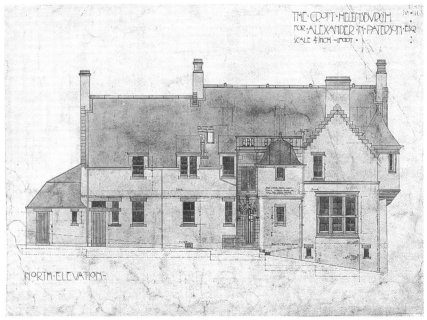

NORTH·ELEVATION·

FIGURE 26.2   A. N. Paterson's design for the entrance front of the Longcroft, 1902.

windows, although seemingly stamped by a pastry cutter, reflect carved seventeenth-century examples, and, predictably, the date (1901) is carved on the centre one.

The house sports five different forms of turret which give drama to the skyline (see Figure 26.2). The entrance is in a stumpy canted turret with widely spaced balusters, a type beloved of Burnet, in the crowning balustrade. Eschewing slavish copying from tower-house sources, and fulfilling the need for plumbing for the studio and the guest bedroom above, Paterson abutted a distinctly seventeenth-century bellcast-roofed, square angle tower against the entrance. The very bold turret at the south-west is at first sight, apart from its dimensions, a fairly common design with the first floor corbelled; the octagonal lower part is not, however, a usual form, and may well owe something to Charles McKim's house for Mrs Frances L. Skinner at Newport Rhode Island of 1882 or to his Osborn estate gate lodge (1883–5).[18] On the west elevation, a traditional corbelled turret clasps the angle between the inner hall and the studio, while on the south front a very restrained two-storey turret with a shallow roof marks the change from living to service area, a distinction which is carried up into the roof, the service roof being lower than the main one. These roofs are covered very effectively with a mixture of bluish-grey Ballachulish and dark green Aberfoyle slates. A further traditional detail, particularly singled out in the lecture, is the use of crow or corbie steps on the east and north gables and on the garden-front roof pitch. In houses of relative simplicity, the window design is of particular importance; at the Longcroft, although the shapes vary according to function, the sash window is used throughout, with the exception of oblong leaded lights to the landing. The idea of the leaded lights for thoroughfares may have come from Philip Webb, who made this distinction at Standen.

The internal arrangement continues the logical approach combined with sparing but effective ornament. It is built on well-vented foundations, and, because of the slope of the land at the west, there are two good basement rooms as well as storage for coals, wine etc. Underneath the large angle turret is a store for garden tools entered from the terrace. The interior design is the most imaginative, combining the skills of the architect with the decorative ability of his wife and the craft of the plasterer Bankart.[19] The main part of the house has no corridors, all communications being by the hall or the inner hall. From the canted vestibule, it is possible to go either into the lobby adjoining the studio or into the entrance hall, which occupies a pivotal position in the plan. The hall shows the influence of Paterson's time in London and assimilation of Queen Anne detailing seen in the two-storey arcaded screen with simple fretwork spandrels and carved bosses on the upper landing (see Figure 26.3). It is three-quarter panelled, with niches housing ornaments to catch the eye. All this woodwork, combined with the timber stair, gives the entrance a dark yet warm and welcoming character, in contrast to the bright light which floods the reception rooms. The form is a free interpretation of the tower-house design for re-entrant angle entrance combined with a newel stair.

The inner 'living' hall leads off the entrance hall through a wide, arched opening and itself provides a spacious sitting area as well as a lobby to the drawing-room and access to the balcony and the garden. This use of a hall as a sitting area is uncommon in Scotland and is more naturally an English or American tradition. Like the hall, it is three-quarter panelled, and on the north wall is a wide chimneypiece, all part of the panelled scheme, over which is set one of a series of embroidered panels. It is a symmetrical composition with doves and sinuous flowers and plants, a calmer design than the restlessly twisting tendrils beloved of the Macdonald sisters. The shallow barrel ceiling makes it altogether more airy than the entrance hall, and the expanse is subtly broken by delicate straps of plasterwork.

From the inner hall, a triple door opens out into the drawing-room, allowing for the creation of a large room for entertaining and reminiscent of the open planning of American houses.[20] The drawing-room has all the informality of an Arts-and-Crafts-inspired room. The ceiling is low, although

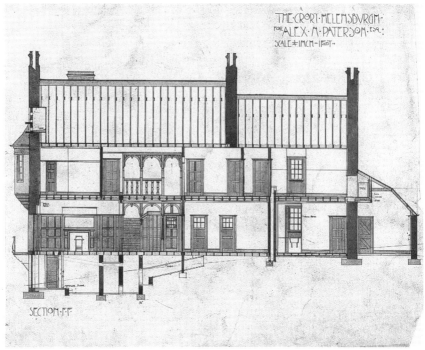

FIGURE 26.3   Section of the Longcroft showing the stair: working drawing by A. N.
Paterson.

an impression of height is created by the shallow cove, only to be countered
by the flattened late seventeenth-century-style plasterwork created by Bankart. Originally, the walls were dark up to the picture-rail, giving a great sense
of intimacy and a richness to two exotic embroidered panels. On the east wall
was a large rectangular panel of scrolled abstract design, while on the west,
set into the wide, shallow-arched Shavian chimneypiece which provides
a powerful focus to the room, are decorated carved panels framing the
jewel-like embroidered inset, as though enclosing the centrepiece of an
illuminated manuscript. The jewelled quality continues in the windows of the
turret, where the upper panes of painted glass depict architecture, embroidery, painting and music, all arts which the family practised. This turret
area is drawn together by the semi-domed ceiling and the circlet of plaster,
and a further decorative delight is found in the tiny plaster floral tondos over
the arched window heads.[21]

   In contrast to the decorative detail of the drawing-room, the dining-room
is sombre, with more panelling. Beyond the dining-room lay the service
quarters, which, like the house, were planned to suit their function, with a

FIGURE 26.4   Snapshot photograph of A. N. Paterson at his drawing-board in the study
at the Longcroft, c. 1908.

service stair to the upper floor. After the First World War, Paterson replanned
them to suit a household which no longer had resident staff. The studio too
was functional: it is in the northern wing with its own entrance off the
entrance lobby, a large bowed window at the north and a small window
looking west over the garden, in front of which Paterson had his drawing
board (see Figure 26.4). This room has a very rich grate, probably one of
those known to have been provided by George Walton.

The upper floor is puritan by contrast with the living areas. The only
decoration is in the main bedroom, which again has a floral overchimney
panel, and in the guest room, which has a barrelled ceiling and walls
delicately stencilled in a manner closest of all the designs in the house to the
more familiar Glasgow style, using rose leaves and flowers twined around
stylised tendrils. The guest room also has a similarly detailed embroidered
panel in the pseudo-inglenook seat. The house was liberally provided with
bathrooms, perhaps a further spin-off from the American experience. The
original design allowed for expansion into the attic with the insertion of swept
dormers. In 1937, Paterson drew up just such a scheme for two additional
rooms in the roof which was not executed.[22]

Alexander Paterson demonstrated his personal perception of a national style as put forward in the 1895 lecture more fully at the Longcroft than in any of the houses which he designed for clients. The logic, humour, imagination, parsimony and restrained character which he associated with the Scots are all to be found in the house, which is an echo of the particular type of lifestyle of a comfortable, middle-class family of discerning and artistic taste. Did Alexander Paterson go any way to achieving a universal national style at the Longcroft, or did he in fact prove that the creation of a twentieth-century national style was an impossibility? There is no doubt that, within the parameters which he set himself, he achieved a house that was unquestionably Scottish in essence; it owed much to seventeenth- and eighteenth-century Scottish domestic architecture and to his east-coast contemporaries,[23] but there was more to it. His wide experience at the Beaux Arts, in London and in the USA all provided the sources for a personal input into the design. Like Voysey before him, he provided a design which was at once both traditional and original. But it could only be the source of a national architecture if his concepts of Scottishness were understood and reinterpreted for every commission. Paterson joined a group of Scottish architects who clearly established a Scottish Free Style demonstrating the power of Scottishness and the variety of interpretation which it allowed. What they all achieved in their various ways was a new awareness of the spirit of history and its value in contemporary architecture.

NOTES

1. RIBA *Journal*, 1895, vol. 2, 3rd series, pp. 246–9. Part of the Presidential address to the Glasgow Architectural Association: *Style, Individuality and Tradition*.
2. Dumbarton Dean of Guild, 1900.
3. Hermann Muthesius, *Das Englische Haus*, 1904–6 (English translation 1979), pp. 61–2.
4. Op. cit.
5. Op. cit.
6. Op. cit.
7. Alexander Paterson, *Some reminiscences of an uneventful life*, a fragment by Alexander Paterson, manufacturer, Glasgow, 1819–1907. A continuation of the story of his life and an appreciation of his personality by his youngest son Alexander Nisbet Paterson, 1937–8, p. 53. Copy in NMRS.
8. The Paterson Family, 100 years of Scottish Painting 1877–1977. Exhibition Catalogue (Belgrave Gallery and the Fine Art Society Scotland), p. 3.
9. RIBA Fellowship Nomination papers, 25 November 1909.
10. Op. cit. The Paterson Family.
11. RIBA Associateship and Fellowship papers, 22 January 1890, 25 November 1909.
12. Op. cit. RIBA *Journal*.

13. Op. cit. RIBA Nomination papers.
14. Julian Holder, 'Architecture, Myth and Mysticism', in Sylvia Backemeyer and Theresa Gronberg (eds), *W. R. Lethaby 1857–1931: Architecture, Design and Education*, 1984, p. 58.
15. RIBA *Journal*, vol. 5, 3rd series, 1898, pp. 309–31.
16. Muthesius, op. cit., p. 8.
17. Dr Mays tells me that John Kinross introduced similar child portraits of the 3rd Marquis of Bute's children at Falkland.
18. M. Roth, *McKim, Mead and White Architects*, 1984, p. 77.
19. James Nicholl (ed.), *Domestic Architecture in Scotland*, 1908.
20. Op. cit. RIBA *Journal*, vol. 5.
21. In the 1980s, during Miss Paterson's life, a magnificent embroidery frame, said to have been found washed up on the shore, stood in the room with Maggie Hamilton's last piece of work still on it.
22. Copy of drawings in NMRS.
23. Paterson attended a number of visits arranged by the Edinburgh Architectural Association. I am grateful to Dr Mays for this information.

Lindsaylands, near Biggar, designed by William Leiper, 1869.

APPENDIX

Chronological List of Houses in Scotland Designed by William Leiper

JOHN R. HUME

This is a list of all houses known or confidently believed to have been by William Leiper, including major extensions. The sources quoted are in each case the earliest references found, and are as referred to in the footnotes, with the exception of RSA, which refers to works exhibited at the Royal Scottish Academy. Sources are also given for illustrations of houses now demolished.

Kirktonhill House, Helenslee Road, Dumbarton, NS388753, built 1866 for John McAusland, a director of William Denny and Bros, shipbuilders. Early French Gothic, two-storey, with octagonal balconied tower. Demolished.

D. MacLeod, *Dumbarton Ancient and Modern*, 1893.

The Elms, Cairnie Road, Arbroath, NO632417, built 1864–6 for Provost D. Corsar, linen manufacturer. Early French Gothic, two-storey, using motifs similar to those at *Kirktonhill*. Now a children's home. Lodge in similar style dated 1868, extended.

Fellowship papers, RIBA.

Colearn Castle (also Col Earn), Auchterarder, NN947132, built 1869 for Alexander Mackintosh, advocate. Baronial, one-, two- and three-storey, with many allusions to authentic Scots vernacular. Good Aesthetic Movement glass and interior work. Lodge and dovecote in similar style. House now a hotel.

Fellowship papers, RIBA.

Lindsaylands, Biggar, NT027373, built 1869 for J. M. Little. Early French vernacular, with bold projecting bay, two-storey, addition to a plain earlier nineteenth-century house. Lodge in similar style, and plain stable block. Dated window in house; RSA 1873.

Ranochlea House (also Rannochlea), 1 St Andrews Drive, Glasgow, NS576637, built for James McGregor, timber measurer. French Gothic, two-storey and attic. Lodge canted bay with attic window. Demolished.
Post Office Directory 1870; RSA 1871; photograph in NMRS.

Cairndhu, Rhu Road Lower, Helensburgh, NS284827, built 1871 for John Ure, flour miller and merchant, Lord Provost of Glasgow. François I Renaissance, two-storey and attic, with large curved bay. Magnificent interior with good glass and Anglo-Japanese ceiling, in Aesthetic Movement style. Now a nursing home. Lodge similar to that at Colearn.
RSA 1873.

Cornhill House, Biggar (Coulter Parish), NT018352, built 1871 for Alex Kay of James Finlay and Co, cotton manufacturers and merchants. Early French Gothic with some Renaissance details, elaborate two- and three-storey addition to plain early Victorian house which it dwarfs. Turret corbelled from short column, as later used in Templeton's Carpet Factory. Now an old people's home. Lodge similar to that at The Elms, home farm in simple Arts and Crafts style.
Fellowship papers, RIBA.

Redholm (now Westermillig House), 18 Millig Street, Helensburgh, NS292833, built 1871. Early French vernacular, very similar to Lindsaylands, but more elaborately detailed. Now flatted. Stables at 25 Queen Street (now domestic), also by Leiper, built 1898–9, later Arts and Crafts with Baronial details similar to stables at Piersland and The Croft.
Information from part-owner; RIBA obituary. Stables: Helensburgh Dean of Guild plans.

Terpersie (also Terpersy, Thurloe), 1 Sutherland Street North, Helensburgh, NS290837, built around 1871 for Leiper himself. Early Arts and Crafts, two-storey, simple, good Aesthetic Movement glass.
Post Office Directory; *British Architect*, 26 January 1883.

Bonnyton (also Bonnington, now Rhuarden), 1 Sutherland Crescent Upper, Helensburgh, NS291832, built around 1871 for John McGregor JP. Greek Revival, two-storey. Leiper's only house in this style so far identified. Later Leiper conservatory.
Post Office Directory; RIBA obituary.

Balgray House, Crossloan Road (now Cleveden Road), Glasgow, NS561679, built around 1873 for A. D. Dean, printer. François I Renaissance, two-storey, a more modest version of Cairndhu. Demolished.
RSA 1873; photograph in *Kelvinside*.

Dalmore, Rhu Road Lower, Helensburgh, NS281833, built 1873 for Robert Little. Baronial two- and three-storey, similar in layout to Colearn Castle, but with simpler massing and detail. Prominent rounded bay later used at Kinlochmoidart and Glendaruel. Now flatted. Lodge and coachman's house (1894) in similar style.

Fellowship papers, RIBA.

Castlepark, 80 Broomgate, Lanark, NS879434, built around 1880 for Hugh Renwick. A remarkable house in Swiss/American/Japanese style, two-storey and attic, low-pitched gable with decorated bargeboards. Now flatted. Lodge in plain vernacular style as lean-to on garden wall.

RIBA obituary.

Ruthven Tower, Auchterarder, NN952130, built 1882 for J. Halley, of Halley and Co., power-loom weavers, Ruthvenvale Works, Auchterarder. Baronial, one- and two-storey and attic, finely-detailed with good Anglo-Japanese glass by William Cottier. Now a nursing home, with large additions in garden.

Wheatpark, Wheatpark Road, Lanark, NS878440, built 1882 for Thomas Watson JP. Gothic addition to earlier Jacobean house, two-storey and attic, rather ungainly. Now flatted. Lodge and stables in simple Arts and Crafts style.

Date on addition; RIBA obituary.

Clarendon, 83 James Street, Helensburgh, NS296831, extended 1883 and 1891 for John Anderson. Jacobean, two-storey and attic, additions to plain earlier Victorian villa. Now a school.

Helensburgh Dean of Guild plans.

Tordarroch, Douglas Drive, Helensburgh, NS301836, built around 1883 for Mrs R. Smith. Later Arts and Crafts, one- and two-storey and attic. Leiper's first house in this style.

RIBA obituary.

Dorlecote (also Dovelcote, later St Bernard's, now Albion Lodge), 134 Luss Road, Helensburgh, NS303836, built 1883 for Quentin Galbraith, and later extended. Later Arts and Crafts, two-storey. Smaller version of Tordarroch, almost doubled in size by extension.

Helensburgh Dean of Guild plans.

Kinlochmoidart, Arisaig and Moidart parish, Inverness-shire, NM717723, built 1884 for Robert Stewart. Baronial, one- and three-storey and attic. Enlarged version of Dalmore, but with less academically correct and more stylish entrance elevation. Service wing incorporates pioneer hydro-electric plant. Good, original interiors and furnishings. Two lodges, one Baronial, one tile-hung, boathouse, school and schoolhouse.

Date on house; *British Architect*, 13 September 1889.

Aros, Aros Drive, Rhu, NS265848, built around 1885 for Sir G. B. McLeod, professor of surgery, University of Glasgow. Later Arts and Crafts, two-storey, similar to Dorlecote, but not extended later.

RIBA obituary.

Ganavan, Oban, NM857324, built 1888 for Mrs McDougall, proprietrix of the Columba Hotel, Oban. Later Arts and Crafts, one- and two-storey, similar to Aros.

Information from owner; RIBA obituary.

Glenkin, 76 John Street, Helensburgh, NS294824, extended 1889 for William Anderson. Substantial one- and two-storey additions to mid-Victorian villa. Tower with 'coolie hat' roof and Shavian wing. Good Jacobean interiors.

Helensburgh Dean of Guild plans.

Moredun, Stanley Road, Paisley, NS478628, built 1890 for John Brown JP, of Brown and Polson, starch and cornflour manufacturers. Jacobean, two-storey and attic, very massive. Now a nursing home. Plain Arts and Crafts lodge.

RIBA obituary.

Kelly House, Wemyss Bay, NS194686, rebuilt and extended 1890–1 for Alexander Stephen, of Alexander Stephen and Sons, shipbuilders. Jacobean, two-storey, treatment similar to 1891 addition to Clarendon but larger. Demolished.

The Builder, 24 February 1900; photographs in Watt Library, Greenock.

Queensberry, Park Road, Kilmacolm, NS353696, built 1893. Simple two-storey villa with Baronial and Arts and Crafts details. Now flatted.

Date on building. Identified in thesis by Greig and Clarkson.

Westbreak, Park Road, Kilmacolm, NS352696, built 1893, probably for Archibald Annan, solicitor and notary, of W. E. and A. J. Annan, Glasgow. Plain two-storey villa with 'coolie hat'-roofed corner tower. Similar in plan to Queensberry. Demolished.

RIBA obituary.

Brantwoode, Munro Drive West, Helensburgh, NS299833, built 1895 for J. Alexander of Jamieson and Co., oil refiners, Clyde Street, Glasgow. Later Arts and Crafts, two-storey. Larger, linear version of Dorlecote design. Good original interiors.

Helensburgh Dean of Guild plans.

Tighnabruaich House, Tighnabruaich, Argyll, NR983732, built 1895. Later Arts and Crafts, one- and two-storey and attic. All-stone version of Brantwoode. Simple panelled interiors.

RIBA obituary; information from owners.

Knockderry Castle, Cove, NS217835, extended 1896 for John S. Templeton of James Templeton and Co. and J. and J. S. Templeton, carpet manufacturers, Glasgow. Baronial, three-storey and attic extension to Alexander Thomson/John Honeyman Baronial house for William Miller, Glasgow warehouseman. Leiper addition had splendid interiors. Garden cottage, tile-hung.

RSA 1897.

Knockderry House, Cove, NS217835, extended 1897 for John Anderson JP. Later Arts and Crafts, two- and three-storey extension to earlier Baronial house. Now a hotel.

Stylistic attribution.

Viewfield (now Langgarth), St Ninian's Road, Stirling, NS797927, built 1897 for William Renwick. Baronial, two-storey and attic with bold rounded bay on garden elevation. Now Central Regional Council Offices. Lodge in 'Queen Mary's Bath' style; cf. Robert Lorimer's Balcarres Lodge.

RSA 1910.

Auchenbothie, Kilmacolm, NS350709, built 1898 for H. B. Collins. Baronial one-and two-storey and attic, on complex plan, harled. Derelict. Stables in 'Queen Mary's Bath' style, now flats.

RSA 1910.

The Croft, Park Road, Kilmacolm, NS352696, built around 1898 probably for John Binnie, stockbroker, Glasgow. Baronial, two-storey, harled.

Stylistic attribution; similar details in Piersland and Redholm stables.

Ballimore, Otter Ferry, Kilfinan parish, Argyll, NR928834, extended 1898 for Major McRae Gilstrap. Baronial, two-storey and attic reworking and extension of early Victorian Baronial house by David Hamilton, of which *porte-cochère* survives unaltered.

RSA 1899.

Piersland, Craigend Road, Troon, NS331299, built 1898–9 for Alexander Walker, whisky distiller and blender, of John Walker and Sons Ltd, Kilmarnock. Late Arts and Crafts, two-storey and attic, with extensive half-timbering somewhat Voysey-esque. Elaborate interiors. Now a hotel. Lodge, range of offices and mews in similar style. Mews has details like The Croft; now flatted.

RIBA obituary.

Red Tower, Douglas Drive, Helensburgh, NS299386, built 1898–1900 for James Allan, provision merchant. Eclectic Baronial/Arts and Crafts, two- and three-storey, with conical-roofed drum tower. Now a drug rehabilitation centre.

Helensburgh Dean of Guild plans.

Deroran (now Endrick Lodge), Polmaise Road, Stirling, NS787924, built 1900 for Charles A. Buchanan, stockbroker, of Buchanan and Fergusson, Glasgow. Scots Renaissance/English Arts and Crafts, two-storey with

entrance tower in re-entrant angle. Half-timbered lodge in Devey/Nesfield style.
RSA 1910.

Ard Luss, 135 Luss Road, Helensburgh, NS302838, built 1900 for William Russell JP, factor for the Luss Estates. Later Arts and Crafts, one-storey and attic and two-storey, a late and simple version of the Dorlecote style.
Helensburgh Dean of Guild plans.

Glendaruel, Kilmodan, Argyll, NS000870, rebuilt and extended 1900–1 for Lewis D. Wigan, shipowner. Baronial, three-storey and attic reworking of older house, with features from Dalmore and Red Tower. Demolished. Stables and coach house, home farm, gamekeeper's cottage, henhouse, corn and sawmill, all harled. Chapel, simple Gothic, 1912.
RSA 1910; information from owner of site of house.

Ard Choille, Clynder, NS241857, built 1900–2 for George MacGregor of the West of Scotland Fire Office, 131 St Vincent Street. Later Arts and Crafts, two-storey and attic.
Information from owner.

Morar Lodge (now Drumadoon), Colquhoun Street Upper, Helensburgh, NS299839, built 1903 for Thomas G. Bishop, grocer, of Coopers Ltd, Glasgow, additions in 1907. Eclectic Arts and Crafts/Baronial/Scots Renaissance/French Gothic, with some American influence, two-storey and attic, massive. Now a nursing home. Motor house and laundry in similar style, 1904, extended 1906.
Helensburgh Dean of Guild plans.

Rockbank, Charlotte Street and Abercromby Street East, Helensburgh (now 41, 43 and 45 Charlotte Street: Ortona, Comarach and Hilden), NS303829, built from 1906 for John Jack, factor to the Luss Estates. Latest Arts and Crafts, a group of three two-storey houses, Voysey-inspired variants of the Dorlecote type. Later billiard-room extension to Hilden.
Helensburgh Dean of Guild plans.

Uplands, 15 Abercromby Drive, Bridge of Allan, NS797977, built 1907 for William L. Puller JP. Shavian Arts and Crafts, two-storey and attic, on a steeply-sloping site. Now flatted.
RSA 1910.

Polkemmet (now Lynton), 6 Colquhoun Street Upper, Helensburgh, NS299834, built 1908 for Major J. F. Duncan. Latest Arts and Crafts, one- and two-storey, a Voysey-inspired version of the Brantwoode type.
Helensburgh Dean of Guild plans.

ALPHABETICAL LIST OF HOUSES

Albion Lodge, see Dorlecote		Kinlochmoidart	1884
Ard Choille	1900–2	Kirktonhill House	1866
Ard Luss	1900	Knockderry Castle	1896
Aros	c. 1885	Knockderry House	c. 1897
Auchenbothie	1898	Langgarth, see Viewfield	
Balgray House	c. 1873	Lindsaylands	1869
Ballimore	1898	Lynton, see Polkemmet	
Bonnington, see Bonnyton		Morar Lodge	1903
Bonnyton	c. 1871	Moredun	1890
Brantwoode	1895	Ortona, see Rockbank	
Cairndhu	1871	Piersland	1898–9
Castlepark	c. 1880	Polkemmet	1908
Clarendon	1883 (1891)	Queensberry	1893
Col Earn, see Colearn Castle		Ranochlea	c. 1870
Colearn Castle	1869	Redholm	1871
Comarach, see Rockbank		Red Tower	1898–1900
Cornhill House	1871	Rhuarden, see Bonnyton	
The Croft	c. 1898	Rockbank	1906 on
Dalmore	1873	Ruthven Tower	1882
Deroran	1900	St Bernard's, see Dorlecote	
Dorlecote	1883	Terpersie	c. 1871
Dovelcote, see Dorlecote		Thurloe, see Terpersie	
Drumadoon, see Morar Lodge		Tighnabruaich House	1895
The Elms	1864–6	Tordarroch	c. 1883
Endrick Lodge, see Deroran		Uplands	1907
Ganavan	1888	Viewfield	1897
Glendaruel	1900–1	Westbreak	c. 1893
Glenkin	1889	Westermillig House, see Redholm	
Hilden, see Rockbank		Wheatpark	1882
Kelly House	1890–1		

Acknowledgements

From the inception of the idea of a Festschrift to honour Kitty Cruft and the outstanding contribution which she has made to Scottish architecture through the work of the National Monuments Record of Scotland, a great many people have helped to further our scheme. The contributors were invited with the advice of an informal 'committee of honour' comprising Anne Riches, Dr Deborah Howard and Dr Debbie Mays. Inevitably the selection tended to be representational, and we regret that we were unable to include a true representation of younger scholars whom Kitty might also have hoped to see.

Kitty's period with the NMRS spanned forty of its fifty-three years. Since 1966, the NMRS has found a safe haven within the Royal Commission on the Ancient and Historical Monuments of Scotland, and indeed is now central to its activities, but it has had spells within the Scottish National Portrait Gallery and the Ministry of Works (now Historic Scotland). Kitty and the NMRS also worked closely with the other national institutions in Edinburgh, including the Scottish Record Office and the National Libraries of Scotland. In 1991, to celebrate the first fifty years, one of the co-editors of this volume attempted the first history of the NMRS as an introduction to the *NMRS Jubilee Guide to the Collections* (HMSO), but we hope that, during her retirement, Kitty may feel inclined to fill out this official history with her personal recollections. Rather as the collections now reflect these many contacts and friendships, we hope that this book will also illustrate the NMRS's close links with other institutions.

We are, of course, greatly in the debt of our fellow contributors; but, as we had anticipated, it was a cause with strong popular support and enormous goodwill. In the hope of attracting a publisher, the editors and their advisers decided that it was essential to set a fairly tight theme; but it was entirely fortuitous, since no pressure was brought to bear on the authors, that an effective chronological spread resulted.

From the outset, we were fortunate in having the support of the then Secretary of the RCAHMS, John G. Dunbar, and this personal interest has been continued by his successor, Roger Mercer. We are most grateful to the Earl of Crawford and Balcarres, Chairman of the Commissioners, for agreeing to supply the foreword.

Anne Riches steered us towards Edinburgh University Press, and Dr Deborah Howard's support was also of service here, but we owe a personal debt of gratitude to its Publisher, Vivian C. Bone, for her faith in the delivery of a manuscript which the editors privately despaired of. Dr Rosalind Marshall, it is only fair to record, has the honour of being first past the finishing post, but the staple binding her manuscript was already rusting by the time the entire team completed the course, although we knew that Kitty's patience would not be tested. We must also sadly record the death of Colin McWilliam during the preparation of this book. Joining the NMRS shortly after Kitty, he had an outstanding impact on its development during the few years when he served as its Director, and he continued to be a frequent and most welcome visitor. He has a modest memorial here because Christine McWilliam has kindly agreed to let us reproduce one of his photographs.

We are very grateful to Edinburgh University Press for publishing this volume, and the production has been rendered enjoyable through not only Vivian's close involvement but also that of Penny Clarke and our copy-editor, Ivor Normand, who have endeavoured to set us a high standard. Within our own institutions, we have received a great deal of support. At the Edinburgh College of Art, Renee Macmillan heroically transferred many of the typescripts onto disk. At the RCAHMS, Victoria Collison Owen, Tahra Duncan, John Keggie, John Hamilton, Dr Graham Ritchie, Shona McGaw, Steven Thomson, Veronica Steele, John Stevenson, Jane Thomas and Ruth Wimberley have all assisted with the illustrations, the majority of which are drawn from the collections of the NMRS. The Editors and Edinburgh University Press are grateful to Roger Mercer for so kindly agreeing to waive reproduction fees on the NMRS illustrations and to the many other institutions and owners of private collections who have permitted illustrations to be reproduced and whose contributions are acknowledged by individual contributors.

IAN GOW
ALISTAIR ROWAN

Photographic Credits

Duplicate entries will usually refer to material copied for The NMRS *Photographic Survey of Private Collections*.

Ashmolean Museum, Oxford: 5.5
British Architectural Library: Drawings Collection: 17.4, 17.5
British Museum: 10.1–5
John Hume: 24.1–5, p. 336
James Hunter Blair: 15.6
Charles McKean: 1.1–5
The late Colin McWilliam: 23.1
National Galleries of Scotland: 9.1–3, 9.5, 14.2
National Trust for Scotland: 2.4, 6.1 (Haddo Collection), 6.3 (Georgian House), 8.4, 8.5, 19.2–7 (Craigievar Collection)
Private Collections: 3.4–5, 4.1–5, 6.2, 11.1–3, 12.1–5, 14.2–4, 15.1–2, 15.3a–d, 15.5, 16.1, 20.2–5, 21.2, 22.4–5
Joe Rock: Portrait of Kitty Cruft (jacket), 22.4, 22.5
The Royal Commission on the Ancient and Historical Monuments of Scotland (RCAHMS): National Monuments Record of Scotland (NMRS): 1.6, 2.1, 3.1–4, 5.1–3, 6.1–3, 7.1–3, 8.1–3, 9.4, 11.1–4, 12.1–5, 13.3, 14.1, 14.3–5, 15.1–7, 16.2–4, 17.1–3, 18.1–5, 19.1–7, 20.1–5, 21.1–3, 23.2–3, 25.1– , 26.1–4
Scottish Record Office: 16.1
Sir John Soane's Museum, London: 13.1–2, 13.4–6
Professor David M. Walker: 25.1

Index of Designers and Buildings

Page numbers in bold denote main references. Page numbers in italics denote illustrations.

347